CI/CD as a Control System

Designing Cloud, DevOps, and DevSecOps Platforms for Scale, Stability, and Autonomous Delivery

Sundeep Bobba
Naga Sujitha Vummaneni

Apress®

CI/CD as a Control System: Designing Cloud, DevOps, and DevSecOps Platforms for Scale, Stability, and Autonomous Delivery

Sundeep Bobba
Allen, TX, USA

Naga Sujitha Vummaneni
Tracy, CA, USA

ISBN-13 (pbk): 979-8-8688-2841-6
ISBN-13 (electronic): 979-8-8688-2842-3
https://doi.org/10.1007/979-8-8688-2842-3

Managing Director, Apress Media LLC: Welmoed Spahr
Acquisitions Editor: Anandadeep Roy
Editorial Assistant: Jessica Vakili

Cover designed by eStudioCalamar

Cover image designed by Magnific

Distributed to the book trade worldwide by Springer Science+Business Media New York, 1 New York Plaza, New York, NY 10004. Phone 1-800-SPRINGER, fax (201) 348-4505, e-mail orders-ny@springer-sbm.com, or visit www.springeronline.com. Apress Media, LLC is a Delaware LLC and the sole member (owner) is Springer Science + Business Media Finance Inc (SSBM Finance Inc). SSBM Finance Inc is a **Delaware** corporation.

For information on translations, please e-mail booktranslations@springernature.com; for reprint, paperback, or audio rights, please e-mail bookpermissions@springernature.com.

Apress titles may be purchased in bulk for academic, corporate, or promotional use. eBook versions and licenses are also available for most titles. For more information, reference our Print and eBook Bulk Sales web page at http://www.apress.com/bulk-sales.

Any source code or other supplementary material referenced by the author in this book is available to readers on GitHub. For more detailed information, please visit https://www.apress.com/gp/services/source-code.

If disposing of this product, please recycle the paper

To my parents, whose sacrifices, values, and encouragement shaped my journey.

To my wife, Tejaswi, and my sons, Dhruv and Devansh, for their love, patience, and constant inspiration.

And to Michael Erdman, whose passion for automation, innovation, and engineering excellence inspired many of the ideas explored in this book.

—Sundeep Bobba

For my parents, who taught me that knowledge is the one investment that never depreciates.

For my husband, whose patience and partnership made every late night at the desk possible. And for my daughter, who asks "why" before she believes anything and "how" before she touches anything.

—Naga Sujitha Vummaneni

Table of Contents

About the Authors

Sundeep Bobba is a technical leader in Cloud and DevOps engineering with over 16 years of experience designing and operating large-scale cloud-native platforms and enterprise software delivery systems. He has led DevOps and DevSecOps modernization initiatives for mission-critical, high-availability systems supporting multi-billion-dollar digital businesses.

His work focuses on treating software delivery as an engineered system, integrating CI/CD, security controls, observability, and governance into cohesive, scalable platforms. Sundeep has architected and operated complex delivery pipelines, platform engineering frameworks, and risk-aware release systems in highly regulated and high-throughput environments.

Sundeep is an invited speaker at international DevOps and Cloud conferences and has authored technical publications and industry case studies on modern CI/CD and cloud automation practices. He actively contributes to the global DevOps and platform engineering community through technical writing, peer review, and advisory roles.

He holds a master's degree in computer science and is a Fellow of the British Computer Society and an IEEE Senior Member. His current work explores system-level approaches to software delivery, focusing on feedback loops, decision boundaries, and control mechanisms for enterprise-scale DevOps and DevSecOps platforms.

Naga Sujitha Vummaneni is a Cloud security architect with over ten years of experience designing and implementing enterprise-scale security automation frameworks across multi-cloud environments. She has led security engineering and infrastructure automation initiatives for high-growth technology companies, safeguarding critical systems and sensitive data across AWS, Azure, and GCP.

Her work focuses on operationalizing security through intelligent automation, integrating vulnerability management, threat detection, and incident response into cohesive, scalable security platforms. Sujitha has architected and deployed advanced WAF automation systems, Zero Trust security frameworks, and comprehensive PKI management solutions that dramatically reduce manual overhead while strengthening security posture across complex cloud infrastructures.

Sujitha has demonstrated measurable impact through her security innovations, including reducing incident response times by 95%, automating the remediation of 85% of vulnerabilities, and building security frameworks that increased team productivity by 50% while reducing security incidents by 70%. Her expertise spans cloud security policy development, automated compliance monitoring, and cross-functional security team leadership.

She holds an MBA from Cornell University and a Master of Science in Computer Science from the University of Toledo and maintains multiple industry certifications including AWS Certified Security, CISM, and Advanced Computer Security from Stanford University. Her current work explores AI-enhanced security automation, advanced threat detection systems, and the intersection of cloud infrastructure and proactive security engineering.

About the Technical Reviewer

Krishna Kosaraju is a senior Cloud, infrastructure, and site reliability engineer and architect with over 14 years of experience designing and operating scalable, secure, and highly available systems across cloud and on-premises environments. He specializes in AWS, Kubernetes, and DevOps practices, with deep expertise in container orchestration, infrastructure as code, and CI/CD automation. Krishna has led large-scale cloud migrations and built resilient multi-region architectures supporting modern microservices platforms. He is also experienced in Python and Go-based automation, enabling efficient infrastructure management and operational excellence. Passionate regarding emerging technologies, he actively explores AI/ML integrations within cloud-native ecosystems while driving best practices in reliability, security, and performance.

Acknowledgments

Writing this book has been both a technical and personal journey. The ideas presented throughout these chapters were shaped through years of experience designing, securing, automating, and operating large-scale cloud and software delivery platforms across complex enterprise environments.

We are deeply grateful to the many engineers, architects, security professionals, platform teams, and technology leaders we have collaborated with throughout our careers. Their innovation, curiosity, and commitment to building resilient and scalable systems continuously inspired the perspectives shared in this book.

This work was also influenced by the broader DevOps, cloud, and cybersecurity communities whose ongoing contributions continue to redefine how modern software systems are built, governed, secured, and operated.

We would like to sincerely thank the Apress editorial and production teams for their guidance, support, and patience throughout the publishing process.

We are especially thankful to our families for their encouragement, understanding, and unwavering support during the many long evenings and weekends dedicated to writing this book. Their patience and belief in us made this journey possible.

Finally, we hope this book encourages engineers, architects, and technology leaders to think beyond automation alone and toward building software delivery systems that are intelligent, resilient, secure, and responsibly governed.

Foreword

The world operates on code and security, and code effectiveness relies on observability. *CI/CD as a Control System* blends together modern solutions to address the rapid pace of development. We are in a technological explosion driven by AI, with daily changes and quick adaptation requirements. Following the practical advice outlined enables us to move fast, remain focused, and pivot quickly while sustaining strong security. Observability allows us to address errors and their source so that we move toward a "bug-free" world.

I am excited regarding the source of truth to enable the future during this monumental change. The material presented by Sundeep Bobba and Sujitha Vummaneni combines more than 25 years of evolving development methodologies. Sundeep brings forth transformational techniques from his time with Southwest Airlines, being highly recognized for delivering platforms for complex environments. He is a forerunner for AI-augmented software delivery initiatives. Sujitha, having worked across Ripple, Nike, Google, and eBay, continues to advance solutions using AI across cloud infrastructures. Their experiences showcase proven techniques for our fast-paced evolution.

I recommend this book for developers, security practitioners, and CIOs as we embrace AI change.

—Mignona Cote

Mignona Cote is a world-class security pioneer spanning multiple industries such as telecom, finance, healthcare, and high tech through companies such as Bank of America, AWS, AIG, Aetna, NetApp, and Verizon (GTE). Mignona has been instrumental in building strong security integration into the development processes, leveraging her cloud and hybrid experiences.

Introduction

Modern software delivery systems are becoming increasingly complex. Applications no longer run as isolated deployments on static infrastructure. Today's platforms operate across distributed cloud environments composed of microservices, APIs, infrastructure automation, observability systems, security controls, and continuously evolving CI/CD pipelines. Every change triggers a chain of automated decisions, validations, deployments, and operational responses that need to work reliably at scale.

Yet many organizations still approach software delivery using an outdated mental model. CI/CD is usually seen only as automation. DevOps is largely linked to tooling. DevSecOps is often reduced to plugging security scanners into pipelines. Teams optimize individual stages of delivery while struggling to understand the behavior of the delivery system as a whole. This book introduces a different perspective: software delivery as a control system.

Traditional engineering disciplines build control systems to maintain stability in dynamic environments, utilizing feedback loops, telemetry, corrective actions, constraints, and decision boundaries. Modern software delivery systems behave very similarly. CI/CD pipelines are execution mechanisms. Observability platforms are feedback signals. Governance and security policies are operational constraints. Deployment strategies regulate risk, stability, and system behavior across increasingly complex environments.

When viewed through this lens, many modern engineering challenges become easier to understand. Pipeline instability, delayed feedback, operational drift, noisy telemetry, deployment risk, and the growing difficulty of balancing speed with control are not isolated tooling problems. They are system behavior problems.

Rather than focusing on specific vendors or technologies, this book provides a reusable systems-level mental model that applies across cloud platforms, engineering organizations, and delivery ecosystems. The concepts explored throughout these chapters are intentionally platform-agnostic because the underlying operational patterns remain consistent regardless of tooling choices.

The book begins by examining why software delivery requires a new architectural mindset and how principles from control system engineering apply naturally to CI/CD and DevOps environments. From there, it explores observability as feedback, pipelines as actuation mechanisms, governance and security as operational constraints, and decision-making inside modern delivery systems. The later chapters focus on operational instability, recovery patterns, enterprise-scale platform design, and the long-term evolution of software delivery systems.

This book is written for senior DevOps engineers, DevSecOps engineers, platform engineers, site reliability engineers, cloud architects, and engineering leaders responsible for designing and operating delivery platforms at scale.

One of the central ideas throughout this book is that automation alone is not maturity.

True operational maturity comes from understanding how delivery systems behave under changing conditions, how feedback propagates through platforms, where control boundaries should exist, and how organizations maintain stability while continuing to move quickly.

As software delivery increasingly incorporates intelligent automation and AI-driven operational systems, these ideas become even more important. The future of software delivery will depend not only on faster automation but on designing systems that remain observable, governed, adaptable, and trustworthy at scale.

CHAPTER 1

Why Software Delivery Needs a New Mental Model

1.1 Chapter Objective

In this chapter, We talk about the problems with traditional DevOps and automation in modern businesses and why we need to think about software delivery in a new way. DevOps and CI/CD have made things faster, more productive, and easier to work together, but they aren't enough to deal with the complexity and constant change of modern cloud-native systems.

1.2 Introduction: Evolution of Software Delivery Paradigms

Software delivery has changed in accordance with the increasing need for speed, reliability, and scalability. Early systems were monolithic, and the components were tightly coupled and rarely released. These systems were relatively easy to maintain; however, their tightly coupled architecture and lack of independent deployability severely constrained adaptability, limiting controlled, component-level changes in response to evolving business requirements and user demand.

The transformation to service and microservices architectures altered the software building and delivery approach. Cloud computing made this shift faster with the ability to provide on-demand resources, scaling up and down, as well as global distribution

S. Bobba and N. S. Vummaneni, *CI/CD as a Control System*, https://doi.org/10.1007/979-8-8688-2842-3_1

(Prakash & Sharma, 2023). Because of this, the contemporary systems have become decentralized, dynamic, and always changing.

Organizations embraced the DevOps practices in order to cope with this complexity. DevOps encourages the development and operations to work closely with each other and automate the build, test, and deployment actions. This approach made continuous integration (CI) and continuous deployment (CD) pipelines a priority, which allowed releasing products faster and more regularly (Kolawole and Fakokunde, 2024).

These enhancements made delivery faster and quicker in turnaround. But today, systems are required to work in an environment that is not just fast. They should be strong and consistent even in the face of constant change.

Cloud-native systems introduce several challenges:

- Multisensory services in multiple distributed settings
- Temporary infrastructure that is controlled by containers
- System changes that occur constantly and simultaneously

These properties give rise to non-linear and emergent behavior, in which even minor changes in behavior can cause unpredictable behavior. This complexity cannot be effectively governed using traditional linear workflows, which assume isolated and sequential validation of changes, failing to capture continuous system interactions and emergent behavior in dynamic environments.

Multi-cloud environments also make operations more difficult. It is systems that are distributed across various providers, and their configurations and failures are not uniform. Such fragmentation increases invisibility and makes behavior in systems more difficult to predict.

DevOps also introduced infrastructure as code (IaC) and automated monitoring; although those devices allow making things faster and more efficient, they do not actually change the situation. They do not entirely discuss system behavior or stability. They, in others, increase the risk by increasing the rate of change.

This leads to a critical question:

What are the issues related to the software delivery systems to achieve stability with high-velocity operations in complex environments?

It takes a change of mindset to answer this. Delivery of software can no longer be considered a series of automated actions. It ought to be subjected to constant control as a dynamic system instead.

A control-oriented approach focuses on

- Continuous monitoring of system outputs
- Adjustment of inputs based on feedback
- Maintaining stability under changing conditions

This perspective reframes software delivery as a closed-loop system, where

- Code changes serve as inputs
- System performance represents outputs
- Observability data provides feedback
- CI/CD pipelines act as control mechanisms

In this way, the proactive regulation of the system is possible instead of the reactive management of failures. It changes the intention of merely implementing code to making the system behave predictably in the face of constant change.

1.3 The Promise and Plateau of DevOps

DevOps has been created in response to historic inefficiencies between software development and operations departments. Historically, there were two opposing sides in terms of developers and operations teams: developers were interested in providing features, and the operations team was interested in the stability of the system. This division produced wrong objectives, postponed releases, and often failed. DevOps has brought about a new framework that relies on the principle of collaboration, automation, and shared responsibility, which can deliver software faster and more reliably (Ugwueze & Chukwunweike, 2024).

DevOps fundamentally encourages continual incorporation, automated testing, and repeated releases. The practices lower the manual workload, enhance consistency, and assist in gradual delivery. CI/CD pipelines are also core in processing the automation of build, test, and deploy processes across the environments (Sannapureddy et al., 2021).

DevOps-adopting organizations claim to be able to live shorter deployment cycles and have quicker responses to market needs. Smaller releases with smaller increments minimize the potential risk of big deployments (Kolawole and Fakokunde, 2024).

Collaboration is another area that DevOps is enhancing by silo busting and enhancing cross-team transparency, resulting in a quicker resolution of issues and more reliable systems.

All these advantages notwithstanding, DevOps is becoming a limitation in contemporary settings.

1.3.1 Achievements of DevOps in Modern Software Delivery

DevOps has contributed greatly to the delivery of software. Its effects can be most observed in speed, reliability, collaboration, and consistency.

To start with, DevOps hastens delivery. Software can be released constantly through automated pipelines. This pace is essential in the competitive world where time to market is important.

Second, DevOps enhances the reliability of deployment. Automated testing and deployment minimize the human factor and provide continuous releases. This has minimized the failure rates and the use of rollback.

Third, DevOps changes the culture of the team. It fosters system performance and interdepartmental cooperation in both development and operation. Such alignment enhances the communication and system results.

Lastly, standardization is made possible by DevOps. Infrastructure as code (IaC) is one of the practices that provide consistency between the development, testing, and production environments (Kumar, 2024).

These successes have rendered DevOps crucial to contemporary software engineering. Its limitations are however becoming apparent as systems become increasingly complicated.

1.3.2 The Plateau: Limits of DevOps in Complex Systems

DevOps is effective in enhancing processes, but it cannot cope with system complexity. The modern software systems are not easy and predictable anymore. They are adaptive complex systems that have the following characteristics:

- High interdependence of microservices
- Constant scaling and coordination

- Several and repetitive changes
- Unpredictable component interactions

These properties bring in behavior that can hardly be predicted or controlled. This complexity cannot be fully controlled using pipeline-based DevOps. The larger the size of the systems, the harder it becomes to have visibility and control (Sanghi & Chaurasia, 2025).

1.3.3 Structural Limitations of DevOps

There are a number of structural constraints as to why DevOps goes to a plateau in complicated situations.

One of the biggest problems is the management of interdependent microservices. When something changes in one service, it may influence other services in some unanticipated manner. These system-wide interactions are not reflected in CI/CD pipelines, which usually work at the service level (Banerjee & Chatterjee, 2025).

A lack of system-wide visibility is another weakness. Monitoring tools create data that in most cases are scattered. Teams can hardly anticipate the behavior of the entire system or identify emerging problems in time (Chandrashekar, 2023).

The other type of risk is automation, which is dangerous when it is not regulated. CI/CD pipelines are fast at implementing changes, and they do not have strong feedback. Consequently, mistakes may be propagated quickly throughout the settings, making systems less stable (Tyagi, 2021).

Moreover, DevOps is based on the linear workflow. Such workflows fail to capture the non-linear nature of systems of today, where results are a result of various interacting factors.

Lastly, the DevOps ecosystem is now disjointed. A vast variety of tools are used by teams to control versions, CI/CD, monitor, and protect. These tools are usually autonomous, which complicates and raises cognitive load (Bajpai et al., 2024).

1.3.4 The Gap Between Process Optimization and System Control

These constraints indicate an inherent loophole:

DevOps streamlines processes and fails to regulate the behavior of systems.

Process optimization enhances the flow of software in the pipeline. It is however not a guarantee that the system will act as it is expected to act after deployment.

A process perspective deployment may be successful but will still result in suboptimal system performance. The space between these systems increases with the complexity and dynamics of the system.

In order to solve this problem, software delivery should not just be process execution. It should be concerned with the behavior of systems and their control.

1.3.5 Toward a New Paradigm

The DevOps plateau is not an omen of failure. Rather, it points out the necessity of evolution.

In order to deliver modern software, a software delivery model should focus on

- Constant feedback and response
- Global visibility and observability
- Feedback-driven and controlled interventions

These demands agree with the theory of control systems that aims at the management of dynamic systems based on feedback and control.

Organizations can no longer rely on process efficiency by considering software delivery as a control system. They are capable of creating systems that are fast and more so stable, resilient, and adaptive.

1.4 Pipeline-Centric Models: Capabilities and Limitations

The current DevOps practice is built on the model that is pipeline based and reflects software delivery as a series of automated processes, such as build, test, integration, deployment, and monitoring. This model has changed software engineering into an automated and repeatable process, as opposed to a manual and error-prone process. Due to this, organizations are able to provide software at a higher speed and with a higher consistency (Bajpai et al., 2024).

Practically, this model is applied by using CI/CD pipelines which determine a set of structured phases of the system through which the code will pass to the production phase after its development. Every stage has a particular role, e.g., compilation of the code, automated testing, configuration check, or artifact delivery. Such efficiency, traceability, and reproducibility have been enhanced in software delivery environments through standardization and the use of less human intervention (Sannapureddy et al., 2021).

Other important practices that have been achieved through pipeline-driven delivery include shift-left testing in which validation is done early on in the development lifecycle and automated quality gates in which only accepted code moves through the pipeline. Interstage feedback enables teams to detect and correct mistakes quickly.

Although these strengths exist, the models of the pipeline are based on a linear and reductionist perception of software delivery. This poses great constraints to complex and distributed systems.

1.4.1 Foundational Assumptions of Pipeline-Centric Models

Various software delivery simplifications are based on a number of underlying assumptions in pipeline-centric models. Although such assumptions may work in small-scale, controlled systems, they get problematic in large-scale cloud-native systems.

a. *Assumption of Deterministic System Behavior*

   Pipeline-centric models assume predictable system behavior, where a given input - such as a code change - produces a consistent and repeatable outcome. This assumption underpins automated testing and deployment, and implicitly relies on determinism across environments, which does not hold in distributed systems characterized by dynamic conditions, non-linear interactions, and infrastructure variability.

   Non-deterministic behavior is, however, common with distributed systems. Variables like network latency, resource contention, and asynchronous interaction may have different results under varying conditions. Consequently, the identical deployment can be different in different settings (Banerjee & Chatterjee, 2025).

b. *Assumption of Immediate and Reliable Feedback*

   CI/CD pipelines are created to give a fast response at every stage, enabling the developers to identify and fix the problems promptly. Such feedback is usually provided by automated tests, monitoring tools, and static analysis.

In reality, it is usually delayed, incomplete, or noisy feedback, particularly in a production setting. The real world is not the same as a test platform, and there are challenges that cannot be noted until after implementation. Such slowness diminishes the efficiency of validation by means of pipelines (Chandrashekar, 2023).

c. *Assumption of Component Independence*

Pipeline models assume that system components can be developed, tested, and deployed independently. This assumption simplifies pipeline design and supports parallel workflows.

In reality, modern systems consist of interdependent microservices. A change in one component can affect others in unexpected ways. These dependencies are difficult to capture in linear pipelines and often create blind spots in testing and validation (Kumar, 2024).

1.4.2 Capabilities of Pipeline-Centric Models

Pipeline-based models offer some significant advantages even though they have limitations.

Pipelines make the software delivery process standardized in the sense that all code changes go through the same validation and deployment procedures. This enhances reliability and lowers variability.

Efficiency is enhanced through automation, which gets rid of manual repetitive tasks. It eliminates human error and enhances quicker delivery cycles, especially in high-frequency deployment settings.

There is also enhanced traceability in pipelines. Execution logs offer a comprehensive account of each step, and it is possible to trace the changes and diagnose the problems with the help of execution logs. This is especially significant when industries are controlled.

Moreover, pipelines encourage scalability. Changes can be developed and deployed in parallel by the teams without the need to vary when applied to different environments.

The mentioned abilities explain why pipelines will continue to be useful in process optimization. Nevertheless, they are not as productive in the control of the dynamic behavior of modern systems.

1.4.3 Limitations in Modeling Complex System Behavior

The fact that pipeline-centric models do not provide a way to represent and control the behavior on a system-wide level is the primary drawback of these models. Modern software systems are complex adaptive systems, in which interactions between components yield results that are not predictable using linear analysis.

a. *Non-linearity and Emergent Behavior*

   Interactions within a distributed system give rise to behavior in services, infrastructure, and external dependencies. These are non-linear interactions, i.e., minor alterations have big and unpredictable consequences (Banerjee and Chatterjee, 2025).

   This complexity cannot be entirely reflected in pipeline models which have a step-by-step structure. This sets up a discrepancy between anticipated and observed system behavior.

b. *Fragmented Feedback and Limited Observability*

   Pipelines give feedback in certain steps, yet they do not allow one to see the entire picture of the system. However, observability tools produce massive amounts of data that are usually fragmented and hard to process.

   This constraint decreases the capability of the teams to identify the problems on time, learn about the root causes, and make knowledgeable decisions on deployments.

c. *Reactive Rather Than Proactive Risk Management*

   Models based on pipelines are reactive by nature. They are responsive to problems that arise. Some defects can be detected using automated tests but, again, not complex system failures.

   The contemporary systems have demanded proactive risk management in which possible problems are spotted and dealt with before they affect performance.

d. *Inability to Regulate System Behavior*

   One of the major drawbacks of pipeline-based models is that they do not have control mechanisms. Pipelines follow a set of steps without making changes according to the system feedback. They are open-loop systems in which the actions are not continually manipulated in response to performance.

This is especially important in high-velocity environments where fast rollouts can cause instability before the problem is diagnosed and resolved.

1.4.4 Reconceptualizing Software Delivery Beyond Pipelines

These drawbacks underscore the fact that it is time to go beyond pipeline-centric thinking. Software delivery cannot be considered a series of steps and actions but rather a dynamic system that has ongoing interactions and feedback.

This shift involves moving from

- Process execution → System behavior
- Stage-based validation → Continuous feedback
- Reactive correction → Proactive regulation

This perspective aligns with system-oriented delivery models, which emphasize adaptability, resilience, and stability.

As shown in the Table 1-1, system-oriented delivery models differ from traditional pipeline-centric models by emphasizing continuous feedback, adaptive behavior, and overall system resilience rather than linear process execution.

Table 1-1. *Pipeline-Centric vs. System-Oriented Delivery Models*

Aspect	Pipeline-Centric Model	System-Oriented Model
Structure	Linear workflow	Dynamic, interconnected system
Feedback	Stage-based, discrete	Continuous, multi-source
Behavior	Predictable, deterministic	Emergent, non-linear
Focus	Process efficiency	System stability and resilience
Risk Handling	Reactive	Proactive and adaptive

1.4.5 Implications for Modern Software Engineering

Sustenance of pipeline-based thinking in complex environments leads to a discrepancy between the management of systems and the way they operate. This results in high system fragility, low predictability, and high reliance on reactive troubleshooting.

Software delivery should undergo a change to meet these demands by adopting models that focus on continuous feedback, system-wide observability, and adaptive control mechanisms.

These demands justify the use of the control systems view that offers the means of controlling complex and dynamic software environments.

1.5 Complexity in Cloud-Native and Distributed Systems

Developments in modern software delivery are not in settings that are similar to the traditional centralized systems. Cloud-native and distributed architecture has presented new degrees of dynamism, scale, and interdependence. These developments have transformed the behavior of software systems and how they should be handled.

Cloud-native architectures are flexible, scalable, and resilient. They, however, also create complexity, which cannot be managed effectively in linear, pipeline-centric models. The behavior of a system is no longer predictable and stable. Rather, it changes constantly according to the fluctuation of work demands, infrastructure statuses, and service interactions.

There are usually three characteristics that define cloud-native systems. To begin with, applications are now executed in multi-cloud and hybrid environments. This distribution enhances the availability but makes operations more complex and unpredictable. Second, both containerization and orchestration facilitate dynamic scaling and automated resource management. The infrastructure is virtual, and resources are generated and deleted on demand. Third, the systems are based on distributed service architectures, especially microservices, wherein components communicate with each other via loosely coupled relational dependencies.

These attributes provide environments in which system behavior becomes adaptive and emergent. Any change can be transmitted between two or more services and may lead to unforeseen effects. Components often have dependencies that are not explicitly seen, and thus, it is not easy to know how a system will react to a new deployment or even configuration changes.

Moreover, real-time orchestration and continuous scaling cause the continuous change of state of systems. It complicates everything when it comes to staying consistent and reduces the probability of configuration drift and cascading failures. The failures are not an isolated occurrence anymore; they can propagate swiftly through the interrelated services.

This means that the software systems of the new era cannot be handled through process automation. It demands system-level knowledge in terms of interactions, dependencies, and feedback. Conventional pipeline-based methods that depend upon predictable and linear behavior are not able to cope with these issues completely.

1.5.1 Multi-cloud and Distributed Infrastructure Complexity

Multi-cloud strategies are more widely adopted nowadays as organizations are aiming to maximize performance, minimize vendor lock-in, and increase resilience. Nonetheless, the process of allocating workloads to different cloud providers also leads to a high level of operational complexity. All providers have unique services, configurations, and performance features which lead to a heterogeneous environment that can hardly be standardized and managed.

In such environments

- Resource provisioning is decentralized
- Network latency varies across regions
- Failure modes differ between platforms

Such diversity makes observing the system more complicated and troublesome to diagnose and fix the problems. Consequently, the system behavior starts to occur within the context, that is, the same deployments can produce varying results based on the infrastructure.

1.5.2 Containerization and Orchestration Dynamics

Software delivery has also been changed by the broad usage of container technologies and orchestration systems (e.g., Kubernetes). The containers allow the packaging of applications along with their dependencies, and this makes them consistent across environments. Orchestration platforms coordinate the deployment, scaling, and lifecycle of these containers to enable systems to dynamically react to demand changes.

These technologies bring about extreme dynamism and abstraction, even as they come with immense levels of advantages. The infrastructure is not permanent but volatile, as the resources are established, expanded, and shut down in the process of real time (Kumar, 2024).

This dynamism introduces several challenges:

- Rapid changes in system topology
- Difficulty in tracking resource states over time
- Increased complexity in debugging and incident analysis

Additionally, the orchestration decisions that include load balancing, scheduling, and auto-scaling can create unintended service–service interaction, which is another cause of system unpredictability.

1.5.3 Distributed Service Architectures and Interdependencies

The most common cloud-native systems are constructed today based on microservices architectures, in which applications are split into loosely coupled, independently deployable services. This is a good way to make things more modular and more scalable, but it also leads to complicated interdependencies between services.

Each service may

- Communicate with multiple upstream and downstream services
- Depend on shared infrastructure components (e.g., databases, message queues)
- Operate under different scaling and failure conditions

The interdependencies form a network of interactions that are hard to predict and model. Consequently, it creates system behavior that arises due to the collective behavior of components and not due to the behavior of individual services (Banerjee & Chatterjee, 2025).

This phenomenon, known as **emergent behavior**, implies that

- System-level outcomes cannot be fully understood by analyzing components in isolation
- Small changes in one part of the system can propagate and amplify across the network
- Failures may manifest in unexpected and indirect ways

1.5.4 Emergent Behavior and Non-linearity

The non-linear behavior of cloud-native systems is one of the defining characteristics of this type of system. Contrary to traditional systems, when cause and effect relationships are relatively very simple, distributed systems have behaviors that are driven by a number of interacting factors which include

- Network conditions
- Resource availability
- Concurrent workloads
- External dependencies

With this kind of system, the disproportionate and cascading effects can be caused by a small perturbation, like a change in configuration or an increase in traffic. The non-linearity poses a challenge to the classical methods of system design and management, which have a tendency to be predictive and stable.

Emergent behavior further complicates this landscape. For example:

- Incidentally, any deployment that passes all tests can be degraded by the real-life situation.
- Localized breakdown of a single service could have a trickle-down effect across the entire system.
- Auto-scaling systems can act unwittingly to increase the load imbalance.

These dynamics point out the shortcomings of pipeline-based validation which tests the components individually as opposed to testing them as part of the overall system.

1.5.5 Infrastructure as Code and Ephemeral Environments

One of the enablers of cloud-native delivery has been the adoption of infrastructure as code (IaC). IaC enables the definition of infrastructure, its provision, and management with code, and it is consistent and repeatable across environments (Kumar, 2024).

But IaC also adds to system complexity by allowing

- Quick and sustained changes in infrastructure
- Dynamically provide and decommission resources
- Automated reconfiguration of system components

This is causing contemporary landscapes to become more ephemeral, i.e., temporary and in a state of constant flux. This increases scalability and efficiency, but it presents a number of threats:

a. *Configuration Drift*

   With automation, there may be differences between the desired and actual system settings, especially in large-scale settings. Such inconsistencies may cause erratic behavior and instability of the system.

b. *Hidden Dependencies*

   Automated provisioning may hide links between elements, and it can be hard to determine the interactions between services and the propagation of changes within the system.

c. *Cascading Failures*

   Failure in a tightly coupled distributed system can spread quickly between services. In case of a single service failure, other dependent services could be overloaded, causing a domino effect and causing the entire system to be disrupted.

1.5.6 Implications for Software Delivery Models

Cloud-native and distributed systems are complex systems that reveal a fundamental limitation of traditional software delivery models:

They are not designed to manage dynamic, interconnected, and non-linear systems.

The approaches based on pipelines with their linear processes and stages validation are not adequate to describe the behavior of such systems. Specifically, they fail to

- Account for system-wide interactions
- Incorporate continuous, real-time feedback
- Adapt dynamically to changing system conditions

This causes an increasing disconnect between the delivery of systems and the behavior of systems in the production environment.

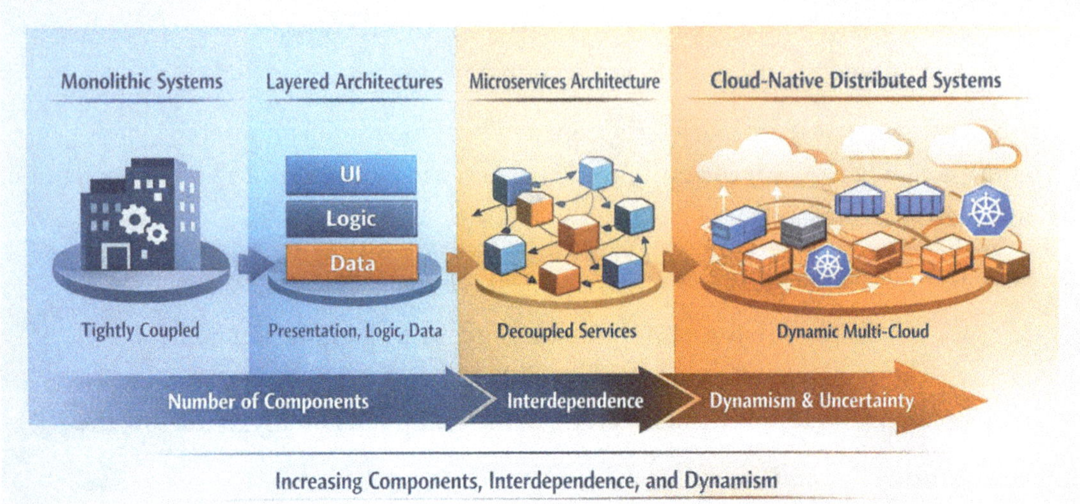

Figure 1-1. *Evolution of Software System Complexity Across Architectural Paradigms*

This figure demonstrates the gradual transformation of software system architecture models between monolithic models and completely distributed models based on a cloud. It provides a stratified perspective of four essential architectural patterns monolithic systems, where all components within an application are tightly coupled with each other layered architectures, where there is separation of concerns among presentation, logic, and data tiers microservices architectures, where an application is broken down into independently deployable services with a clear interface cloud-native distributed systems, where systems operate in dynamic and multi-cloud environments, and where each service is orchestrated by containers.

The figure underscores the way architectural evolution results in a dramatically growing system complexity that is expressed in three key dimensions: (i) the number of components and services being added to the system, (ii) the degree of interdependence among components and elements of the system, and (iii) increased dynamism and uncertainty due to continuous deployment, temporary infrastructure, and a distributed execution environment. All these changes together highlight the shift toward relatively predictable systems of relatively high adaptability and non-linearity and the need to design more sophisticated systems, monitor them, and control them.

1.5.7 Toward a New Approach to Managing Complexity

The issues presented in this section help to understand why a new approach to software delivery is important, and it must explicitly consider complexity, dynamism, and uncertainty. This should go beyond the level of workflow and encompass the mechanisms of

- Constant feedback and monitoring
- Adaptive system regulation
- Proactive system behavior management

The described requirements are very similar to the concepts of control systems theory, which gives an approach to handling dynamic and complex systems by means of feedback and control.

1.6 Failure Modes in Modern Software Delivery Systems

As software failures with highly distributed, cloud-native systems, the character of this type of failure has been transformed dramatically. The traditional failures were frequently local and deterministic, and their diagnosis was easier. They were usually restricted to one component layer or system layer. Modern software delivery environments, in contrast, are complex and interrelated systems. Failure in such environments is now non-linear, systemic, and unpredictable.

The reason behind this change is accelerating complexity, interdependence, and dynamism in the system, which has been mentioned in the section above. The failures are no longer a single event. Rather, they are the consequences of interactions among various components, layers of infrastructure, and external dependencies. This has led to failure analysis becoming system-level in place of component-level.

1.6.1 Characteristics of Modern Failure Modes

Modern software delivery systems exhibit distinct failure characteristics.

a. *Distributed Nature of Failures*

The failures in cloud-native systems have a tendency to diffuse to several services and are not easily localized. One fault may take different forms based on system dependencies. As an illustration, the latency spike in one service can cause the downstream services to fail, leading to a multi-point failure (Banerjee & Chatterjee, 2025).

b. *Difficulty in Detection*

Contemporary failures can be hard to spot during the act. Most are not capable of crashing systems instantly. Rather, they deteriorate performance over time or impact a certain group of users. These nuanced problems are usually not captured by traditional monitoring techniques, which are based on a predetermined set of thresholds (Chandrashekar, 2023).

c. *Delayed Manifestation of Issues*

One of the most important aspects of the modern modes of failure is the lag in cause and effect. A deployment can seem to be functioning well and satisfy all validation tests, yet still have latent problems. Such problems tend to arise later during certain conditions of running. This latency makes root cause analysis more difficult and riskier and makes instability potentially more long-term.

1.6.2 Common Failure Patterns in CI/CD-Driven Systems

The combination of CI/CD pipelines has enhanced the speed of deployment. Although this enhances responsiveness, it also brings new failure patterns that are associated with rapid and frequent changes.

a. *Deployment-Induced Failures*

Automated pipelines incorporate changes in production at a rapid rate. When a defect goes undetected at earlier stages, it may lead to the instant failure of the system when released. End users are usually impacted by these failures and rendered inefficient (Sannapureddy et al., 2021).

b. *Silent Performance Degradation*

Failures cannot be seen at once. Several deployments result in a progressive degradation of performance, i.e., longer latency, memory leakage, or lower throughput. Such problems might not raise an alarm but can seriously impact customer experience in the long run (Pereira, 2025).

c. *Cascading Failures Across Services*

Microservices architecture builds high interdependencies. A malfunction in any of the parts may sprawl throughout the system. As an illustration, a failure of the database can overload the dependent services, leading to an outage in the entire system. Such cascade failures are hard to predict and manage.

d. *Monitoring Overload and Alert Fatigue*

The modern systems produce masses of telemetry data, such as logs, metrics, and alerts. Although this data can be used to support observability, it may overwhelm engineers unless they are handled appropriately. A large number of alerts (including false positives) may result in alert fatigue and may cause important problems to be overlooked (Tyagi, 2021).

Software delivery systems experience a variety of failure modes, each affecting system reliability in different ways. Table 1-2 summarizes the most common failure types, their characteristics, and the operational impact they can have on enterprise environments.

Table 1-2. *Failure Patterns in CI/CD Systems*

Failure Type	Description	Impact
Deployment Failure	Errors during release	Immediate downtime
Silent Degradation	Performance issues post-deployment	User dissatisfaction
Cascading Failure	Dependency-triggered failure	System-wide outage
Alert Fatigue	Excessive alerts masking critical signals	Missed critical incidents

1.6.3 The Role of CI/CD Velocity in Failure Propagation

The modern world of software delivery is characterized by high deployment velocity. CI/CD pipelines facilitate regular and fast releases. Though this might enhance the speed of innovation, it also augments the chances of spreading the error.

The old systems had slower release cycles and thus more time to identify and correct problems. Modern pipelines on the other hand implement changes themselves on demand – sometimes several times a day. This minimizes the time taken to detect and rectify flaws before they get to production (Kolawole & Fakokunde, 2024).

According to Pereira (2025), the transmission of failures can occur in high-speed pipelines in various ways:

- Incorrect changes are implemented more often.
- Problems propagate in environments and are not noticed.
- The changes are overlapping, and this complicates recovery.

This interaction makes software delivery a high-frequency and risky process in which failures can grow exponentially.

1.6.4 Limitations of Traditional Failure Management Approaches

The conventional failure management methods depend on traditional reactive identification and human intervention. They make assumptions of cause and effect, immediate visibilities into failures, and individual components of a system. But the assumptions are not true with the current software systems. Such failures can be non-linear and have multiple factors contributing to them and are not visible because they are not observable. Failures are not usually localized. Due to this, organizations have a major problem in finding root causes within a short time frame, containing failures before they blow out, and ensuring the stability of systems in a world of constant change.

When the velocity of deployment is high in CI/CD, these restraints become more evident due to the limited time to detect and respond to threats. Traditional methods have problems with such environments, failing to cope with

- Overlapping changes that obscure cause-and-effect relationships

- Delayed or noisy feedback signals that hinder timely decision-making
- Tightly coupled dependencies that allow failures to propagate across services

As a result, the implementation of reactive methods only contributes to the rise of operational risk and constrains the capacity of an organization to have resilient and stable systems. This solidifies the necessity to have more active, feedback-based failure management methods.

1.6.5 Toward Proactive Failure Management

The key to curbing modern failure modes lies in the transition from reactive ways to troubleshoot to proactive ways to manage the system. This entails making systems more observable, using early warning systems, and creating systems that can endure and recover from failure.

Organizations have to be more visible in order to identify valuable signals at an early stage. They must also incorporate anomaly detecting and automatic response systems to make the process of reactions quicker. Moreover, the systems should be resilient in design to manage and overcome disruption.

These strategies are consistent with the principles of control systems, where the behavior of the system is constantly observed and modified according to the feedback.

The subsequent emergence of a new system architecture is also indicated by the growth of the complexity of failures. The shift toward monolithic systems to distributed cloud-native environments as shown in Figure 1-1 adds more and more components, interdependencies, and system dynamism. This has a direct increase in the probability and influence of system failures.

1.7 Limitations of Automation-Driven Delivery

Automation is considered to be one of the main pillars of DevOps. It allows organizations to automate the delivery of software, minimize manual labor, and launch systems at unprecedented speed. Software delivery has become more predictable, faster, and highly scalable through the use of CI/CD pipelines, infrastructure as code (IaC), and automated testing frameworks. Nevertheless, regardless of such advantages, automation creates systematic risks in case of its uncontrolled functioning, particularly in complex, cloud-native systems.

Fundamental to automation, software delivery is turned into an accelerated execution platform, where the changes are quickly diffused across the settings. Although this makes the code more efficient, the risk of introducing mistakes and exponential growth is elevated. The high-velocity pipelines prompt successful deployments and fault spreading, and in the case of the lack of safeguards, the system may be degraded in a short period of time (Tyagi, 2021).

1.7.1 Automation as an Unregulated Amplifier of Change

Automation eliminates friction in the delivery process, enabling tasks to be executed automatically within seconds with minimal human intervention. While this increases system responsiveness, it also amplifies the impact of incorrect changes by accelerating their propagation across environments and weakening traditional feedback and control mechanisms that previously mitigated risk.

In automated setups, code is constantly integrated and deployed, validation processes are defined and restricted, and human monitoring is minimized. Due to this, automation may be something that amplifies change without control. With minor defects, they can spread quickly through systems, configuration mistakes can occur in many environments at the same time, and faulty updates may make it to production and be discovered.

This is an even greater issue in distributed systems where one error can spread through several layers of service and infrastructure.

1.7.2 The Risks of High-Speed CI/CD Pipelines

The work of CI/CD pipelines is quick and efficient, enabling organizations to launch changes several times a day. Nonetheless, this focus on speed creates a number of severe risks.

To begin with, higher deployment frequency diminishes the time during which extensive validation is possible. Automated tests are able to detect the known problems but fail to represent the complex interactions of the system.

Second, overlapping changes are caused by high deployment velocity. Several updates can be brought at the same time, which will make it hard to single out the source of failures (Pereira, 2025).

Third, mistakes have the ability to spread rapidly within settings. Developed faulty staging configuration may easily leak to production and impact end users.

These dangers bring out one of the main shortcomings of automation-based delivery:

Speed destroys the stability of a system when there is a lack of feedback and control systems.

1.7.3 AI-Driven Automation: Opportunities and Emerging Challenges

The automation has been further improved with the adoption of artificial intelligence (AI) in DevOps. The AI-based systems have the potential to streamline pipelines, anticipate failures, and automatically make decisions, enhancing their efficiency and flexibility (Allam, 2025).

Nevertheless, AI also presents other problems.

AI systems tend to be based on acquired patterns as opposed to rules. This may result in the unplanned behavior of the system, especially in the new environment. Besides that, AI-based decision-making is not easily understandable, making it more challenging to debug and analyze incidents.

The greater the autonomy of automation, the less visible and controllable people are. Although this minimizes the overhead of operation, it hinders the capacity of the engineers to intervene in real time and rectify failures (Mittal, 2025).

These issues demonstrate the necessity of paying close attention to the aspects of AI integration into software delivery systems to make sure that the process of automation increases, but does not decrease the level of system reliability.

1.7.4 The Illusion of Control in Fully Automated Systems

One of the most widespread myths about contemporary DevOps is that the more it is automated, the more control it has. As a matter of fact, automation without a relevant feedback system gives an illusion of control. Systems can be seen to be functional, and yet there might be structural problems.

This illusion is because automated processes are applied without regard to context, with a monitoring system being unable to pick subtle anomalies, and feedback connections are frequently incomplete or lagging.

Consequently, organizations might still be implementing changes when they think that it has become stable, only to realize they end up failing in the future. The difference between perceived and actual system condition is a major hazard in automation-based environments.

1.7.5 The Need for Feedback-Driven Regulation

The automation should be supported with powerful feedback and control to counter the limitations. The process of automation must be more of a closed-loop process, with actions being constantly adjusted by real-time feedback.

Key requirements include

- Constant observability to give correct and proper computer system insights
- Dynamic control systems in response to changes in the system
- Critical operation decision-making that involves a human in the loop

By incorporating these aspects, organizations can turn automation, as a strictly execution-based process, into a regulated and reconfigurable framework.

1.7.6 Toward Controlled Automation in Software Delivery

The deficiencies of automation-based delivery emphasize that automation should be switched to controlled automation. This change demands a departure from speed as the central goal and putting stability and resilience of the system at the forefront.

It also entails the incorporation of feedback loops in all the delivery processes so that the behavior of the system is monitored and controlled constantly. This strategy is consistent with the control systems theory, in which the performance of the system is sustained by the constant feedback mechanisms and correction.

1.8 Introducing Control Systems Thinking

The increasing complexity, dynamism, and interdependence of modern software systems necessitate a paradigm shift as they demand a system-oriented approach as opposed to the traditional process-based approach. The control systems theory offers a well-established paradigm for understanding and managing complex adaptive systems. Control theory was initially adapted in engineering to control physical systems and is concerned with ensuring desired system behavior by continually monitoring, feeding back, and controlling.

In essence, the goal of any control system is to maintain the system output at a desired state in the face of disturbances, uncertainties, and variable conditions. This is done by means of closed-loop control in which outputs are monitored and returned into the system to provide corrective action. This method is specifically applicable in modern software delivery where systems are run in dynamic environments where change and uncertainty are the norm.

1.8.1 Fundamental Principles of Control Systems

Control systems are based on some fundamental principles that dictate the response of the systems to the inputs and how systems are maintained over time. These are feedback loops, stability, adaptation, and regulation. Feedback loops register the outputs of the system, and the data are employed to modify the inputs. Stability is the capacity of the system to behave in a similar way when exposed to different conditions. Establishing a dynamic final response to any changes inside and outside the system is made possible through adaptation and sustained correction through regulation, respectively.

In contrast to open-loop systems, which carry out actions without regard to consequences, closed-loop systems constantly compare the actual system activity with the expected performance and make corrections. The feedback that is continuous allows the control and the performance of the system to be better.

1.8.2 Mapping Control System Components to Software Delivery

The control systems thinking applied to software delivery necessitates a solid mapping of the traditional components of a control system to the aspects of the current DevOps environment. Such mapping allows a conceptual transformation of the perspective on software delivery as the chain of actions and the interpretation of the delivery as a controlled system of interactions.

Core Components

- **Inputs**

  In software delivery, inputs are the changes in code, changes in configuration, and changes in infrastructure that are added to the system. These are the major sources of system evolution.

- **System (Process)**

  The system is composed of the runtime environment, which consists of applications and services, infrastructure, and orchestration platforms that consume inputs and produce outputs.

- **Outputs**

  Outputs can be defined as the visible results of system behavior, e.g., performance measures, system reliability, latency, and user experience.

- **Feedback**

  Observability mechanisms such as logs, metrics, traces, and alerts are used to derive feedback. These indicators give information on the system status.

- **Controller**

  It is the controller that modulates the inputs using feedback. CI/CD pipelines, deployment strategies, and automated decision-making mechanisms are playing this role in software delivery by controlling the way changes are introduced and handled.

This mapping establishes a direct analogy between control systems and software delivery, enabling the application of control-theoretic principles to improve system stability and performance.

Software delivery can be viewed as a closed-loop control system in which every deployment generates operational feedback that influences subsequent delivery decisions. Rather than treating deployment as the end of the process, the system continuously measures outcomes, evaluates operational signals, and refines future actions to maintain stability and reliability. Figure 1-2 illustrates how closed-loop control principles are applied to software delivery, with CI/CD acting as the controller that continuously adjusts the system based on runtime feedback.

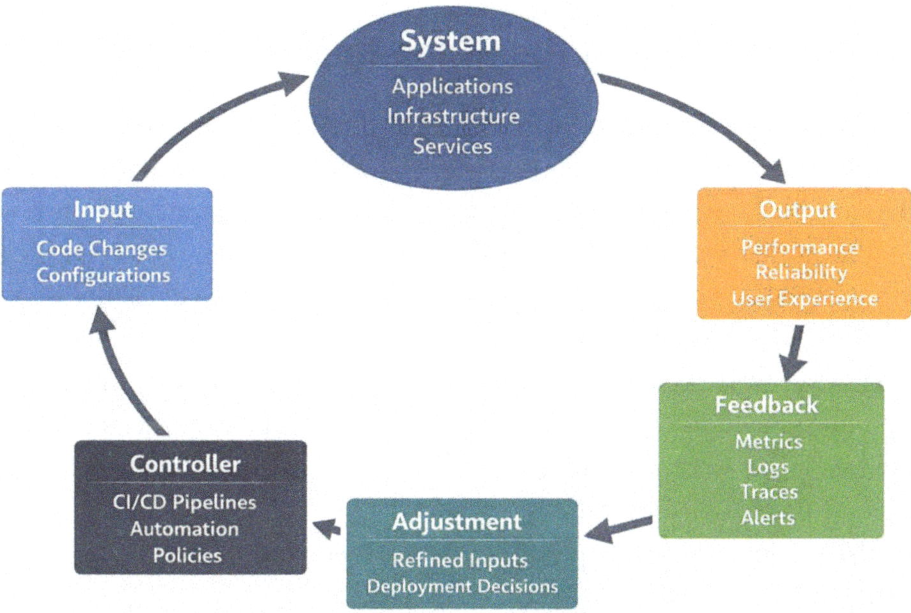

Figure 1-2. *Closed-Loop Control Model Applied to Software Delivery Systems*

This figure represents a conceptual model of software delivery as a closed-loop control system, by showing the constant interplay of inputs, system processes, outputs, feedback controls, and control activities. It starts with inputs as the model takes the shape of code changes, configuration changes, and infrastructure changes which are injected into the system. The system receives these inputs and generates outputs, including system performance, system reliability, and user experience.

Feedback mechanisms such as metrics, logs, traces, and alerts are used to monitor these outputs and provide real-time visibility into system behavior. The controller interprets the feedback and is embodied by CI/CD pipelines, automated deployment strategies, and governance policies and sets corrective actions accordingly. Such activities lead to configuration of system inputs, including refined deployments, rollbacks, or changes of the system, and thus the loop is closed.

This figure highlights the shift between a conventional linear delivery pipeline toward a dynamic, feedback-based control system, with three essential qualities: (i) dynamic feedback mechanisms that make the system self-aware, (ii) active response to observed system behavior by dynamically adjusting inputs, and (iii) continuous control of system behavior and stability. The closed-loop view offers a baseline to approach the architecture of software delivery systems which are responsive, robust, and able to sustain the desirable effect in a dynamic and highly dynamic environment.

1.8.3 From Open-Loop Pipelines to Closed-Loop Systems

The classical CI/CD pipelines may be perceived as the kind of open-loop systems when the pre-defined set of steps gets performed, but it is not continuously modified in accordance with the outcomes of the system. Although such pipelines may have validation phases (like testing and quality checks), they are usually not dynamically adjusted to the dynamically running system. This leads to making decisions depending on set rules instead of the actual running of the system.

Conversely, a control systems approach modifies software delivery into a closed system. System behavior is continuously monitored, and actions in this model are changed in relation to feedback. This helps the delivery process adapt to the varying conditions and ensures system stability.

A closed-loop delivery system is defined by the following:

- Ongoing observation of the system outputs, such as performance, reliability, and user experience
- Decision-making that relies on observability data, deploying, and operating based on this feedback
- Adaptation modifications, including rolling back, scaling, or altering the configuration to sustain the required system performance

Combining these aspects, software delivery transforms into dynamic regulation instead of being conveyed in a fixed manner. This methodology helps overcome one of the main drawbacks of pipeline-based models, which is the use of continuous control instead of a pre-defined workflow.

Finally, the replacement of open-loop pipelines with closed-loop systems can help organizations to get beyond process automation and to actively manage system behavior and guarantee a higher degree of stability, resilience, and adaptability to complex environments.

1.8.4 Benefits of Applying Control Systems Thinking to Software Delivery

There are important benefits to applying principles of control systems to the delivery of software, especially in dealing with complexity, uncertainty, and ongoing change. By moving away from the execution based on the process approach to feedback-based regulation, organizations will be able to enhance the performance of the system as well as its reliability.

A major advantage is that there is constant control of system behavior. Control systems also provide the ability to monitor and make changes continuously, to keep the system outputs consistent with the expected results. This minimizes the chances of unnoticed deviations and enhances the reliability of the entire system.

The other significant benefit is that it has enhanced stability in dynamic situations. The control systems through feedback loops ensure that the behavior is maintained as the workloads, infrastructure conditions, and deployment patterns vary. This is particularly important in cloud-native systems, where the behavior of the systems is non-linear and not predictable (Banerjee & Chatterjee, 2025).

An adaptive response to feedback is also supported by control systems. Software delivery mechanisms can even be dynamically adapted in real time using system data. As an example, the deployment strategies can be adjusted based on the performance metrics, so the teams could resolve possible issues before they become critical.

Besides that, control systems improve decision-making. Feedback-driven methods offer precise and punctual information about how the system behaves so that engineers can make rational choices about deployments, rollbacks, and optimization of the system.

All of these advantages indicate that control systems thinking can change the software delivery process, which is traditionally a process-oriented and static activity, to a dynamic and adaptive system that can retain its stability even in the context of a complex environment.

1.8.5 Addressing Limitations of DevOps Through Control Systems

The concept of control systems thinking directly responds to some weaknesses found in the traditional DevOps methodologies. Feedback-based control allows organizations to shift the focus away from process efficiency and into efficient system control.

Key improvements include

- Increased system-wide visibility, which is gained by the extensive feedback and observability mechanisms that give a sense of the overall system behavior
- Less overdependence on automation, through the inclusion of feedback-managed automation that varies responses according to the current conditions in the system
- Better control of non-linear behavior, via adaptive control strategies that react to complex and unpredictable interactions of the system

Organizations may go beyond process optimization by integrating these control principles within the software delivery so that they can be able to transition to regulation at the system level. Such a shift allows creating delivery systems that are efficient, yet stable, resilient, and adaptable to dynamic environments.

1.8.6 Toward a Control-Oriented Software Delivery Paradigm

Control systems thinking is a paradigm change in the way software delivery is treated and thought. It does not see delivery as a series of activities, but instead, it redefines it as a feedback mechanism that needs constant monitoring and regulation.

The aspects of this paradigm include

- The significance of quality feedback signals that give precise and prompt information on the system behavior
- Responsive and adaptive control mechanisms, which should be able to cope with the changing conditions of the systems
- Automation is incorporated in a larger control system, where automated processes are controlled, not autonomous

This view is consistent with the new movements in platform engineering, DevSecOps, and resilience engineering where the emphasis has been on ensuring that systems are stable in the face of complexity, uncertainty, and constant change.

1.9 From Pipelines to Control-Oriented Delivery Systems

The complexity and the dynamism of modern software systems demand an original change in the understanding and management of software delivery. Pipeline-based models are conventional ways of delivery, depicting it as a sequence of automated steps that are pre-defined. Although these models are effective at enhancing efficiency and speed of deployment, they lack the capability to handle the system-wide behavior, uncertainty, and continuous change.

The control-oriented delivery systems change the focus of perspective on the stability of workflow to dynamic feedback systems. This strategy is consistent with the control systems theory, under which the behavior of a system is actively observed, analyzed, and corrected in order to provide the desired results.

1.9.1 From Static Workflows to Dynamic Systems

Pipeline-based models understand software delivery as a process that is linear and deterministic; software flows through phases of the process, including build, test, and deployment. This framework is consistent and repeatable but requires that the behavior of the system can be predicted and that system behavior can be validated at the various levels.

As a matter of fact, modern software environments are non-linear and dynamic. The factors that determine system behavior are as follows:

- Persistent variation of the state of the system.
- Answers to this question can be found in distributed interactions.
- Unstable workload and infrastructure factors.

Consequently, the workings of the delivery systems should be more of a flexible system that responds to real-time alterations instead of taking predetermined paths of execution. This change makes the emphasis less on the execution of processes to control the behavior of a system.

1.9.2 From Reactive Processes to Proactive Regulation

Conventional DevOps is more or less reactive. They are based on incident response and monitoring to solve the problems that arise. Although this is needed, it is not enough in environments where failures can be transmitted quickly.

Control-based systems of delivery are proactive in nature. They

- Eliminate possible problems by means of constant feedback
- Implement remedial measures too early to prevent failures
- Control system behavior to be stable

Such proactive control can be facilitated by feedback mechanisms that enable the systems to observe the difference between the desired state and make corrections. Ongoing monitoring of system behavior decreases the possibility of unforeseen failures and enhances resilience.

1.9.3 Continuous Feedback Loops as a Core Mechanism

Control-oriented delivery systems are based on continuous feedback loops. Control-oriented systems combine feedback throughout the delivery lifecycle, as opposed to the case with traditional pipelines, where feedback is confined to particular steps.

There are various sources that provide feedback, and this includes

- System performance metrics
- Application logs and traces
- User experience indicators
- Security and compliance indicators

These indicators give a full picture of system behavior. They facilitate making decisions in time and in an informed manner.

Continuous feedback ensures that

- System state is always monitored
- Deviations are detected early
- Adjustments are applied in real time

This transforms software delivery into a closed-loop system, where actions are continuously guided by outcomes.

1.9.4 System-Wide Visibility and Observability

Control needs a system-wide perspective. Pipeline-based models tend to have very little visibility and are restricted to a particular stage or component. This is because it becomes hard to comprehend how changes spread throughout the system.

System-wide observability is the focus of control-oriented delivery systems. They combine information from several sources to give a single perspective of system performance and behavior.

This includes

- Service inter-service tracing
- Aggregated performance and reliability measurements
- Correlated logs to analyze and debug

Enhanced observability helps organizations discern trends, detect deviations, and system-wide effects of changes. It minimizes uncertainty and facilitates better regulation of systems.

1.9.5 Adaptive Decision-Making in Software Delivery

One of the characteristics of control-oriented delivery systems is adaptive decision-making. The decisions are made on the basis of the system feedback in real time as opposed to predetermined rules.

Examples include

- Reconfiguring deployment policies on performance measures
- Rolling back changes automatically in case of anomalies
- Resource scaling based on changes in workload

This flexibility is necessary in places where changes occur very quickly. It enables the delivery systems to react to the emerging issues and to remain stable in different circumstances.

1.9.6 Integrating Control Principles into CI/CD Ecosystems

The move to control-driven delivery is not an alternative to CI/CD pipelines. Rather, it adds control mechanisms to them. Changes are still carried out by pipelines, but control systems provide a layer of regulation that governs the way and timing of change application.

This integration involves

- Integrating feedback loops in pipeline stages
- Making deployments based on observability data
- Using policies to control the behavior of a system

Organizations are able to achieve a balance between speed and stability by integrating pipelines and control mechanisms, as well as guaranteeing the stable delivery of software.

1.9.7 Implications for Modern Software Engineering

The shift toward control-based delivery systems has an important impact on software engineering practices.

The emphasis of engineering has changed to the control of the behavior of a system rather than the optimization of the process. Observability turns out to be a requirement and not an auxiliary feature. Control mechanisms accompany automation to make sure that it is carried out safely. The process of decision-making has been turned to adaptive and data-driven instead of being rule-based.

These shifts demand new skills, tools, and practices in the organization. They also need a change of thinking in which the delivery of the software is perceived as a system that is constantly controlled.

1.10 Organizational and Engineering Implications

The change to a control systems approach to software delivery is not only a technological change but also a very important change in the organization's structure. Shifting away from the pipeline-based execution to the feedback-driven, control-oriented systems implies altering the way the teams are organized, decisions are made, and the way the systems are designed, monitored, and controlled. This paradigm redefines software delivery as an evolving and dynamic process, where the engineering practice and capabilities of an organization have to be aligned.

In its essence, a control-oriented approach implies that organizations should be able to go beyond their fixation on process efficiency and focus more on the behavior of systems, their stability, and their resilience. Such a change would require the concerted movement along several fronts, such as platform engineering, observability, decision-making models, and maturity of DevOps.

1.10.1 Emergence of Platform Engineering as a Control Layer

One important consequence of the control systems thinking taught is that platform engineering has become a core competency. Platform engineering is concerned with the design and management of internal developer platforms (IDPs), standardized and reusable tools and services used to deliver software.

In a control-based paradigm, platform engineering is treated as a control layer that allows uniform and controllable behavior of a system. It supports

- Deployment process standardization
- Malaysian key figures: The feedback mechanism is centralized
- Implementation of governance policy and operational restrictions

Platform engineering removes the cognitive effort of development teams by abstracting underlying complexity and providing self-service capabilities, but ensures consistency and control throughout the organization (Rusum & Pappula, 2024).

Moreover, platform engineering provides the opportunity to combine the main elements of the delivery ecosystem. These are CI/CD pipelines, observability tools, and security and compliance mechanisms. This integration enhances the visibility of the system-wide and facilitates coordinated control of the distributed environment.

1.10.2 Investment in Observability as a Foundational Capability

Observability is not an option in a control-oriented delivery system: it is a requirement. To gain control, it is important that feedback on system behavior is accurate, timely, and actionable. In the absence of quality observability data, organizations would not be able to track performance consistently or identify when they are not in the desired state.

In order to facilitate this, organizations are required to invest in observability infrastructure of full scale. This includes

- System performance and reliability metrics
- Detailed event logs and event analysis logs
- Trace distributed to know about the service-to-service interactions

Such abilities will assist in real-time detection of anomalies, enhance the root cause analysis, and improve the general situational awareness throughout the system.

Notably, observability needs to grow out of a tool-focused approach. It must be considered as a strategic ability that is woven into the software delivery lifecycle. This will make feedback available at all times to aid in decision-making, system control, and stability in the long run.

1.10.3 Feedback-Driven Decision-Making Models

Traditional software delivery is mostly premised on prescribed rules and fixed decision-making procedures, in which processes are determined by presumption or by prior behavior. Conversely, control-based systems demand decision-making that is driven by feedback, wherein actions are constantly tuned with reference to real-time system data.

This change has a number of implications.

To begin with, the process of making decisions becomes informed. The choices involved in deployment, rollback, and scaling are informed by metrics and system signals and no longer by intuition. It enhances precision and minimizes the possibility of wrong action.

Second, regular assessment takes the place of periodic assessment. The organizations implement continuous monitoring and adjustment instead of measuring the performance of the system at predetermined intervals. This enables problems to be detected and dealt with when they arise.

Third, dynamic adaptation is accepted. Changing conditions are adjusted in real time, with systems and processes adapting to the changing conditions to maintain more flexible and resilient operations.

Consequently, the type of decision-making based on feedback enhances the capacity of an organization to

- Detect issues early
- React positively to risks that arise
- Maintain system stability under varying conditions

1.10.4 Evolution of DevOps Maturity Toward System-Level Thinking

The movement toward the control-based delivery system means that organizations need to take DevOps maturity further than simple automation and collaboration. The maturity models of traditional DevOps focus on pipeline automation, continuous integration and deployment, and collaboration between teams. These factors still play a crucial role, but they are not enough to handle the complexity of modern software systems.

Organizations need to take a system-level approach in order to fill this gap. It will consist of putting more emphasis on the study of system-wide interactions, the ability to manage feedback loops effectively, the stability, and resilience of dynamic environments.

According to Oyewole et al., mature DevOps organizations expand their capabilities by inculcating observability in the main workflows, incorporating feedback into the process of decision-making, and instituting governance systems that aid adaptive control.

This development shifts DevOps from a set of practices to a system management approach and is well-related to the guidelines of the control systems theory.

1.10.5 Organizational Alignment and Cultural Transformation

The adoption of a control systems approach also necessitates a change in organizational culture on a large scale. Conventional organizational frameworks that tend to isolate development, operations, and security functions are not conducive to dealing with dynamic feedback systems.

Key organizational implications include

a. *Cross-Functional Collaboration*

   Teams must work collaboratively across disciplines, sharing responsibility for system outcomes and leveraging collective insights to manage complexity.

b. *Emphasis on System Thinking*

   The mindset developed by engineers and those in charge should put the emphasis on the interdependencies and behavior on the system level, as opposed to the emphasis on the parts.

c. *Continuous Learning and Adaptation*

   Organizations must embrace a culture of experimentation and continuous improvement, where feedback is used to refine processes and enhance system performance.

1.10.6 Engineering Practice Transformation

Engineering-wise, the process of switching to control-based delivery systems necessitates fundamental modifications in the design and functioning of systems. Functionality and performance were the major concerns of traditional approaches. Conversely, the contemporary systems should also be engineered to sustain ongoing feedback, flexibility, and robustness.

The design principles that are highlighted in this transformation include the following:

- **Design observability**: The systems are designed to produce meaningful and useful feedback.

- Design resilience, such that systems can withstand failure, isolate failure, and recover.
- Design to be adaptable so that the architectures can be dynamically scaled and reconfigured.

Besides the architectural transformation, the engineers must acquire new skills to work in the field of control. These include

- Knowledge of feedback loops and system dynamics
- Making sense of observability data to make decisions
- Creating self-governing systems

Combined, these changes transform the engineering practices as they are no longer concerned with the creation of fixed systems but rather with creating dynamic systems that are driven by feedback and capable of functioning under constant change.

1.10.7 Integrating Governance and Control Mechanisms

Control-based delivery systems demand that governance mechanisms that are compliant, secure, and reliable be incorporated which do not restrict system agility. These mechanisms act as the restriction in the control system, which determines the behavior of the system, but it remains flexible and adaptable.

Governance in this case is directly incorporated into the delivery process and is not used as an external or manual checkpoint. This will allow the uninterrupted implementation of standards without interruption of delivery.

Common examples include

- Policy as Code frameworks, or written and executed rules
- Systematic verification of compliance, which guarantees that the systems comply with the regulatory and organizational standards

Controlled releases risk-based deployment controls, where release strategies are varied according to the risk level of the system.

These mechanisms are put in place to make sure that the systems can work within a set limit, yet they can respond to changing environments. Because of this, organizations are able to remain both in control and agile in dynamic and complicated environments.

1.11 Chapter Summary and Transition

This chapter has critically analyzed how practices of software delivery have evolved and how there is an increasing disalignment between the old DevOps paradigm and the nature of a modern, cloud-native system. Although DevOps and CI/CD pipelines have provided significant benefits in terms of automation, collaboration, and deployment speed, they are deeply entrenched in pipeline-based and process-based thinking. As has been revealed in this chapter, these methods are becoming inadequate when it comes to handling systems of high complexity, interdependence, and constant change.

A number of major limitations have been identified in the analysis. First, pipeline-based models are based on the simplification of assumptions, including deterministic behavior, component independence, and instant feedback, which cannot be true in a distributed environment. Second, there is the growing use of microservices, multi-cloud architecture, and automated orchestration which has brought about emergent and non-linear system behavior that cannot be effectively described or controlled by linear workflows. Third, automation, although efficient, may raise the risk of systems that are not supported by well-established feedback and control systems.

To address these issues, this chapter has proposed control systems thinking as a more competitive and stronger conceptual framework for the current software delivery. With the reformulation of delivery systems to dynamic feedback-based control systems, it can be possible to move the focus to not only the implementation of processes but to actively control the behavior of the system. The significance of this viewpoint lies in the importance of

- Continuous feedback loops for real-time system awareness
- System-wide observability to capture holistic behavior
- Adaptive decision-making to respond to changing conditions
- Controlled automation to balance speed with stability

In addition, the chapter has discussed the larger organizational and engineering consequences of this change, such as the rise of platform engineering, the centrality of observability, and the demand for feedback-based operational models. Overall, these developments lead to a new paradigm where the software delivery systems would also be created in a way that ensures resilience, stability, and flexibility, in addition to being fast and efficient.

To conclude, the shift of pipeline-based DevOps toward control-based delivery systems is one of the paradigm shifts in the design, deployment, and management of software systems. It has been a transition toward dynamic systems with dynamic workflows and reactive processes into proactive regulation, isolated parts of the ecosystems that are holistically managed.

This chapter is followed by the next chapter which develops upon this foundation by introducing the main principles of the control systems theory, such as feedback loops, stability, signal processing, and control boundaries. It also builds a stringent mapping of these principles and software delivery systems, which gives the theoretical basis that is needed to create scalable, stable, and adaptable delivery platforms.

References

Bajpai, G., Schildmeijer, M., Mishra, M., & Piwosz, P. (2024). *CI/CD design patterns.* Packt Publishing.

Banerjee, R., & Chatterjee, T. (2025). Comparative evaluation of cloud-native and VM-based CI/CD pipelines. *Asian Journal of Research in Computer Science, 18*(11), 153–171.

Chandrashekar, P. (2023). CI/CD integration in DevOps workflows. *International Journal of Advanced Research in Science, Communication and Technology, 3*(3), 1366–1376.

Gajula, S. (2025). Cloud-native technologies and multi-cloud strategies. *International Journal of Advanced Computer Science and Applications, 16*(4), 75–81.

Kolawole, I., & Fakokunde, A. (2024). Improving software development with CI/CD. *International Journal of Computer Applications Technology and Research, 14*(1), 25–39.

Kumar, M. (2024). Automated deployment pipelines for AWS using GitOps.

Mittal, A. (2025). AI-driven DevOps automation. In *International Conference of Global Innovations and Solutions* (pp. 130–147). Springer.

Oyewole, T., Akokodaripon, D. A., Babatope, O. M., & Mayo, W. A. DevOps maturity framework.

Pereira, L. (2025). Impact of CI/CD automation on performance and scalability.

Prakash, M. D., & Sharma, N. (2023). DevOps and cloud computing convergence. In *Proceedings of ICIIP* (pp. 800–805). IEEE.

Rusum, G. P., & Pappula, K. K. (2024). Platform engineering and developer platforms. *International Journal of AI, Big Data, Computational and Management Studies, 5*(1), 89–101.

Sanghi, S., & Chaurasia, D. (2025). *Enterprise DevOps architecture.* Yashita Prakashan.

Sannapureddy, R., Nelavelli, S., & Kovvuri, V. (2021). Optimizing CI/CD pipelines. *International Journal of AI, Big Data, Computational and Management Studies, 2*(4), 117–129.

Tyagi, A. (2021). Intelligent DevOps. *Journal of Emerging Technologies and Innovative Research, 8,* 367–385.

Ugwueze, V. U., & Chukwunweike, J. N. (2024). CI/CD strategies for DevOps. *International Journal of Computer Applications Technology and Research, 14*(1), 1–24.

Allam, H. (2025). AI-augmented CI/CD systems. *International Journal of AI, Data Science, and Machine Learning, 6*(1), 137–146.

CHAPTER 2

Control System Thinking for Software Engineers

2.1 Chapter Objective

The new software delivery systems are no longer predictable pipelines. They act as dynamic systems - dynamically changing, responsive to inputs, and responsive to the real-world conditions. However, they continue to be handled by the majority of teams through linear workflows on the basis of stability and predictability.

This chapter presents another approach to the thinking of software delivery.

We do not view delivery as a series of steps that are automated; rather, we view it as a controlled system - a system of uninterrupted observability of behavior, reference to feedback in making decisions, and real-time adjusting actions. This is the essence of thinking about control systems.

Using the concepts of feedback, stability, signal quality, and control boundaries, the software delivery will not be based on execution but rather on active control of the systems. It results not only in faster delivery but in stable, flexible, and predictable systems even when they are under constant change.

2.2 Foundations of Control Systems Theory

The current behavior of software delivery does not act as a fixed process; instead, it resembles more of a living system. It constantly changes, it is responsive to change, and it frequently acts in a manner that is not easily predictable. To manage such a system, one needs more than pipelines, and it needs control. Control systems theory offers such a foundation since it achieves this by continuously monitoring system outputs, comparing

S. Bobba and N. S. Vummaneni, *CI/CD as a Control System*, https://doi.org/10.1007/979-8-8688-2842-3_2

actual outputs against desired system states, and applying corrective input adjustments to maintain alignment. Within its essence, a control system performs only one thing efficiently, i.e., makes sure that a system remains to act as it is meant to do, even when environmental circumstances change. It does this by undertaking a process of constant monitoring of outputs, comparing them to expectations, and correcting inputs. It is this loop, observe, compare, and adjust, that keeps the system under control. This is not being provided in most current software delivery environments, and that is why systems tend to get unstable even though their delivery environment is highly automated.

2.2.1 Definition and Scope of Control Systems

A control system is not merely a technical term but a behavioral management system.

Control systems are employed in the engineering discipline to control aspects such as temperature, speed, or pressure. They operate under the principle of continually checking the status and rectifying anything that deviates from the desired state.

The same concept is directly applicable to software systems.

Any deployment, configuration adjustment, or infrastructure modification serves as an input. Some of the outputs that the system reacts to include performance, reliability, and user experience. Control is intended to make sure that those outputs remain within reasonable boundaries.

Practically, a control system has three things to do:

- **Regulation**: Maintaining the behavior of the system within particular limits
- **Stability**: Ensuring the system does not drift and become unpredictable
- **Performance**: Maximizing system response in various conditions

These are not abstract goals. They are the same problems that a team of engineers operates with on a day-to-day basis.

What changes is how you approach them.

Conventional systems are based on pre-set processes. The control systems are based on constant adjustment.

Traditionally, control systems were used in physical systems: machines, electrical circuits, and aerospace systems. However, nowadays, the same thing can be said about modern software systems:

- They are being constantly fed with inputs (code changes, configurations, deployments).
- The behavior of these changes depends on load, dependencies, and environment.
- As they are constantly changing, they need to be monitored and adjusted.

That is, modern software systems are dynamic systems, and dynamic systems cannot be handled well in terms of fixed workflows.

They need to be constantly regulated; that is why control systems thinking is becoming a must in the delivery of software. It offers a means of no longer performing changes but proactively controlling system behavior.

2.2.2 Open-Loop vs. Closed-Loop Systems

Among the most crucial differences when it comes to control systems and the one that reveals the borders of conventional software provision directly, there is the distinction between an open-loop and a closed-loop system. It is not a mere theoretical concept. It describes why most contemporary delivery pipelines cannot be stable after systems scale.

An open system performs actions without evaluating the result. It uses a predetermined format: input enters the system, the system processes it, and an output results. The problem here is just a matter of fact: there is no way of checking whether this output is right or optimal. The system presupposes that, in case the steps were taken, the outcome should be satisfactory.

This works in predictable environments. It breaks down into dynamic ones.

This is what the majority of CI/CD pipelines in software delivery behave like. They perform build, test, and implementation steps in that order. Once all the stages are successful, the system proceeds.

However, once code is deployed to production, the pipeline loses visibility into runtime system behavior and does not incorporate production feedback into its decision-making. As a result, deployments may pass all pipeline stages yet still degrade system performance, introduce instability, or negatively impact user experience.

The constraint is not automation - it is the lack of control based on feedback.

A closed-loop system does not work in the same way. It monitors system outputs and compares them to a desired condition. Deviations are corrected by varying the inputs. This brings about a continuous observation, assessment, and rectification cycle that keeps the system stable even in dynamic conditions.

Software delivery. In software delivery, this does not end with the deployment of the system. It keeps track of actual performance such as performance, reliability, error rates, and user experience and uses this information to make decisions. When a thing is not acting as per the expected condition, the system will react. It can decelerate releases, cause a rollback, scale, and/or configurations.

Here, observability comes into play. In addition to being monitoring tools, metrics, logs, and traces are the feedback signals that enable control. In this case, CI/CD pipelines cease to be mere execution engines and become components of an extended control mechanism.

The distinction between the two approaches is empirical and is evident in actual systems. Open-loop delivery supposes that the correctness is attained prior to the deployment. The closed-loop delivery acknowledges the fact that once things are deployed, correctness should be continuously checked.

Engineering-wise, the trade-off is obvious. Open-loop systems are less complex and less demanding to deploy, although they are extremely dependent on assumptions. Closed-loop systems are more complex, however, more flexible and resilient. That trade-off is not a choice in the environments in which the change is a constant and the behavior of the systems cannot be predicted fully.

This difference is critical when it comes to the software systems of the modern world, where unpredictability is a standard. In the absence of feedback, systems drift. They can be controlled with feedback.

Traditional CI/CD pipelines often operate as open-loop systems, where predefined stages execute without continuously adapting to runtime outcomes. A closed-loop model changes this pattern by using feedback from monitoring, analysis, metrics, and logs to adjust delivery decisions. Figure 2-1 compares open-loop pipeline execution with closed-loop, feedback-driven delivery.

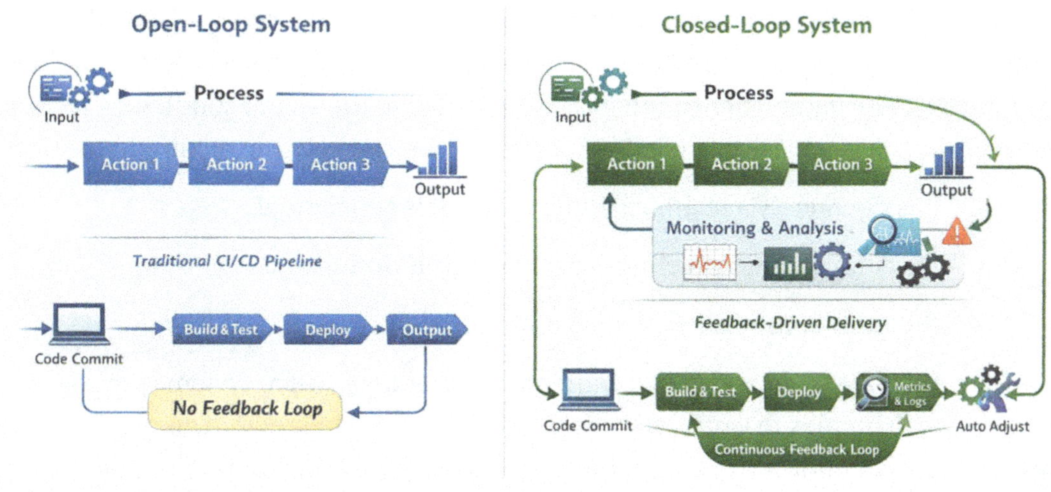

Figure 2-1. *Open-Loop vs. Closed-Loop Systems (General vs. Software Mapping)*

This figure generates a variance between the open-loop system and the closed-loop system; it shows how the variance is realized in terms of the delivery of software.

The open-loop model on the left is a linear execution path. There is no continuous verification of actual system behavior, and inputs pass through predefined steps. And that is how the majority of conventional CI/CD pipelines work; they run a build, test, and deployment process, but they are not modified to respond to what has really taken place in production.

The closed-loop model on the right adds feedback on a continuous basis. Outputs are real-time measured and fed to the system as a way of providing corrective measures. This is an indication of the feedback-oriented delivery strategy, where the decisions are informed by the actual performance of the system, as opposed to the assumptions when implementing the pipeline.

2.2.3 Mapping to Software Delivery Paradigms

The difference makes it evident that the delivery of software must be perceived differently.

In DevOps that are pipeline-centric, delivery is considered a linear process. Systems follow a set of predefined steps, feedback is restricted to a few checkpoints, and problems are resolved after they have arisen. It is concerned with getting the pipeline through instead of managing system behavior.

Contrarily, control-based delivery systems view software delivery as a feedback loop. Monitoring of system behavior is always carried out, and system actions are modified dynamically. The deployment strategies are adjusted to the actual conditions, and the behavior of the system is controlled before failure instead of being repaired.

- It is not merely a technical difference but is conceptual.
- Execution within pipeline-based models is optimized.
- Behavior is controlled in control-oriented models.

Such a change is necessary in a contemporary setting, where systems are too dynamic and complex to work with a set of workflows on their own. The pipelines can only perform, and not guarantee stability, without the control that is based on feedback.

2.3 Feedback Loops in Software Delivery Systems

Feedback is, perhaps, the single concept that distinguishes between a stable system and an unstable one.

Control in control systems is made possible by feedback. In the absence of it, systems are blind. Through it, they are able to identify change, rectify action, and hold on to it when the pressure hits. This is the same case with regard to software delivery.

The contemporary software systems evolve. Code is deployed frequently. The infrastructure is dynamically scaled. The behavior of the user changes in real time. You cannot be content to work by pre-set procedures in this environment. You must be constantly conscious of what is really going on - and be able to answer it.

This is what feedback loops offer.

They transform the delivery of software into an execution process that is fixed and not capable of self-observation and learning about its actions, but can do so and adapt itself.

2.3.1 Concept of Feedback in Control Theory

Feedback is, in its most basic form, very straightforward; you measure the output of a system and use the information to act upon that future output.

However, in reality, it is how you exploit feedback that will either stabilize your system or send it into a downward spiral.

Feedback is divided into two types.

Systems are held constant by negative feedback. It recognizes when something is going out of the desired state and brings it back. This is what doesn't allow minor problems in software delivery to become a huge failure. A failed test puts the pipeline to a halt. Action is triggered when performance decreases. Systems scale or roll back when there is an increase in error rates. This is control in action.

On the contrary, positive feedback intensifies behavior. It supports the process that already occurs. This proves useful in certain situations, such as scaling systems that experience rising load, but it can also be dangerous. Otherwise, it will cause runaway effects. One system fails, causes more failures, and becomes increasingly unstable faster than it can be addressed.

In nature, the two types coexist in a real-world system. The idea is to not remove the positive feedback, but to offset it with the powerful negative feedback processes to ensure that the system is kept in check.

2.3.2 Feedback Mechanisms in CI/CD Environments

Feedback in its simplest form is extremely direct; you gauge the output of a system and, based on this information, act upon the future output.

But in real life, it is the manner in which you use feedback that will either stabilize your system or put it in a free fall.

Feedback is categorized into two.

Negative feedback keeps systems unchanging. It identifies when a person is going out of the intended condition and restores it. That is what does not make minor issues in software delivery a very big failure. A defective test halts the pipeline. When the performance declines, action is instigated. Systems go up or down with an increase in error rates. This is control in action.

Quite on the contrary, positive feedback amplifies behavior. It helps in the process that has been taken already. This can be handy in some cases like scaling systems that see an increased load, but it can also be dangerous. Otherwise, it will bring about runaway effects. A failure in one system causes more failure and becomes less stable sooner than it can be dealt with.

The nature of such a system in the real world is that the two types coexist. The concept is not to eliminate the positive feedback, but to counter it with the strong negative feedback processes to be able to maintain the system in check. It is not essential to have feedback but utilize it.

2.3.3 Continuous Feedback in Modern Delivery Systems

The conventional models of delivery view feedback as an occurrence at certain checkpoints. You develop, you test, you release - and you verify at every step.

That model no longer works.

Feedback has to be continuous in contemporary systems. It has to exist before deployment, during deployment, and long after deployment. Once code has been released, systems do not cease to change. So much more often, that is when the actual behavior commences.

This is the reason why observability has occupied the place of contemporary delivery systems. It is no longer true that metrics, logs, and traces are monitoring tools, but the signals that are used to make decisions.

Feedback is incorporated correctly:

- Real performance data is utilized in making deployment decisions.
- Abnormalities cause automatic reactions.
- Systems are self-adaptive.

This is whereby pipelines develop into control systems.

Feedback loops provide the foundation for applying control systems thinking to software delivery. To make this concept practical, each control system component can be mapped to a software delivery equivalent. Table 2-1 shows how sensors, controllers, actuators, and feedback signals correspond to observability tools, CI/CD automation, deployment mechanisms, and runtime telemetry in modern delivery systems.

Table 2-1. *Mapping Feedback Loops (Control Systems vs. Software Systems)*

Control Component	Software Equivalent	Function
Sensor	Monitoring/observability tools	Collect system data
Controller	CI/CD pipelines/automation	Adjust system inputs
Actuator	Deployment mechanisms	Apply changes
Feedback Signal	Metrics, logs, traces	Inform decision-making

2.3.4 Feedback as the Foundation of Control-Oriented Delivery

Software delivery is about control, and the feedback transforms the execution into control.

Pipelines do not stop running without feedback. They take actions, implement changes, and move forward. It is later found out too late or too late that the system will either be improved, degenerate, or fail. This is what renders automation threatening in the case of operating without sight. It becomes fast, but blind.

As soon as the feedback is introduced into it, the nature of delivery is altered.

The system is no longer just an action-performing system. It observes self-behavior, perceives signs, and adapts to them. At this point, delivery has stopped being a pipeline and is a managed system.

Within a practical setting, feedback makes possible three important abilities:

- What it does is to offer constant knowledge of system state, not only at deployment time but across the system lifecycle.
- It promotes the use of the data to make decisions, as the decisions are made based on actual circumstances and not presumptions.
- It also lets you take control proactively so that the system can correct itself before things get out of hand.

This is the difference between responding to failures and avoiding them. Control-oriented environments do not have feedback as an addition, but rather as a layer. Deployment decisions are the outcome of observability. Releases are affected by the behavior at runtime. Scaling and configuration changes are directed by system signals.

The outcome is the opportunity to have a self-regulating system. Without it, the most sophisticated automation is always curtailed. It is able to run at a faster rate but is not stable. Strong feedback loops make systems more than automated, though the systems are adaptive, resilient, and ever turning a system upside down.

2.4 Stability and Behavioral Dynamics

The only difference between systems that can scale and those that are too complex to scale is stability. Stability is not a side-by-side concern in the current software delivery strategy, as change is constant and the environment is extremely dynamic, with the minimum requirement of reliability and trust.

Speed, automation, and frequency of deployment are the key considerations of most teams. However, in the reality of things, it is not how quickly you can deploy. It is whether or not the system is predictable after you do. It is stability that prevents continuous change from becoming continuous disruption.

Stability in control systems is concerned with maintaining behavior within reasonable limits, even with varying conditions. Exactly the same principle is relevant to software delivery. Systems are always presented with new inputs: code changes, configuration changes, and infrastructure changes, and the question always remains, "Is the system under control?"

2.4.1 Definition of Stability in Control Systems

Practically, a stable system is one that returns to its expected state following a disturbance, through continuous feedback and timely corrective adjustments. Neither does it drift away, nor does it escalate minor disturbances into major issues. Instead, it takes change in, self-corrects, and gets into a comfortable state of operation predictability.

There are three aspects that are normally interpreted by this concept. Firstly, there is steady-state behavior, in which the system runs on a long-term basis without any intense variation. Such is the state that teams strive to achieve in production: predictability of performance, constant latency, and consistent results.

Second is the system's response to disturbance. There is no actual system that works in an ideally controlled environment. Peaks in traffic, infrastructure problems, and unforeseen interactions are standard. The factor of stability lies in the ability of the system to absorb these disturbances without being rendered out of control.

Lastly, there exists an equilibrium. This is where the system has been balanced, and correction mechanisms keep the deviations within reasonable limits. It is neither an absolute nor a permanent condition, but a sustained one that is reinforced by feedback.

Although these concepts are based on conventional engineering, they directly correlate to software systems. Modern delivery environments are dynamic systems, in which change is inevitable and stability should be an ongoing effort and cannot be considered a given.

2.4.2 Stability in Software Delivery Systems

When it comes to software delivery, stability does not mean avoiding change, but rather the ability to control change without going out of control. Systems are continuously updated, at times several times a day, and every modification may present a possible variation in the behavior. Stability is what makes such variations fall within acceptable limits.

A consistent delivery system delivers constant results once deployed. The performance stays constant, the error rates do not exceed the thresholds, and the user experience cannot fail unexpectedly. This does not imply that the system does not change. It is an indication that the effects of change are managed and perceived.

A volatile system works in a different manner. Minor changes cause random outcomes. The performance varies, the incidents become a common occurrence, and teams depend so much on rollbacks to get back. The problem of instability in most instances is not due to one failure but rather a result of small deviations that accumulate.

The lack of effective feedback and control is usually the issue that lies behind the deployment. In the absence of early indications and corrective mechanisms, systems are unable to control their performance. In the long run, this causes drift, inconsistency, and failure.

It is due to this that stability should be a continuous property. It does not happen once. It is what you keep by continually watching and changing.

2.4.3 Behavioral Patterns in Dynamic Systems

After systems have started to operate in dynamic environments, they start to exhibit familiar patterns in their behavior. This is important to understand the patterns of loss of stability and the ways it can be restored.

One of the trends is oscillation. This occurs when a mechanism is overcorrecting with feedback. It oscillates rather than stabilizes and goes through deploy, rollback, scale up, and scale down without stabilizing. This is usually occasioned by a slow or inappropriately tuned feedback, in which the system responds too slowly or too violently.

Another pattern is drift. Drift is gradual and often difficult to detect, occurring when feedback signals are weak, delayed, or not acted upon, allowing small deviations to accumulate until they manifest as significant instability.

Sudden failure is the worst trend. Here, the system seems to be steady until a stimulus event causes it to reach its breaking point. This might be a poor deployment, or a spike in traffic, or even a problem with infrastructure. Since modern systems are highly networked, these failures can propagate rapidly through services and disrupt many services.

These trends are not incidental. They arise as a consequence of the way feedback, delay, and interactions with the system are addressed. Oscillation is amplified when feedback is weak or slow. Drift is not detected when only part of the monitoring is carried out. Lack of control mechanisms leads to failure of small problems in small systems.

One of the primary objectives of any control system is to maintain stability despite disturbances and changing operating conditions. In software delivery, this means ensuring that deployments, infrastructure changes, and workload fluctuations do not cause the system to deviate from its desired operating state. Figure 2-2 illustrates the contrasting behavior of stable and unstable systems, highlighting how effective feedback and control mechanisms enable recovery from disturbances, whereas inadequate control can lead to oscillation, system drift, and eventual failure.

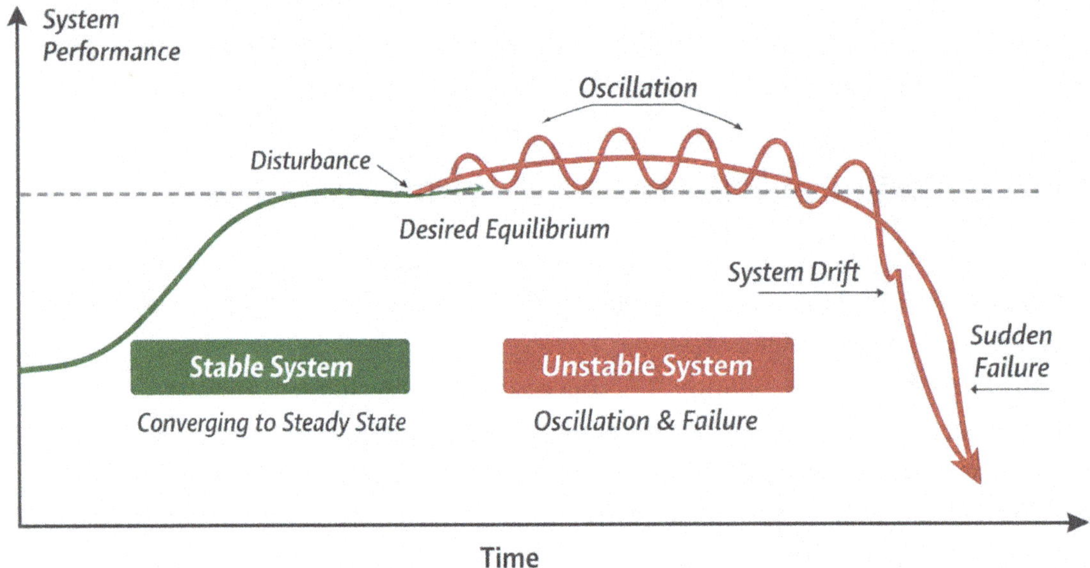

Figure 2-2. *Stability Behavior over Time in Software Systems*

This figure illustrates how software systems behave over time under different control conditions. A stable system responds to disturbance and gradually returns to a steady operating state, maintaining consistent performance with minimal fluctuation. In contrast, an unstable system fails to settle. It either oscillates due to repeated overcorrection or diverges entirely, leading to degradation or failure.

What this highlights is straightforward but critical: stability is not accidental. It is the result of effective feedback and control. In environments where change is continuous and uncertainty is high, systems without proper feedback mechanisms will not converge—they will drift, oscillate, or break.

2.5 Signal-to-Noise Ratio in Software Systems

Feedback alone is not enough to control a system. What matters is the quality of that feedback. In theory, control systems rely on signals to understand system behavior. In practice, those signals are often mixed with noise—irrelevant, misleading, or excessive data that makes it harder to see what is actually happening. This is where the concept of signal-to-noise ratio becomes critical.

In modern software delivery, decisions are increasingly driven by observability data. Metrics, logs, and traces provide a continuous stream of information about system behavior.

In many environments, the real problem is not lack of data - it is an excess of low-value data, unless signals are filtered and explicitly aligned with control objectives.

A high signal-to-noise ratio allows teams to act with confidence. A low ratio creates hesitation, confusion, and poor decisions.

2.5.1 Signal Processing in Control Systems

Within the control systems, a signal is meaningful data regarding the system status, and noise is anything that prevents or distorts that data. The success of the control loop will be the ability of the system to be able to differentiate the two.

Systems are able to detect deviations at a young stage and take the necessary action when the signals are clear. At a point where noise is overpowering, the system reads the wrong way. This brings about slow reaction, wrong adjustment, and even instability.

This difference is frequently ignored in providing software. There is a huge amount of telemetry that is collected by teams, and not all of it is beneficial. The system responds to the incorrect signals or does not respond at all, unless it is filtered and interpreted properly.

That is why the principles of signal processing such as filtering, prioritization, and noise reduction are as significant in software systems as they are in conventional engineering circles.

2.5.2 Signal Quality in Observability Data

Practically, whether a signal can be utilized as a control depends on the quality of the signal.

There are three properties of a useful signal. It is realistic, it is timely enough to be doable, and it makes obvious what should be done. The system can respond when in these conditions.

Observability platforms are created to produce signals of various types: metrics, logs, and traces. They form an elaborate picture of system behavior. They are, however, very noisy.

The usual causes of noise are unnecessary alerts, unclear thresholds, too much logging, and metrics that are not directly relevant to the decision-making process. There are too many alerts or a lack of context in most systems. In the long run, this leads to a decrease in trust in the signals.

When systems are large in size and are getting automated, the amount of data is increasing exponentially. It can be further enhanced with sophisticated pipes and AI tooling that will make it even more difficult to distinguish between meaningful signals and background noise (Allam, 2025).

2.5.3 Impact on Decision-Making

The quality of the signal determines the decision made directly. When the signals are accurate and reliable, then decisions are made faster and more accurately. Teams have the capability of identifying problems early enough, responding with certainty, and ensuring the stability of the system. Automation, in such settings, works as desired since it is based on reliable inputs.

Under circumstances of weak, delayed, and ambiguous signals, decision-making fails. The deployments are done with incomplete information. The performance problems are not noticed until they grow. The root causes are more difficult to detect, and the response time is extended.

Meanwhile, what causes alert fatigue is excessive noise. Engineers start to disregard signals since most of them are not relevant. Once it occurs, there is a risk of missing even critical alerts and reducing the chances of system failure.

Increasing the signal-to-noise ratio is not only a technical job – it is an operational goal. It involves attaching attention to indicators that are directly related to the behavior of the system itself, minimizing the redundant noise, and making the feedback useful.

This improves the whole control system when it is effectively done. Decisions are more accurate, the responses are faster, and the system does not collapse even when there is a change in the system.

Table 2-2 Effective control depends not only on collecting telemetry but also on distinguishing meaningful information from background noise. High-quality signals enable accurate assessment of system behavior and timely corrective actions, whereas excessive or irrelevant telemetry can obscure important events and delay operational responses. Table 2-2 compares the characteristics of high-quality signals and noise in software telemetry, highlighting their impact on decision-making and system control.

Table 2-2. *Signal vs. Noise in Software Telemetry*

Aspect	High-Quality Signal	Noise
Accuracy	High	Low
Actionability	Clear and decision-oriented	Ambiguous or misleading
Frequency	Controlled and relevant	Excessive and redundant
Impact	Improves decision-making	Degrades decision-making

2.5.4 Signal Quality as a Foundation for Control

In control-oriented delivery systems, signal quality is not a secondary concern - it is the foundation on which control depends. Feedback loops only work when the signals they rely on are accurate, timely, and meaningful. Without that, even well-designed control mechanisms become unreliable.

In practice, every decision in a modern delivery system is driven by signals. Whether to proceed with a deployment, trigger a rollback, scale resources, or investigate an anomaly - all of these depend on how clearly the system communicates its current state. If the signals are strong, the system can respond quickly and correctly. If they are weak or misleading, the system reacts too late or reacts in the wrong way.

High-quality signals make control possible because they provide clarity. They allow teams and automated systems to detect deviations early, understand what is actually happening, and apply the right corrective actions without hesitation. This leads to more stable behavior, faster recovery, and consistent system performance.

When signal quality is poor, the opposite happens. Decisions are delayed because the system state is unclear. Incorrect actions are taken because signals are misinterpreted. Small issues grow into larger problems because they are not detected early enough. Over time, this erodes system stability and reduces confidence in both automation and observability.

This is why signal quality must be treated as a core design concern, not just an operational detail. A system cannot be controlled if it cannot be understood. And it cannot be understood if the signals it produces are unreliable.

2.6 Delayed Feedback and System Oscillation

In control systems, it is crucial to have feedback as well as to have it in a timely manner. Feedback is of no value when it arrives late since it cannot represent what is prevailing in the system. Rather, it is a state of the past, and this may result in a decision that is not aligned with actuality. This misalignment is a significant cause of instability in dynamic systems, like modern software delivery systems, where changes take place continuously and at a fast pace.

Delayed feedback will interfere with the alignment of the system state and corrective action. In case of systems reacting to obsolete information, corrections made will not be responsive anymore. This misalignment is a major source of instability in dynamic systems and can introduce oscillatory behavior due to overcorrection, as the system reacts to outdated states rather than current conditions. Such delays are more significant in high-frequency delivery settings, and feedback latency can be considered one of the most important factors affecting system stability.

2.6.1 Time Delay in Control Systems

The delay in responding to a change in system behavior is also known as feedback latency and is commonly defined to describe how long it takes a change to be detected and responded to. This latency can be caused by the fact that the data is being collected, transmitted, processed, or that corrective measures have been taken.

Delayed feedback causes the system to persist with the previous assumptions about the system. Consequently, corrective measures are implemented at too late a stage, or they are implemented in a way that is no longer suited to the prevailing circumstances. This can cause either overcorrection, in which case the system is in a state of surplus over-desired response, or undercorrection, in which case the reaction is inadequate to recover equilibrium.

The control theory proves that too much delay can make even the most designed systems unstable, as the controller will always respond to the previous states instead of the current situation. In those situations, the system is not able to approach the equilibrium, but rather is characterized by swings or erratic behavior. This concept applies directly to the software delivery systems, where feedback must be provided in a timely fashion due to the changes that happen very quickly.

2.6.2 Effects in Software Delivery Systems

Delays in feedback are experienced in software delivery environments in various real practice and highly disruptive ways. Late detection of the problems is one of the most prevalent effects, as defects added in the course of deployment cannot be noticed instantly and only become apparent based on certain runtime conditions. When these problems are identified, it is possible that they have already affected users or spread among various services (Bajpai et al., 2024).

Incident response is also influenced by delayed feedback. Whenever the alert or performance signals are not produced in a timely or even accurate way, the corrective action becomes delayed. This further prolongs the time of disruption and the magnitude of disruptions in the system as the system continues to run in a suboptimal condition before it is subject to intervention.

The other disastrous impact is the discrepancy between deployment and outcome. In a world where there are a high number of deployments, several changes can be implemented before the implications of the previous changes are even realized. This introduces grayness in cause-and-effect relationships and makes the root cause analysis difficult and decreases the credibility of decisions made. The less that feedback is linked to real-time system behavior, the less the delivery process can serve as an effective control mechanism (Miah, 2026).

2.6.3 Oscillation and Overcorrection

Among the most serious effects of slow feedback is the phenomenon of oscillation, where the system is over and over again responding to the perceived deviations. The system, rather than settling down, constantly oscillates around the desired state as corrective measures which are too violent or too slow are implemented.

Examples of patterns in software delivery systems where oscillatory behavior is apparent can include repeated deployment and rollback cycles, multiple and unnecessary scaling, or failed and repeated configuration changes. These trends represent a sign that the system is responding to old or incorrect signals.

Due to overcorrection, the system tries to counteract a deviation that has already been corrected or that has already become another state. This leads to unneeded modifications that bring in more instability. As an illustration, scaling down the resources due to a performance problem that has already been solved may cause inefficiencies and lead to subsequent corrective measures, further cementing the cycle of instability.

Oscillation is much more likely to occur in high-velocity, CI/CD environments because of both the speed of change and the delay in feedback. The lack of feedback control in such environments, as noted by Sannapureddy et al. (2021), may cause long-term instability, despite the fact that even individual parts may apparently work properly.

The interaction between the timing of feedback and system behavior is basic. Feedback received too late does not merely postpone a response, but changes the character of that response, usually resulting in wrong or disabilitating actions. In the current software delivery systems, to achieve stability, the gap between system change and system awareness should be minimized. The more this gap is to the real time, the more effectively the system can control itself and deliver a consistent performance even in the context of constant change.

2.7 Control Boundaries in Distributed Systems

With the further decentralization of software systems, it is no longer about how to control them but where to apply control. Control in centralized systems is rather easy, as the boundaries are evident. Those boundaries are broken in distributed environments, both in services, infrastructure, and teams. Even properly designed control mechanisms cannot work effectively without well-defined control boundaries.

Control boundaries determine the boundaries within which the decision is made, actions are implemented, and system behavior is controlled. They establish the control of things that can be directly controlled, the coordination of things that have to be coordinated, and the responsibility. These limits occur both technically and organizationally in the present-day software delivery, and their design directly affects the stability of the system, its ability to scale, and performance.

2.7.1 Definition of Control Boundaries

A control boundary is the area around a system or component that is able to keep track of its condition and take corrective measures. It determines the boundaries of visibility, power, and accountability within a bigger system.

Pragmatically, control boundaries can respond to three very important questions: what exactly is being controlled in the system, who or what controls that, and how do we use feedback to control behavior within that range. Predictability in how systems work can be achieved when there is clarity in defining boundaries, since the control mechanisms are in tandem with the system structure.

The significance of control boundaries is more evident as systems become increasingly more complex. Their absence creates diffuse and inconsistent control. Several parts can be trying to control the same behavior, or worse, none of the parts is in charge. This creates control lapses, sluggishness, and volatility of systems.

Boundary alignment with the system architecture and operational responsibilities is crucial for effective control in a distributed system. This makes sure that the feedback loops are working in significant scopes and corrective measures are timely and suitable.

2.7.2 Technical Control Boundaries

On the technical level, system architecture defines control boundaries. The modern software systems are generally built around micro services, layered infrastructure, and platform abstractions, each of which brings its control boundary.

Microservices architectures establish natural boundaries for single services. Every service possesses its logic, data, and runtime behavior. This makes it possible to control it locally, with services being able to measure their performance and act independently. Nevertheless, since services are interdependent, local control should still be in line with system-wide behavior to prevent inconsistencies (Bajpai et al., 2024).

Another level of control is created by infrastructure layers. Computer resources, networking, and storage are controlled by separate control mechanisms, which are often controlled via orchestration platforms. The layers affect the behavior of the system indirectly, yet in a strong way, particularly with respect to scalability and resilience.

There is also another difference between the platform and application layers. Platform engineering offers common functionality like deployment pipelines, observability, and governance controls, whereas application teams emphasize business logic and service behavior. This division forms a model of control with a structured platform where consistency and standards are enforced, and applications maintain flexibility within said limits (Rusum & Pappula, 2024).

The control is more effective when these technical boundaries are clearly defined since each layer has a clear scope of operation. Their lack of definition leads to fragmented control, and the behavior of the system is more difficult to control.

2.7.3 Organizational Control Boundaries

Control boundaries are technical and at the same time organizational. The manner in which teams are organized and the distribution of responsibilities will have a direct impact on the manner in which control is exercised throughout the system.

The issue of team autonomy vs. central control is one of the main contradictions of modern software delivery. DevOps practices prompt teams to have their services as an end-to-end application, which is more swift and responsible. Nevertheless, in the absence of any form of centralized coordination, this autonomy may result in inconsistency of practices and disjointed control.

Platform engineering is one of the solutions to this problem that proposes a common layer of control. Platform teams establish standards, tooling, and governance, whereas application teams are allowed to work within those limits. This forms a model that gives distributed control but coordinated control.

The difference between the DevOps and platform engineering positions is hence vital. DevOps focuses on the idea of ownership and teamwork, whereas platform engineering concentrates on empowerment and control of consistency throughout the system. In the event that these roles are aligned, control mechanisms are scaled well throughout the organization. In the event that they are not, control gaps and overlaps arise.

2.7.4 Challenges in Distributed Environments

Distributed systems pose some natural challenges that complicate control to maintain. Fragmentation is the most short-term problem. The ownership of control is distributed among several services, layers, and teams, and it is hard to have a single perspective of system behavior.

This division raises the complexity of coordination. Decisions made in one area of the system can only create unwanted effects in others, particularly when dependencies are not highly apparent. In the absence of effective feedback mechanisms and clear boundaries, these interactions may cause instability.

The other problem is a lack of consistency in system behavior. The system is no longer homogeneous when the control mechanisms in a service or team are different. There are some components that can react promptly to problems, and others are slow. This incompatibility lowers predictability and complicates the overall stability of the system.

It needs conscious boundary design to tackle such challenges. Control should be decentralized with no ties cut. Any boundary has to be in favor of local autonomy, and yet, it has to play a role in the behavior of the global system.

Controlling is not scalable without clearly defined boundaries. Stability in distributed systems is not only a matter of feedback and automation but also the way the system is structured in terms of control. In aligning boundaries to architecture and organization, systems are predictable. This lack of the same results in control that is disjointed and hard to hold together.

This is not a centralized control or full autonomy; it is coordinated control within clearly demarcated limits.

2.8 Modeling CI/CD as a Control System

The majority of organizations consider CI/CD as a delivery mechanism - a means to move code through development to production. That view is incomplete. CI/CD is not a pipeline; at scale, it is a component of a control system. It is change, brought to the dynamic environment, which monitors the result and has to adapt to what is really occurring.

The concept of CI/CD being a control system is relevant because when system execution is replaced with system regulation, the emphasis is placed on the latter. It is not only about deploying faster but also making sure that all changes do not disrupt the system stability, performance, and reliability. This point of view is necessary in contemporary settings, where the behavior of a system cannot be predicted entirely in advance and has to be regulated.

2.8.1 System Representation

CI/CD can be considered a control system, and it is beneficial to divide it into its primary elements.

In all delivery systems, there are inputs. These inputs in software environments are not abstract inputs but rather concrete inputs that are added to the system. Code changes, configuration changes, infrastructure changes, dependency changes, and code updates are all types of inputs that make systems behave differently.

Outputs are generated once all these inputs have been put into the system. These outputs indicate the behavior of the system in practice and usually contain system performance properties, including latency, throughput, error rates, availability, and general user experience. These are the outputs that finally dictate whether a deployment is successful or not.

In between the inputs and outputs is the system, the application, infrastructure, and services that process change. But it is the existence of the feedback that makes this a control system. Measures of change: observability data (metrics, logs, traces, and alerts) will provide ongoing knowledge of system behavior. It is this type of feedback that enables the system to determine whether the current state is in line with the expected results.

By being linked together, software delivery ceases to be linear and turns into a circle. The inputs manipulate the system, the result is revealed in the form of outputs, and what should next be done is informed by feedback.

2.8.2 CI/CD Pipelines as Controllers

In a control system, the controller has the role of adjusting the inputs according to the feedback. As of software delivery, this task is carried out by CI/CD pipelines, though that requires them to be designed to do more than merely run a set of predetermined procedures.

Conventionally, pipelines are engines of execution. They create, test, and release code in a predetermined order. This enhances consistency, but not control. The pipeline is run irrespective of the behavior of the system once it is deployed.

The pipeline is transformed into a controller in a control-oriented model. It does not merely implement, but reviews and modifies. System feedback drives deployment decisions, and actions are changed according to real-time conditions.

This involves pipelines and observability systems integration. Stages of deployment are not separated anymore in terms of runtime behavior. On the contrary, it informs them. As an example, the release progression can be based on performance indicators, automatic rollbacks can occur as a result of anomalies, and the scaling choices can be directly linked to the perceived system load.

The important change is the following: the pipeline is not simply a moving code anymore; it is actively controlling the behavior of the system.

2.8.3 Closed-Loop Delivery Model

Software delivery is a closed-loop system when the inputs, outputs, feedback, and control mechanisms have been completely incorporated. In this model, deployment is not a conclusive process, but instead, it is a continuous process of observation and revision.

The system is self-observing in the sense that it continuously checks its condition, it measures actual behavior against the expected result, and it takes corrective measures in case deviations are noticed. This forms a feedback-driven delivery model where the decision is taken based on actual conditions rather than assumptions taken in the execution of the pipeline.

This practically implies that deployment strategies are made adaptive. Changes are checked not only prior to release but during release, as well as after release. Systems are able to automatically reduce releases, rollbacks, or change configurations via live feedback.

This is a highly valuable way of enhancing stability since the difference between change and response is minimized. The system does not respond to failures once they happen but rather constantly needs to control itself to avoid instabilities spiral out of control.

Software delivery systems generate large volumes of telemetry, but not all data contributes equally to effective decision-making. The value of a feedback loop depends on its ability to distinguish meaningful signals from irrelevant or redundant information. Table 2-3 compares the characteristics of high-quality signals and noise in software telemetry and highlights their impact on feedback-driven decision-making

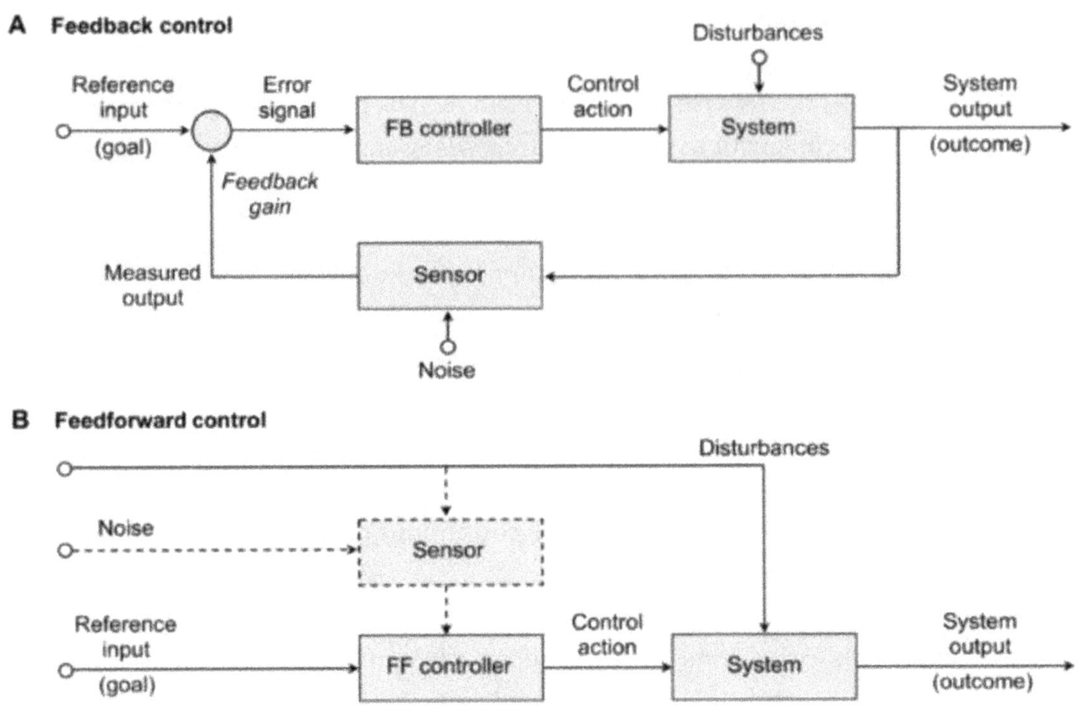

Figure 2-3. *CI/CD as a Closed-Loop Control System*

This figure is used to show software delivery as a closed-loop control system. Starting with inputs like code and configuration changes, these changes are applied to the system. The outputs of the system are performance, reliability, and user experience. Those outputs are continuously checked by the use of feedback, such as measurements, records, and traces. The controller, modeled as CI/CD pipelines and related automation, then uses this feedback to modify future inputs and deployment selections. It is the cyclic nature of this loop that helps maintain control over the behavior of the system, keeping it stable, adaptable, and within the target results.

CI/CD is not a stability maker; it is a change maker. The success or failure of the change maker hinges on the success of the change controller. When the pipelines are run without feedback, they increase the risk. When they are used in a closed-loop setup, they facilitate never-ending, managed evolution.

That is the distinction between execution delivery and the delivery as a controlled system.

2.9 Trade-Offs Between Speed, Stability, and Control

The contemporary software delivery is under overall stress to deliver faster. Rapid releases allow faster innovation, reduced feedback time, and responsiveness to business requirements. Speed is risky, however. The higher the rate of change introduced, the greater the chances of instability. This provides a basic conflict between delivery speed, system stability, and the amount of control needed to handle either.

This is not a trade-off in theory. It is a functional limitation that all engineering organizations have to sail through. The systems, which are not controlled enough yet, are focused more on speed and are fragile. Those systems that are stressed on stability but not on flexibility end up being slow and uncompetitive. The goal is not to maximize one of them, but to balance them.

2.9.1 Speed vs. Stability Dilemma

On a high level, when control is weak, the relationship between speed and stability is inverse. Higher deployment velocity brings additional changes to the system that increase the potential risk of defects, unforeseen interactions, and variable performance. In the absence of effective feedback and control mechanisms, such changes pile up at a rate that the system can absorb.

Little problems can spread rapidly in the fast-paced environment. Before it is noticed, a faulty deployment can potentially impact a variety of services. Root causes may be concealed by changes in a way that makes it more difficult to recover. Consequently, uncontrolled high velocity can easily result in multiple accidents, poor performance, and loss of trust in the delivery process.

Conversely, the need to focus on stability through a reduction in the speed of delivery is limited in itself. The delay in feedback, decreased responsiveness, and larger and more complex changes are all effects of longer release cycles. This has the potential to complicate the diagnosis and resolution of failures when they arise.

It is not the speed per se that is the problem, but the speed out of control. At higher deployment frequency, with feedback and adaptive control used to properly regulate the system, instability is not a necessary result. Rather, it can enhance stability by limiting the effects of individual changes and hastening correction.

2.9.2 Over-optimization Risks

Most organizations are trying to automate and optimize throughout in the quest to enhance efficiency. Although automation is necessary, too much dependence on it without proper feedback would pose great risks.

The challenge of assuming that automation ensures the rightness is one of the frequently encountered problems. Pipelines are predictable in following the given set of steps, yet they do not necessarily have a sense of understanding of how the system works. When the feedback mechanisms are either weak or slow to respond, automation can scale errors and errors before being identified.

The other threat is diminishing human visibility. With increased automation of systems, the engineer may no longer have any clue about the manner in which the system is making its decisions or the current state of the system. It complicates the process of debugging and enhances the use of reactive intervention.

There is also over-optimization, whereby the systems are optimized toward speed and not control. When this happens, the frequency of deployment rises, but the ability to detect, interpret, and react to changes occurring in the system does not improve similarly. Such an imbalance brings about weak systems that are perceived to be effective but very sensitive to failure.

It is not about automation per se, but unregulated automation. Automation will hasten success and failure without effective feedback loop and decision controls.

2.9.3 Achieving Balance

Avoiding speed, stability, and control would demand a careful design. It is not through slowness and lack of automation, but through control mechanisms incorporated in systems to enable them to safely run at high-velocity rates.

Controlled deployment strategies are an effective method. Canary releases, blue-green deployments, and phased rollouts are some of the techniques that can be used to implement changes progressively as the behavior of the system is observed. This will minimize risk and give a chance to identify problems at an early stage.

Feedback-informed decision-making is also important. System signals should be used to make deployment decisions instead of assumptions that have been made. The metrics, logs, and traces should be incorporated in the delivery process in such a way that the actions can be adjusted dynamically according to the real results.

The balance also needs to be attained by balancing system design with control principles. This involves the provision of high-quality signals, feedback latency reduction, and having clear boundaries of control across services and teams. With such elements in place, the systems are able to run fast without compromising on stability.

2.10 Practical Implications for Engineers and Architects

It is only when control systems thinking alters the design and operation of systems that the approach can be considered valuable. It is to engineers and architects that this implies a shift in thinking from creating functional systems to creating systems capable of controlling themselves in the face of constant change. It is no longer about carrying out deployments, but about behavior, not about adding features, but maintaining them, and not about responding to failures, but avoiding them.

To achieve this in reality, this demands careful design decisions in feedback loops, signal quality, system flexibility, and robustness. These are not isolated issues, but are closely interrelated and have to be handled.

2.10.1 Designing Effective Feedback Loops

Proper control begins with feedback loops that are well-designed. In their absence, the systems will be blind whether the automation is highly developed or not.

The instrumentation is the starting point of designing feedback loops. Systems should have the capacity to monitor themselves in a significant manner. This is achieved by incorporating observability into applications and infrastructure itself to have the performance, reliability, and health of the system visible at all times. The metrics, logs, and traces must not be considered as optional extensions but as part of the system output.

Another factor that is equally significant is the feedback on the delivery process. The idea of feedback cannot stay in the periphery of the tools of monitoring; rather, it needs to actively shape the decisions about the pipeline. Real-time signals should be made in the deployment processes, where the system can assess the outcomes and make corrections. In the event that feedback is highly interwoven, pipelines change into control mechanisms that govern system behavior as opposed to being engines of execution.

2.10.2 Improving Signal Quality

Feedback effectiveness is determined by the quality of the signals that it conveys. The difficulty in most systems does not lie in the lack of data but rather in a situation where there are large amounts of irrelevant data.

To enhance the quality of signals, it is necessary to minimize the noise and pay attention to the information that directly contributes to the decision-making process. This will entail the removal of unnecessary notifications, the optimization of thresholds, and the alignment of measurements with the purpose of the system. Signals must be understandable, prompt, and operative and must give a direct view of what is occurring inside the system without wasting time in complexity.

Prioritization is critical. Not every measurement is useful, and not every alarm needs to be addressed. The systems should be in such a way that they bring out the most vital signals and leave low-value noise behind. Once this equilibrium is attained, a human operator as well as automated systems are able to respond better and take control in a dynamic situation.

2.10.3 Building Adaptive Systems

Modern software systems should have the capability to adapt on a real-time basis. The current environments have been dynamic and cannot be served by the use of static systems that merely adhere to pre-existing rules.

Adaptive systems are constructed on the basis of feedback. They keep a watch over themselves and dynamically modify their behavior in response to a shifting state of affairs. This involves scaling resources according to demand, changing configuration based on performance indicators, and changing deployment plans whenever anomalies are identified.

Automation is a major part of this process, but it has to be driven by feedback. Automation based on feedback also makes sure that the actions are not just performed efficiently but also in accordance with the real conditions of the system. This would over time allow the creation of self-regulating systems capable of remaining stable without much human intervention.

2.10.4 Engineering for Stability

The stability has to be a design. It does not just surface itself through automation or the complexity of the system.

Stability in design entails integration of patterns of resilience in the system design. This encompasses redundancy, fault isolation, graceful degradation, and automated recovery systems. The systems are meant to be resilient to failure, mitigate the effects of failure, and rebound promptly.

It is also necessary to develop a failure-conscious attitude. Engineers have to take responsibility for failures and design systems. This is done by looking at the possible areas where the system might fail, the system dependencies, and by having in place mechanisms of feedback that can lead to early detection and reaction to problems.

Stability is not the lack of failure in control-oriented systems, but rather the possibility to deal with failure without the loss of control.

In the case of engineers and architects, control-oriented delivery does not involve using new tools. It is concerned with the change in system design.

The systems should also be visible, feedback-based, adaptive, and resilient in nature. In cases where these are adhered to, software delivery ceases to be a series of operations but a system capable of managing itself, being stable, and working efficiently when subjected to constant change.

2.11 Chapter Summary

This chapter provided a working basis for the meaning of software delivery as a control system. The key change is evident: contemporary systems of deliveries cannot be operated as linear pipelines. They should be perceived as dynamic systems, which should be regulated.

This approach is characterized by a number of fundamental principles. Feedback systems are able to monitor their behavior and react to change. Stability guarantees that the systems are predictable regardless of the new inputs being added. The quality of the signal defines the accuracy and the timeliness of decisions. Control boundaries refer to the place and method of regulation in distributed environments. These factors have been integrated to create an effective system control.

The chapter has also demonstrated how these principles are applicable to real-world software delivery. CI/CD pipelines transform into execution mechanisms for controllers.

Observability forms the origin of feedback on which the decision-making is based. The behavior of the system is not assumed anymore; it is constantly being measured and modified. This turns the process of delivery into a controlled system that is able to sustain performance in the face of constant change.

Trade-offs also are vital to be identified. Stability, speed, and control have to be traded off. Feedback should direct automation. The systems should be made to evolve rather than be done. In the absence of such considerations, the rate of complexity grows quicker than control, causing instability.

Now the emphasis is laid on the application rather than on theory.

In case the control is based on feedback, then the observability is the process that allows feedback. The second step toward developing control-oriented delivery systems involves an understanding of how to design, measure, and utilize observability signals.

References

Bajpai, G., Schildmeijer, M., Mishra, M., & Piwosz, P. (2024). *CI/CD design patterns.* Packt Publishing.

Sannapureddy, R., Nelavelli, S., & Kovvuri, V. (2021). Optimizing CI/CD pipelines. *International Journal of AI, Big Data, Computational and Management Studies, 2*(4), 117–129.

Allam, H. (2025). AI-augmented CI/CD systems. *International Journal of AI, Data Science, and Machine Learning, 6*(1), 137–146.

Miah, M. R. (2026). AI and ML pipelines in CI/CD-enabled cloud infrastructures. *International Journal of Scientific Interdisciplinary Research, 7*(1), 234–279.

Rusum, G. P., & Pappula, K. K. (2024). Platform engineering and developer platforms. *International Journal of AI, Big Data, Computational and Management Studies, 5*(1), 89–101.

CHAPTER 3

Observability as Feedback

3.1 Chapter Objective

The current software delivery systems are not controllable without effective feedback. With the increasing distribution, dynamism, and continuous change of systems, real-time observability and interpretation of system behavior becomes critical. Observability is no longer a supporting capability, but the primary source of feedback is required for effective system control.

This chapter establishes observability as the most essential feedback layer in control software delivery. It describes the use of telemetry as metrics, logs, and traces as structured signals that help reflect the actual state of the system. Such signals allow teams and automated systems to go beyond assumptions and make decisions that are grounded in real system behavior.

This chapter focuses not on observability as a set of tools, but as a system's ability to allow a constant sense and control. Effectively designed, observability gives the basis to comprehend system reactions to change and identify deviations at an early stage and provide corrective actions on the fly. This is what enables the modern deliverys systems to stand steady even during constant deployment and changing workloads.

This chapter creates its contribution to facilitating adaptive delivery by redefining observability as an element of the control system, instead of a post-deployment checking feature. It demonstrates that with quality signals, the accuracy of decisions is provided, uncertainty is minimized, and systems are self-regulated. This is no optional ability in complicated cloud-native settings, as it is what enables the delivery of software under control and reliability.

S. Bobba and N. S. Vummaneni, *CI/CD as a Control System*, https://doi.org/10.1007/979-8-8688-2842-3_3

3.2 Observability as the Feedback Layer of Software Delivery

Observability is no longer the supporting feature in contemporary software delivery; it is the mechanism that enables control. With more and more distributed systems becoming dynamic, it becomes a necessity to be able to see what is going on within them in real time. In the absence of such visibility, the delivery systems are run on assumptions. It is with it that they act on evidence.

The old monitoring was created to be used in comparatively stable settings. It concentrated on predetermined metrics, hard thresholds, and when something went wrong. The same strategy is no longer adequate. Contemporary systems never fail in predictable manners, and they seldom work under given conditions. Instead, it needs observability, which will enable systems to reveal their inner workings in a manner that will support continuous interpretation, diagnosis, and decision-making.

The movement toward observability is really the movement toward active system awareness as opposed to passive observation. Movies inform you when something is wrong. Observability will make you know why it is a mistake and what needs to be done next. The difference is essential in situations where systems are under constant development and failure is often due to an interaction of complexes and not isolated cases.

From a control system point of view, observability is the feedback layer. It gives the indicators to know whether the system is acting as expected or a corrective action is necessary. Metrics, logs, and traces are not operational data per se, but formal descriptions of system behavior. When used in the right way, they can enable human beings as well as automated systems to identify deviations, gauge system health, and react in real time.

This is what makes it possible to be aware of the system at all times. Observability enables continuous monitoring of performance, reliability, and user experience instead of measuring the state of the system at set time intervals. It also fills the gap between system behavior and decision-making so that the actions are made based on prevailing conditions and not based on old assumptions.

Practically, observability is incorporated in the feedback loops. Telemetry is the result of system behavior. Telemetry is analyzed into signals. The decisions are informed by those signals. Actions are motivated by decisions which also determine the behavior of systems. This recurrent loop is what creates the difference between software delivery as a series of actions and a controlled system.

Such a shift is more significant in complicated settings. Observability is the sole certain means of learning the system-wide behavior, in distributed systems, where there are many services and dependencies that can be hidden. It enables engineers to track the effects of the changes, locate the bottlenecks, and notice any anomalies before they become critical. In its absence, the control mechanisms work with incomplete information, and therefore, the probability of instability rises (Bajpai et al., 2024).

Finally, observability does not involve gathering an increase in data. It is a matter of allowing more control. When properly designed, it will make the feedback correct, timely, and useful. This is what enables software delivery systems to evolve continuously, remain stable, and be continuously reliable in an ever-changing environment.

Service mesh architectures provide a powerful foundation for collecting telemetry across distributed applications, but observability can be implemented using different deployment models. The two most common approaches are sidecar (proxy-based) observability, which captures telemetry through dedicated proxies, and agentless (non-sidecar) observability, which relies on application instrumentation. Figure 3-1 compares these two approaches, illustrating how metrics, logs, and traces are collected and routed to the observability backend in each model.

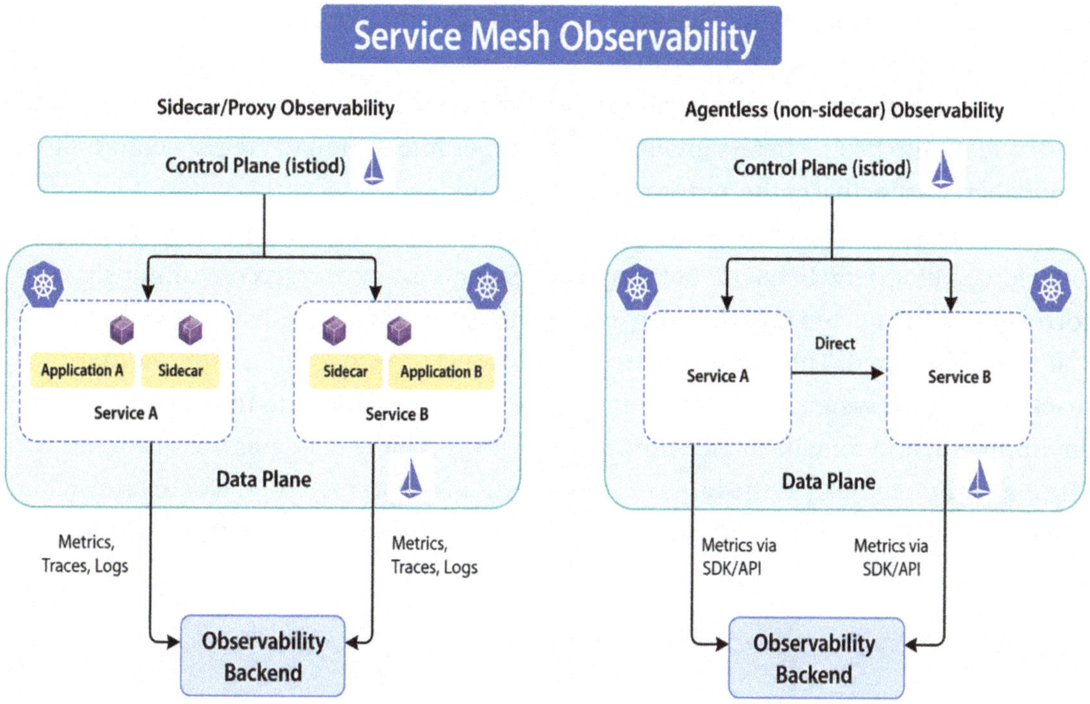

Figure 3-1. *Observability as a Feedback Layer in Software Delivery Systems*

This figure demonstrates observability as the feedback layer of a software delivery system designed for control. The behavior of the system produces telemetry (metrics, logs, traces) that are made into valuable signals. These signals indicate the decision-making processes of taking corrective measures like deployment changes, scaling, or rollback. Actions resulting in the behavior of a system cause a complete loop of feedback that is in turn able to provide real-time regulation, stability, and adaptive control of the system.

3.3 Telemetry as System Signals

Telemetry should be interpreted as structured signals representing measurable system outputs that directly inform control decisions. Each measure, log record, and trace is an indicator of the way the system is operating in the actual circumstances. The issue is not gathering telemetry, but correctly interpreting it and drawing conclusions to make appropriate decisions. Conventional methods consider telemetry as operational output, which is to be read after something has gone wrong. In contemporary systems, such a perspective is no longer adequate. Telemetry should be interpreted as defined signals that are fed directly into control loops. These indicators enable systems to identify deviations, measure performance, and induce corrective actions on the fly. The various kinds of telemetry offer various views into how the system works. No one signal is adequate unto itself. These signals require proper integration to create a coherent, actionable perspective of the system to be controlled.

Once this integration has occurred, telemetry will no longer be a source of insight, but a force behind the behavior of the system. Signals are processed continuously, correlated, and injected into decision-making mechanisms that affect the way the system is developed. This allows one to move toward proactive control rather than reactive analysis; systems are able to anticipate problems, adjust to the changing environment, and remain stable without necessarily having to be hand-controlled. Through this, telemetry is the basis of a feedback-based architecture, where knowledge and response are closely intertwined, and real-time evidence constantly provides guidance to system behavior.

3.3.1 Metrics: Quantitative Signals of System State

The most basic and easiest to scale form of telemetry is the metrics in the modern software systems, which are aggregated, numerical data regarding the functionality of the system. They are useful in continuous monitoring as they gauge the key performance indicators such as the latency, throughput, error rates, and resource utilization. The measures enable metrics to give an answer to a broader question of operation: Is the system working as intended? They are also necessary to have real-time visibility at scale because they are lightweight and can be readily aggregated in a distributed environment.

One of the key advantages of metrics is speed and simplicity of metrics. They allow teams and automated systems to know that a normal behavior is not behaving normally, thus very helpful in alerting and high-level monitoring. The metrics in particular come in handy when identifying the trends in a given time span, e.g., the slow decline in the performance, sudden rise in the error rate, or the change in the rate of consumption of a resource. This will aid in detecting the issues early enough and be in a position to react promptly to the issues before they can impact the system on a mass level.

Nevertheless, measures are not sufficient to understand system behavior. Even though they could show that something is not right, they do not provide the depth that can be used to explain why something has gone wrong. This is particularly evident in distributed, complicated systems where there is a variety of interactions between several components that are non-linear. Consequently, metrics can be considered as the gateway to the system analysis, as opposed to being a solution on its own. They are the initial alert in the control loop and provide areas of concern, but have to be supplemented with logs and traces to facilitate further diagnosis and successful resolution.

3.3.2 Logs: Contextual and Event-Based Signals

Logs give metrics the contextual richness that they lack. Whereas metrics provide system performance in aggregate form, these entries are gathered and analyzed over time; they can allow engineers to have the ability to recreate the series of events that triggered a certain state of the system. This renders logs essential in debugging, incident investigation, and interpretation of complex system behavior.

Logs document discrete events, enabling contextual interpretation of system behavior by capturing what occurred, when it occurred, and often why it occurred across system interactions. Logs are even more critical in the distributed and cloud-native environments where numerous services interact dynamically and can be quite unpredictable. They reveal much of the logic of the application, error situations, and interactions between services that are not available just based on high-level metrics. With this level of granularity, logs enable engineers to go beyond the stage of knowing that there is a problem to the cause behind that problem.

The usefulness of logs however comes with a great trade-off. Contemporary systems produce a high amount of log data which may often be in an overwhelming quantity in both the storage as well as in the human operators. The existence of valuable signals can easily be buried in the irrelevant or redundant information unless there is proper structure, standardization, and filtering of the available information. To overcome this, productive logging must be practiced through disciplined logging, which entails the use of structured formats, the same schema, and correlation identifiers that bind events between services. By keeping logs, one can find a very useful source of understanding; by keeping logs unmanaged, one can only add to the noise and impede the understanding of the system.

3.3.3 Traces: End-to-End Visibility Across Distributed Systems

Distributed systems are becoming more common, and isolated metrics or logs are not sufficient to understand their behavior. This is the point where traces are necessary. Traces provide end-to-end visibility by correlating interactions across distributed components, enabling full reconstruction of request flow across services. They show the interactions between components and delays and the contribution made to system performance by each part of the system. Traces can be the only effective method of knowing how a system behaves because, in microservices architectures, a single request can pass through many services.

Traces reveal bottlenecks, sources of latency, and failure points in a request that would not have been seen otherwise by mapping the entire lifecycle of a request. They allow engineers to go beyond outward signs and get a better idea of the effect of various elements on results. It is also useful, especially when it comes to diagnosing issues of performance and uncovering hidden dependencies that cannot be detected by metrics or logs themselves.

Nonetheless, more insightful information is offered with a greater complexity of traces. Successful tracing involves proper instrumentation, consistent transference of contexts across services, and strong analysis tools. Trace data may be hard to understand without appropriate integration into the wider observability system on a large scale. Consequently, the usefulness of traces is determined not only by their collection but also by the extent to which they are organized, cross-linked, and co-aligned with other telemetry indicators to be useful in meaningful analysis and decision-making.

Effective observability requires multiple forms of telemetry, each providing a unique perspective on system behavior. Table 3-1 compares the primary telemetry types and highlights their roles, strengths, and limitations in supporting feedback-driven software delivery.

Table 3-1. *Telemetry Types and Their Roles in Feedback Systems*

Telemetry Type	Role in Feedback	Strength	Limitation
Metrics	Real-time state visibility	Fast, scalable	Limited context
Logs	Event-level insight	Rich detail	High volume and noise
Traces	End-to-end flow analysis	System-wide visibility	Higher complexity

Controlling the systems well requires that the behavior of the systems is clearly understood and accurately. Measurements reveal that something is going on by giving real-time quantitative reports. The logs provide an explanation of what occurred by recording the system activities and events. Traces move a step further and show how it occurred, the direction of the request, and the interaction between services. Each of the forms of telemetry provides an incomplete picture of the system individually. Combining them together, however, results in a complete signal system that allows to control properly, in time, and with all information. This integration, in turn, in the context of modern software delivery, transforms observability from a mere data collection process to a mechanism of real-time system regulation.

This is a cohesive perspective that is crucial in distributed and complex environments, whereby the behavior of systems cannot be viewed in just one way. Engineers and automated systems can use the comparison of metrics, logs, and traces to determine the pattern, diagnose, and make decisions confidently. In the absence of this integration, signals are left in bits, and control is not consistent. It provides systems with the capability to continuously evaluate their own state, effectively respond to changes, and be stable even when under constant evolution.

3.4 Signal Quality and Noise in Observability

The value of observability is only achieved in cases where the signals produced by it are trustworthy. In a control-based approach to software delivery, the issue is not so much a lack of data but the incapacity to find significant signals in the noise. The telemetry created by systems is very large, and with no clarity, this becomes a liability instead of an asset. The precision is the key to control. The most sophisticated pipelines and automation mechanisms will make bad decisions in case the signals are weak, delayed, or misleading.

Signal quality is foundational to system stability, as control actions rely directly on the accuracy and timeliness of signals. It either allows the feedback loops to be successful or degenerate into reactive and error-prone processes. In the contemporary setting - where systems are distributed, highly dynamic, and continuously changing - it is the capacity to draw correct and practical signals that makes the difference between controlled systems and unstable systems.

3.4.1 Defining Signal and Noise in Software Systems

The control-oriented software delivery puts an emphasis on the concept of signal and noise as the core part of the understanding of system behavior and effective control. A signal is a piece of relevant information that conveys the meaning of the status of a system. It represents performance, reliability, or user experience which can be directly used to guide decisions and corrective action. Noise on the other hand is a set of irrelevant, redundant, or misleading data. Instead of making the system behavior clearer, it clouds it and makes it more challenging to establish what really counts.

As a matter of fact, it is hardly ever easy to differentiate between signal and noise. Technically correct data is not necessarily operationally useful. For example:

- A metric can also give a realistic report of the activity of the system but not whether it is a healthy or a problematic activity.
- When a log entry happens, it can capture an event, but it might lack adequate context that can be used to comprehend its meaning.
- A trace can show the route that a request takes but not necessarily the source of latency or failure.

The value of a signal is not really whether it is there or not, but whether it can support control. A real signal makes meaning, creates less uncertainty, and results in action.

The quality of signals is always characterized by three characteristics:

- **Precision**: They include a reflection of what is going on in the system without distortion or misrepresentation.
- **Timeliness**: They can be obtained as fast as possible to make a difference in the decision before the circumstances can change.
- **Actionability**: They give a clear direction of what or what not to do.

The feedback loops work well when such attributes exist. Deviations can be identified early and interpreted in the right way and made to correct the situation through the systems. Feedback is, however, unreliable when signals are unclear, as is the case with delay, ambiguity, or distortion. The process causes delays in decisions or poor information, and the system slowly becomes out of track.

Separation of signal and noise in modern and complicated environments is not merely an operational issue; it is a fundamental prerequisite of stability as well as the well-being of control mechanisms working as designed.

3.4.2 The Impact of Signal Quality on System Control

The stability of control systems depends on the feedback, and the quality of the feedback is predetermined by the quality of the signals that it transmits. With good signal quality, systems can tell that something is going wrong, understand system behavior, and use corrective measures with precision. This is because it allows faster reaction time, enhanced dependability, and stable performance even in settings where there is constant flux. The use of high-quality signals can minimize uncertainty which enables automated systems and engineers to take action with confidence and retain control in different conditions.

In case of poor signal quality, the effects are direct and multiplying. Systems do not see the problems, or more importantly, they are not able to understand the information they get. This results in late reactions, wrong judgments, and unwarranted or even damaging corrective measures. All these impacts compound over time, bringing in instability and undermining trust toward automation and observability. Feedback is a cause of confusion as opposed to control.

The effects of signal quality are also evident in the software delivery environments. For example:

- A deployment decision that is made on faulty or wrong signals may bring defects into the production process.
- Delayed feedback may cause other services to experience performance degradation or failures before they can be detected.
- Ambiguous signals may lead to wrong corrective actions, including unnecessary rollbacks or incorrect scaling which have the additional effect of destabilizing the system further.

This is where a very important fact comes into play, which is that control is as powerful as the signals that enlighten it. Weak signal quality does not merely lower the efficiency, but it is an active contributor to undermining the stability of the systems.

This is the reason why signal quality should be considered a fundamental design consideration and not an operational consideration. The systems have to be designed in such a way as to generate actionable, accurate, and timely signals. The feedback loops can only work then, as systems can continue to be in control, respond well to change, and operate with confidence in complex and dynamic environments.

3.4.3 Sources of Noise in Observability Systems

There is seldom an occurrence of noise in observability systems; it is usually a result of the design and generation as well as management of telemetry. The more systems change, the more data is gathered by a team in the effort to become more visible. But, unless organized in a very coherent fashion and mission, such a collection brings noise that obscures significant signals instead of contributing to clarity.

Excessive alerting has been cited as one of the most frequent noise sources. A large number of notifications, many of which cannot be acted on, are the consequence of poorly defined alert thresholds, and these are duplicated across systems. This in the long term causes alert fatigue, where engineers no longer give attention to alerts. Such environments may fail to notice critical issues because they are lost among the sea of low-value signals.

Another serious cause is unstructured or irregular logging. System behavior is difficult to interpret using logs that are not contextualized, not standardized, or do not have correlation identifiers. They do not make it clear but add to the cognitive load and retard incident analysis. In the absence of homogeneous formats and valuable metadata, logs are disjointed fragments of information and not coherent signals.

The metrics could also be noisy where they do not match the system objectives. Gathering metrics in such quantity with no clear objectives will be a pile of rubbish and will lead to a lack of focus. The teams might also have to monitor indicators that do not directly indicate the health of the system or the user, thus resulting in confusion in troubleshooting and decision-making.

Fragmentation also increases noise in distributed systems. Various services tend to produce telemetry in different formats, naming conventions, and standards. These signals are not linked together unless there are adequate correlation mechanisms, e.g., shared identifiers or unified schemas. This complicates the process of rebuilding system-wide behavior or finding out what is causing problems.

These challenges increase with the size of the system. The volume of data is increasing exponentially, interactions between systems are becoming more and more complicated, and the distance between the accessible information and operational knowledge becomes even larger. Unless consciously controlled to deal with noise, observability systems are prone to being an object of perplexity instead of a control mechanism.

3.4.4 Signal Clarity and Decision Accuracy

There is a direct, causal relationship between signal clarity and decision-making. Well-defined and structured signals can lead to accurate and timely decision-making, whereas vague or unsteady signals create unpredictability that retards reaction and increases the chance of making a mistake. Control-oriented systems rely on the signals that make decisions only as dependable as the signals that make them. Clarity of signals minimizes ambiguity and enables the engineers and automated systems to operate with confidence.

Signals in high-quality contexts are not only accurate but can also be interpreted in context. The engineers do not have to waste time analyzing the system state and identifying deviations, as it can be done within a short time. On the same note, automated systems are also able to react in real time according to pre-set conditions and backed by trusted inputs. This results in quicker response, better remediation, and increased stability in the system in general. The process of decision-making is simplified since the signals in themselves are clear directions.

On the other hand, poor-quality signal environments cause tension in decision-making. The teams waste time on data analysis and data validation rather than taking action. Signals can be conflicting, out of context, or too late to be of use. This causes the root cause analysis to be slower, and corrective measures are usually either delayed or implemented incorrectly. In certain instances, the process of making decisions is put on hold until there is a great deal of confidence that arises as a result of the available information. This reactive and intermittent methodology raises the operation risk and lessens system reliability.

This effect is even greater in automated systems. Automation is based on deterministic and clear inputs to operate properly. Automatic processes can stop not when they are required or perform wrong actions when signals are vague or noisy. This does not only decrease the efficiency of automation but may also cause a new manner of instability. In these situations, control is lost, not due to a lack of mechanisms, but due to a lack of reliability of signals that control them.

The quality of feedback depends not only on the availability of telemetry but also on the quality of the signals it provides. Table 3-2 compares the key dimensions of signal quality and illustrates how they influence effective observability and decision-making in software delivery systems.

Table 3-2. *Dimensions of Signal Quality in Observability*

Dimension	High-Quality Signal	Low-Quality Signal
Accuracy	Reflects actual system state	Misleading or distorted
Timeliness	Available in real time	Delayed
Actionability	Enables clear decisions	Ambiguous

3.4.5 Managing Signal Quality in Practice

Enhancement of signal quality is a planned process. It is not attained through the use of additional tools or the gathering of more data. It involves prioritizing what is important and doing away with what is not.

This starts with the establishment of meaningful measures that directly point to the system objectives. Measures must be linked to performance, reliability, and user experience and not arbitrary system outputs. The structure, context, and inter-service correlation of logs should exist. Traces should be constructed to bring out important paths and dependencies.

Filtering and prioritization are also important. Systems have to know the difference between critical signals and background noise. The alerting mechanisms should be programmed to activate only when there is a need to do so. Unnecessary or unnecessary signals ought to be eliminated.

Incorporation is also important. Various sources of signals should be correlated in order to obtain a single image of system behavior. Even the high-quality signals will be incomplete without this integration.

In control-based systems, signal quality is what defines the extent to which feedback can be useful in influencing system behavior. The amount of data does not help in control but the clarity and usefulness of the data. When signals are accurate, timely, and actionable, systems can regulate themselves effectively and maintain stability even under continuous change. But once signals are delayed, ambiguous, and misleading, control starts to collapse, resulting in poor decisions and greater instability. In current software delivery settings, the distinction between stable and unstable systems is frequently in the capacity to produce clear, dependable signals and respond to them with certainty.

3.5 Observability-Driven Decision: Signal Quality and Noise in Observability

Decisions made in modern software delivery cannot be based on assumptions or any fixed rules. Systems are run in changing conditions where the conditions are not constant and the behavior is determined by the combination of different components. Observability in this context forms the basis of the decision-making. It delivers the dynamic cues that are needed to assess the state of the system, compare the results, and take the necessary steps in a specific manner.

The transition is evident. It is not made in a place of intuition and established expectations; it is made in a place of evidence that is provided by telemetry. Cumulatively, metrics, logs, and traces are present as a continuous stream of information that exhibits the actual behavior of the system. With such signals in place, making a timely and accurate decision is made possible. In the event that they do not, the decision-making process becomes indecisive, slow, and ineffective.

3.5.1 From Intuition to Signal-Driven Decisions

The conventional software delivery was largely experience-based and rule-driven and lacked dynamism. The decision made by engineers was guided by the past occurrences, anticipated system operation, or definite operational boundaries. This method proved to be successful in quite predictable and stable environments, but it is not scaled to the modern systems where variability is high, dependencies are complicated, and behavior is frequently non-linear. The use of assumptions creates a risk in this type of environment because system conditions may change more quickly than the predefined rules can keep up with them.

The core aspect of observability is the shift in this dynamic where the decision-making process is based on real-time system indicators. Rather than wondering what has to occur, according to expectations, teams can assess what is actually occurring according to live telemetry. Such a transition diminishes uncertainty and allows making decisions that are in line with the current system state and not historical trends or fixed settings.

Practically, the decision-making based on the signals will alter the way the major operational activities are processed. Decisions are no longer individualized but ongoing processes that are informed by feedback. For example:

- **Deployment Decisions**

  Releases are considered on real-time performance metrics including latency, error rates, and system load as opposed to pipeline completion.

- **Rollback Actions**

  The rollbacks are also initiated as a result of perceived degradation of the system behavior rather than predefined failures.

- **Scaling Strategies**

  The allocation of resources is done dynamically on the basis of demand and performance of the system rather than on the basis of fixed schedules or thresholds.

- **Incident Response**

  Live signals help in detection and remediation, thus allowing quicker identification and resolution of problems.

Such a strategy allows changing reactive to proactive operations. Systems and teams can identify warning signs in time and intervene before failures happen instead of responding once they have taken place. It also enhances uniformity because decisions are made on objective data of a system and not subjective judgment.

Finally, signal-based decision-making has software delivery consistent with the realities of the modern system. It also holds to the fact that activities are constantly informed by system behavior so that more accurate, timely, and controlled responses can be made in the environment where change is continuous and unpredictability is the norm.

3.5.2 Observability in Deployment Validation

Control fails or succeeds at deployment validation. Traditional definitions of success rely on a pipeline completion, i.e., build passes, test passes, and deployment passes. In the real world, that definition is not complete. The true assessment of the success is the behavior of the system after introducing a change in the real traffic and under real conditions.

Observability bridges this gap by making validation a process where validation is ongoing and evidence-based. Rather than assuming that something was correct when it is released, systems check results in real time with telemetry signals. The rate of errors, latency, saturation, and throughput are metrics used to know whether the system is operating within acceptable parameters of performance. The logs give a contextual understanding of anomalies and exceptions, whereas the traces show the impact of new changes on service interactions, dependencies, and important request paths.

This allows a transition from a point-in-time validation to continuous validation. The system not only uses pre-deployment checks but actively measures the impact of a release as it occurs. Decisions are then dynamically modified on the basis of the observed behavior. Practically, this brings in a control capability set:

- **Post-deployment health check-up**: Instantaneous evaluation of system performance as per the set service objectives
- **Incremental rollout assessment**: Drip-by-drip exposure of changes with real-time monitoring

- **Anomaly detection at release**: The detection of anomalies in their initial stages
- **Adaptive decision points**: Capability to proceed with, suspend, or cancel a deployment using live feedback

This methodology will lead to substantial minimization of risk. If problems are identified in an earlier stage, the blast radius is restricted, and corrective measures may be taken before the system-wide effect takes place. It also enhances confidence in delivery since the decisions taken are based on the real system behavior as opposed to assumptions.

Finally, observability changes deployment validation into a binary result to a regulated feedback mechanism. It makes sure each release is not only carried out, but constantly checked, and systems can be stable and in constant motion of change.

3.5.3 Linking Telemetry to Operational Decisions

In order to achieve real value, telemetry has to be closely aligned with operational decision-making. Signals should be gathered, but they should then be put into perspective and converted into actions that will affect system behavior. In the absence of this relationship, observability is passive, which means that it provides visibility but not control.

In control-driven systems, telemetry is made an active input in working processes. This will involve integrating observability into delivery and runtime processes such that real-time system signals make decisions continuously. Systems are not fixed by some rules or interpreted manually, but are dynamic and react according to what the telemetry tells them to do.

In practice, this integration enables several key capabilities:

- **Alert-Driven Actions**

  Observability signals can be automated to respond to specific conditions, which minimizes the response time and reduces the need to be handled by humans.

- **Deployment Control**

  CI/CD pipelines have real-time metrics and system health to determine whether or not to keep going, stop, or retract a release.

- **Dynamic Scaling Decisions**

  The distribution of resources is reconfigured according to the real system load and performance as opposed to predetermined schedules or presumptions.

- **Incident Response Coordination**

  Telemetry gives direct context on the diagnosis of problems, which can be remedied faster and more efficiently.

The success of this strategy is based on alignment. Telemetry should be modeled in terms of system goals: performance, reliability, and user experience, but the decision mechanisms should be able to react accordingly to these indicators. Once this alignment is reached, then decisions can be consistent, repeatable, and based on actual system behavior as opposed to gut feeling.

This integration will turn observability into a monitoring capability and a control mechanism. It guarantees that all operational decisions are made based on the right, opportune, and pertinent signals, and therefore, the systems can react positively to the change and sustain stability in the presence of continuous delivery conditions.

3.5.4 Enabling Faster and More Accurate Incident Response

The incident response is one of the most obvious evidence of the real control of the system. In contemporary conditions where systems run 24 hours a day and their crashes may reach a large scale quickly, the rate of response and response accuracy serve as the key factors in overall system resilience. Observability is the key component of this process as it gives the indicators needed to identify, comprehend, and address incidents efficiently.

Quality telemetry means that it is possible to notice anomalies at an early stage. Rather than relying on observable failures, systems are able to detect the minor changes in performance, error rates, or resource behavior as they occur. This early information lowers the mean time to detection (MTTD) and enables corrective measures to be initiated before things get out of control and cause extensive interruptions.

In case signals are clear, timely, and correlated well, incident response is much more efficient. Without wasting time to investigate the problem, engineers can easily check on the state of the system, identify the cause of the problem, and decide on the right step to undertake. Simultaneously, automated systems may respond to these signals in real time, with such capabilities as

- Automated rollback of faulty deployments based on degradation signals
- Dynamic traffic routing or load balancing adjustments to isolate failing components
- Auto-scaling responses to mitigate performance bottlenecks
- Alert prioritization that surfaces the most critical issues first

However, bad signal quality presents major problems in contrast. Late, imprecise, or discontinuous signals slow down the process of detection and make diagnosis difficult. The time spent in interpreting data instead of solving the issue is made more critical, which adds time and magnitude to the incidents. In other situations, wrong interpretations may cause ineffective or counterproductive behavior which only makes the system even more unstable.

Finally, observability is a characteristic that defines the speed and accuracy of a system's response to failure. In control-based delivery, incident response is not merely a response, but an accurate response, one that is steered by clear and consistent indicators that allow the systems to be rejuvenated and brought back to normal levels.

3.5.5 Supporting Continuous System Optimization

In addition to incident response, observability allows to continuously optimize the performance of the system. Trend analysis. The analysis of time-based telemetry can help teams to pinpoint trends, discover inefficiencies, and optimize the behavior of the system.

This involves optimization in the use of resources, better performance at different loads, and performance in deployment strategies. Observability offers the feedback needed to assess the effect of these changes so that optimization actions result in quantifiable changes.

In this respect, observability is not reactive only but proactive. It also facilitates continuous system improvement, which is important in enabling the system to grow and at the same time be stable.

Observability makes the decision-making a subjective process, a controlled and data-driven functionality. Systems can be predictable when decision-making is informed by well-defined and dependable signals, faster response, and more predictable results are realized.

In control-based software delivery, decisions are directly related to the quality of the signals. It is not the failure of systems to make decisions but rather the failure because they make decisions without proper information. Observability makes decisions based on reality, which makes the systems run with certainty under the conditions of constant change.

3.6 Observability in Release and Deployment Control

The points when change is introduced into the system are release and deployment. This is also the riskiest in control-oriented delivery. Any deployment is an element of uncertainty that cannot be effectively handled without real-time feedback. Observability bridges this gap by making deployments a controlled operation as opposed to a one-way execution.

Once observability is incorporated into the release processes, deployment ceases to be a binary process, with success or failure, and becomes an ongoing assessment of system behavior. The system does not assume that a successful pipeline run will ensure stability, but the system is actively monitored for its response to change and adjusts to change accordingly. This is the distinction between issuing code and regulating its effect.

3.6.1 Observability as a Gating Mechanism in CI/CD Pipelines

In classic models of delivery, CI/CD pipeline gates are determined by fixed checks, e.g., test outcomes or policy validation. Although such checks are essential, they are not enough. They ensure that they are right but give no guarantee of how the system will behave once a change has been introduced.

This is further extended in observability, which implements dynamic gates on the basis of the real system behavior. Rather than depending on pre-deployment validation, pipelines can utilize runtime signals in order to decide to either continue with a deployment, terminate it, or reverse it.

An example is that a deployment can only continue its progress when key performance indicators (i.e., error rates or latency) stay within specified limits. In case there is a deviation in these signals, the system will automatically stop additional rollout. This converts the pipeline to a control system that is sensitive to real-time results and not merely applying the programs that are preprogrammed.

This method ensures that the deployment decisions are made in accordance with the real conditions of the system and minimizes the use of assumptions, making them more stable.

3.6.2 Real-Time Validation of Deployment Outcomes

It is not until a deployment is taken to production that the actual effect can be realized. Real-time validation assures that this effect is being measured on a continual basis as opposed to being assumed.

This is made possible through observability, which gives real-time feedback on the performance of the system after release. Measures show whether the performance has been maintained, logs show any unforeseen mistakes, and traces show how new changes will impact the current services. These signals as a collective can give a holistic picture of the behavior of a system.

This ongoing validation enables teams to identify problems at a young age and in many cases before they turn to full-blown incidents. It also allows gradual decision-making in which deployments are not reviewed at once but gradually.

This is vital in high-frequency delivery settings. The lack of real-time validation causes systems to be run with slow awareness, which further contributes to the probability of cascading failures and an extended recovery time.

3.6.3 Feedback-Driven Release Strategies

Observability makes it possible to have a new release strategy that is safer and more adaptable by definition. These plans are based on constant feedback to help in determining the way changes are implemented into the system.

A typical example is canary deployments. A change is not rolled out to the whole system at once, but instead, it is initially rolled out to a small group of users or services. System behavior is then measured using observability signals. The deployment is slowly increased in case the signals do not exceed the acceptable limits. Otherwise, corrective measures are implemented in advance before the wider effect takes place.

Progressive delivery is based on the same principle, but it takes it to an even greater extent. Releases become a controlled experiment with feedback to control the speed and scope of release. This enables organizations to trade speed and stability, whereby they introduce change fast while being in control of how systems behave.

The effectiveness of these strategies lies in the fact that they view deployment as a process as opposed to an event. Observability provides the feedback needed at every step, allowing decisions to be made based on the actual state of affairs rather than guesses.

3.6.4 Automated Rollback and Adaptive Adjustment

Response time is important in control-oriented systems. In the case of deviations, corrective measures should be implemented as fast as possible so that the escalation is avoided. This can be made possible through observability, which makes available the signals that are necessary to support automated response mechanisms.

One of the simplest applications is automated rollback. In case the degradation is detected by a key metric (e.g., error rates increase or latency), the system can restore to a previous stable point without manual intervention. This decreases the downtime and reduces the effects of failures.

In addition to rollback, observability also promotes adaptive adjustments. Systems are able to adjust configurations, scale resources, or change traffic routing according to real-time signals. These steps enable the system to stabilize, but not necessarily revert the deployment, which gives more flexible and more nuanced control.

These mechanisms are dependent on the quality and timing of the signals. When the signals are accurate and prompt, the adjustments made will be accurate, whereas when the signals are poor, the response may be incorrect or delayed. This supports the role of observability as a control basis.

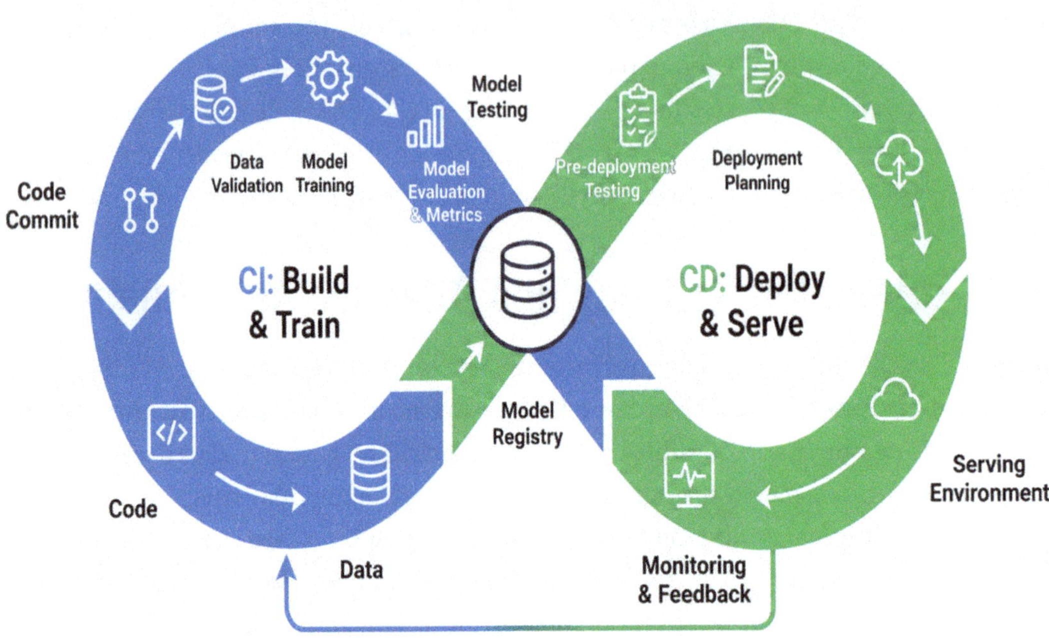

Figure 3-2. *Observability-Driven Deployment Control Loop*

This figure depicts how observability can be used to regulate software releases. The deployment activities inject changes into the system, and thereafter, telemetry (metrics, logs, and traces) records system behavior dynamically. The results of these signals are used to assess the performance of the system with reference to what is expected. According to this assessment, the decisions are made to proceed, suspend, readjust, or undo the deployment. This recurring cycle allows the release processes to be dynamically controlled to ensure system stability is maintained as changes are being made.

Change comes into a system at deployment, but observability is what can cause change to be contained or cause chaos. Without feedback, releases are only blatant exercises. The code is translated into production according to some set of steps, and the degree of knowledge on how the system will really react in a real-life scenario is very minimal. This leads to the occurrence of a disconnect between the implementation and the realization where a problem may arise but go unnoticed until it grows into a bigger problem.

Observability bridges this gap by giving continuous feedback about system behavior. It converts deployment into a single event but an evaluation and adjustment process. Having solid indicators of metrics, logs, and traces, systems will be able to identify deviation early, evaluate the effect of changes in real time, and react accordingly. This allows a transition between problem-solving reaction and proactive control.

Speed in the modern software delivery is no longer a goal, but controlled speed. Rapid deployment that lacks feedback enhances risk, and deployment that is feedback-based ensures stability. It is this balance that observability allows to be achieved, as the entire basis of every release decision should be based on actual system behavior. Consequently, deployments are made safer, more predictable, and reflective of the system performance goals, enabling organizations to move swiftly without jeopardizing reliability.

3.7 Challenges in Observability Implementation

Control requires observability, which, however, is not easily applied to real-world systems. The size of systems and their distribution raise the amount of telemetry, its type, and speed to large levels. Unless they are well designed, observability systems may add complexity instead of clarity, and it is no longer easier, but harder, to know how the systems behave.

It is not the mere gathering of data but rather the maintenance of meaning, action of the data, and conformity to the system objectives. Once such alignment fails, observability systems start to create noise, add overhead to operations, and diminish the performance of feedback-based control.

3.7.1 Data Overload and Alert Fatigue

Among the most pressing issues in observability, data overload must be mentioned. Modern systems produce numerous metrics, logs, and traces that may be overwhelming in magnitude and that teams are not always capable of working with effectively. Although such data can be useful, its large amount with no effective filtering decreases the signal-to-noise ratio.

The result of this overload is alert fatigue. Engineers start to ignore unnecessary alerts when there is an excess of alerts generated by their systems, in particular, the alerts that can be ignored, alerts that have low priorities, or alerts that cannot be acted upon. This in the long run undermines confidence in the observability system itself and heightens the potential of missing critical signals.

A lack of observability does not cause this problem, but an inadequately constructed signal management does. To achieve effective observability, priority should be given to signals, and only important deviations should raise alerts, and operational significance must be linked to the signals (Tyagi, 2021).

3.7.2 Fragmentation Across Tools and Platforms

Contemporary observability is typically spread over various tools and platforms. The metrics can be gathered in one system, the logs in another system, and the traces in another system. Although every tool has its worth, disintegration is a result of its absence.

This fragmentation contributes to the fact that it is hard to come up with a cohesive picture of system behavior. The engineers are required to move through several interfaces, match data manually, and infer signals independently. This delays the process of decision-making, and the chances of misinterpretation become high.

Fragmented observability, that is, in distributed systems, where system behavior is shaped by interactions between services, restricts visibility of system-wide dynamics. In the absence of integration, the effectiveness of feedback loops is limited because the feedback loop is not complete and will be ineffective in informing control decisions (Bajpai et al., 2024).

3.7.3 Difficulty in Correlating Signals Across Distributed Systems

With the emergence of microservices architectures in systems, behavior can only be understood by correlating signals across multiple components. A single user request can go through various services, and each service will produce its own metrics, logs, and traces.

The difficulty is in relating these signals in order to create a coherent narrative. Signals are isolated without the appropriate correlation mechanisms, e.g., trace identifiers or structured logging. It becomes hard to determine root causes, comprehend dependencies, and determine the overall impact of changes.

This problem is even more acute in failure situations, in which many components can fail concurrently. In the absence of a clear correlation, the source of the problem is time-consuming and prone to errors.

Effective observability involves not only data collection but data correlation. There should be mechanisms to connect signals between services in order to have a common interpretation of behavior.

3.7.4 Cost and Scalability Considerations

Observability systems are performed at scale, which presents technical and financial issues. It is important to note that infrastructure needs are high in order to collect, store, and process large amounts of telemetry data. These costs escalate with the development of systems.

Scalability does not necessarily consist of being able to handle the volume of data, but being able to maintain performance and responsiveness. The observability systems should be able to give real-time insights without creating a latency or a bottleneck. This demands the use of efficient pipelines of data, optimum storage plans, and selective retention of data.

It is the role of organizations to therefore trade off between visibility and cost. There is no need for the practicality of gathering all the data that can be gathered. Rather, observability systems need to be targeted to high-value signals that aid directly in control and decision-making.

3.7.5 Managing Complexity in Observability Systems

In addition to the personal problems, there is the bigger problem of complexity. With the development of observability systems, they tend to be complex systems on their own. There are several layers of data sources, processing, and visualization tools that add more failure points and operational overhead.

Otherwise, such complexity may compromise the very concept of observability. It introduces an extra layer of complexity in the system understanding, which is what engineers have to cope with.

This must be taken care of through a planned design. Observability systems should be as simple as possible, cross-layered, and objective-driven. It is not desired to develop more sophisticated systems, but to develop systems that give a clear understanding and actionable insight.

Effective control in contemporary software systems requires observability, yet observability alone does not ensure significant results. An increase in the amount of data does not enhance visibility, as the increase in the number of tools does not always result in insight. The real worth of observability is its design, integration, and alignment with the system goals. Once applied wisely, it can create concise and practical messages that can be used to make informed decisions and take constant control over the system. Though when ineffectively applied, it may add noise, complexity, and uncertainty, which will eventually erode the control it is intended to back up. The challenge of implementing observability is not in taking place in the modern software delivery setting, but rather making it work at scale without losing clarity or utility.

3.8 Toward Intelligent Observability Systems

Traditional methods of observability, based on dashboards, thresholds, and manual analysis, are limited as systems scale and delivery speed increases. The size and sophistication of telemetry have become so large that it cannot be interpreted by human operators with any degree of reliability in real time. To ensure proper control, observability should transform passive visibility into active, intelligent, adaptive, and responsive signal interpretation, prioritization of what is relevant, and acting accordingly with a minimum of delay.

This change does not substitute engineers; it complements them. The decrease in cognitive load, reduced time to decision, and improvement of feedback loops are what define intelligent observability because this is accomplished by ensuring that the relevant signals are relayed to the relevant control mechanisms at the right time.

3.8.1 AI-Driven Anomaly Detection

Fixed thresholds cannot work in a moving environment. Normalcy varies according to traffic patterns, deployments, and the behavior of users. The intelligent observability applies machine learning to predict normal behavior and identify any deviations, which would be otherwise invisible.

These models compare the trends in metrics, logs, and traces in context and not independently. As an example, increased latency can be normal when the load is at peak but abnormal when the load is normal. The systems can learn such patterns and differentiate between anticipated variation and real deterioration.

The outcome is the early diagnosis and reduced false positives. Systems identify minor changes in behavior, rather than responding to the breach of the threshold, and present them as actionable indicators (Allam, 2025).

3.8.2 Automated Correlation and Signal Prioritization

The related signal association between distributed systems is one of the most challenging in observability. One incident can cause hundreds of alerts across services, each representing a dissimilar symptom of the identical underlying issue.

This is dealt with by intelligent observability with automated correlation. It connects signals between metrics, logs, and traces to create a comprehensive picture of system behavior. Instead of showing individual pieces of data, it recognizes connections, what was changed, at what location, and in what way it spread.

Prioritization is important as well. Not everything has to be acted upon. Smart systems also prioritize signals with respect to impact, urgency, and relevance to system goals. This will minimize noise, alert fatigue, and ensure important issues are handled at the first instance.

This is a necessary feature in large-scale settings where manual correlation can no longer be done and interpretation is delayed, which has a direct effect on system stability.

3.8.3 Predictive Insights for Proactive Control

Intelligent observability also facilitates prediction in addition to the identification of existing problems. Systems will be able to predict possible failures ahead of time by analyzing past trends and current trends in real time.

Forecasting capabilities enable the teams to shift from response mode to proactive control. Rather than waiting until the system starts to slow down or crash, systems can detect leading indicators, e.g., slowing resource saturation or a growing error rate, and preemptively take corrective action.

This can be such as preemptive scaling, configuration change, or a controlled release pause. Effectively, the system starts to control itself according to the future states of expectation and not only the present ones.

These features greatly enhance resilience, especially in systems where swift transformation can swiftly escalate minor problems into system-wide problems (Miah, 2026).

3.8.4 Integration with Delivery Pipelines and Control Mechanisms

Intelligent observability can be most effective when it is closely connected to delivery systems. Signals are not to be kept inside monitoring platforms; they should directly influence the process of introducing and managing changes.

Under this model, CI/CD pipelines are made to be sensitive to observability insights. Real-time and predictive signals are used to determine deployment decisions. As an example, the release can be slowed down, halted, or reverted automatically, either due to anomaly detection or based on forecasted risk.

This integration makes delivery a closed-loop system. Observability is what gives the intelligence, and pipelines do the actions. The combination of them allows the sustained system behavior control.

Automation in this case has taken center stage, yet not a blind execution. It is a feedback-based automation where each action is based on the system state and the control goals.

3.8.5 Toward Self-Regulating Systems

The next logical step of intelligent observability is the development of self-regulating systems. These systems are self-monitoring, provide interpretation of the signals, and take corrective measures without necessarily having to be operated by human beings.

This does not remove the human control but changes its focus. The engineers shift to system design and governance where the control mechanisms are verified to be in proper operation and the signals are also reliable.

Self-regulating systems are especially useful in those environments that are of high scale, high velocity, and high complexity. They allow stable control when the system changes so that the stability is not lost, but the delivery does not slow down.

Observability is becoming more of an advanced capability that builds upon visibility. The main aim of the previous systems was to observe what was going on using dashboards, alerts, and logs. Although this gave it some sort of awareness, it is no longer relevant to the highly dynamic environment in the present times. Modern systems produce massively huge quantities of telemetry, and looking at this information is not a guarantee of comprehension. The thing is that it is important to be able to perceive the behavior of the system in the context, what is important and what is irrelevant, and what are the important signals and what is background noise.

It is at this point that smart observability is required. It converts raw telemetry into something useful by analyzing trends, matching signals, and ranking what is worth paying attention to. More to the point, it incorporates these insights into the control mechanisms, as a result of which the systems can react to them in real time. Systems are able to identify anomalies, predict possible problems, and automatically take corrective action as opposed to depending entirely on human interpretation. In contemporary software delivery, this change enables organizations to go beyond passive monitoring to active feedback-based control to ensure that systems are stable, adaptive, and resilient to constant change.

3.9 Observability as a Foundation for Control-Oriented Systems

Observability is no longer an optional ability in modern software delivery; it is the keystone on which control is constructed. In control-based systems, all decisions, corrections, and adjustments are based on the fact that we can adequately comprehend the behavior of the system in real time. In the absence of observability, feedback loops do not work well, and in the absence of feedback, control degenerates to an assumption-directed performance.

This part unites the main concepts of the chapter, placing observability at the forefront of the feedback-driven delivery systems. It is the process that makes software delivery a series of actions to a controlled system that can be held together through constant change.

3.9.1 Observability as the Enabling Layer for Continuous Control

The control systems follow the process of constant monitoring, assessment, and modification. Observability is the layer of observation that underlies this cycle within the software delivery setting. It allows systems to release their internal state in terms of structured and interpretable signals and to have both engineers and automated processes make accurate judgments of system behavior at any given time. Lack of this visibility means that control is unable to operate efficiently since there is no sure method of knowing whether the system is operating as planned.

Practically, observability means that any change that is made to the system, whether it is through deployment, configuration changes, or scaling operations, is immediately coupled with feedback. It is this feedback on results that forms the basis of evaluating the results and determining whether the system is within acceptable performance and reliability limits. Observability provides responses in control mechanisms when deviations are encountered.

This continuous feedback loop supports several critical control capabilities:

- **Real-Time System Awareness**

  Immediate visibility into system performance, reliability, and user impact after any change.

- **Continuous Evaluation of Outcomes**

  Ongoing assessment of whether system behavior aligns with defined objectives and thresholds.

- **Responsive Control Actions**

  Integration with mechanisms such as CI/CD pipelines, auto-scaling systems, and recovery processes to adjust system behavior dynamically.

- **Early Detection of Deviations**

  Identification of anomalies before they escalate into larger failures.

The control mechanisms run unconsciously without any observability. They are able to carry out activities, but they cannot analyze the outcomes of such activities. This will cause a slow response time, an erroneous change, and greater instability of the system. When it comes to the environment where such systems seem automated, the systems are not under control.

By the presence of observability, control becomes adaptive and continuous. The systems are no longer restricted to predetermined behaviors but are capable of responding dynamically to changing environments, can regulate themselves in real time, and can stay stable even at the point of constant evolution.

3.9.2 Observability Maturity and System Stability

The maturity of observability capabilities is also directly related to the effectiveness of the system control. Where basic observability can offer visibility on system state, advanced observability can offer much more insight into it, correlations between signals, and actionable insights. This visibility to intelligence transition determines the ability of the system to remain stable with constant change.

On the lower maturity levels, observability tends to be restricted to single-metric observability and ad hoc alerting. Such systems are able to show that something is not right but fail to tell why or how various components are adding to the problem. This is an outcome of delayed recognition, disjointed knowledge, and response delays. Such environments tend to make reactive decisions, and they are usually inconsistent because the signals do not have the clarity and context needed to give specific actions.

As observability matures, several key improvements emerge:

- **Structured and Correlated Signals**

  Metrics, logs, and traces are integrated to provide a unified view of system behavior.

- **Alignment with System Objectives**

  Telemetry is designed to reflect performance, reliability, and user experience rather than arbitrary indicators.

- **Faster and More Accurate Detection**

  Anomalies are identified earlier, reducing the time between issue emergence and response.

- **Improved Root Cause Analysis**

  Correlated signals enable a deeper understanding of system interactions and dependencies.

At more mature stages, more sophisticated functionality like distributed tracing, automated signal correlation, and anomaly detection is the norm. These capabilities enable systems to understand behavior in context, spot patterns across components, and be able to respond with more precision. This minimizes the use of manual processes and increases the efficiency of automated control systems.

The influence of this development on the stability of the system is important. Mature observability systems have a higher degree of resiliency in that they allow detecting and rectifying deviations before they develop into fatal failures. Conversely, systems that are not highly observable tend to exhibit instability as a result of sluggish, partial, or misguided feedback. The reliability in the current environment of software delivery depends on the possibility to correlate and interpret system signals on a large scale, as emphasized by Bajpai et al. (2024).

Finally, observability maturity is not an operational enhancement only; it is a condition of attainability of consistent, managed, and adaptive software systems.

3.9.3 Supporting Adaptive and Self-Regulating Architectures

The current software systems are supposed to be operating under constant change. There is no longer a need to have static architectures that are based on fixed rules. Systems need to be dynamic in response to evolving conditions, and this demands that there is a robust foundation of feedback.

This adaptability can be achieved through observability which gives the signals required to steer the behavior of the system. These signals are utilized by adaptive systems to make changes to the allocation of resources, adjust configurations, and fine-tune deployment strategies. This enables them to keep performance and reliability even when the conditions change.

On a higher level, observability assists in the creation of self-regulating structures. Feedback is also incorporated directly in the control mechanisms in such systems, thereby providing the possibility of automated responses to conditions of the system. As an example, anomaly detection may cause scaling measures, performance degradation may cause rollback operations, and predictive metrics may orchestrate deployment pacing.

This method lessens the use of handover and makes systems stable on their own. It is also consistent with the general trend in smart DevOps and AI-based automation where feedback is utilized to improve the resilience and efficiency of the system (Allam, 2025; Miah, 2026).

3.9.4 From Visibility to Control

The development of observability is an extension of a larger change in software system management. In the beginning, observability was employed to give insight into the behavior of the system. It has now become evident that it is not about visibility only. It is the manner in which such visibility is deployed.

Observability is not a final state in control-oriented systems, but rather a feed. It pours into the decision-making and the control. This changes observability from a passive capability to an active system regulation component.

The implication of this change is enormous. It mandates organizations to design observability systems in a manner that is control-oriented where signals are not merely recorded but also processed and reacted to. It also demands cross-functional coverage between the layers of the system, and thus, feedback should be able to impact activities at all levels of the delivery process.

The control in modern software systems is based on observability. Without it, the systems can run the changes effectively, yet they cannot manage their behavior according to actual results. Implementation is not a sure way of ensuring stability but is merely a way of bringing change. Observability gives the needed amount of visibility to system behavior, allowing it to be continuously assessed in terms of performance, reliability, and user experience. With such feedback, systems are able to identify deviations, comprehend their effect, and respond suitably.

Observability introduces the systems to adaptation over execution. They become able to stabilize within different conditions and adapt to the ever-changing conditions. This feature is necessary in an environment where complexity, scale, and frequency of deployment are high. In this situation, the control process should not be based on the use of some predefined rules; it should be activated by the real-time signals. This control performance relies on the quality of observability design, integration into the layers of the system, and compliance with operational goals. When applied properly, observability is not merely a toolset, but the fundamental capability that makes software delivery systems based on feedback, resilient, and self-regulating.

3.10 Chapter Summary

The chapter has defined observability as the primary feedback mechanism in the contemporary control-oriented software delivery systems. With the increasing distributed, dynamic, and constantly changing software environments, the capacity to learn system behavior on a real-time basis is no longer a luxury. Observability makes this possible by converting telemetry (metrics, logs, and traces) into the structured signals that depict the actual system state. These indicators help systems to stop relying on assumptions in their execution and instead control with evidence.

Without observability, control loops remain incomplete, as systems lack the feedback required to evaluate real-world behavior. Without complete control loops, stability cannot be guaranteed in dynamic, distributed environments where continuous change is the norm.

One of the most important lessons that we can gain in the course of the chapter is the fact that the success of control is not directly related to the amount of data, but rather the quality of signals. The quality of signals, that is, accurate, timely, and actionable signals, enables systems to diagnose deviation early, respond accordingly, and remain stable when a system is in constant change. On the other hand, low signal quality creates noise; latency in decision-making and stability are more likely to occur. This explains why it is important to create observability systems with the principles of clarity, relevance, and alignment with the objectives of a system.

Telemetry also enabled real-time decision-making throughout the software delivery lifecycle, as was shown in the chapter. Observability provides a foundation for deployments to be validated and decisions to be made based on actual system behavior, from guiding the release strategies to being able to respond quickly to an incident. This is essential in fast-paced environments, where slow or inaccurate information can easily result in domino effects.

Finally, observability goes beyond visibility. It is the basis of active regulation of the system. Observability allows systems to adjust, stabilize, and continuously evolve by incorporating feedback into control systems. This establishes a distinct separation between monitoring as a passive operation and observability as an active force in system control that preconditions the following chapter, where the CI/CD pipelines are discussed as the forces that take action on this feedback to introduce controlled change.

References

Allam, H. (2025). AI-augmented CI/CD systems: Enhancing observability and automation in modern DevOps environments.

Bajpai, G., et al. (2024). CI/CD design patterns: Scalable and resilient software delivery architectures.

Miah, M. R. (2026). AI-driven pipelines and real-time feedback systems in CI/CD environments.

Tyagi, A. (2021). Intelligent DevOps: Managing complexity through automation and observability.

CHAPTER 4

CI/CD Pipelines as Actuation Mechanisms

4.1 Chapter Objective

In this chapter, CI/CD pipelines are redefined as actuation components of control loops, and their responsibility is explained in terms of applying changes that affect the behavior of the system. It explains the effect of actuation frequency, the structure of the actuation process itself, and its control coordination on stability.

4.2 Introduction: From Execution Pipelines to Actuation Systems

Pipeline-based thinking has been applied to modern software delivery systems. Programs pass through different phases, including building, testing, and deploying them. When all these stages are successful, then the system can proceed to production. Under this model, pre-deployment validation is expected to provide adequate confidence that the software will behave acceptably once it reaches production.

In distributed, cloud-native, and dynamically scaled environments, that expectation has become increasingly difficult to sustain.

In modern times, systems tend to be dynamic. This means that automatic scaling, dependency changes, and user activity can impact the performance of systems. Therefore, under these circumstances, it would be impossible to know beforehand the results of deploying the program in such a system. It is not just a question of the success of the pipeline, but also of its behavior following that success.

This is where the concept of actuation becomes essential.

S. Bobba and N. S. Vummaneni, *CI/CD as a Control System*, https://doi.org/10.1007/979-8-8688-2842-3_4

In control systems, actuation is how decisions are executed to control the system. Sensors monitor the system, while the controller makes the necessary decisions for altering the system. However, there cannot be any control without actuation. Monitoring on its own does not alter system behavior, and even well-reasoned control decisions remain operationally inert until they are translated into concrete actions on the running system.

Similarly, CI/CD pipelines are actuation processes.

These processes take decisions that have been made about changing a system into action, applying the changes through code deployment, configuration changes, scaling, or even rollbacks. Every one of these acts affects the state of the system and, therefore, acts upon it. Therefore, these processes are not just automation processes but an integral part of a control system.

It is crucial to understand.

If pipelines are considered execution processes, then the emphasis is placed exclusively on speed and execution itself. A success criterion for this process will consist of whether the pipeline worked correctly or not. But if the pipeline is considered an actuator, then the emphasis will be on controlling the process. This means that the question is not whether the process was correct, but whether the system is still under control after that.

It is this problem that modern delivery systems face.

Automation makes it possible to make much faster changes in the operation of the system. Using CI/CD, we get constant evolution and several updates per day. When the velocity of change outpaces the mechanisms available to govern it, the resulting operational risk compounds. Recovery becomes harder to coordinate, the behavior of the system grows less predictable, and the margin available for safe correction narrows.

In such a system, pipelines perform much more important tasks.

Each update creates new conditions. Any change in settings causes some modification of the dynamics of the system. Scaling changes performance criteria and, in turn, affects other components of the system, creating a complex interaction.

That is why actuation needs to be deliberately designed.

Good actuation carefully implements changes. This means it synchronizes execution with feedback; it makes execution reversible; and it minimizes the impact of each individual change. It takes into account not only what execution happens, but when and how execution happens. In poor actuation, however, changes happen too quickly; corrections are made too late or too soon; and the system falls into various unstable conditions, including oscillations, drift, and cascading failures.

This chapter aims to lay a foundation for our discussion about CI/CD pipelines as actuation processes in a control system. The previous chapter talked about feedback, stability, signals, and the boundary of control. Now let's talk about the execution aspect of software delivery systems.

In practical terms, this means rethinking how pipelines are designed and evaluated. Instead of asking

- Does the pipeline execute successfully?

We must ask

- Does the pipeline apply changes in a way that maintains system stability?
- Are actions aligned with real-time system feedback?
- Can the system recover quickly when changes introduce unintended behavior?

These questions shift the focus from automation to control.

The difference between the two types of pipeline becomes crucial as the complexity of and changes in the systems increase. Pipelines optimized solely for execution throughput may deliver reliably under predictable conditions, yet they tend to become fragile once runtime signals or operational circumstances deviate from the assumptions embedded during design. Pipelines that are instead engineered as actuation mechanisms within a broader control architecture stand a better chance of detecting such divergence early and compensating for it before instability takes hold.

This is what the current chapter focuses on.

Firstly, the concept of actuation as understood in control systems will be introduced and linked to the software delivery environment. Next, the types of actuation, as well as the influence of the latency of actuation on the stability of control systems, will be considered. Finally, rollbacks, progressive delivery, and other actuation methods will be covered.

The core concept is always the same:

CI/CD pipelines do not have neutral effects on execution. They are dynamic parts that influence system performance. Their structure decides whether the system will maintain stability amid constant transformation or become more and more chaotic.

Recognizing this difference is vital when designing delivery systems capable of operating effectively at large scales.

4.3 Actuation in Control Systems Theory

Control systems theory offers a particularly instructive framework for examining how software delivery processes observe behavior, arrive at decisions, and carry out changes against live infrastructure.

Whereas decision-making and feedback govern observation and understanding of behaviors, it is the element of actuation that allows for change to occur based on the understanding.

Actuation enables a system to do more than just observe and understand; it makes the system have an effect.

This chapter introduces the concept of actuation and lays out its key attributes within the context of software delivery.

4.3.1 Definition of Actuation

In classical control systems, an actuator is a mechanism that transforms control signals into actions. It is where theoretical decisions become actualized.

In mechanical control systems, actuators can include mechanisms that change positions or forces; in electrical control systems, actuators can control voltages, currents, and signals. However, whatever type they are, their function is the same - applying transformations that affect system operations.

The simplest control system has only three interacting parts:

- Sensors: They monitor system outputs and give feedback.
- Controllers: They analyze feedback and make control decisions.
- Actuators: They implement those decisions through actions.

These parts are involved in an ongoing interaction.

Sensors monitor for any departures from the desirable state of affairs. Then the controller analyzes these departures and makes decisions regarding necessary adjustments. The actuator implements these decisions, transforming the system so that it moves toward the desired state (Ogata, 2010).

Such an interaction is essential.

A control system equipped with sensors can observe, and one equipped with a controller can compute decisions, but neither observation nor decision-making alters the controlled process. Only when those decisions are carried out through actuation does the system exert real influence over its own behavior.

Hence, actuation is what gives efficacy to control. In a dynamic environment, which entails constant disturbances and where the behavior of the system cannot be known, actuation becomes even more important. It has to function continuously, turning decisions into actions that can help stabilize and control the system. This idea holds true for software delivery as well.

4.3.2 Characteristics of Effective Actuation

Not every act of actuation yields a stable or desirable result. Whether the outcome trends toward equilibrium or toward further deviation depends on how well the actuation aligns with the dynamics of the system it is meant to govern, a principle that holds across both classical engineering and software delivery contexts.

The following are some of the main features of good actuation:

Responsiveness

Responsiveness is the rate at which an actuator reacts by carrying out a corrective measure once it is decided.

There are certain disadvantages associated with delayed actuation in control processes. When delayed, actuation may cause a gap between the state of the system and the action being applied.

In software delivery, responsiveness is reflected in

- Deployment speed
- Rollback execution time
- Scaling reaction latency

Slow actuation leads to delayed recovery, prolonged incidents, and increased system exposure to failure conditions (Forsgren et al., 2018).

Precision

Precision is about how well the actuator executes the intended change.

Improper actuation results in deviation from the intended change rather than fixing the deviation. When we talk about physical systems, this can be represented by overshoot/undershoot. In terms of software, precision is demonstrated by

- Corrupted configurations
- Incomplete deployment
- Dysfunctional scaling

Precision makes sure that the fix brings us closer to our target state without adding extra problems.

Stability Impact

Actuation directly influences system stability.

Well-designed actuation

- Dampens disturbances
- Reduces variability
- Guides the system toward equilibrium

Poorly designed actuation

- Amplifies fluctuations
- Causes oscillations
- Introduces cascading failures

In control theory, excessive or poorly timed actuation can lead to **overcorrection**, where the system repeatedly overshoots the desired state and fails to stabilize (Åström & Murray, 2008).

In software delivery, this is observed in

- Repeated deploy–rollback cycles
- Rapid scaling up and down
- Continuous configuration adjustments without convergence

Efficiency (Energy/Control Analogy in Software)

Physical systems measure efficiency through the energy required for control. In software systems, efficiency is measured in terms of

- Resource usage (CPU usage, memory usage, network)
- Pipeline execution cost
- System disturbance due to changes made

Efficiency in actuation means making a minimum of unnecessary changes to accomplish the task. Inefficient actuation means making unnecessary changes, causing disturbance in the system. These attributes are interrelated.

Efficiency will not be possible without proper actuation and feedback. Making systems more responsive but less precise results in greater instability. Making actuation faster without considering system stability results in oscillations.

This highlights a key principle:

Actuation must be designed as part of a control system, not as an isolated execution mechanism.

4.3.3 Mapping Actuation to Software Systems

The principles of actuation translate directly into software delivery when systems are viewed through a control lens.

In this mapping:

- **Inputs** correspond to system changes:
    - Code commits
    - Configuration updates
    - Infrastructure modifications
- **System** represents the runtime environment:
    - Applications
    - Services
    - Cloud infrastructure
- **Outputs** reflect system behavior:
    - Performance (latency, throughput)
    - Reliability (error rates, availability)
    - User experience
- **Feedback signals** are provided by observability:
    - Metrics
    - Logs
    - Traces
- **Actuators** are implemented through CI/CD pipelines and deployment mechanisms.

The CI/CD pipeline serves as the mechanism for implementing changes into the system. But from a control systems point of view, the CI/CD pipeline doesn't just implement; it interprets actions in terms of system behavior.

Every action taken via the pipeline is actually an actuation process:

- Application of new code → application logic changes
- App scaling → system capacity change
- App configuration update → system parameter change
- Rollback → system state reset

These processes affect the system in real time.

The above mapping makes it clear that

Traditional view:

- Pipelines execute predefined steps

Control-oriented view:

- Pipelines apply controlled changes based on system feedback

This distinction is not theoretical – it has direct operational consequences.

In systems where pipelines operate without feedback integration

- Changes are applied blindly
- Stability depends on assumptions
- Failures are detected after impact

In systems where pipelines function as actuators within a control loop

- Actions are informed by real-time signals
- Changes are applied progressively
- Stability is actively maintained

Control systems provide a useful framework for understanding how software delivery continuously monitors, evaluates, and adjusts system behavior. Figure 4-1 maps the core components of a control system to a CI/CD pipeline, illustrating how observability, decision logic, deployment mechanisms, and runtime feedback work together to maintain system stability.

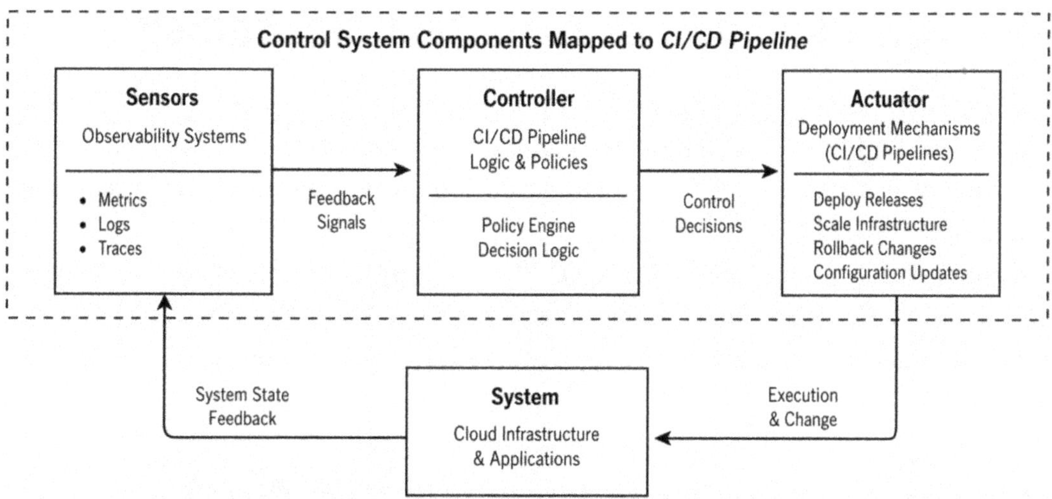

Figure 4-1. *Mapping Control System Components to CI/CD-Based Software Delivery Systems*

Mapping of sensors, controllers, and actuators to observability, pipeline logic, and deployment mechanisms in CI/CD systems.

Section Summary

In this section, we demonstrated the necessity of actuation as one of the core elements of control systems and directly linked it with the software delivery environment.

The main takeaways from this section are

- Actuation is the means of controlling
- Effective actuation calls for responsiveness, precision, proportionality, and sustained alignment with the feedback signals that inform it
- CI/CD pipelines act as actuators in the software delivery environment
- System behavior is affected by how actuation works

On the basis of this understanding, we can further explore how various kinds of actuation work.

In the following section, we will look into the types of actuation in software delivery systems and their impact on system behavior.

4.4 CI/CD Pipelines as Actuation Mechanisms

CI/CD pipelines are most often described as automation frameworks that build, validate, package, and deploy software changes into target environments. That description is operationally accurate, yet it leaves out a dimension that becomes critical at scale and in dynamic settings.

If one were to examine a CI/CD pipeline from the point of view of control theory, then it should be understood as an actuator rather than just a sequence of processes. An actuator is a mechanism used to effect change within a system, constantly shaping its behavior.

4.4.1 Pipelines as Execution Engines vs. Control Components

The traditional paradigm used in CI/CD pipelines hinges on execution. In such cases, the pipeline is coded in such a way that tasks will be executed following a predetermined procedure: first build, execute tests, package the artifact, and deploy it to the deployment environment. The ultimate aim is to succeed at each of these stages.

This paradigm is inherently process-driven, anchored in the expectation that thorough validation before release will be sufficient to ensure acceptable production behavior. Such an expectation holds reasonably well for deterministic workloads but loses reliability when deployment outcomes hinge on runtime conditions that only materialize in distributed or cloud-native environments.

The core limitation is that execution-centric pipelines tend to verify artifact correctness and workflow completion without continuing to evaluate how the system behaves once the deployment is live.

Execution-based pipelines do not analyze if the system is behaving properly after being deployed into the operational environment. They make changes according to the predefined logic, regardless of the runtime status of the system. Hence, even if they pass all validation procedures, they end up making the system unstable.

On the other hand, control-oriented pipeline works in a closed-loop setting. This means that it incorporates feedback from the system during its execution process and reacts to the feedback.

Here is how these two types of pipelines differ:

- Execution-centric pipelines rely on decisions made prior to execution, which are dependent on assumptions and preconditions.
- On the other hand, control-oriented pipelines rely on decisions that are constantly made with feedback incorporated into it.

A control-oriented pipeline is not just about making the deployment but also about evaluating whether the deployment is effective, and if needed, even intervening. This makes the deployment conditional.

In doing so, it reflects the basic nature of control theory where actions are constantly modified to maintain performance and stability (Åström & Murray, 2008).

4.4.2 State Transitions in Software Systems

For pipelines to be understood as an actuator for the system, there must be a way to consider the software system in relation to state transitions.

The state of a system is a description of the current status of the system, which is dependent on its code, configuration, infrastructure, and runtime.

Pipelines are the main method through which this transition of states happens.

Deployment as State Change

Deployment results in the addition of a new application behavior to the existing system. It is not simply a matter of code change but rather the alteration of the behavior of the entire system.

Even the smallest code change can affect

- The execution flows
- The resource consumption
- The communication between different services

And this may lead to unexpected system behavior, even though everything was tested before deployment. That is why deployment should be considered as an actuation event (Humble & Farley, 2010).

Configuration as Behavioral Modifier

Configuration changes often have a more immediate and widespread impact than code changes.

Adjustments to

- Feature flags
- Resource limits
- Routing rules

These changes can influence the system's behavior without making any changes to the program itself. Such modifications have been referred to as behavioral modifiers; they offer flexibility but, if used improperly, may cause instability.

Unlike the deployment process, the configuration process usually occurs much faster and with minimal precautionary measures.

Infrastructure Changes

Infrastructural actuation could comprise rescaling resources, altering network configuration, and modifying storage and computational parameters.

These actions directly influence the ability of the system, the robustness of the system, and system performance. For example, rescaling affects how the system behaves under load, while changing network configurations alters latency and availability.

Actuation at the infrastructural level is particularly important when working in the cloud environment since such systems are highly flexible and actuation is constant.

In all cases, the essential takeaway is clear:

Every step taken by a pipeline implies a change in system state, which inevitably produces behaviors.

Thus, when designing pipelines, one must ensure that such changes in state are made in a manner that does not destabilize the system.

4.4.3 Actuation Scope in Modern Systems

Modern architectures implement actuation at different levels of the stack, where all levels play an important role in the whole process of achieving the desired behavior.

It is important to comprehend such a range of scopes because it helps implement effective systems of controls.

Application Layer

The application layer deals with code deployment and feature activation.

The actions implemented on this level affect the operation of business logic and the user's interface with the system.

Due to the direct impact of the actions taken at the application layer, their effect becomes apparent quite quickly.

Infrastructure Layer

At the infrastructure level, actuation involves resource management and system capacity.

This includes

- Auto-scaling mechanisms
- Load balancing adjustments
- Resource allocation changes

These actions influence system performance under varying conditions. They are critical for maintaining stability in the face of fluctuating demand.

Platform Layer

The platform layer represents the foundation upon which both applications and infrastructure run. This layer contains such components as CI/CD tools, orchestration software, and governance tools.

The actuation performed on the platform layer can be described as follows:

- Pipeline implementation
- Policies implementation
- Environment configuration

The coordination role is provided by the platform layer as it ensures that all activities carried out in both layers are aligned with the goals set for the entire system (Bass et al., 2015).

Nevertheless, it is worth mentioning that the layers are interdependent, as any action performed in one layer will affect the others.

This is why coordinated actuation is crucial owing to the aforementioned dependency.

CI/CD pipelines influence system behavior through a variety of actions that serve as control mechanisms within a feedback-driven delivery system. Table 4-1 maps common pipeline actions to their corresponding actuation types and illustrates how each action affects system behavior and operational stability.

Table 4-1. *Pipeline Actions as Actuation Types*

Pipeline Action	Actuation Type	System Impact
Deployment	Direct	Changes runtime behavior
Scaling	Adaptive	Alters system capacity and responsiveness
Rollback	Corrective	Restores the previous stable state
Configuration Update	Conditional	Adjusts system performance and behavior

Section Summary

In this part, CI/CD pipelines are considered as actuation devices that facilitate state transition and affect the overall behavior of systems in several layers.

Important points include:

- Pipelines should be considered not just in terms of execution but as active participants in affecting behavior.
- State transitions induced by pipelines carry tangible operational consequences.
- Actuation is multi-layered and spans applications, infrastructure, and platforms.
- Successful delivery systems entail coordination between actuations.

In the following section, the behavior of these types of actuation under different scenarios will be examined.

4.5 Types of Actuation in Software Delivery

Software delivery systems employ several distinct forms of actuation, each characterized by different control properties, operational risk profiles, and governance considerations.

These differences arise out of various factors such as differences in how control can be exerted over these systems, how feedback is integrated, and the risks associated with a particular delivery system.

Organizations that depend exclusively on a single actuation model often encounter brittleness when delivery risk, runtime variability, or compliance requirements evolve beyond the assumptions that the model was built on.

In this part, we will explore the main actuations that are involved in software delivery.

4.5.1 Deterministic Actuation

Deterministic actuation is the oldest and most commonly used type of actuation in software deployments. With the deterministic method, actions are triggered by a sequence of predetermined workflows, which do not vary depending on the state of the system.

A deterministic workflow consists of a linear pipeline wherein the code is built, tested, and deployed in accordance with predetermined guidelines. Execution will continue if all requirements are satisfied; otherwise, execution will stop. It is assumed that the pipeline behavior will yield a correct system result upon successful completion.

The main strength of deterministic actuation is its consistent and predictable nature. Since there is a predetermined action for a specific set of circumstances, behavior within the pipeline can easily be reasoned about.

However, this predictability comes at the cost of rigidity.

Deterministic workflows that lack runtime feedback mechanisms are unable to adapt when system performance, user traffic patterns, or external dependencies shift after deployment begins. As a result, their reliability rests almost entirely on the validity of assumptions established during design and testing.

This would not cause any problem in case of a stable environment. It can become risky in case of a changing system.

For instance, the deployment could succeed in passing all pipeline tests but still fail when actual production loads are applied. The deterministic pipeline would still go ahead with the deployment because of its lack of awareness of the current condition of the system. When deterministic actuation proceeds without incorporating runtime feedback, it functions as an open-loop mechanism whose outcomes are governed entirely by preconditions rather than observed system state.

4.5.2 Feedback-Driven Actuation

Feedback-enabled actuation solves the problems associated with deterministic systems by utilizing real-time system feedback as a key input to action executions.

Here, actions are no longer determined only through a predefined workflow but by feedback obtained from observability systems. The metrics used, along with logging and tracing, provide information on how the system functions at all times, providing the pipeline with the ability to make decisions regarding its operations on the fly.

The result is a feedback loop that raises the probability of each action reflecting the actual operating state of the system at the moment it is applied, though the quality of that alignment depends on the timeliness and fidelity of the signals involved.

There are multiple benefits provided by such an approach when implementing actuation. First of all, the deployment of the system becomes more versatile, as changes can be introduced depending on the performance level of the system.

However, feedback-enabled systems also have some significant drawbacks, the most important one being that they depend greatly on accurate feedback data (Forsgren et al., 2018).

Moreover, higher levels of complexity within decision-making require proper implementation in order to prevent unwanted interaction between feedback loops.

Despite the added complexity it introduces, feedback-driven actuation represents a meaningful shift away from assumption-based execution and toward delivery that is informed by observed runtime conditions.

4.5.3 Conditional Actuation

Conditional actuation operates at the intersection of deterministic and feedback-driven models. In this approach, actions are triggered when specific conditions or thresholds are met.

These conditions may be defined by

- Policy rules
- Performance thresholds
- Security requirements
- Compliance constraints

Whereas strictly deterministic systems do not allow any room for decisions, conditional actuation allows for decision-making steps that are contingent upon system status or criteria. However, contrary to pure feedback systems, such decisions are generally conditioned upon pre-specified criteria rather than continuous feedback analysis.

This approach is quite common in practical applications, especially in scenarios requiring proper governance and risk management.

Examples include deployment which is only executed if certain security criteria are met. On the other hand, scaling is executed in case of particular levels of resource utilization.

Conditional actuation offers a way of imposing limitations without losing complete flexibility.

The strength of this approach relies heavily on the quality of defined conditions. An inaccurate definition of thresholds may cause both excessive triggering and inadequate responses to the criteria. Both scenarios pose risks regarding system stability.

In sum, conditional actuation poses an important challenge related to the balance between sensitivity and stability.

4.5.4 Human-in-the-Loop Actuation

Though automation technology has made impressive progress, there still exist areas where human intervention becomes important. Actuation involving humans in the loop involves including human decision-making in the control process.

In this approach, there are some operations that need approval from humans before being performed. The examples of such activities are risky deployments, production launches, or dealing with critical events.

The first benefit of using human-in-the-loop actuation is judgment.

Human review continues to add value in situations that demand business context, regulatory interpretation, customer-impact assessment, risk acceptance judgments, or coordination across organizational boundaries, areas where automated decision logic is often too narrow to operate safely on its own.

Nevertheless, there is an important drawback to this benefit, which is latency.

Human decision-making cannot be as fast as automated operations, and when it comes to high-frequency deliveries, this might become an issue.

Moreover, human involvement could bring in inconsistencies and variations, especially under stressful conditions.

There is a conflict between control and speed.

The system with extensive human involvement might ensure better controls but will be less agile. On the other hand, the system that involves fewer humans might be quicker but prone to errors and wrong decisions.

The difficult task is to ascertain when human discretion is required and when automation should prevail.

4.5.5 Hybrid Actuation Models

However, in practice, many current software delivery platforms utilize hybrid actuation schemes that integrate aspects from deterministic, feedback-based, conditional, and human-controlled forms of actuation.

There is no coincidence in the existence of such hybrids. They are created as a means of balancing conflicting requirements:

- Determinism vs. adaptability
- Expediency vs. controllability
- Fully automated processes vs. human oversight

For instance, a software delivery pipeline might incorporate deterministic pipelines for compilation and testing, feedback-based methods for adjustments during deployment, conditional actuation for policy enforcement, and human actuation for major releases.

By combining these approaches, software delivery systems can utilize the benefits of all types of actuation while compensating for their respective weaknesses.

Nevertheless, hybrid actuation schemes involve more complicated mechanisms and thus increase the number of possible problems.

Specifically, the interaction of multiple forms of actuation can generate unwanted feedback effects that destabilize the system instead of adding to its stability.

For hybrid actuation models to function reliably, they require explicit coordination mechanisms such as shared deployment state, Policy as Code enforcement, deployment locks, clearly defined approval boundaries, rollback ownership assignments, and observability-based gating criteria.

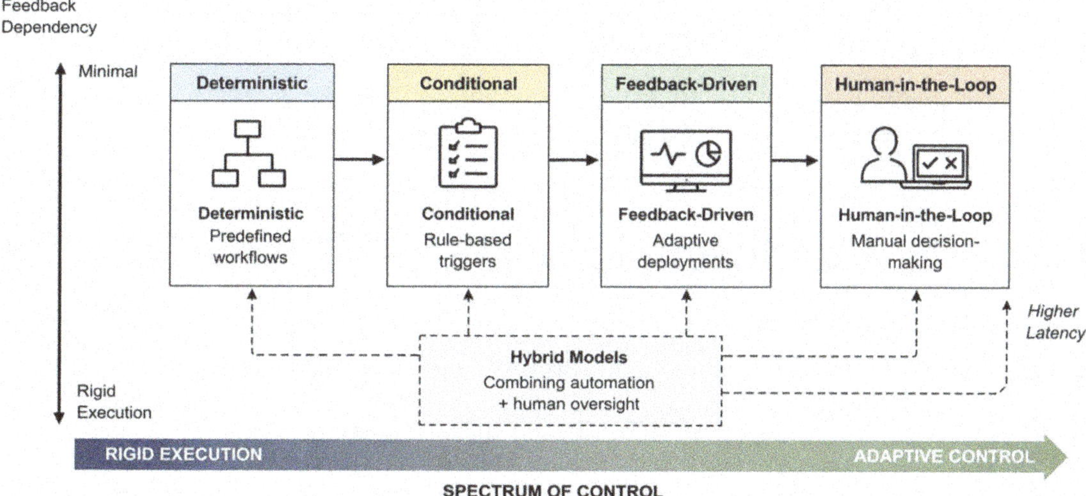

Figure 4-2. *Types of Actuation in CI/CD Systems*

Comparison of deterministic, conditional, and feedback-driven actuation modes in CI/CD systems based on their level of feedback dependency and control adaptability.

This diagram shows how these types of actuations can be found along a continuum of control mechanisms.

Section Summary

In this section, the main kinds of actuation in software delivery control systems have been discussed.

Main takeaways include the following:

- Deterministic actuation is predictable, yet inflexible.
- Feedback-based actuation is dynamic, yet its operation depends on the quality of the received signals.
- Conditional actuation is characterized by systematic decision-making processes.
- Actuation with human input brings flexibility into the system while causing delays.

Hybrid methods may be considered as a combination of all those approaches mentioned above, thus accounting for multiple system parameters.

With this understanding of the principal actuation types established, the next section turns to the role of actuation speed and timing in system stability.

4.6 Actuation Speed, Latency, and System Stability

When dealing with control-based delivery systems, it is not enough to figure out what actions have to be taken. It is equally important to figure out when these actions will occur. The speed and latency of action make a huge difference in how the system operates.

A technically correct action applied after the system has already transitioned to a different operating state can prove ineffective or even counterproductive. In dynamic environments, delays that accumulate across observation, decision-making, and execution create temporal misalignment between the intended correction and the condition it was meant to address, and under certain feedback conditions, such misalignment can contribute to sustained instability or oscillatory behavior.

This section will focus on actuation latencies in control systems and how this topic is related to software delivery.

4.6.1 Actuation Latency in Control Systems

Actuation latency refers to the elapsed time between the point at which a control decision is reached and the point at which the resulting action takes effect on the target system.

In classical control systems, such latency can be due to various causes: signal propagation time, processing time in the controller itself, and physical properties of actuators. No matter what causes the problem, latency creates a time interval between system behavior and the control activity.

Such an interval has fundamental consequences.

A control system is effective only when it works in correspondence with the actual behavior of the system. As a result, a delay in actuation results in additional evolution of the system during the time when the control action remains pending. By the time control action finally comes, the system could become significantly different from its initial state.

This results in temporal inconsistency, i.e., application of control actions to the old states of the system.

A useful distinction can be drawn between these two sources of delay. Feedback delay degrades the accuracy of the system picture on which decisions are based, whereas actuation latency erodes the relevance and effectiveness of the action that follows. When implementation lags far enough behind the triggering condition, even a well-founded decision may no longer match the state it was designed to correct.

As per control theory, too much delay might even destabilize otherwise robust systems. If corrective action always lags behind system changes, then there is the possibility of oscillation or inability to reach an equilibrium state (Åström & Murray, 2008).

This phenomenon is applicable to software delivery systems.

4.6.2 Impact on Software Delivery

Actuation latencies in software delivery systems appear in different ways.

While not as easily noticeable as in physical systems, actuation latencies have significant implications for the operation of the delivery system.

One of the most typical examples of an actuation latency problem is a delay in reaction to a degraded system state. As soon as there start to be problems with the delivery of software, in terms of errors or latency, for example, action must be taken to correct the problem before further deterioration occurs.

A further negative result of actuation latencies is the discrepancy that occurs between the actions taken and the actual state of the system.

When working in an environment where the system frequently undergoes changes due to the high frequency of software updates, different events may take place simultaneously. If there are delays in actuation, then the system will begin implementing a corrective action based on a non-existent condition. For instance, the implementation of a rollback due to high latencies may occur after the system has recovered from the initial problems.

This mismatch impacts efforts toward finding root causes, lowering the reliability of automation. Engineers will find themselves at a loss trying to decide if an exhibited behavior resulted from the change, from the delayed fix, or from interaction between several simultaneous changes.

Latency during actuation also has a negative impact on the effectiveness of incident response processes. When an organization has efficient detection but slow actuation, the resulting recovery process will be lengthy, rendering moot any advantages offered by observability and feedback, since understanding without action cannot solve the problem.

It demonstrates the following concept:

The efficiency of control in software deliveries is based not only on decision quality but also on action execution timeliness.

4.6.3 High-Frequency Delivery Environments

In today's software delivery systems, the frequency of delivery is higher than ever due to the adoption of continuous integration and continuous delivery approaches. The frequency of delivery is high as changes are delivered many times during short time intervals.

It is thus important to consider the timing of actuation in this context.

There are many benefits of high-frequency delivery, which include reducing the magnitude of each change, shortening the feedback loop, and speeding up iterations. On the other hand, there are many dangers associated with the high-frequency actuation approach.

The first risk is the accumulation of changes.

If changes are being delivered continuously and the effects of those changes are not understood until all the previous changes are delivered, then it will be very difficult to manage these changes. The presence of actuation delay might mean that corrections will take place after a series of changes, which makes the process harder.

Another risk associated with high-frequency actuation is instability.

If there is actuation without appropriate feedback alignment, it leads to cycles of delivery and correction because systems keep changing state in response to an action.

The link between speed and control plays an important role here.

Raising delivery frequency without a corresponding strengthening of actuation control tends to widen the window of exposure to undetected or uncorrected faults, thereby increasing the potential for instability. On the other hand, reducing speed in order to increase stability reduces innovation as well. The goal is neither to increase nor decrease speed, but to coordinate speed with control capabilities (Forsgren et al., 2018).

4.6.4 Synchronization with Feedback Loops

Effectiveness in control depends on synchronization of feedback and actuation. Feedback is an informational component that contains data about a system's state, whereas actuation influences this state through changes. Misalignment in terms of timing negatively affects the control's effectiveness.

Synchronization allows

- Feedback to reflect the current state of a system
- Informative decisions to be made
- Control actions to take place before system states can significantly change

This involves the synchronization of observability and CI/CD pipelines in software delivery. Metrics, logs, and traces should be processed in a timely manner and be subject to action within system dynamic timescales.

System stability occurs when synchronization is ensured. System deviations get detected early, control measures are taken quickly, and the system achieves its desired state.

The instability of the system occurs due to a problem with synchrony. There are delays in feedback, delays in performing actions, and oscillations begin to occur in systems.

This emphasizes one basic necessity in the design process:

The timing of actuations should correlate with the speed of system evolution.

For systems with a high speed of evolution, both feedback and actuation processes need to happen fast. In stable systems, this timing can be larger.

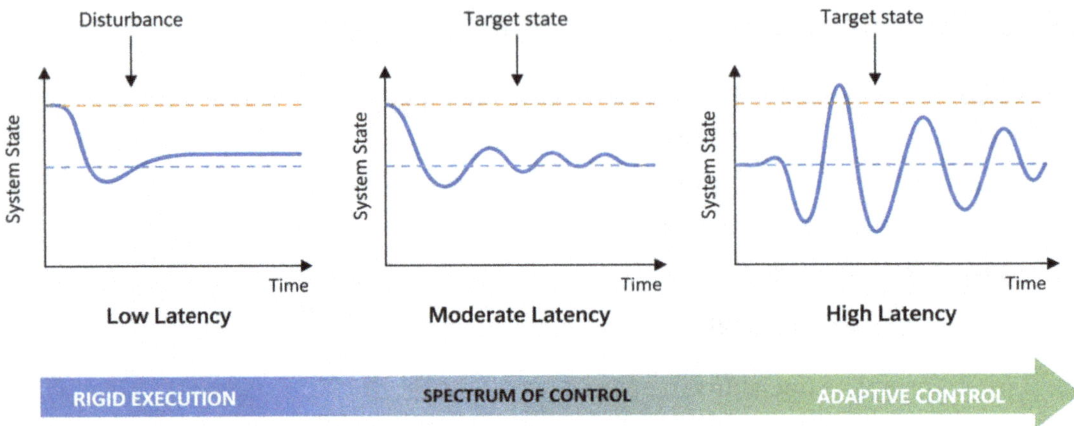

***Figure 4-3.** Effect of Actuation Latency on System Stability*

Comparison of system stability under low, moderate, and high actuation latency, showing convergence, delayed response, and oscillatory behavior.

It is evident that the stability of the system decreases as actuation latency increases. This happens even if the control logic is appropriate, but there is a delay in executing the command.

Section Summary

This section discussed how the actuation rate and latency can affect the stability of control-centric delivery mechanisms.

Key observations include the following:

- Actuation delay results in misalignment of decisions and the state of the system.
- Latency decreases the effectivity of the corrections made.
- The effects of latency are pronounced in high-frequency delivery settings.
- Synchronization of actuation and feedback is essential for stability.

All these contribute to highlighting that pipelines should be designed not only in terms of accuracy and speed but also with respect to actuation latency.

The following sections will elaborate further and demonstrate how improper actuation contributes to destabilization.

4.7 Over-actuation and System Instability

The goal of control-based delivery is not only to make sure the changes are implemented properly but to implement them in a way that sustains the stability of the system. **Just as insufficient actuation can leave a system slow to recover, excessive or poorly coordinated actuation introduces its own hazards: heightened instability, diminished predictability, and an elevated probability of compounding failures.**

When there is over-actuation, changes are made more often than necessary or without adequate integration with the system's status. In these instances, rather than stabilize the system, the actuation itself becomes a disruption.

This section will discuss how over-actuation arises in control systems, how it is exhibited in CI/CD pipelines, and how the difference between feedback and actuation causes practical instability.

4.7.1 Overcorrection in Control Systems

Overcorrection in classical control theory is a situation whereby an automated system tries to compensate for deviation with a disproportionate level of corrective action. Instead of stabilizing around a desired value, the system goes past it and creates new deviations.

The phenomenon results from inappropriate controller tuning, delayed feedback, or too much gain in the feedback loop (Ogata, 2010).

The logic behind it is simple. Whenever a system notices a deviation from the set values, it tries to make up for the discrepancy through correctional action in terms of inputs. If such inputs are too aggressive or do not take into account system dynamics, they push the system beyond its set point, leading to further deviations.

Ultimately, this causes the system to oscillate or diverge.

It should be noted that lack of control is not always to blame for instability. Often, the problem results from excessive control that is uncoordinated.

Such is the case of a software delivery system, whereby pipelines are seen as actuators in a closed-loop control process.

4.7.2 Oscillation in CI/CD Systems

Overcorrection in CI/CD appears as oscillations in the operation of the system.

This becomes especially noticeable in the case of a frequent actuation process in a situation where there is no feedback or where feedback is delayed or partial.

For instance, the deploy and rollback processes represent one of the most frequent occurrences of such a situation.

A new deployment causes some degradation in the performance of the application. The observability layer detects the degradation and surface signals that may prompt the deployment controller, release automation, or pipeline logic to initiate a rollback. However, due to the delayed or partial feedback, the rollback is triggered not right away but later, after other changes to the application have been made. As a result, the application goes through several stages of the deployment process and rollback without stabilizing.

Another example would be the process of auto-scaling.

In the cloud environment, auto-scaling acts as an actuator of the system. It adjusts its capacity according to what the system observes in terms of load. When scaling thresholds are set too aggressively, input signals carry excessive noise, or cooldown and stabilization windows are inadequately tuned, the platform may enter a cycle of repeated scale-up and scale-down events that waste capacity without improving service quality.

These trends are not isolated cases. This is because there is a fundamental problem - a mismatch between actuation strength and system behavior. In a stable system, the actuations are proportionate and immediate. In an unstable system, the actuations are inappropriate and/or tardy.

4.7.3 Feedback–Actuation Mismatch

One main reason for over-actuation in software delivery systems is the inconsistency between the feedback signal and the actuation process.

The former generates the information needed for making a decision, while the latter puts that decision into effect. In the case of poor-quality feedback, the decision will be inaccurate, and when actuation happens continuously under such circumstances, the system ends up multiplying mistakes instead of resolving them.

Low-level signals tend to bring about many actions.

An instance of this could be when there is an ongoing stream of weak alerts that cause many corrections in spite of the absence of any problem. Another case would be an unclear signal causing a pipeline to make extensive modifications.

This mismatch creates a feedback loop in which

- Poor signals lead to incorrect decisions
- Incorrect decisions trigger unnecessary actions
- Unnecessary actions introduce further instability

In time, this process leads to deterioration in the reliability of the system and automation in general.

According to control theory, proper control involves not only correct feedback but also correct scaling in actuation. Otherwise, the system will become unstable (Åström & Murray, 2008).

4.7.4 Real-World Failure Patterns

The theoretical notions of overcorrection and feedback mismatch translate into tangible patterns in real-world software delivery infrastructures. Such patterns give evidence of the effect of over-actuation on destabilization.

An example of such a pattern is the deployment storm.

Under conditions of high deployment frequency, pipelines generate a series of deployments, either in response to small-scale changes or insufficient feedback information. The interaction between these states results in overlapping state transitions, which are hard to control. The problems resulting from previous deployments might be exacerbated by new deployments, creating an unstable state of affairs.

Another typical example of a pattern in question is configuration thrashing.

The values of configuration parameters are constantly altered in reaction to variable signals. For example, in an attempt to achieve stable performance, limits on resources are repeatedly raised and reduced.

More extreme examples lead to cascades, whereby the destabilization in one module affects other services that depend on it.

This is further exacerbated by fast actuation, where corrective actions taken in one part of the system unexpectedly impact others.

It becomes clear from these examples that one of the fundamental facts about contemporary delivery systems is as follows:

In environments where automation is already extensive, instability more often traces back to poorly coordinated or ungoverned actuation than to a shortage of automated capability.

Table 4-2. *Instability Patterns from Poor Actuation*

Pattern	Cause	Impact
Oscillation	Overcorrection	Repeated instability and failure to converge
Drift	Weak feedback	Gradual degradation of system performance
Cascade failure	Rapid, uncoordinated actuation	Widespread system outages

Section Summary

This section examined how excessive or poorly coordinated actuation introduces instability into control-oriented delivery systems.

The key insights are as follows:

- Overcorrection leads to oscillatory or divergent system behavior.
- High-frequency actuation amplifies instability when not aligned with system dynamics.
- Feedback–actuation mismatch is a primary driver of excessive corrective actions.

Real-world instability patterns emerge from uncontrolled actuation rather than a lack of automation.

These results underscore the significance of pipeline design, which seeks to maintain a balance between responsiveness and control to ensure that responses are proportional, timely, and in keeping with the system's current state.

4.8 Rollbacks, Pauses, and Controlled Releases

In control-centric delivery systems, stability does not result from the absence of change but from the management of change itself. As described previously, actuation is the process used to alter the state of the system. While actuation is dependent on accuracy, it is equally important for actuation to be reversible and timely.

Unmanaged actuation results in an unstable state. On the other hand, managed actuation, where actuation happens incrementally, continually, and reversibly if necessary, allows systems to develop within a constantly changing environment.

This chapter explores three important factors that make managed actuation possible in software delivery systems, namely, rollbacks, managed pauses, and strategic deployments. Collectively, these factors turn pipelines into control systems that maintain stability.

4.8.1 Rollback as Corrective Actuation

Rollback is among the most direct corrective actuation mechanisms available in software delivery. It attempts to return the affected service, configuration artifact, or release path to a previously validated operating condition, though the completeness of that restoration can vary depending on statefulness, data coupling, and downstream dependencies.

Viewed through a control system lens, rollback is a corrective actuation event triggered by negative feedback signals - elevated error rates, latency degradation, health-check failures, or SLO breaches - rather than being a form of feedback itself. When post-deployment telemetry indicates that system behavior has crossed predefined tolerance boundaries, release automation or pipeline logic may initiate rollback or suspend further rollout until conditions stabilize.

What makes rollback effective is the speed of its implementation.

In contrast to other types of corrective processes, rollback allows going back to the state before the issue occurred rather than dealing with the problems while staying in the problematic state.

Yet, rollback has its own limitations as well.

It can be used only if a stable state is available. If there are high interdependencies between different components or data changes continuously, then a rollback cannot restore the full behavior of the system to the required level. Moreover, too many rollbacks can mean that there are problems with the actuation design, which should be solved.

However, despite all the disadvantages associated with rollback, it remains an essential mechanism that ensures stability. The advantage of reversibility is one of the fundamental features of any effective control mechanism (Humble & Farley, 2010).

4.8.2 Deployment Strategies

Rollback is one way of addressing instability when it arises; however, deployment approaches seek to prevent or minimize instability from occurring. The changes are introduced gradually into the system such that their effects can be seen and monitored.

The common types of deployment approaches include canary release, blue-green deployment, and progressive delivery.

Canary Releases

Canary releases refer to making any changes to a smaller group of users or systems prior to complete deployment. In this way, the risks are reduced, since one is able to see how the systems operate in real situations.

With each increase in exposure level, decisions regarding next steps are made based on feedback. In case everything goes well, then further deployment takes place. Otherwise, necessary measures can be taken to correct the situation at an earlier stage.

This technique corresponds greatly to the operation of a control system when changes are made step by step.

Blue-Green Deployments

The major advantage associated with the blue-green deployment strategy is that two parallel states can be created: the active one that is currently being used and the other one that is used to test the new version.

When the new version passes all the tests, then the workflow will be switched to the new version.

In such a way, the present state will be easily distinguished from the future state and reverted when necessary.

Under a blue/green model, the incoming version is provisioned in a parallel environment where it undergoes validation; once confidence thresholds are met, production traffic is shifted from the incumbent environment to the new one, with the original retained as an immediate fallback.

Progressive Delivery

Progressive delivery builds on the concepts behind canary releases by incorporating feedback into the decision-making process around deployments. Instead of making decisions based only on predetermined deployment stages, progressive delivery makes decisions about deployments based on real-time observability data.

In effect, deployment becomes a form of closed-loop control, where the actions taken are influenced by the current state of the system.

Progressive Delivery works well in complicated systems, in which interactions between various pieces could lead to unpredictable behavior (Forsgren et al., 2018).

4.8.3 Controlled Pauses and Feedback Windows

In addition to having deployment techniques, there is an additional need for pauses which are controlled within the operation of the system.

A pause allows a delay between one point in the process and the next point of actuation that gives the system time to achieve an equilibrium prior to another actuation point. It is through the pause that we are able to obtain feedback on the performance of the system after one actuation.

If there were no pauses, then feedback would be hard to establish since all changes occur within the pipeline. It will not give enough time for the changes to show themselves so that they are attributed correctly.

This can be achieved through

- Allowing stabilization of feedback
- Minimizing the possibility of cumulative mistakes
- Making decisions that are more accurate

This is from the perspective that the feedback cycle can easily cause oscillations when it is not timed accurately.

Pauses need to be carefully timed. Too much time results in low responsiveness, while too little time fails to give any meaningful feedback.

4.8.4 Risk Mitigation Through Gradual Actuation

The one commonality among rollbacks, deployment approaches, and pauses is that of gradual actuation.

Rather than implementing sudden shifts in drastic ways, gradual actuation implements changes through small increments. This provides sufficient opportunity for adaptation in the system before the next shift. It minimizes the potential dangers associated with the process of change.

Gradual actuation enhances the stability of the system by increasing its predictability.

It is relatively easy to analyze small changes and their implications because they impact small parts of the system only. Troubleshooting becomes straightforward and fast due to the fewer possibilities for errors.

However, this may not be possible when large changes occur abruptly.

Large changes can cause unforeseen interactions, thereby causing problems within the system. These make it difficult to identify the exact problem.

Herein lies another important principle.

For a dynamic system to stabilize, control over its changes must be maintained.

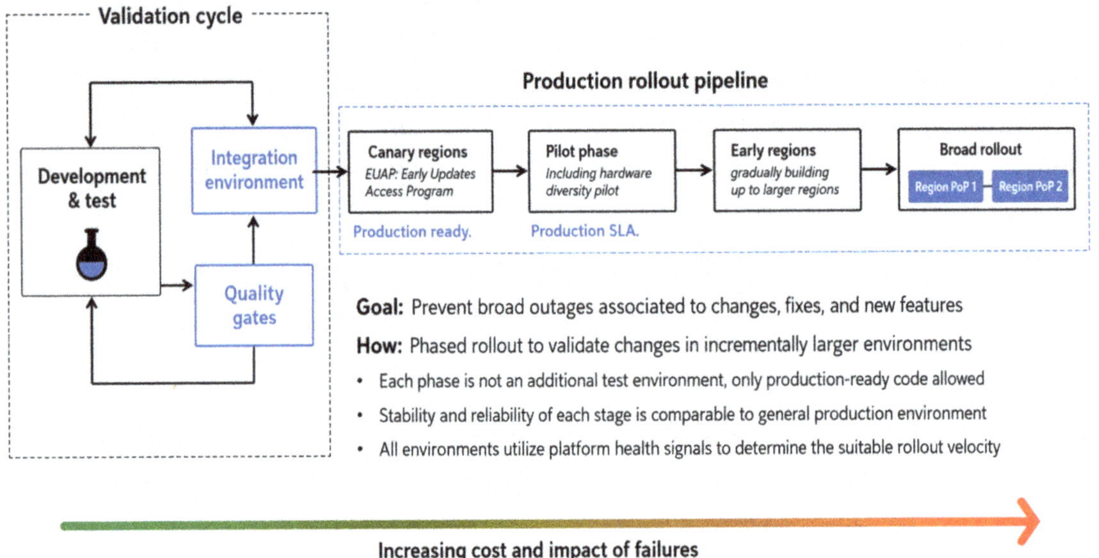

Figure 4-4. *Progressive Delivery as Controlled Actuation*

Progressive deployment with staged rollout and continuous observability, enabling feedback-driven advancement, pause, or rollback decisions.

Progressive delivery is demonstrated in the figure as a feedback mechanism in the actuation process of CI/CD. The method limits the impact of changes while continuously evaluating the results, thus minimizing risks of instability in the system.

4.8.5 Section Summary

In this section, techniques for facilitating controlled actuation within software deployment systems were considered.

The main points include the following:

- Rollback acts immediately and is reversible.
- The method of deployment lowers risks by gradually making changes.
- The timing of feedback and actuation is synchronized through controlled pauses.
- Actuation is made gradual for better stability and predictability.

These processes turn the CI/CD process into a control-aware process that manages changes without affecting stability.

The upcoming section continues the discussion by considering the design of actuation techniques for achieving system resilience and adaptability.

4.9 Designing Effective Actuation Mechanisms

The previous sections have shown that actuation is the way in which changes get applied to the system, and too little and too much actuation can result in instability. The next step that needs to be taken is to establish what kind of actuation is needed in order to maintain stability and responsiveness as well as reliability at the same time.

Good actuation does not just happen by chance. On the contrary, it requires a conscious approach, where execution takes place in conjunction with feedback, reversibility to provide for safety, a limited scope of influence, and adaptation to changing conditions. These criteria help convert pipelines into control-oriented means of operation amid continuous change.

The following section describes the basic design principles behind an efficient actuation system.

4.9.1 Feedback-Aligned Actuation

At the very heart of all control loops sits the interplay between feedback and actuation. For actions that directly affect runtime behavior, actuation should draw on reliable, timely system feedback rather than depending solely on static assumptions or hard-coded progression logic. Deterministic pipeline stages such as linting, unit testing, artifact signing, and static analysis remain valid without runtime signals, but deployment and scaling decisions benefit substantially from observed system state.

In conventional delivery pipelines, events such as commits or scheduled releases are what trigger the process of actuation. While this approach works well from an operational perspective, it fails to account for the state of the system at any given point. This means that any actuations may end up being done irrespective of the condition of the system, which would lead to inconsistencies.

By aligning actuation with feedback, we can achieve a system that reacts properly to various states through its observability signals.

Signals like latency, errors, throughput, and resource usage give us real-time information about our systems. By incorporating these types of metrics into our pipeline logic, we can ensure that actuation will be aware of the situation of the system and make decisions accordingly.

This alignment makes sure that whatever is done is right not only by theory but also by context.

Feedback alignment does have certain limitations. The feedback should be of high quality, and it must be processed at low latency with well-defined thresholds. Ineffective and untimely feedback may result in wrong decisions, thus defeating the very purpose of feedback alignment.

However, feedback alignment remains essential for control-centric systems. It makes sure that pipelines react based on what actually happens in the system.

4.9.2 Reversibility and Safety

No actuation process can be flawless. Even a good pipeline can lead to unexpected behavior because of unknown side effects or environmental changes. This is why there should always be a way to reverse an actuation process.

Reversibility provides a path for the system to recover toward a previously known stable condition, although the completeness of that recovery may be constrained by stateful dependencies, irreversible data mutations, or side effects that have already propagated to external consumers. In practice, organizations pursue reversibility through rollback procedures, versioned configuration management, and immutable deployment artifacts.

The design of rollback procedures is especially important.

A robust rollback system must satisfy several conditions:

- It must be **fast**, minimizing the duration of instability.
- It must be **reliable**, consistently restoring the intended state.
- It must be **isolated**, avoiding unintended side effects.

In addition to rollback, safety can be enhanced through techniques such as

- Immutable deployments, where new versions are introduced without modifying existing ones
- Versioned configurations, enabling precise control over system parameters
- Automated validation checks that prevent unsafe actions

Taken together, these mechanisms materially improve the safety and dependability of the actuation process when failures arise, though they reduce rather than eliminate residual risk.

Reversibility may be considered an important stabilizer from the control systems perspective. In fact, this feature allows addressing deviations without having to make elaborate forward corrections, thus avoiding potential cascades of instability (Humble & Farley, 2010).

4.9.3 Isolation and Blast Radius Reduction

Among other challenges with respect to actuation, the biggest threat is related to the influence that actuation could have on all other components of the system. When dealing with decentralized architectures, one alteration will spread across many different services and therefore create an extensive impact.

Isolation is what helps in avoiding such a problem.

Isolation ensures that whatever changes occur, they remain limited to a certain perimeter and thus do not create a wide-scale effect.

Isolation can be achieved through architectural and operational strategies such as

- Service segmentation, where components operate independently
- Traffic partitioning, allowing selective exposure to changes
- Environment separation, isolating production, staging, and testing systems

Isolation is usually achieved via deployment techniques such as canary deployment and blue-green deployment, which were mentioned in the last segment on CI/CD pipelines.

The advantages of isolation come down to two major aspects.

For one thing, it increases safety by reducing the consequences of failure. For another thing, it facilitates monitoring by helping identify any behavior to particular modifications.

This follows the tenets of control systems, whereby localized correction is preferable to global change management for enhanced controllability.

4.9.4 Gradual and Adaptive Execution

It will be erroneous to deploy actuation through a one-shot approach that covers everything in one big actuation event. It will be prudent to execute actuation gradually, which means allowing time for adaptation during every step of actuation.

This strategy decreases uncertainty through incrementalism, as every small portion is executed separately. This way, it is easier to observe the progress in every small unit and give time for necessary adjustments along the way.

This strategy becomes more relevant when working with complex systems, because there might be unintended consequences from the interaction of various elements.

In turn, adaptive actuation means allowing some flexibility and ability to change the process as it goes, depending on the observations and results that have been attained so far. In other words, adaptive actuation means adjusting the rate of progress, depending on the situation.

For instance, actuation may move quickly if everything seems to work well, while the actuation process may stop if anomalies occur.

4.9.5 Integration with Observability Systems

The process of actuation is impossible in isolation. It should be thoroughly integrated with observability systems that allow gaining constant insights about the way the system behaves.

Observability systems produce feedback signals that determine how to proceed with actuation. This integration ensures that pipelines work in a closed loop by adjusting themselves depending on the effect of their actions.

Integration is not only about collecting data but also

- Processing the information provided by metrics, logs, and traces
- Correlating signals coming from different parts of the system
- Interpreting feedback automatically within the pipeline

Such integration allows observability systems to turn pipelines into closed-loop control systems. They can constantly analyze their actions based on the behavior of the system, making appropriate changes to ensure stable functioning.

Moreover, integration contributes to greater transparency and accountability since engineers can easily find out what effect each action produces.

Table 4-3. *Design Principles for Actuation Systems*

Principle	Description	Benefit
Feedback alignment	Uses real-time system signals to guide actions	Improves decision accuracy and relevance
Reversibility	Enables rollback and recovery mechanisms	Reduces recovery time and limits impact
Isolation	Limits the scope of changes to specific components	Enhances stability and reduces risk
Gradual execution	Applies changes incrementally	Improves predictability and control

4.9.6 Section Summary

This section outlined the fundamental rules that should be used in order to create reliable actuation mechanics for software delivery systems.

The critical lessons are as follows:

- Actuation should be linked to timely feedback in order to be relevant.
- Reversibility is necessary in case of safety considerations when there is uncertainty about the consequences.
- Isolation helps minimize the effects on the system.

- Timely and gradual execution leads to better control and more predictable outcomes.
- Integration with observability tools allows for creating a closed-loop system.

All of these rules together allow us to design pipelines for managing our system not just executing changes.

The final section of this chapter outlines how control over system behavior is provided by actuation.

4.10 Actuation as a Driver of System Behavior

As we have seen earlier, actuation refers to how changes can be made to a system, but this does not tell the full story about its importance. Modern CI/CD pipelines are considered to be reactive systems that carry out a certain workflow based on events such as committing code or changing configurations. That perspective, while operationally functional, is too limited to account for the continuous behavioral influence that pipelines exert in dynamic, cloud-native delivery environments. The truth is that pipelines influence the system's behavior instead of simply reacting to it by adding new conditions to the process and making it evolve further. Therefore, pipelines cannot be viewed separately from system behavior but rather should be regarded as key elements of the latter.

Speaking in terms of control systems theory, pipelines serve as continuous inputs into a system that change its dynamics with time. Deployments, configuration changes, and scaling are ongoing processes that are always influenced by previous conditions in a system and therefore have a significant impact. Thus, modern software systems can no longer be regarded as being static since they constantly develop throughout time. Therefore, all deployments should be approached as controlled behavioral inputs.

The difference between continuous change and controlled evolution will become especially important here. Whereas continuous delivery will allow for quick iterations, continuous change without any sort of regulation means instability, unpredictability, and variability. However, controlled evolution is all about structuring the process of change through feedback mechanisms, incrementally deploying new changes, and implementing reversible decisions. In other words, the key idea is being able to make a system evolve quickly while still maintaining stability in this process.

In other words, system dynamics cannot be understood merely in terms of their design. Dynamics is more about how changes get implemented over time, and actuation is precisely what determines the dynamics of the system. Therefore, the important idea here is that actuation simultaneously responds to observed system behavior and introduces new conditions that reshape subsequent dynamics, making it both a consequence of and a contributor to the trajectory the system follows.

4.11 Transition to Control-Oriented Delivery Systems

The history of modern software delivery systems is indicative of a larger change in practices toward automation, from those centered on control. Conventional DevOps practices focused on automation of repeatable processes to gain speed, cut down on manual labor, and enhance consistency. Although automation is still critical, it is no longer adequate in a world where change is constant, distributed, and unpredictable system behavior. In these situations, implementing changes effectively is not the key concern, but making sure that the changes lead to consistent and predictable results.

This change creates a new paradigm: delivery systems have to be architected as control systems, with automation being done in a designed system of feedback, decision-making, and actuation. Instead of performing pre-defined workflows independently, pipelines need to constantly be in contact with the system state, varying their behavior in response to real-time signals. Such transition re-characterizes the role of CI/CD pipelines, as it is no longer used to move code through phases but to control the behavior of systems in dynamically changing circumstances.

The main elements of this transition are uniting three basic elements. First, feedback systems allow you to have constant visibility of system performance in terms of metrics, logs, and traces. They are signals that reflect the present state of the system and are used to make informed decisions. Second, automated or human-based decision-making mechanisms process these signals and decide on appropriate actions. Third, actuation mechanisms are deployed by CI/CD pipelines, which use these actions on the system, changing its state and impacting subsequent behavior. These elements should work together and complete a single control loop.

The close interrelationship between these components determines the success of this model. Feedback should be prompt and precise, choices need to be situational, and actuation should be responsive and regulated. Under these conditions, the system proceeds to a closed-loop delivery model, where each action is tested based on its effects on system behavior, rather than an open-loop model, where actions are applied without any further validation.

Under closed-loop, deployment is not an eventual activity but a continuous process of monitoring, evaluation, and refinement. The changes are implemented in stages, and the impact of the changes is constantly monitored, and further steps are adjusted accordingly. This allows systems to be stable even when there is a high rate of change since deviation is identified early and corrected quickly.

This transition has serious consequences. The delivery systems should be developed with the control principles considered and with the focus on the feedback integration, accuracy of decisions, and the quality of actuation. Pipelines should not be considered by the capability to perform work but by the capability to ensure the stability of the system and direct the system evolution.

Finally, the shift to control-oriented delivery systems is a change of mindset. It shifts the emphasis from the speed at which changes can be implemented to the effectiveness of those changes. By so doing, it gives a base upon which to construct systems that are not only fast and scalable, but also stable, predictable, and resilient to constant change.

4.12 Chapter Summary

This chapter marked the transition in the understanding of CI/CD pipelines, from being seen as mere automated processes toward recognizing pipelines as actuation elements in a control system, which are responsible for introducing changes affecting the behavior of the system. While it might seem trivial that pipelines have to change the state of systems, this view also entails the consideration that actuation involves more than just executing operations but also making decisions about how the changes happen and deciding on how safe it is to apply them.

Throughout the chapter, one common theme was the idea that systems could not be expected to stabilize by virtue of having automation in place, but through proper actuation design. Pipelines that do not take into account feedback signals and timing, as well as system conditions, cannot ensure stable operation, even if they do their job correctly from an execution point of view. On the other hand, those pipelines that adhere to control-related considerations such as feedback, reversibility, gradualness, and isolation of change can help systems evolve safely.

The connection between speed and control was also analyzed in detail. Although modern DevOps focuses on speedy deployment of software changes, the analysis presented in this chapter has argued that delivery velocity, when it outpaces the control structures meant to govern it, can erode reliability and amplify operational risk rather than accelerate value. The objective is not to throttle the pace of delivery but to ensure that each increment of speed is matched by proportionate control measures, so that rapid evolution and operational stability advance together.

In analyzing various forms of actuation, effects of latency, over-actuation, and controlled deployment, the chapter revealed that pipelines play an active role in determining the direction of system evolution. Deployment was interpreted as behavioral input into the system and the evolution of the system as actuation in the long run. As a result, this approach yielded the general conclusion that pipelines were more than mere instruments - they were the active agents of system evolution.

Lastly, the notion of control actuation was presented, in which pipelines function under a closed-loop actuation scheme involving feedback, decision-making, and implementation of actions. Through such an approach, delivery systems gain the ability to transcend mere automation and become adaptive, driven by feedback. Once the actuation process is correctly designed, the conditions are set for the realization of desirable results, such as predictability, resilience, and scalability of delivery systems.

In conclusion, this chapter proves that the efficiency of contemporary software delivery systems does not lie in how fast changes can be implemented; instead, it revolves around their control. By viewing CI/CD pipelines as an actuation process within the context of a control system, businesses will have the opportunity to create delivery platforms that can sustain themselves through stable operations under high-speed circumstances.

References

Humble, J., & Farley, D. (2010). Continuous delivery: Reliable software releases through build, test, and deployment automation. Addison-Wesley Professional. ISBN: 978-0-321-60191-9.

Bass, L., Weber, I., & Zhu, L. (2015). DevOps: A software architect's perspective. Addison-Wesley Professional. ISBN: 978-0-134-04984-7.

Forsgren, N., Humble, J., & Kim, G. (2018). Accelerate: The science of lean software and DevOps: Building and scaling high performing technology organizations. IT Revolution Press. ISBN: 978-1-942788-33-1.

Ogata, K. (2010). Modern control engineering (5th ed.). Prentice Hall. ISBN: 978-0-136-15673-4.

Åström, K. J., & Murray, R. M. (2008). Feedback systems: An introduction for scientists and engineers. Princeton University Press. ISBN: 978-0-691-13576-2.

CHAPTER 5

Policy and Governance as System Constraints

5.1 Chapter Objective

This chapter applies the architectural vocabulary of control systems theory to reframe policy and governance as constraint mechanics within software delivery. While software delivery environments are discrete, distributed, and socio-technical rather than continuous physical plants, the control system model offers a productive lens for reasoning about how constraints shape decisions and bound change application. Under this framing, governance is treated not as a peripheral or retrospective activity but as something structurally woven into the processes through which decisions are made and changes are carried out.

The chapter examines how constraints shape actuation by restricting the set of system states that may introduce danger, compromise safety, or produce undesirable outcomes. This perspective positions governance as a stabilizing function responsible for maintaining predictability and preventing uncontrolled behavior, provided that the policies underpinning it are versioned, tested against representative scenarios, enforced consistently across environments, auditable for traceability, and aligned with clearly assigned risk ownership.

Furthermore, the chapter discusses how well-designed constraints can enable a system to remain stable even when operating at high delivery velocity. When constraints are codified, version-controlled, continuously tested, and enforced through automated mechanisms that are auditable and aligned with organizational risk ownership, they allow organizations to incorporate governance directly into decision-making and delivery execution. Under those conditions, systems can sustain rapid change while preserving safety and controllability.

S. Bobba and N. S. Vummaneni, *CI/CD as a Control System*, https://doi.org/10.1007/979-8-8688-2842-3_5

5.2 Introduction: From Governance to Control Constraints

In many contemporary software delivery settings, governance has functioned as a peripheral service that runs alongside development and operations rather than being woven into them. It tends to manifest as compliance checks, approval of workflows, and audit mechanisms that engage only after changes have been designed or deployed. While this approach offers a degree of retrospective assurance, it remains fundamentally reactive. It presupposes that risks can be detected and remediated after the fact rather than being addressed proactively as part of the processes that govern system behavior. For governance to serve as genuine control, its policies must be versioned, tested, enforced consistently at every decision point, auditable for traceability, and aligned with clearly defined risk ownership.

This model becomes inadequate when governance remains external to the execution flow, retrospective in its timing, and disconnected from the automated processes through which changes reach production.

Modern software systems are dynamic, distributed, and subject to continuous evolution. Changes flow at high frequency through automated pipelines, infrastructure scales elastically, and observable system behavior emerges from the interaction of many loosely coupled components. In mature delivery organizations, the objective is not to maximize the velocity of change in isolation but to optimize flow under acceptable thresholds of risk, reliability, compliance, and recovery capability. Risks in such environments do not materialize solely at discrete control gates; they develop continuously as the system evolves. Governance that operates only after the fact cannot keep pace with this rate of change, opening a widening gap between actual system behavior and the controls meant to govern it.

This control gap can materially increase the risk of instability.

When governance operates outside the execution path, the constraints it imposes arrive too late to shape the actions that matter. Policies may discourage certain behaviors but cannot prescriptively govern how actions are carried out unless those policies are codified, version-controlled, enforced at each decision point, and backed by auditable evidence of consistent application. In the absence of those conditions, systems can operate within nominal compliance boundaries yet still exhibit undesirable behavior such as performance degradation, latent security exposure, or inconsistent operation across environments. This underscores a key distinction: passing a compliance check is not the same as maintaining control.

Overcoming this shortcoming requires redefining how governance participates in the delivery process. Rather than serving as an external review layer, governance must be restructured so that its policies are versioned alongside application and infrastructure code, tested as part of the delivery pipeline, enforced consistently across all environments, fully auditable, and tied to accountable risk ownership.

Rather than functioning as an external review layer, governance can be modeled as a system of constraints embedded within the delivery architecture itself. Drawing control systems theory as an architectural analogy rather than a literal equivalence, constraints define the envelope of allowable system behavior. They establish the boundaries within which the system must operate and prevent transitions into states that would be unsafe or unstable. Crucially, these constraints do not take effect after a decision has already been made; they participate in shaping the decision as it forms.

The role of policy and governance shifts meaningfully when this concept is applied to software delivery, provided that the policies in question are maintained as versioned, testable artifacts, enforced through automated mechanisms at each stage of the pipeline, auditable for regulatory and operational traceability, and aligned with designated risk ownership across the organization.

Policies, when codified, version-controlled, continuously tested, and enforced through automated mechanisms with auditable outcomes and clear risk ownership, function as processes that govern actuation so that changes flowing through CI/CD pipelines remain within safe and acceptable limits. Under this model, governance no longer confines itself to ratifying or rejecting actions after they have been carried out; instead, it establishes the terms under which actions may be initiated in the first place. This repositions governance from a reactive review function to a proactive controlling role embedded in the execution path.

This shift is especially consequential in delivery environments where organizations seek to optimize flow under acceptable levels of risk, reliability, compliance, and recovery capability rather than pursuing raw deployment speed as an end.

As the rate of change increases, the cost of delayed intervention rises correspondingly. Errors propagate more quickly, and the consequences of incorrect actions become harder to contain. Embedding constraints within pipelines and decision-making processes is designed to keep governance operating at the same cadence as execution, thereby reducing the likelihood that changes outpace the controls meant to govern them. When this alignment is achieved, systems stand a materially better chance of remaining safe and stable even under conditions of continuous change.

Simultaneously, constraints need to be formulated.

Constraints that are unnecessarily complex, poorly scoped, or ambiguously defined can limit a system's flexibility, slow delivery throughput, and introduce operational complexity that outweighs the protection they provide. Conversely, constraints that are absent or inadequate leave the system exposed to preventable risk and instability. The objective is not to maximize restriction but to arrive at an optimal constraint design in which boundaries are clearly defined, consistently enforceable through automated mechanisms, version-controlled and testable alongside delivery artifacts, auditable for traceability, and aligned with both system objectives and accountable risk ownership.

The control-oriented delivery systems are based on this balance.

Actuation operates within the framework established by constraints, provided those constraints are codified, version-controlled, tested, enforced consistently, and backed by auditable evidence. Under these conditions, constraints help direct changes toward outcomes that strengthen system stability rather than undermine it. By defining acceptable margins of behavior, they allow systems to change and adapt without exceeding safe operational boundaries. The relationship between properly implemented constraints and system stability is therefore both structural and direct.

Applying control theory as an architectural model rather than a direct physical equivalence, stability is understood to depend not only on actuation and feedback but also on the presence of well-defined boundaries. Such boundaries limit the magnitude of permissible deviations and guide the system toward its intended operating state. Governance in software delivery performs an analogous function within a discrete, distributed, and socio-technical context. It establishes the operational boundaries within which pipelines execute, so that rapid and continuous change does not give rise to unchecked or divergent behavior.

This brings us to the main point of this chapter:

Well-designed governance is not merely restrictive; when its policies are clear, enforceable, and proportionate, it serves as the mechanism through which actuation is made safe, controlled, and aligned with organizational objectives.

When governance is introduced as a constraint mechanism within the delivery architecture, using control theory as an organizing model rather than a literal physical equivalence, the effect can be facilitative rather than suppressive. Under this framing, systems can sustain high delivery velocity without forfeiting stability, provided that speed is pursued within boundaries that protect reliability, security, and compliance.

Building on this foundation and continuing to treat control theory as an architectural model rather than a literal equivalence, this chapter examines how constraints function within delivery systems, how policies can be implemented as enforceable mechanisms within pipelines, and how governance can be scaled across complex, distributed environments. Viewed through this lens, policy and governance emerge as core structural elements of contemporary software delivery, vital to sustaining safe, scalable, and controlled evolution in the face of continuous change.

5.3 Constraints in Control Systems Theory

To appreciate the relevance of policies and governance in software delivery, it is helpful to begin with the concept of a constraint as it is understood in control systems theory. Although software delivery systems are discrete, distributed, and socio-technical rather than continuous physical plants, control theory provides a valuable architectural model for reasoning about boundaries and safe operating envelopes. Within that model, constraints are not secondary considerations or external additions; they are foundational components that define the boundaries within which a control system may operate. Without them, the system would be free to assume any state, regardless of whether that state was safe, efficient, or aligned with operational objectives.

Constraints, in this sense, define the boundaries that limit the range of permissible system operations. Their importance in system design stands alongside that of feedback and actuation, though they deliver genuine control only when they are codified, version-controlled, consistently enforced through automated mechanisms, and auditable for traceability.

5.3.1 Definition of Constraints in Control Systems

In classical control systems theory, which serves here as an architectural model rather than a direct physical equivalence, constraints represent the limits imposed on system variables, inputs, or outputs. These limits arise from two principal sources.

The first source is physical constraints. In mechanical systems, actuators cannot exceed defined limits of force and velocity; in electrical systems, voltage and current are similarly bounded. These limits are inherent to the system and, if exceeded, can cause irreversible damage. When this concept is mapped to software delivery, the analogous constraints are those imposed by infrastructure capacity, network bandwidth, storage throughput, and computational resources. To function as effective controls in that domain, such constraints must be codified, monitored, and enforced through automated mechanisms with auditable outcomes.

The second source is operational constraints, which are imposed to ensure that the system operates safely and effectively within its intended parameters. In software delivery, operational constraints encompass rules governing deployment cadence, resource utilization thresholds, change approval criteria, and rollback conditions. These constraints deliver control only when they are versioned, tested, enforced consistently at each decision point, and aligned with accountable risk ownership.

In both categories, constraints bound the range of permissible values for system variables, typically expressed as upper or lower thresholds that the system must not breach. Effective constraint management requires that these boundaries be codified in a form amenable to automated enforcement, version-controlled for auditability, and tested to confirm they behave as intended. Systems operating under properly implemented constraints adjust their behavior within these boundaries rather than exceeding them.

This definition highlights a critical characteristic of constraints that applies equally in classical control and, by architectural analogy, in software delivery: constraints do not function in isolation but rather shape and bound the operation of other control elements, provided they are implemented with the versioning, testing, enforcement consistency, and auditability required to make them operationally effective that they do not operate on their own but rather constrain the operation of other control functions.

5.3.2 Role of Constraints in Stability and Safety

Constraints are among the fundamental mechanisms through which stability and safety are supported in control systems, though they cannot guarantee these outcomes in isolation and must work in concert with feedback, actuation, and properly calibrated decision logic.

First, applying control theory as an architectural model, constraints serve a stabilizing function. By restricting the set of behaviors available to the system, they help keep potential deviations within manageable levels and allow corrective actions to operate more effectively within a bounded range. In software delivery, this stabilizing effect materializes when constraints are codified, enforced consistently, and aligned with observed system dynamics.

Second, constraints function as safety barriers in dynamic environments. Within classical control and, by architectural analogy, within software delivery systems, rapid or unexpected operational changes and external disturbances can push a system toward unstable or undesirable states. Well-implemented constraints reduce the probability of such outcomes by preventing the system from transitioning beyond its defined safe operating envelope.

Finally, the relationship between constraints and system equilibrium merits attention. In classical control theory, equilibrium denotes the operating state toward which a properly governed system tends to converge. When this concept is applied as an architectural model to software delivery, equilibrium corresponds to the steady operating condition in which performance, reliability, and resource consumption remain within their intended ranges.

In control theory, equilibrium signifies that the system is operating within its intended parameters and converging toward a stable state rather than diverging from it. When constraints are clearly defined, consistently enforced, and well-aligned with system objectives, they help guide the system toward equilibrium. In the absence of adequate constraints, the system is less likely to reach or sustain a stable operating condition (Ogata, 2010). While software delivery systems differ from continuous physical plants in their discrete, distributed, and socio-technical nature, this principle translates architecturally: delivery systems lacking well-implemented governance boundaries tend to exhibit greater variability and reduced predictability.

5.3.3 Hard vs. Soft Constraints

Within the control-theoretic framework adopted here as an architectural model, constraints can be classified into two broad categories, hard constraints and soft constraints, each with distinct implications for how delivery systems are designed and governed.

Hard constraints denote restrictions that must be observed at all times. They represent absolute boundaries whose violation typically results in severe consequences for the system, ranging from operational failure to safety incidents. Classic examples include maximum temperatures in a reactor vessel or maximum structural loads. In software delivery, analogous hard constraints might include mandatory security scan thresholds, regulatory data-handling requirements, or production access controls. For hard constraints to function as reliable safeguards, they must be codified, version-controlled, enforced through automated prevention mechanisms, and auditable so that compliance can be demonstrated continuously rather than asserted retrospectively.

Because hard constraints carry the highest operational consequence, control systems are designed to prevent their violation through deterministic enforcement mechanisms. In practice, however, failures, defects, race conditions, or enforcement gaps can still result in violations, which is why defense-in-depth strategies, redundant enforcement layers, and continuous monitoring are essential. The intent is to implement measures that block actions that would lead to a hard-constraint breach before those actions can take effect.

Soft constraints, by contrast, introduce a degree of flexibility. They define preferred operating ranges within which the system performs most effectively, rather than absolute boundaries whose breach causes immediate harm. Exceeding a soft constraint typically does not produce catastrophic consequences but may degrade efficiency, increase latency, or reduce the margin available for absorbing future disturbances. As with hard constraints, soft constraints deliver meaningful control only when they are codified, monitored, and enforced through mechanisms that are auditable and version controlled.

Soft constraints are particularly relevant in optimization scenarios where competing objectives require deliberate trade-offs. A system might, for instance, tolerate a temporary breach of a latency target in order to preserve availability during an unexpected traffic surge. Such trade-offs should be governed by policies that are explicitly codified, versioned, and enforced through automated logic with auditable decision records, so that each relaxation of a soft constraint is intentional, traceable, and aligned with organizational risk priorities.

The distinction between hard and soft constraints reflects a broader design requirement: combining strict, non-negotiable enforcement over parameters critical to safety, security, and compliance with more flexible governance over parameters that influence efficiency and performance. Realizing this balance in practice demands that both categories of constraint are versioned, testable, enforceable through automated mechanisms, and auditable, differing primarily in the severity of consequence and the tolerance for temporary deviation.

This layered approach is especially valuable in software delivery, where it enables organizations to enforce critical policies without unnecessarily constraining the flexibility that teams need for rapid iteration, provided that the policies themselves are versioned, tested, consistently enforced, auditable, and aligned with designated risk ownership.

Control systems maintain stability by ensuring that system behavior remains within predefined operating boundaries despite disturbances and changing conditions. Figure 5-1 illustrates how control constraints define safe operating regions and guide corrective actions that keep the system within acceptable performance and safety limits.

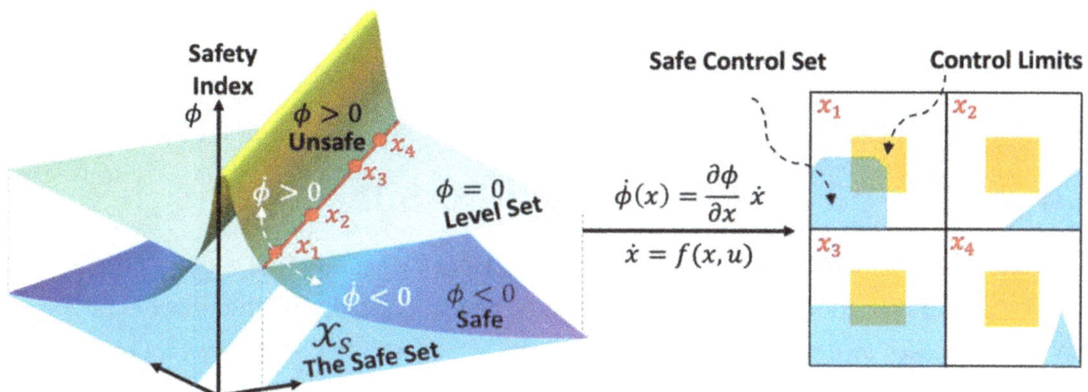

Figure 5-1. *Constraints as Boundaries in a Control System*

Architectural model illustrating a delivery system operating within defined constraint boundaries, using control-theory concepts to represent how governance limits maintain system behavior within safe and stable operating regions.

5.3.4 Section Summary

In this segment, the concept of constraints was presented, drawing on control systems theory as an architectural model rather than a literal physical equivalence, as an integral element of system governance that outlines the limits within which system activities must operate.

The major ideas include the following:

- When properly codified, version-controlled, and enforced through automated mechanisms, constraints determine the allowable range of operation of a system.
- Their role is critical in sustaining stability and reducing the likelihood of unsafe conditions, functioning through architectural boundaries, automated enforcement, feedback-informed thresholds, and consistent remediation behavior across environments.

- Constraints affect equilibrium and direct control measures
- Hard and soft constraints offer a compromise between strict adherence and adaptability.

This theory forms the foundation for explaining the working of policies and governance as constraint instruments in software delivery systems, which will be discussed in the subsequent segment.

5.4 Policy as a Control Mechanism

In control-based software delivery architectures, policy does not just represent a list of guidelines and requirements. Policy acts as a means of control that dictates decision-making processes and processes in the delivery system. While constraints set out the limits of allowable activities, policies provide a mechanism to enforce these limits through the implementation of logic.

The distinction is critical. Constraints state what should not be done, but policies state how it should not be done in the system. This way, policies act as the interface through which governance and system activity meet.

5.4.1 Policy as Enforcement Logic

At its very foundation, policy is nothing but governance made executable. Governance is baked into the very fabric of the pipeline, platform, and runtime, ensuring automated, consistent governance.

Traditional governance involves manual, discretionary actions that include human judgment and approval. The consequence of such an approach is inconsistent, slow, and discretionary decisions. Policy as a governance mechanism helps enable deterministic governance, making decisions consistently.

Pipeline policies can also be viewed as filters that apply to decision-making processes. All decisions that can be made within the pipeline, such as deploying applications, configuring them, or scaling the infrastructure, are filtered according to the policies set forth. An action is accepted by the system if it adheres to policy guidelines, but it is changed or delayed otherwise.

This allows us to turn pipelines into environments that have both execution and evaluation mechanisms. Thus, making policies an inherent part of decisions, not an external one.

5.4.2 Static vs. Dynamic Policies

There are two main types of policies that could be defined by their adaptability to the system state.

The first type of policy is known as static policies. Such policies are predefined and almost constant over time. Static policies usually help to define some fundamental principles related to security, compliance, architecture, and other areas. Since such policies do not take into account the current state of the system, they are relatively stable and predictable. However, due to the absence of adaptive mechanisms, they might lack flexibility.

The second type of policies is known as dynamic policies. Dynamic policies adjust themselves depending on the behavior of the system and additional context. These policies include feedback signals such as performance levels, error rates, or workloads to change their enforcement strategy. For example, a deployment policy might allow fast deployment of software components when performance metrics are stable but prohibit any changes when the level of system performance decreases.

Dynamic policies help to achieve more flexible operation of the system. Nevertheless, they are more difficult to implement because they are highly dependent on feedback signals.

5.4.3 Policy Placement in Delivery Systems

It should be noted that the effectiveness of policy as an instrument for control is determined not only by its quality as a whole but also by the location where this or that type of policy will be used in the implementation process. Policies can serve different purposes, depending on the stage at which they are enforced.

The pre-deployment level includes policies that work as validation gates. At this level, the artifact validation takes place, checking whether code, configuration, and other artifacts satisfy certain conditions. The pre-deployment level is oriented to preventing any potentially dangerous actions from taking place.

When we talk about the stage of deployment, policy acts in real time, controlling action execution in some particular way, defining the allowed rollout strategy, exposing to changes, and setting up a threshold for actions. At the deployment level, the behavior of actuation is influenced by policy.

The post-deployment level allows monitoring and assessing the system behavior from the perspective of such metrics as reliability and performance.

5.4.4 Policy as Part of the Control Loop

The full potential of policy is realized when it becomes part of the closed-loop control system for the software delivery process.

In this scenario, policy interacts with feedback and actuation as follows:

- Feedback is used to obtain information regarding the state of the system.
- The policy interprets this information under certain constraints.
- Actuation acts upon the information based on policy.

Thus, instead of just being rules to follow, policies become dynamic decision-makers.

Policies monitor the system's performance constantly and dictate how pipelines react to changing circumstances.

For instance, when feedback shows a high error rate, the policy could prevent new deployments or reverse previous ones. When performance stays consistent, the policy may speed up deployment.

Ultimately, the policy guarantees that decisions made are consistent with the system's goals and constraints.

Through this process, a control loop driven by policy is formed, which makes governance an integral part of the system itself. This leads to a system that is self-regulated and able to maintain its stability amid constant changes (Åström & Murray, 2008).

Software delivery systems must operate within defined constraints to maintain stability, reliability, and safe operation under changing conditions. Figure 5-1 illustrates how control constraints establish safe operating boundaries and guide system behavior to prevent instability while maintaining desired performance.

Table 5-1. *Types of Policies in CI/CD Systems*

Policy Type	Description	Control Function
Security policy	Defines vulnerability thresholds and security checks	Risk control
Compliance policy	Ensures adherence to regulatory requirements	Legal alignment
Operational policy	Governs deployment processes and workflows	Stability control
Performance policy	Enforces SLO/SLA thresholds	Quality assurance

5.4.5 Section Summary

This section established policy as a core control mechanism within software delivery systems.

The key insights are as follows:

- Policy translates governance into enforceable execution logic.
- It acts as a decision filter within pipelines, shaping system behavior.
- Static and dynamic policies provide a balance between consistency and adaptability.
- Policy must be applied across all stages of the delivery lifecycle.
- Integration with feedback and actuation enables closed-loop control.

These principles demonstrate that policy is not an external constraint but an embedded component of system control, enabling delivery systems to operate safely, consistently, and at scale.

5.5 Policy as Code and Automated Governance

With the advancement in software release systems toward higher rates of frequency, wider distribution, and higher levels of complexity, the conventional mode of governance involving manual inspection and retrospective enforcement proves inadequate. Within such contexts, changes come at a rate faster than that which can be achieved through human-driven monitoring and governance. The disparity leads to an important gap between governance and its implementation, where policies are established without being enforced adequately.

Policy as Code (PaC) serves as a means to bridge this gap.

Policy is transformed into machine-executable code, allowing for automation of the process of governance. Policy moves from being a piece of documentation or guidance to becoming part of the code running the application or system under management. This allows for governance to keep pace with the rate of change within a complex system.

5.5.1 Evolution from Manual Governance to Policy as Code

Traditional approaches in governance depend heavily on manual procedures. Code review, approvals, and audit checks are implemented to make sure that the requirements imposed by organizational standards are met. Such a model works quite well for rare occurrences; however, if applied in modern deployment systems, it will cause inconsistencies due to latency.

Manual enforcement faces a series of shortcomings. First, it depends on people's availability and ability to understand what should be done; second, its implementation could vary across various teams or environments. Finally, it happens outside of the execution flow, which means that governance does not affect decision-making at all.

This problem becomes critical in the case of high-frequency systems that can deliver their products several times a day. In such a situation, a system would require tools that provide continuous, deterministic, and execution-related governance.

Policy as Code provides a solution to this challenge by turning governance into a form of programming. Policies are codified, stored together with application assets, and executed during deployment. Thus, they are guaranteed to act consistently and without any delay.

5.5.2 Policy as Code Frameworks

Implementation of the concept of Policy as Code has been facilitated by the creation of an ecosystem of frameworks and tools, which aim to implement policy enforcement in the delivery process.

Policy as Code is based on the principle of implementing constraints in pipelines and platform layers, so they are able to check and evaluate the proposed action in real time. In turn, such policies act as control mechanisms, impacting the actions prior to their execution.

Two prominent frameworks serve as an example of this approach:

Open Policy Agent (OPA) is a universal framework for defining policies using a declarative language and enforcing them in the required parts of the system. With the help of Open Policy Agent, it is possible to incorporate policies into CI/CD processes, API gateways, and other infrastructure components.

Admission controllers of Kubernetes are a set of tools for enforcing governance controls in Kubernetes at the infrastructure level. The main idea of admission controllers is the interception of actions sent to the Kubernetes API and evaluation in accordance with the provided policies.

In both cases, it is possible to see that the control mechanism has been implemented at multiple levels of the system.

5.5.3 Real-Time Enforcement vs. Post-Hoc Auditing

One of the primary benefits of Policy as Code is its capability to move governance from being retrospective, which involves auditing, to being proactive, which involves enforcement.

Under the existing paradigm, there will always be an audit process for detecting violations that have occurred, and these can subsequently be fixed. In essence, compliance is determined after the occurrence of the event, but it will not stop the undesirable activity.

On the contrary, enforcing policy via the code entails checking compliance prior to execution, and only compliant actions are allowed. The distinction between the two methods is substantial. Auditing means that something went wrong already, and we need to do something about it afterward, while enforcement means that we validate all actions before they happen. Enforcement helps us avoid the risk of instability because we don't allow the actions that can potentially cause instability.

In control systems theory, this paradigm shift is called transitioning from open-loop governance to closed-loop control (Åström & Murray, 2008).

5.5.4 Benefits and Risks of Policy Automation

Policy as Code brings some key advantages. First of all, policy automation makes it possible for policies to be applied consistently across all kinds of environments without variations caused by human intervention. Moreover, Policy as Code makes scalability easy, which means that governance can take place in a large-scale environment consisting of numerous teams and services.

It should also be noted that policy automation increases transparency and traceability. In this case, policies are recorded in code and can be tracked and traced as usual. This allows making it clear why some decisions were taken and how they were taken.

Nevertheless, there are some risks associated with the implementation of Policy as Code that should be considered.

First of all, one should mention over-constraint. Over-constraint means excessive use of constraints that might hinder system behavior. In such a situation, some required operations will be impossible to perform. Thus, over-constraint results in low system reactivity.

Another significant risk is policy complexity. With the increase in dynamics and situationality of policies, their complexity grows. This can lead to unexpected interactions and dependencies, resulting in contradictory decisions and incorrect reactions to stimuli.

Software delivery systems must operate within defined constraints to maintain stability, reliability, and safe operation under changing conditions. Figure 5-2 illustrates how control constraints establish safe operating boundaries and guide system behavior to prevent instability while maintaining desired performance.

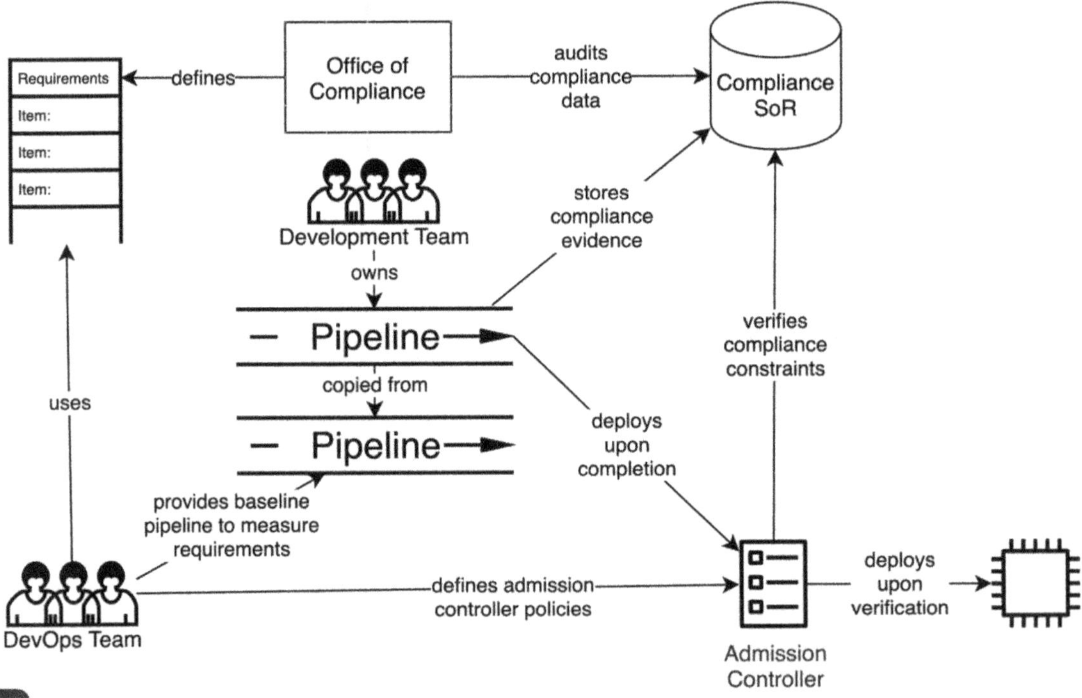

Figure 5-2. Policy as Code Integrated into CI/CD Pipeline

Integration of policy as code across CI/CD stages, enabling feedback-driven validation, enforcement, and control of pipeline actions.

5.5.5 Section Summary

This section examined the transformation of governance through Policy as Code and its role in modern delivery systems.

The key insights are as follows:

- Manual governance is insufficient in high-frequency, dynamic environments.
- Policy as Code embeds governance directly into system execution.
- Frameworks such as OPA and Kubernetes enable real-time enforcement.
- Real-time policy enforcement improves system control and stability.
- Policy automation enhances consistency and scalability but requires careful design.

These findings reinforce the role of policy as an integral component of control systems, enabling governance to operate continuously and effectively within modern software delivery environments.

5.6 Balancing Control and Delivery Speed

The primary challenge facing modern software deployment mechanisms includes determining the right balance between control and speed. The rise of CI/CD technologies has seen a significant increase in the rate at which change can be implemented. While this advancement has come with its own set of benefits, allowing organizations to adjust to changes quickly, it has also contributed to making mistakes, errors, misconfigurations, and cybersecurity issues more prevalent.

In light of this, governance models have to evolve to maintain a healthy balance between all these factors. This is due to the very nature of control systems and their inherent trade-offs: more constraints will provide better safety and predictability, but fewer constraints will make processes more flexible and faster.

5.6.1 Over-constrained Systems

Over-constrained systems have too many or overly strict governance controls. In such environments, policies are applied in a very rigid way and without taking into account the situation at hand and the dynamics of the system.

This would mean that people do not take high risks, but at a cost. Lack of flexibility is one of the common effects. Deployment takes time since there are different forms of validation required in the process.

The constraints create issues at all stages of the deployment process. There could be unnecessary waiting for long periods of time, leading to lower productivity. Eventually, the developers will attempt to circumvent the constraints placed on them, failing to observe the governance structure.

Control systems theory tells us that over-constrained systems leave little room for action; this leads to loss of adaptiveness. It is true that in the short term, stability is ensured, but in the long term, over-constraints hinder performance and innovation.

5.6.2 Under-constrained Systems

On the other end of the spectrum, one finds under-constrained systems, in which governance structures have either not been put in place, are insufficient, or are inconsistent.

The use of such a system ensures rapid execution of changes; however, there are many dangers involved.

Under-constrained systems have a higher probability of suffering from problems relating to stability and predictability. Deployment of incorrect configurations could lead to unexpected effects due to the fact that there are no limits for propagating these mistakes throughout the services being operated. Also, configuration changes may be applied without verification.

There is an increased risk of security and regulatory compliance breaches in an under-constrained system. The latter arises due to the absence of any rules, which would make it possible for vulnerabilities to remain unnoticed. The implications thereof are often hard to spot, although they do carry potentially serious consequences.

In terms of control, it is important to note that the system cannot establish limits, which are needed in order to influence its operation and ensure proper performance of its functions.

5.6.3 Optimal Constraint Design

The shortcomings associated with overly constrained and unconstrained systems emphasize the importance of effective constraint design.

Constraint design should not seek to optimize the number of constraints but ensure that they suit system goals and operating conditions. This calls for a different strategy, whereby the constraints are applied in a selective manner.

In such scenarios, it is important to take into account adaptive constraints. Unlike rigid constraints that cannot be modified, adaptive constraints can adapt according to the condition of the system. Therefore, while deployment policies can be strict in a situation where the system is unstable, once the system stabilizes, policies may become more liberal.

Another factor in designing constraints is enforcing policies based on risks. It is apparent that all changes to the system do not have the same level of impact on the system. Therefore, risky changes should be subject to more stringent constraints than non-risky changes.

It is a strategy that is consistent with the real risks associated with the system, making sure that any constraints imposed are both efficient and effective.

When looked at from the control system perspective, efficient constraint management ensures that the system runs safely without losing its dynamic ability to respond to changes.

5.6.4 Trade-Off Between Speed and Safety

Safety vs. speed in the realm of software deployment and delivery systems is not an either/or situation but a sliding scale. One end would involve the greatest amount of governance, which brings about the greatest amount of safety but with little to no agility. The other would be unbridled delivery, which provides maximal speed at the cost of stability.

What is sought is a solution that allows for both safety and speed.

In order to do so, governance needs to be integrated into the feedback control system loop. Here, speed is not sacrificed but controlled.

In order for this to occur, certain things need to be considered. The constraints must be well-defined, yet flexible depending on the conditions of the system. The feedback needs to be accurate and timely to enable proper decision-making. The actuation needs to be under control, allowing for incremental application and retraction.

By doing so, systems will be able to achieve fast-paced operations while maintaining stability. It is a move from perceiving governance as a hindrance to recognizing it as a means for safe and scalable delivery.

Compliance and governance are essential control mechanisms that ensure software changes satisfy organizational and regulatory requirements before deployment. Figure 5-3 illustrates how compliance requirements, delivery pipelines, and admission controllers work together to continuously validate deployments and enforce governance throughout the software delivery lifecycle.

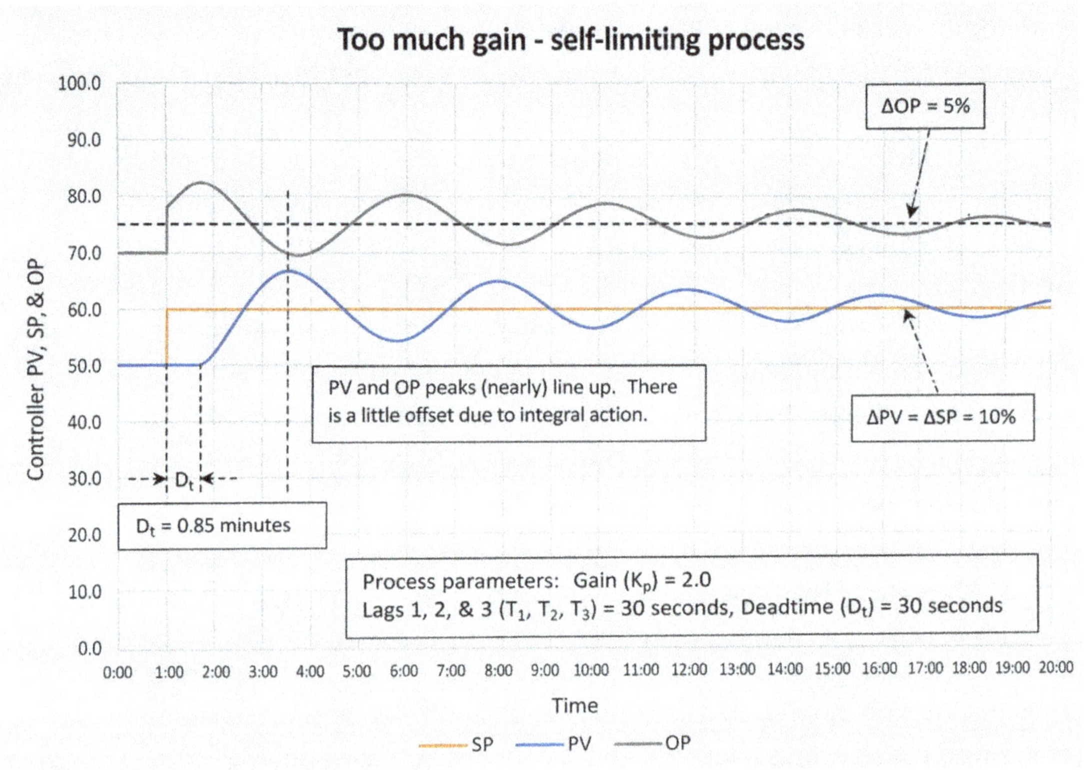

Figure 5-3. *Trade-Off Between Governance Constraint Level and Delivery Speed*

Illustration of how varying levels of governance constraint affect delivery speed and system stability. Over-constrained configurations reduce delivery throughput and create operational bottlenecks, while under-constrained configurations permit higher speed at the cost of increased instability and risk exposure. The optimal region balances sufficient constraint enforcement with sustained delivery velocity.

5.6.5 Section Summary

This chapter discussed the interplay of control vs. speed within contemporary software delivery infrastructures and the consequences of various approaches to constraints.

The salient points are as follows:

- Over-constraining leads to decreased flexibility and creates bottlenecks in the delivery process.
- Under-constraining increases vulnerabilities and instabilities within the system.
- The best approach to constraints is based on adaptability and risk management
- Good systems integrate both speed and control for efficient and reliable delivery.

This emphasizes the need for governance systems that allow for fast delivery while maintaining stability and scalability.

5.7 Governance in Distributed and Scaled Systems

With the expansion of software systems, the role of governance should transition from being a local process to becoming a distributed approach that can work on more than one team, environment, or platform. Contemporary architectures are inherently decentralized because they are built from microservices, cloud-native architecture, and global teams. Although these designs make it possible for organizations to achieve scalability and flexibility, they come with their own set of complexities when it comes to implementing governance.

Governance in this setting does not occur within one boundary but rather among different systems.

5.7.1 Challenges of Distributed Governance

The structure of distributed governance brings about a number of issues that directly impact the efficiency of the control processes.

Firstly, the existence of separate teams, each having its own processes and ways of implementing them, is an important factor. While such an approach promotes innovation and creativity, it can also lead to a situation where there will be no consistent interpretation of policies and their implementation.

Moreover, varying environments can become a source of problems. Distributed systems might use development, testing, and production environments, as well as different clouds or regions. The fact that every one of those environments has its own conditions makes it difficult to implement universal governance, which does not require modification.

Such attributes tend to have a negative effect on the consistency of implementation of policies. The inability to be consistent poses problems such as possible instabilities and weaknesses.

In terms of control systems theory, distributed governance will need to tackle the problem of achieving coherence of control despite being composed of elements operating beyond defined bounds.

5.7.2 Centralized vs. Federated Governance Models

To overcome such issues, there exist various organizational models of governance that strike an appropriate balance between control and decentralization.

The centralized model of governance involves setting policies that are applied across the entire organization. In such a case, all the teams must conform to the policies set by one governing body. The centralized approach streamlines the application of policies.

However, this type of governance can make it difficult for teams to respond to changes quickly since they are governed by policies that may fail to take into account the context within which they operate.

On the other hand, the federated model of governance involves distributing control among teams. Each team is free to develop its own policies to govern its members.

These conflicting interests can be effectively balanced with the help of hybrid governance systems. This type of system involves defining core policies at the center, which define the basic level of constraints, while teams have the freedom to apply such policies.

The hybrid form of governance is consistent with the idea of control system design because it involves global constraints as well as local adaptation.

5.7.3 Standardization and Platform Engineering

The realization of successful governance in distributed environments is achieved through the use of mechanisms that will allow for consistency without sacrificing any flexibility. Standardization and platform engineering become instrumental in achieving this objective.

Standardization refers to the use of common standards or platforms that are adopted by all the teams. Standardization includes standardizing the CI/CD pipelines, policy, and its definition and enforcement mechanisms. In doing so, governance becomes simpler since there is consistency in its execution.

On the other hand, platform engineering is an extension of standardization, as it involves the creation of a central platform that incorporates governance, tooling, and infrastructure. The platform works as a governance layer, incorporating policy in the systems utilized by various teams.

This way, the use of governance becomes easier and more convenient. Through shared pipelines and policy enforcement mechanisms, the platform enables consistent governance execution while retaining simplicity.

In regard to the control aspect, the platform operates as a control layer that enables the coordination of actions in distributed components with constraints in place.

5.7.4 Cross-System Consistency

Consistency among different systems is one of the primary concerns that needs to be addressed when designing a governance architecture.

Cross-system consistency refers to the consistent enforcement of policies irrespective of the location and manner in which changes occur. Consistency is vital in ensuring the overall stability and integrity of the system while also meeting any regulatory requirements.

Consistency requires that policies be designed in such a way that they can be easily applied across different platforms. Additionally, there should be an agreement between the individuals and organizations involved in the development of the policies.

Policies as code can ensure consistency because there will be one common set of policies for implementation in all systems. Furthermore, automation enables the real-time implementation of policies.

Consistency, however, should not be equated with rigidity; there is a need to strike a balance between consistency and flexibility by ensuring local adaptability within the bounds of global consistency.

Different governance models provide distinct tradeoffs between centralized control, team autonomy, and operational flexibility. Table 5-2 compares the characteristics, advantages, and limitations of centralized, federated, and hybrid governance models in software delivery systems.

Table 5-2. *Governance Models Comparison*

Model	Advantages	Limitations
Centralized	Ensures consistency and uniform policy enforcement	Reduces flexibility and responsiveness
Federated	Enables autonomy and adaptability for teams	Risk of inconsistency and policy fragmentation
Hybrid	Balances consistency with flexibility	Increased design and operational complexity

5.7.5 Section Summary

In this part, governance challenges and strategies in distributed and scaled environments have been analyzed.

The main points include

- The presence of complications while achieving a consistent governance of distributed systems
- Different advantages of centralized and federated approaches to governance
- Usage of hybrid models in governance
- Importance of standardization and platform engineering to enforce consistent policies
- Cross-system consistency as an important condition to keep things stable and aligned

From the above information, it can be seen that governance in distributed environments should be approached as a scalable control system to ensure alignment in any conditions.

5.8 Constraints and Risk Management in DevSecOps

However, as software delivery approaches tend to move toward continuous deployment models and distributed systems architectures, security and risk management cannot remain an isolated or after-the-fact process anymore but have to be embedded into the actual control processes governing system operations. In the conceptual model presented above, security and compliance can be interpreted as constraint mechanisms that limit risks and make sure that the system does not enter into a state where safety and compliance conditions are violated.

The adoption of DevSecOps in software development represents an extension of standard DevOps principles by incorporating security at all stages of software delivery. Yet, as stated above, this incorporation is not just procedural but rather structural since it involves security being embedded into the very processes that drive control. Constraints become the main tool used for managing risks within the system.

5.8.1 Security as Constraint

Security in control-oriented systems represents a collection of risk-driven constraints that specify what conditions can be considered acceptable for the operation of the system. These constraints include limitations such as thresholds and rules that reduce potential risks associated with various vulnerabilities and threats.

Firstly, it should be emphasized that risk thresholds are among the most important elements of this security concept. Risk thresholds represent limits on the acceptable levels of risks, which may be represented either quantitatively or qualitatively, e.g., maximum vulnerability severity, acceptable rates of authentication failures, or limited access rights. The presence of risk thresholds allows evaluating any actions of a system, such as deploying new software or making changes to its infrastructure, based on whether the related risks meet these thresholds.

DevSecOps requires constant enforcement of security constraints. While traditional security models involve regular assessments of the risks in question, DevSecOps implies constant monitoring and evaluation. Therefore, security constraints must be enforced constantly to evaluate the security status of each action performed by the system in real-time.

Considering this view, security becomes an integral part of control systems rather than an additional layer.

5.8.2 Compliance as System Boundary

While security concerns the management of risks, compliance concerns the setting of boundaries beyond which the system cannot function. These boundaries are put in place by means of regulations, standards within an industry, and organizational policies.

The constraints involved with compliance are binding and require certain conditions to always be kept in place, including issues like data protection, limitations on access, and audits. Failure to comply with these constraints may result in legal action and costs.

Looking at control systems theory, the constraint of compliance implies rigid boundaries beyond which one cannot go. While some of the constraints, namely, soft constraints, may be broken if needed, compliance demands absolute observance of their boundaries.

Audit capabilities are essential for ensuring compliance. Besides ensuring that the system runs within its established boundaries, it is important that it provides proof of doing so all the time. This involves the use of tools for logging and monitoring system activity.

Constraints associated with compliance play an integral role in providing stability to the system while preventing it from evolving beyond acceptable boundaries.

5.8.3 Integrating Security into Control Systems

The incorporation of security into the control systems involves establishing security feedback loops and decision-making capabilities in real time.

The security feedback loop works like the observability system but uses signals related to risk. The signals may involve vulnerabilities identified through scanning, intrusion events detected, anomalous activities detected, and any form of access violation. Continuous monitoring of the signals makes the system observable from a security point of view.

Next comes the stage of implementing the feedback into the decision-making process. The policies will be responsible for analyzing the security cues and determining whether to deny deployment, initiate rollback, or reconfigure the system settings.

One of the important results of such integration will be the implementation of real-time risk-based actuation. The system is going to adapt its performance based on the risk situation that is happening at the moment. In particular, the deployment policies will be stricter when there are risks and when the system is experiencing an attack, whereas they will be relaxed otherwise.

Such a solution corresponds to the philosophy of control-oriented delivery systems, which Forsgren et al. (2018) describe.

Security controls are most effective when they are integrated directly into the software delivery process rather than applied as separate validation steps. Figure 5-4 illustrates how security policies, automated deployment pipelines, change management, and continuous monitoring form a closed control loop that detects configuration drift and enables automated remediation.

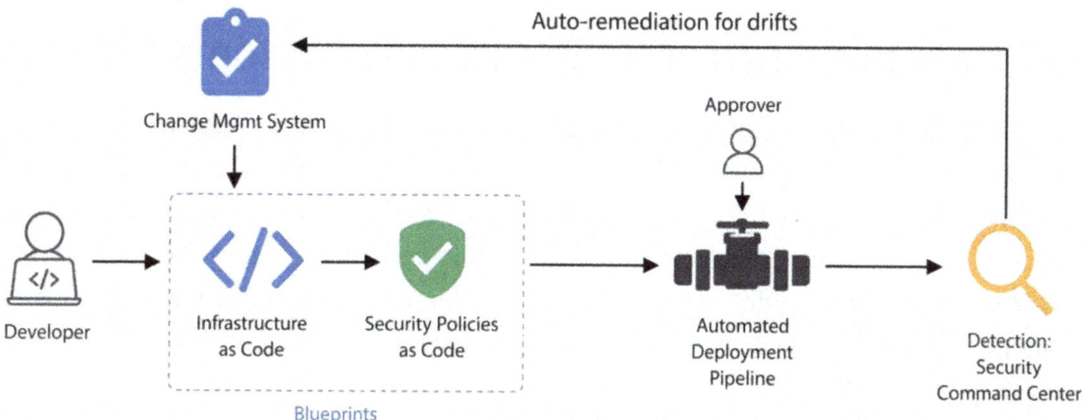

Figure 5-4. *Security Constraints in the Control Loop*

Integration of security feedback, policy enforcement, and actuation within a closed-loop control system to maintain operations within defined risk boundaries.

5.8.4 Section Summary

This section examined how constraints enable effective risk management within DevSecOps environments.

The key insights are as follows:

- Security functions as a dynamic constraint system based on risk thresholds.

- Compliance defines non-negotiable boundaries that must always be enforced.
- Continuous enforcement replaces periodic validation in modern systems.
- Security feedback loops enable real-time, adaptive control.
- Risk-based actuation aligns system behavior with current threat conditions.

These results show that security and compliance are not extraneous considerations but essential elements of control mechanisms. This helps to maintain the security and reliability of software release processes.

5.9 Designing Effective Constraint Systems

The effectiveness of governance and policymaking in contemporary software development systems depends, at the end of the day, on how effectively the constraints have been designed and applied. As outlined above, constraints determine the bounds within which the system behavior can occur. But bad constraints may either be too weak to ensure the system's stability or too strong to hinder its performance. The challenge for developers and engineers thus becomes designing those constraints to allow for control while preserving agility.

A good system of constraints has to fulfill contradictory functions - to ensure safety and agility, to enforce certain behaviors without inhibiting others.

5.9.1 Principles of Constraint Design

The very core of an efficient constraints system is based on two principles: clarity and alignment.

As concerns clarity, it means that constraints are clear, consistent, and easy to understand. Any ambiguity in constraints causes problems since there might be a chance that different people interpret constraints differently, which will create inconsistencies in their application. However, if the constraints are clear and consistent, this allows for establishing a reliable base for decision-making in the system.

The second key element of an efficient constraints system is alignment with system goals. It means that constraints should correlate with the objectives of the system. Misaligned constraints can impose restrictions that seem to be correct but will not allow attaining system objectives.

From the point of view of control theory, the concept of clarity creates a certain pattern in control, whereas alignment moves the system toward the desired state.

5.9.2 Adaptive and Context-Aware Constraints

Although static constraints may be helpful in ensuring that base-level requirements are met, they rarely meet expectations in dynamic environments. Modern systems operate in a variety of environments that may require either overly restrictive or lenient predefined constraints.

As opposed to static constraints, adaptive constraints are based both on the environment that surrounds the system and feedback from the system. While static constraints remain unchanged during system operation, adaptive constraints vary their threshold values according to the state of the system.

For example, deployment constraints enable fast deployment when things are normal and tighten up when the system detects any abnormality. Resource consumption constraints may also vary according to circumstances in order to maximize efficiency while mitigating risks.

Despite being very responsive, this approach does not sacrifice control and even requires proper feedback and careful settings in order not to overreact.

From the point of control theory, this implies that the system can function adequately under different conditions.

5.9.3 Avoiding Constraint Overload

Despite being necessary for effective control, unnecessary and improperly prioritized constraints could have an adverse effect on system operations. Such a situation is known as constraint overload and represents a state where there are numerous constraints on the system, including redundancies and insignificant ones.

Constraint overload can create various problems. These include an increase in the decision-making process complexity, a delay in pipeline processing, and conflict between teams that work on developing a product. In some cases, constraint overload can create rule conflicts, where some constraints contradict others.

To prevent such outcomes from occurring, constraint creation should focus on minimalism and proper prioritization of constraints.

Minimalism implies the imposition of only necessary constraints on a system to achieve its goals. The prioritization of constraints includes imposing rigorous enforcement on crucial constraints like those associated with security and compliance and flexible enforcement on other less important constraints.

The approach taken here is similar to the concept used in control systems, where unnecessary constraints are not applied.

5.9.4 Integration with Actuation Mechanisms

Constraints will fulfill their desired purpose only when they are coupled with actuation. Within software delivery systems, such coupling is achieved through CI/CD pipeline tools and policy engines that analyze actions either before or during their execution.

Under such conditions, constraints affect pipeline execution because they will inform the decision on whether an action is allowed, what steps should be taken, and which conditions must be met for its implementation.

This way, constraints become not just static borders but dynamic control measures. CI/CD pipelines will have to execute actions according to established governance rules because they do not exist in a void but rather within the confines set by constraints.

Such coupling of constraints with actuation processes also allows for a feedback-based form of control in which the latter affects how pipelines operate based on new constraints informed by changes in the system.

From a control system point of view, this kind of coupling closes the control loop because all three elements work together to ensure system stability and development (Åström & Murray, 2008).

Well-designed constraints enable control systems to enforce governance without unnecessarily limiting agility or adaptability. Table 5-3 summarizes the key principles for designing effective constraints and highlights how each principle contributes to reliable and efficient software delivery.

Table 5-3. *Constraint Design Principles*

Principle	Description	Benefit
Clarity	Well-defined and unambiguous rules	Reduced ambiguity and consistent enforcement
Adaptability	Dynamic, context-aware constraints	Improved responsiveness to system conditions
Alignment	Constraints reflect system objectives	Better decision-making and system outcomes
Minimalism	Avoidance of unnecessary constraints	Maintains speed and reduces complexity

5.9.5 Section Summary

This section examined the principles required to design effective constraint systems in modern software delivery environments.

The key insights are as follows:

- Effective constraint design requires clarity, alignment, adaptability, and minimalism.
- Adaptive constraints enable systems to operate under dynamic conditions.
- Constraint overload reduces efficiency and introduces unnecessary complexity.
- Integration with actuation mechanisms ensures that constraints actively guide system behavior.

These principles provide a foundation for designing governance systems that support both control and agility, enabling software delivery systems to scale while maintaining stability and performance.

5.10 Constraints as Enablers of Stability and Scale

This chapter has explored constraints as means of delimiting the allowable system behavior. Although constraints are seen as limiting, this definition is not full. Constraints in control-oriented systems are not simply limiting actions, but they allow scalable, predictable, and stable operation. Systems can be free without restrictions, but they are not guaranteed to be safe, consistent, or reliable.

In terms of control systems, constraints act as stabilizing forces. They avoid entering unsafe or unstable areas of the system and regulate the behavior toward equilibrium. Without such limits, feedback and actuation do not suffice to provide stability because the system might react to perturbations in a manner that exaggerates rather than mitigates deviations. Limitations in the form of constraints give the structural boundaries within which control mechanisms are able to work in an effective manner such that the corrective actions are meaningful and constrained (Åström and Murray, 2008).

This stabilizing part is even more crucial with the size of the systems.

Governance in micro-scaled, humbly sized, and highly centralized settings can be quite hand-controllable, and the consequences of mistakes are comparatively limited. In large-scale, distributed systems, however, the changes spread quickly across several components and teams. This propagation may cause global instability without well-stated limitations, with local activities causing unintended consequences throughout the world.

Constraints allow safe scaling through the introduction of repeated limits throughout the system. With uniform policies established and implemented, the teams can work independently even though they are aligned with the overall system goals. This minimizes the requirement to have centralized control and enables the system to scale without bringing fragmentation or inconsistency.

Here, constraints can be seen as a coordination mechanism. They make sure that components distributed work in a common context and can be coherent in different environments. It is especially relevant when it comes to microservices architecture and systems that are cloud-native, as services are not closely related to each other, yet highly dependable.

The interconnection of constraints and autonomy is also important.

The notion of autonomy is usually regarded as the capacity of teams to work on their own and make choices without any centralized control. Nevertheless, real autonomy means having a clear structure within which it is possible to make secure decisions.

Liberation of autonomy is unbridled and results in the divergent practice, inconsistency, and heightened risk-taking.

Structured autonomy is based on constraints. They help the teams to make decisions without fearing that what they are doing will exceed acceptable limits by establishing clear boundaries. This makes it unnecessary to monitor them all the time and permits teams to be innovative without going off track from the organizational goals.

In this view, governance does not preclude autonomy but is a precondition to autonomy.

Moreover, constraints also ensure predictability, and the latter is fundamental to stability and scalability. Predictability makes the behavior of the systems predictable within different conditions so that the system is reliable and can be easily troubleshooted. Well-designed and enforced constraints minimize variability and offer a stable basis on which systems can evolve.

This predictability also promotes the efficacy of feedback and actuation mechanisms. When the behavior of the system has limits and is predictable, feedback signals are more accurate, and control actions can be exercised more precisely. This enhances the system stability as a whole and facilitates continuous improvement.

Uncertainty compounds at scale due to the lack of limitations. Even minor deviations can spread and multiply, and it may be hard to control them. This risk is alleviated through constraints that restrict the number of possible behaviors, keeping the system within manageable and observable restrictions.

This has a wider implication for the system design.

Scalability is not delivered by the use of infrastructure or architecture alone in contemporary software delivery. It is attained by having the capability of dealing with complexity and retaining control as the system expands. This process heavily relies on constraints, which allow systems to grow and maintain stability and alignment.

Finally, limits convert governance into a limiting role to an enabling capacity. They bring the framework that systems need to be safely run in constantly changing environments, enable distributed decision-making, and coherence in complex environments.

5.10.1 Key Insight

Constraints do not limit systems – they enable controlled, scalable, and predictable behavior.

5.10.2 Section Summary

This section has therefore reconsidered constraints as facilitators of stability and scale as opposed to restrictions on the behavior of systems.

The key findings of this section include

- The fact that constraints serve as forces for stabilization of systems, leading them toward equilibrium states
- Constraining systems makes them amenable to safe scaling due to defined limits across systems
- The fact that governance facilitates autonomy through structured decision-making spaces
- Predictability is improved through constraints, enhancing the control and reliability of systems

These findings reiterate the fundamental argument made throughout this chapter.

5.11 Chapter Summary

The chapter redefined policy and governance as constraint systems in a control system and left behind their conventional understanding as an external or compliance-based process. Instead of post-hoc governance, governance was now used as an active and embedded element that spells out what is acceptable in system behavior. In this context, policy acts as the agent that operationalizes constraints such that everything done in the system is in line with established objectives and acceptable levels of risk.

One of the main points of the chapter is that the system boundaries are determined by governance. These limits define the safe operating space where feedback, decision-making, and actuation take place. Lack of clearly defined constraints will lead to instability in systems, since they can shift to dangerous or unpredictable positions. On the other hand, properly crafted constraints offer the framework that is needed to sustain equilibrium such that the systems can be able to run smoothly with a constant change.

The chapter also addressed the trade-off that is critical between under-constraint and over-constraint. Although stable, over-constrained systems are less agile and lack bottlenecks in their operation which limits their ability to respond to the dynamic environment. Under-constrained systems, conversely, are faster but more likely to be exposed to greater risk, instability, and even security or compliance failures. The goal is to have the best constraints, not to maximize or minimize them, but to design them in the best way possible, to fit the system goals and to adapt to the context and risk.

One of the enablers of this balance is Policy as Code which converts governance into logic that is executed directly within CI/CD pipelines and platform layers. Systems ensure that the delivery and governance are conducted at equal speeds by integrating policies in the execution flow, to enforce constraints in real time. This change in retrospective auditing to continuous validation can allow a closed-loop control model, where feedback is used to make decisions and constraints are used to actuate in a dynamic manner.

Finally, the chapter showed that constraints are not limitations but facilitators of the efficient functioning of systems. Well-designed and combined constraints help to maintain stability by avoiding unsafe states, increase security by imposing risk limits, and allow scalable delivery by imposing consistent governance across distributed systems. This re-framing puts governance as a central aspect of contemporary software delivery, a key to achieving controlled, reliable, and sustainable system evolution.

References

Forsgren, N., Humble, J., & Kim, G. (2018). *Accelerate*

Humble, J., & Farley, D. (2010). Continuous Delivery

Bass, L., Weber, I., & Zhu, L. (2015). DevOps: A Software Architect's Perspective

Open Policy Agent Documentation

Kubernetes Policy Enforcement Docs

Åström & Murray (2008). Feedback Systems

Ogata (2010). Modern Control Engineering

Allam (2025)

Rusum & Pappula (2024)

CHAPTER 6

DevSecOps Through a Control Lens

6.1 Chapter Objective

In this chapter, DevSecOps will be viewed as a control mechanism designed for managing the risks and security of the system, as well as providing stability to the continuous delivery environment. Here, the role of security in DevSecOps is not seen as a phase in itself but rather as an integral feedback-driven constraint mechanism. The process of integrating security into decisions and actuators will be such that any activity performed by the system will be judged against a set of risk limits.

The chapter also explores the relationship between security signals, which function as sensors providing risk visibility; policies, which serve as controller logic interpreting those signals against defined thresholds; and pipeline actions, which act as actuators executing preventive, corrective, or adaptive responses. Together, these elements form a closed-loop control mechanism that helps ensure systems maintain awareness of their risk posture and take proportionate action where necessary. This architecture enables organizations to manage security and risk while sustaining an acceptable delivery pace under the constraints of safety, reliability, and compliance.

6.2 Introduction: From Security Integration to Control Systems

Contemporary software delivery has undergone a substantial transformation through the adoption of DevOps and, more recently, DevSecOps practices Humble, J., & Farley, D. (2010). While the stated objective of DevSecOps is to make security an integral

S. Bobba and N. S. Vummaneni, *CI/CD as a Control System*, https://doi.org/10.1007/979-8-8688-2842-3_6

component of the development lifecycle, implementations in many organizations have remained tool-oriented and stage-based, treating security as a set of discrete activities inserted at predetermined pipeline stages (Bass, Weber, & Zhu, 2015). Practices such as static code analysis, vulnerability scanning, and compliance checks are introduced alongside development and deployment workflows and, in doing so, create the impression that security has been fully embedded. This characterization applies most directly to high-frequency delivery environments, systems handling sensitive workloads, and organizations operating at sufficient platform maturity for the gap between tool presence and genuine integration to become operationally consequential.

Nevertheless, this strategy does not show essential drawbacks.

DevSecOps implementations that remain tool-centric or rely on isolated checkpoint validation can struggle to keep pace with the dynamic and evolving risk landscape of contemporary systems. When security checks are executed only at fixed pipeline stages, their findings may become stale as the system continues to change after the check completes. This introduces temporal gaps between detection and response during which vulnerabilities or misconfigurations can persist. Such gaps tend to widen as delivery frequency increases, progressively eroding the effectiveness of security controls, particularly in environments where deployments occur multiple times per day Forsgren, Humble, & Kim (2018).

This shortcoming reflects a broader conceptual limitation: treating security as a discrete action rather than as continuous system behavior. When security operates only at isolated checkpoints, it cannot account for the cumulative effect of interleaved changes on system risk posture, nor can it detect emergent instabilities that arise from the interaction of architecture, dependencies, workload patterns, feedback latency, and remediation timing.

Risk is not static. It evolves with each change introduced into the system and is shaped by modifications to code, configuration, infrastructure, and the external threat landscape. In high-frequency delivery environments and systems handling sensitive or business-critical workloads, confining security to specific phases of the delivery process becomes increasingly insufficient. In these contexts, security is more accurately understood as a dynamic property of the system, one that requires continuous monitoring, evaluation, and adjustment rather than periodic validation alone (NIST, 2020).

This shift becomes especially pressing in delivery environments where organizations aim to optimize flow under acceptable thresholds of risk, reliability, compliance, and recovery capability. In systems where deployments occur multiple times per day, periodic security validation cannot keep pace with the rate of change. Such environments require mechanisms capable of evaluating and responding to risk on a near-real-time basis, so that each change is assessed in the context of current system conditions rather than assumptions established at the last scheduled check.

This brings about the aspect of real-time risk control.

Real-time risk control refers to the continuous collection of security signals, their analysis against defined policies, and the execution of proportionate responses through automated processes. For this mechanism to function as genuine control rather than passive monitoring, the policies governing it must be versioned, tested against representative scenarios, enforced consistently across environments, auditable for traceability, and aligned with designated risk ownership. When these conditions are met, security becomes structurally coupled to the control system concepts of feedback, decision-making, and actuation, working in concert to support system stability.

In this context, security transitions from a validation layer to a structural participant in the control loop, provided the three elements of closed-loop control are genuinely integrated rather than merely co-located. Specifically, feedback is supplied by security sensors such as vulnerability scanners, runtime monitors, and anomaly detection systems, which provide continuous visibility into system risk. Decision logic resides in policy engines that evaluate incoming signals against codified risk thresholds and governance rules. Actuation is carried out by CI/CD pipelines that implement, restrict, or roll back modifications based on the decisions those policy engines produce.

This perspective builds on and extends the well-established shift-left security approach. Moving security activities earlier in the development lifecycle remains valuable for catching issues before they compound, but early detection alone does not satisfy the requirement for continuous control. Shift-left security should therefore be complemented by continuous controls that span development, deployment, and runtime, so that risk is monitored and managed across the entire system lifecycle rather than validated only at early-stage checkpoints.

This results in a more detailed model: continuous control.

In a continuous control model, particularly one applied to runtime-impacting changes, high-risk environments, or organizations operating at mature platform levels, security is incorporated across operational stages rather than confined to isolated checkpoints. The model works dynamically, adapting to changing conditions to keep risk within acceptable levels. Rather than depending on periodic validation, the system continuously assesses its state and implements corrective or preventive measures as conditions warrant.

This transition has important implications.

In mature DevSecOps implementations, security moves beyond a supporting role or a toolset bolted onto pipelines (Microsoft, n.d.). It becomes an intrinsic element of the processes that govern system behavior, shaping how decisions are made and how changes are carried out. When this integration is achieved through versioned, tested, and consistently enforced policies with auditable outcomes, it helps ensure that security considerations participate in system evolution from the outset rather than being appended as an afterthought.

Key Argument

DevSecOps, in its most effective form, is not merely about integrating security tools into pipelines. It is about embedding security into the control loop of software delivery systems, where security sensors provide continuous risk feedback, policy engines interpret that feedback against codified thresholds, and pipeline actuators execute proportionate responses, together forming a closed-loop architecture rather than a passive monitoring arrangement.

This section introduced the limitations of traditional DevSecOps approaches and established the need for a control-oriented perspective.

The key insights are as follows:

- Traditional DevSecOps remains tool-centric and stage-based.
- Security must be understood as a continuous system behavior.
- High-frequency delivery requires real-time risk control.
- “Shift-left” must evolve into a continuous control model.
- Security must be embedded within the control loop.

These concepts provide the foundation for the next section, which examines how security functions as both a constraint and a feedback mechanism within the architectural framework of control systems theory, applied here as a structural model for reasoning about software delivery rather than as a literal physical equivalence.

6.3 Security in Control Systems Theory

To analyze the significance of security within modern software delivery platforms, control systems theory offers a productive architectural lens, though one that should be understood as a structural model rather than a literal equivalence to continuous physical plants. Within this framework, security is treated not as a standalone process but as a multi-faceted aspect of control that simultaneously serves as a constraint defining acceptable operating boundaries, a feedback mechanism providing continuous risk visibility, and a control objective representing the target risk posture the system aims to maintain. This holistic view enables a deeper understanding of how security governs system dynamics throughout the constant change inherent in modern delivery environments.

Where conventional techniques treat security primarily as a verification function, applying control theory as an architectural model reframes security as an ongoing function that continuously influences system operation. Under this model, security establishes the boundaries within which the system may operate, maintains continuous awareness of the system's risk state, and contributes to the conditions under which stability is sustained. These functions, taken together, constitute the foundational framework of a control-oriented DevSecOps approach, acknowledging that software delivery systems are discrete, distributed, and socio-technical in ways that differ from classic continuous-process examples.

6.3.1 Security as System Constraint

Within the control system model adopted here as an architectural framework, constraints specify boundaries for system behavior that keep it within an acceptable operating range and prevent transitions into prohibited states. Security operates analogously by defining risk-related boundaries beyond which system behavior should not proceed, though the effectiveness of these boundaries in software delivery depends on how consistently they are codified, enforced, and audited.

Security risk-related boundaries are expressed as thresholds for vulnerability severity, configuration risk exposure, access anomalies, and required mitigation actions. For instance, a deployment might be blocked if vulnerability findings exceed a defined severity threshold, or access privileges might be restricted when anomalous user behavior is detected.

As in other engineering disciplines where constraints are vital to avoiding failure, software systems require constraints to operate safely and within acceptable security parameters. These constraints function as security barriers beyond which no system operation should proceed, provided they are versioned, tested, enforced consistently through automated mechanisms, auditable for traceability, and aligned with designated risk ownership.

From this perspective, constraints can be regarded as boundaries that help regulate system behavior and keep it within an acceptable risk range, so long as those boundaries are codified in enforceable form, version-controlled, tested against representative scenarios, and backed by auditable evidence of consistent application.

6.3.2 Security as Feedback Signal

Whereas constraints define the boundaries, the control system model uses feedback to determine whether the system is operating within them. Applying this architectural model to DevSecOps, security feedback is generated by detection and monitoring tools and provides a continuous overview of the system's risk status, enabling the decision logic to assess whether current conditions remain within acceptable thresholds.

The sources of security feedback include vulnerability scans, static and dynamic analysis, anomaly detection, intrusion detection systems, and runtime monitoring. These technologies produce signals that reflect various dimensions of the system's security state, including code quality, configuration integrity, and runtime behavior. For these signals to support reliable control decisions, they must be timely, correlated across sources, de-duplicated to reduce noise, and interpreted against defined SLOs or policy thresholds rather than treated as inherently reliable raw data.

Within the architectural model adopted here, these signals serve as inputs for the decision layer of the control system, which evaluates them against policy rules to determine appropriate pipeline actions. The discovery of critical vulnerabilities may trigger deployment blocking, while anomalous traffic patterns could prompt scaling restrictions or traffic isolation, depending on the thresholds and response logic codified in the governing policies.

The timeliness and accuracy of security feedback are critical determinants of control quality. Delayed feedback allows the system state to drift before corrective action can be applied, while noisy feedback may trigger disproportionate responses or mask genuine threats behind a volume of false positives. In both cases, the resulting decisions become misaligned with the actual system state, and the resulting control actions may introduce instability through mechanisms such as unnecessary rollbacks, deployment oscillation, or missed remediation windows.

Applying control theory as an architectural model rather than a literal equivalence, security feedback serves as the observability layer that informs the decision logic responsible for evaluating system conditions against specified constraints and initiating appropriate adjustments.

6.3.3 Security as Control Objective

Beyond its roles as a constraint and a feedback source, security also functions as a control objective, representing a target risk posture that the system is designed to achieve and sustain. This objective becomes operationally meaningful only when the policies defining acceptable risk levels are versioned, tested, enforced consistently, auditable, and aligned with accountable risk ownership across the organization.

The point here is not absolute security since this concept might prove unreachable. Instead, an acceptable level of risk should be maintained as one of the control variables. This means that the system will constantly need to make certain trade-offs in order to optimize risk management processes.

For instance, tightening security measures will allow for a lower risk but may cause delays or decrease the system's flexibility, while loosening the measures will result in better performance and higher vulnerability to external threats. As a result, it becomes necessary for the system to operate at a certain balance between these two factors.

This balance can be achieved only when both security and performance parameters are factored into the design of the delivery system. In this respect, DevSecOps shares structural similarities with classical control systems when viewed through an architectural lens, though the discrete, distributed, and socio-technical nature of software delivery introduces complexities that classical models do not fully capture. Establishing a control objective provides the system with a defined standard against which its behavior can be continuously assessed. Figure 6-1 illustrates how security operates as a constraint and feedback mechanism within a control-oriented delivery architecture.

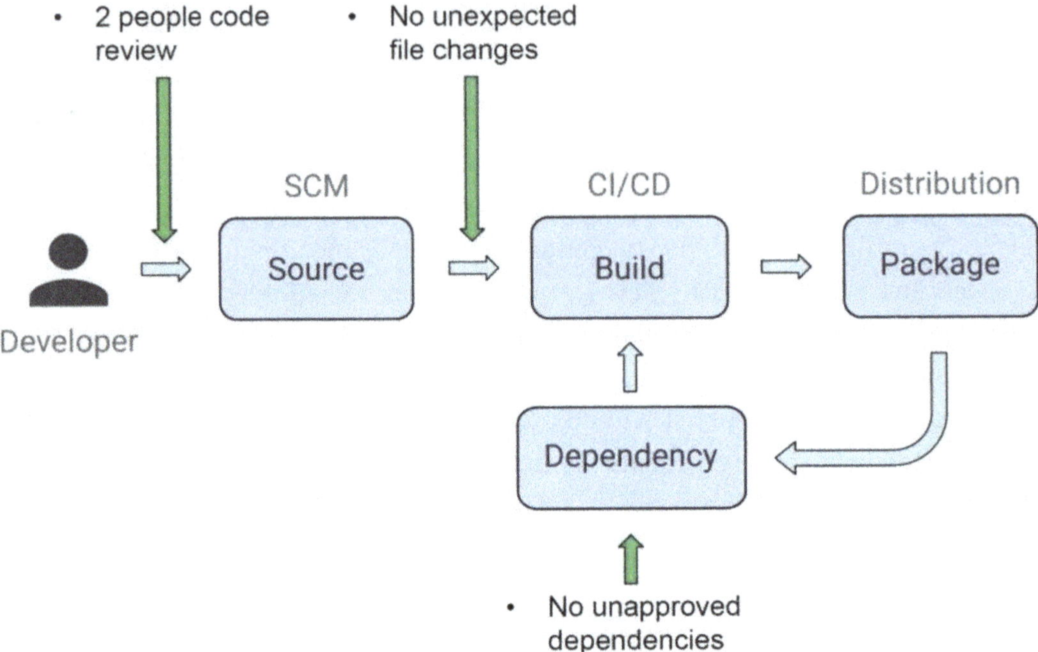

Figure 6-1. *Security as a Constraint and Feedback Mechanism in a Control-Oriented Delivery Architecture*

This architectural model shows, security sensors providing risk feedback, versioned and auditable policy engines interpreting signals against defined thresholds, and CI/CD pipeline actuators executing proportionate responses to enforce risk constraints within a closed-loop delivery system.

Section Summary

This section highlighted, using control theory as an architectural model rather than a literal equivalence, how security functions simultaneously as a constraint, a feedback source, and a control objective within software delivery systems. Under this framing, security cannot be treated as an isolated function or a post-deployment activity but is more productively understood as an inherent process that continuously governs system behavior within acceptable risk boundaries.

A further point concerns security's role as a boundary-setting mechanism. The constraints established through security policies are designed to reduce the likelihood of the system entering unstable or unacceptable states, thereby supporting its safety and stability without guaranteeing these outcomes in isolation. Simultaneously, security serves as a source of continuous feedback, surfacing information about vulnerabilities, configuration issues, and operational anomalies. This feedback enables proportionate and timely decision-making under the conditions prevailing at the moment of assessment.

Moreover, security can be understood as a control objective that orients system operation toward a sustainable balance between risk management and operational performance. In most enterprise delivery environments, security is pursued in conjunction with other control objectives, including performance, efficiency, and delivery throughput, though the relative weighting of these objectives may shift depending on the risk profile of the service, the sensitivity of the environment, regulatory requirements, and organizational context.

When security is applied as a constraint through codified and enforced policies, as a feedback mechanism through continuous monitoring and detection systems, and as a control objective through defined risk posture targets, the resulting architecture takes the form of a closed-loop control system. In this architecture, security sensors supply risk signals, policy engines evaluate those signals and determine responses, and pipeline actuators execute the resulting decisions. This structural integration, rather than merely co-locating tools, distinguishes a control-oriented DevSecOps model from a collection of techniques and technologies.

6.4 DevSecOps as a Closed-Loop System

The growing complexity and dynamism of contemporary software systems call for a more structurally integrated approach to security within development and delivery cycles. While current DevSecOps strategies have made meaningful contributions by introducing security activities into these cycles, many implementations remain constrained by an effectively open-loop posture in which actions proceed without continuous verification against the actual state of the system. This limitation is most consequential in high-frequency delivery environments, systems handling sensitive or business-critical workloads, and organizations operating at sufficient platform maturity for the absence of closed-loop feedback to translate into material risk exposure and reduced operational stability.

It is vital to architect DevSecOps as a closed-loop control system in which security sensors continuously generate risk signals, policy engines evaluate those signals against versioned and auditable governance rules, and pipeline actuators execute proportionate responses. Under this architecture, security is not treated as a static attribute to be verified once but as an ongoing operational process in which detection, evaluation, and response operate in a continuous cycle.

6.4.1 Open-Loop vs. Closed-Loop Security Models

In an open-loop security architecture, actions are performed according to predefined instructions or rules without ongoing feedback from the system's runtime state. Security tests typically execute during designated phases, such as code review or pre-deployment validation. While these tests provide a degree of confidence at the point of execution, they cannot account for changes that occur after the assessed action has been implemented. In high-frequency delivery environments, systems handling sensitive workloads, or architectures where runtime conditions diverge significantly from pre-deployment assumptions, this gap can leave the system exposed to risks that have materialized since the last checkpoint.

Because an open-loop system operates without ongoing feedback, it cannot adjust its actions based on runtime conditions or post-deployment state changes. Any correction relies on the next scheduled test or manual intervention, neither of which can keep pace with continuous change. For this reason, open-loop architectures become increasingly inadequate as delivery frequency rises and the interval between changes shrinks.

In a closed-loop security architecture, feedback is structurally incorporated into the control process through three integrated mechanisms. Security sensors, including vulnerability scanners, runtime monitors, and anomaly detection systems, continuously collect and analyze signals that provide visibility into the risks present in the system. Policy engines, operating as the decision layer, evaluate those signals against versioned and auditable governance rules to determine appropriate responses. Pipeline actuators then execute the resulting decisions, whether that means proceeding with deployment, blocking a release, initiating rollback, or adjusting access controls. It is this integration of detection, evaluation, and response, rather than the presence of monitoring alone, that constitutes closed-loop control.

The structural relationship between feedback, decision-making, and actuation creates the conditions for an adaptive system capable of responding to a wide range of modifications, particularly in high-frequency delivery environments and systems where runtime conditions can diverge materially from pre-deployment assumptions. In these contexts, emerging risks can be identified and addressed promptly, reducing the window of exposure and helping prevent the kind of cascading instabilities that might otherwise escalate into broader system failures.

From the viewpoint of control systems theory, the transition from an open-loop model to a closed-loop one represents the evolution from static, pre-scheduled control to dynamic regulation in which security sensors generate continuous risk signals, policy engines evaluate those signals in near-real time, and pipeline actuators execute proportionate responses on an ongoing basis rather than at isolated intervals (Åström & Murray, 2008). It is this tight coupling of detection, decision, and action that distinguishes dynamic regulation from periodic validation.

Additionally, closed-loop security models exhibit anticipatory and proactive characteristics that emerge from the tight integration of their constituent elements. Security sensors surface trend data and anomaly indicators, policy engines evaluate these patterns against adaptive thresholds informed by historical baselines and current context, and pipeline actuators can pre-emptively tighten controls or delay changes before detected risks escalate to operational incidents. This capability, grounded in real-time observability feeding into codified and auditable decision logic, allows closed-loop systems to identify emerging problems before they propagate into wider system failures. The advantage is particularly pronounced in high-frequency delivery environments, where the rate of change amplifies the cost of delayed detection.

6.4.2 Components of the DevSecOps Control Loop

The closed-loop DevSecOps framework comprises three essential building blocks drawn from control theory and applied here as an architectural model for software delivery. Sensors, realized through tools such as SAST, DAST, vulnerability scanners, and runtime monitors, generate continuous security signals. Controllers, implemented as policy engines with versioned and auditable rule sets, interpret those signals against defined risk thresholds and determine appropriate responses. Actuators, embodied by CI/CD pipeline mechanisms, execute the resulting decisions through actions such as deployment blocking, rollback, configuration enforcement, or access restriction. The distinguishing characteristic of this architecture is not the presence of these components individually but their structural integration into a single feedback loop that ensures constant monitoring, assessment, and adjustment of system behavior in response to evolving conditions.

Sensors gather security-related information about the system under management. Within a DevSecOps environment, sensor implementations include static application security testing, dynamic application security testing, vulnerability scanning, and runtime monitoring systems. The output of these sensors constitutes a stream of data reflecting the current security status of the system, encompassing identified vulnerabilities, configuration deviations, and anomalous runtime behaviors. For this data to support reliable control decisions, signals must be timely, correlated across sources, de-duplicated to minimize noise, and interpreted against defined SLOs or policy thresholds rather than treated as inherently reliable raw input. The effectiveness of the entire control loop depends on the quality, latency, and contextual relevance of these sensor outputs, since downstream decisions and actuations are only as sound as the feedback on which they are based.

Controllers interpret the output of the sensors and derive appropriate decisions from the data they generate. In software delivery environments, controllers are implemented as policy engines, rule sets, and decision-making logic that evaluate incoming signals against defined constraints and objectives. For these mechanisms to function as genuine control rather than advisory guidance, the policies they enforce must be versioned, tested against representative scenarios, applied consistently across all environments, auditable for traceability, and aligned with designated risk ownership. When these conditions are satisfied, controllers determine whether system behavior conforms to acceptable risk levels and respond accordingly, whether by authorizing continued operation, restricting specific actions, or initiating corrective measures. In this capacity, controllers serve as the intelligence layer of the system, translating raw feedback into informed and proportionate control actions.

Actuators implement the decisions taken by the controllers, making actual changes in the operation of the system. The implementation of actuators takes the form of automated actions performed by CI/CD tools in the context of DevSecOps, which include deployment blocking, rollbacks, patches, configuration management, and other tasks.

It should be noted that the cooperation between sensors, controllers, and actuators creates a feedback loop that works constantly, taking into account the current state of the system and correlating the actions with the specified goals of security. The use of such a feedback loop allows systems not only to provide for the security policies' implementation but also to maintain their stability.

6.4.3 Continuous Risk Monitoring

One critical attribute of the closed-loop DevSecOps framework is the continuous risk monitoring mechanism, which ensures that security is treated not as a sporadic testing process but rather as a continuous and real-time control process. Instead of using scheduled or event-driven processes for validating security, continuous risk monitoring enables consistent monitoring of the evolving risk of the system. Such a process is imperative for modern development frameworks, whereby continuous changes to the code base, the underlying infrastructure, and the patterns of use constantly change the risk profile of the system.

The continuous monitoring of risks becomes possible through the high-level integration of security solutions and observability tools, where metrics, logs, and traces are combined with security signals (Beyer et al., 2016), including vulnerabilities, configuration changes, and behavior drifts, thus creating an overall picture of the current status of the system. Combining operational data with security data allows getting a clear idea of what's going on and why, making risk detection easier.

Continuous monitoring provides the ability to make proactive decisions as well as predictive decisions. The analysis of trends and patterns, as well as other signals that the monitoring system receives, allows predicting future events. Slow deterioration in the performance indicators, together with anomalies in access patterns, may suggest some security issues. Early detection of such anomalies gives the ability to implement appropriate measures that prevent possible future problems, such as preventing access, changing settings, or delaying deployments. Thus, proactive measures will move the system from a purely corrective mode to the prevention mode.

The use of continuous monitoring comes with its own problems, which are associated mostly with huge volumes of data and poor quality of signals. With the current volume of data that modern applications produce, it becomes increasingly hard to distinguish valuable signals from useless data. In addition, there is always a risk that some low-value signal will trigger inappropriate actions of the decision systems.

In the context of control systems theory, the process of continuous risk monitoring increases the level of observability in the control system, which gives the right input to make decisions at the right time. Feedback is an important aspect of the control system, and continuous risk monitoring improves the feedback process. Figure 6-2 depicts DevSecOps modeled as a closed-loop control system integrating security feedback, policy-based decision-making, and pipeline actuation.

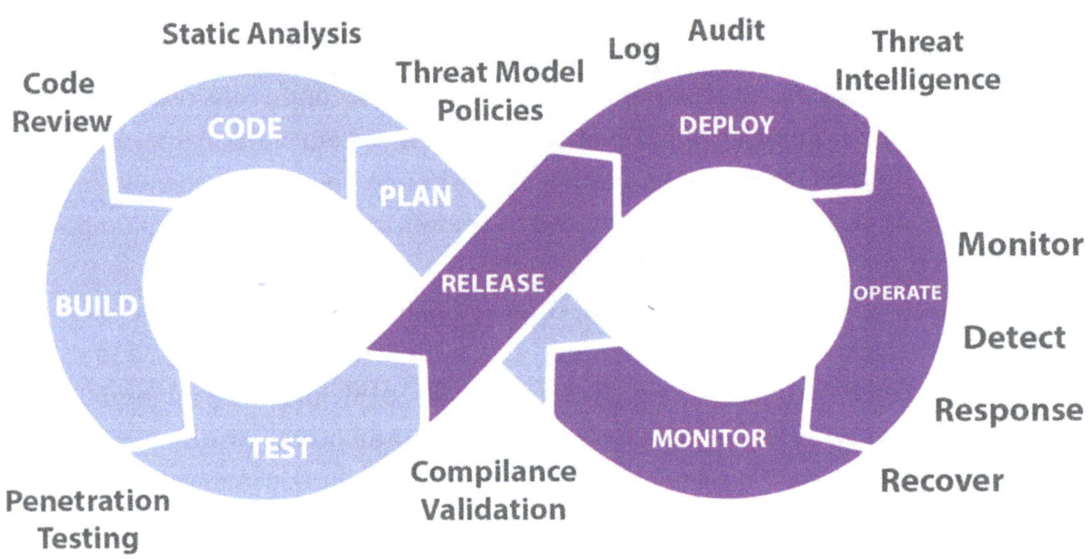

***Figure 6-2.** DevSecOps Closed-Loop Control Model*

DevSecOps is modeled as a closed-loop control system integrating security feedback, policy-based decision-making, and pipeline actuation.

Section Summary

With this regard, this chapter introduced DevSecOps as a closed-loop control system in which feedback, decision-making, and actioning processes are constantly linked to control for the purposes of security in constantly changing software delivery systems. The chapter explained that, beyond the stage-based security model that is common in DevSecOps operations, a more appropriate approach would be the constant application of the closed-loop concept where the state of the system is observed, analyzed, and corrected constantly through control activities.

This means that security becomes an intrinsic aspect of the system itself rather than a separate process. This brings another important realization. Open-loop security models cannot effectively handle the rapidly changing nature of modern systems because they rely on periodically checking changes and validating results. On the contrary, using closed-loop models, the systems can detect any change or deviation from expected risk levels in real time and apply the necessary action to mitigate or prevent any issues.

Additionally, it is stated that the components which include sensors, controllers, and actuators make up the structural part of the DevSecOps loop. Thus, sensors are responsible for security feedback, as monitoring and analytical tools are continuously utilized in order to collect data. Then, it is time to process all the collected information via policy-driven decision-making, which is executed by controllers. Finally, actuators conduct certain actions after the decision is made.

It is important to note that the principle of continuous risk monitoring plays a significant role in supporting this feedback loop and its benefits. With the help of constant surveillance, decision-making becomes proactive in its nature, meaning that the equilibrium can be achieved in the system, and no reactions will be needed.

As we can see from the above discussion, some key principles of security feedback loops have been discussed in detail. Now, let us focus on the structure of the latter.

6.5 Security Feedback Loops in Software Delivery

In control-based DevSecOps frameworks, feedback is the process used to allow continuous awareness of and adjustments to conditions within the system. The security feedback loops are extensions of this concept, offering real-time awareness of risks present within the systems, such that security is not checked at specific intervals but continuously throughout. Feedback loops are a method that connects the process of detecting, assessing, and reacting to risks.

Feedback loops function differently from traditional security approaches, as these are conducted in real time and can react to new threats and risks as they occur. The efficiency of these loops will depend on what type of feedback is offered, when signals are produced, and the nature of the signals being delivered.

6.5.1 Types of Security Feedback

There exist various feedback mechanisms for security within software delivery pipelines that provide visibility at different stages of system operation. Unlike working independently, they combine into an approach that includes several levels of feedback and enables ongoing assessment and control of risks. Using these mechanisms, it is possible to make preventive actions based on the information gained from different parts of the lifecycle and use this information to develop more effective control processes.

Static analysis method, which can also be termed static application security testing, involves analysis at the early stage of the development lifecycle, analyzing source code, library packages, configurations, and many other aspects. The reason why static analysis proves to be quite effective is that it can identify errors even before the actual implementation occurs. As a result, static analysis is quite good in preventing errors from occurring because they can be identified beforehand. On the other hand, the problem with static analysis is that it is an incomplete process, resulting in false positives OWASP (Top 10, DevSecOps guides).

Dynamic analysis (DAST) complements static analysis in that it assesses software during runtime, usually in test environments. The feedback given through dynamic analysis is contextual because the process involves interacting with the system in use; therefore, it will provide information on problems that arise based on how the program operates. The downside here is that feedback is provided much later in the process, especially since runtime issues may take days to surface.

Runtime monitoring and anomaly detection give feedback after deployment when the application is already being used in an operational environment. These processes involve analyzing data streams from the application and detecting any anomalies that arise. The advantages of these processes are that they provide information immediately and are operational in nature. The disadvantage of using this process is that they are reactive and cannot prevent security breaches but can help mitigate them.

The above forms of feedback complement each other to form an overlapping hierarchy of feedback systems. Feedback at the first level ensures that the weaknesses do not become part of the system, while feedback at the second level helps optimize and validate the security posture. Finally, feedback at the third level makes it possible for continuous surveillance and action to be taken.

6.5.2 Feedback Timing and Latency

The time when feedback is provided is critical when determining its efficiency in control because the sooner and faster this feedback is available, the more efficient the responses are. The provision of feedback in an early stage makes it possible to prevent further issues from occurring by addressing them before they can cause harm to other elements of the system. Such actions are cost-effective as well as minimize the possibility of instabilities. On the contrary, delays make it more likely for problems to affect all components of the process and cause even bigger problems.

It is essential to note that this principle is linked to another crucial concept in control systems - latency. When latency grows, it leads to increased delays between the system state and actions to be performed by the controller, resulting in less accurate decisions being made and making it difficult for a controller to provide a proper response. Moreover, such behavior may become problematic when it becomes too late to address problems in an appropriate manner (Ogata, 2010).

Various kinds of feedback work in different places on the time axis. Early feedback, for example, static analysis, provides proactive control in a way that prevents actions that can be harmful. Mid-time feedback, such as dynamic analysis, gives much more accurate information about the issue, but there is a slight time delay caused by the necessity to run the system first. Late feedback includes live system monitoring and anomaly detection. The advantage of such a kind of feedback is that it provides a clear picture of the real situation within the system. At the same time, it cannot help but prevent anything; only corrective actions are possible here.

Thus, it is necessary to maintain a balance between such types of feedback. Excessive dependence on the early types of feedback could be the reason for the lack of identification of some issues in the runtime environment. On the other hand, dependence on the late type of feedback will put the system at risk.

6.5.3 Signal Quality and Noise

In addition to the timing of security feedback, the efficiency of the process depends on the quality of signals received because the quality of decision-making is dependent on their accuracy and relevance. In any case, the signals used for securing software delivery cannot be entirely accurate. There will always be some elements that create noise and make it difficult to differentiate useful from useless signals. This poses certain risks to the functionality of the system.

One of the issues that could affect the use of signals for securing systems is that of false positives. False positives are signals that suggest that there are threats when this is not really the case. While such signals do not pose any threat to the security of the system, they still affect its function since they might lead to blocking deployment, rolling back changes, or issuing many alerts. If such alerts happen regularly, there might be an issue with alert fatigue.

However, the failure to detect real threats would be considered a false negative result. It is especially important as it defeats the purpose of implementing security controls. The problem could spread within the system and become exploited at some point, resulting in major disasters. In terms of control system theory, a false negative arises when there is no possibility of satisfying the condition of observability, since there will be inadequate information to take the necessary steps.

An effective control system must have mechanisms of filtering, validation, and prioritization of the signals received from the component parts of the system. Filtering and validation processes include sophisticated methodologies such as threshold determination, anomaly recognition, and correlation of various data sets. Other forms of sophisticated signal handling may be based on context-aware enrichment of signals or machine learning.

Good quality feedback signals make it possible for one to be able to react proportionately and appropriately to the situation by taking the necessary measures to solve the problem. Poor quality signals will either lead to overreacting or underreacting to the situation. Both types of reactions to signals create instability within a system since they will not bring about the desired results.

6.5.4 Feedback Integration into Pipelines

However, for security feedback to have an impact on the system's behavior, it has to be incorporated deeply within CI/CD pipelines and their associated control functions in order to become a driving force behind the process rather than just an observable factor. In a control-based delivery process, feedback becomes one of the elements used for making decisions.

Namely, in a control-driven delivery process, feedback will trigger specific reactions from the system automatically based on policies created to respond to specific security feedback signals. For example, the presence of critical vulnerabilities found within the process can trigger automatic blocking of a particular release, while any runtime anomalies like traffic surges or high error rates could lead to such decisions as rolling back to a previous version, changing the traffic flow pattern, or adding more resources to cope with the demand.

Validation is an important part of this integration. While conventional approaches involve validating the security measures only at certain points in time, a control-oriented system performs validation throughout the entire process of delivery. In this case, every activity, whether deployment, configuration change, or scaling, will undergo verification relative to the real environment and constraints. With such a continuous verification mechanism, it will be easy to ensure that the system adheres to the security requirements as well as the performance criteria, even when things keep changing.

With such an integration, it will now be possible to implement a feedback-driven method of execution. Rather than executing a predefined set of activities, there is feedback that guides the execution process. All activities along the pipeline become context-aware through feedback mechanisms. It will then become possible to make decisions regarding control actions to take at different times in response to the current state of the system.

It will be possible for the system to achieve the closed-loop control process because of this feedback-driven decision-making and execution process. Security monitoring, assessment, and enforcement will always be present to help facilitate dynamic control of the system. Table 6-1 summarizes the main types of security feedback, along with their timing, strengths, and limitations.

Table 6-1. *Security Feedback Types and Characteristics*

Feedback Type	Timing	Strength	Limitation
SAST	Early	Preventive	Limited runtime context
DAST	Mid	Context-aware	Slower feedback
Runtime monitoring	Late	Real-time behavior	Reactive nature

Section Summary

In this chapter, we focused on analyzing the significance of feedback loops in ensuring security in DevSecOps systems and how feedback loops serve as the underlying platform for achieving dynamic risk management. Security cannot be viewed as a linear process that occurs at certain stages but rather as an adaptable approach that ensures the system operates like a self-regulatory environment where security is constantly controlled.

There are several significant insights gained from the above discussions. The first one is how feedback loops enable the constant surveillance of system risks so that any deviation from the normal system operation is identified early enough. This is crucial in current delivery environments since the environment can easily alter its risk profile.

Another insight is the difference between various feedback loops and how they provide diverse views regarding the nature of system operation. Feedback in the earlier stage provides preventive approaches, while mid-stage feedback enhances knowledge acquisition about system operations, and finally, runtime feedback provides constant surveillance.

The third factor that plays a critical role is the delay and latency of feedback. The longer the feedback takes to return to the controller, the lower its effectiveness becomes. The fourth point related to the issue under discussion is that signal accuracy matters a lot, as the information needs to be correct for the controller to make proper decisions. Low-quality feedback may trigger false alarms or, conversely, ignore serious threats.

The third element is the inclusion of feedback into the CI/CD pipeline itself, which makes it possible to control everything through automation. This means that instead of performing only the assigned tasks, the pipeline will take certain actions based on the actual situation in the system.

In conclusion, it is extremely important to make sure that the concept of feedback loops is taken into account when creating a DevSecOps solution. Simply speaking, one has to make sure that the feedback loop is included in the process of managing risks.

6.6 Risk-Based Decision-Making in DevSecOps

For the control-oriented DevSecOps framework, decision-making processes serve as the most crucial bridge connecting feedback and action initiation. Although previous sections have clarified the importance of security as a limiting factor and a form of feedback, the efficacy of such components largely hinges on the decision-making process itself following feedback from security-related information. In conventional DevSecOps models, there is usually the use of dichotomous decision models that depend entirely on predefined yes or no decision criteria. However, this is ineffective in situations where there are risks, dependencies, and threats that keep changing.

The use of risk-based decision-making is therefore advocated as the best approach in ensuring proper performance of the DevSecOps model. This means that decisions will be made depending on different types of risks. Such an approach is consistent with control system concepts as it facilitates the assessment and management of risk levels through decision-making activities.

6.6.1 From Binary Decisions to Risk Scoring

The security enforcement mechanisms that are commonly used within traditional processes are often binary decision-based. They present the decision process as a simple pass/fail scenario. The benefit of binary-based systems is ease of implementation and straightforwardness; however, such processes also have many drawbacks, especially when applied to a dynamic environment with continuously changing states. In this case, binary decisions often ignore risk variability and thus produce overly tight or overly loose decisions.

In practical terms, this means that a deployment decision will often be made inefficiently since a deployment can be prohibited because of minor vulnerabilities or allowed without any critical vulnerabilities being detected. Therefore, a simple binary decision does not allow one to adequately evaluate complex scenarios of a modern software development process and the risks associated with them.

The introduction of risk-based decision models solves this problem by making decision processes continuous rather than binary. As opposed to simple acceptance/rejection of a deployment decision, a risk-based model evaluates risk as a result of deployment and produces its score using such parameters as vulnerabilities, exploitability, criticality of the system, and exposure.

This multifaceted approach allows for a more accurate depiction of the current risk state of the system.

With the inclusion of risk score calculations on a continual basis, decision-making will become a much more contextualized process. Actions can now be tailored appropriately depending on the nature of the risk faced, rather than applying actions uniformly regardless of the risk involved. Low risk means very few limitations are placed, medium risk requires verification, while high risk could lead to the implementation of blockages or fixes.

From the perspective of control systems, this approach can be said to be moving from a discrete to a continuous control process, where decisions are made based on the status of the system in order to effectively control software deployment activities.

6.6.2 Policy-Driven Risk Thresholds

The decision-making process involving risks is facilitated by having risk thresholds clearly defined, which provides a structure for understanding the degree of risk tolerance that is acceptable for a particular system. Risk thresholds are not arbitrarily assigned but are based on factors such as the objective of the business, legal compliance, and technical constraints that are involved in a particular system. This makes the decision-making process easier and ensures that all criteria are met. Assigning acceptable risk levels provides the basis for developing a structure for interpreting risk assessment outcomes.

Risk thresholds, which are determined according to policy guidelines, form the basis for decision-making. They enable the definition of the actions that are to be taken based on the level of risk that exists within a particular system. For example, a system may have a threshold that permits application deployment if the risk level is below a certain threshold, conduct validation testing if the risk level is between two thresholds, and prohibit application deployment if the threshold is above a critical level.

However, there are situations where static thresholding might not be applicable in the case of dynamic software delivery environments. The factors that may cause rapid changes and affect the system's risk tolerance may include workload, operating environment, or even the nature of external threats. It would therefore become necessary to employ dynamic thresholds in cases like these to ensure that decisions made take into consideration the changing dynamics.

For instance, in situations where everything is normal with no issues whatsoever, the threshold settings should allow for the quick release of software deliverables. But in scenarios where events take place that lead to higher risk thresholds, strict threshold settings are put in place to limit the risk exposure. Dynamic thresholding enables decision-making processes to keep pace with the prevailing conditions.

According to the concepts in control systems, the use of dynamic thresholds would help the control system to adapt to the changing environment by adjusting its control boundaries.

6.6.3 Decision Models

A risk-based approach to making decisions may be put in place using various models, contingent on the degree of automation necessary, the complexity of the system being used, and the tolerance for risk. The models will determine how risk data is evaluated and decisions are carried out, impacting the response times and the consistency of the whole process.

Decision-making models that have been automated utilize predetermined policies and algorithms to analyze risk and choose courses of action. The use of automated decision-making models is crucial in scenarios that involve high-volume distribution since decisions must be consistent and immediate, irrespective of the scope of the system. In this way, the policies that are implemented are enforced uniformly, enabling efficient management and decision-making processes to occur. Thus, decision-making models that have been automated become very important for ensuring efficient operations in continuous delivery workflows.

However, automated decision-making models have limitations. They only function within the defined parameters and may not always understand the situation. Therefore, not all decisions can be automated; indeed, some decisions are more complex than others, and their consequences may be severe.

In situations where there is more risk, uncertainty, or limited information, the models incorporate humans into the loop for an added element of analysis and monitoring. In this case, the computer or machine conducts the risk assessment and makes recommendations, and then human operators analyze the situation and make decisions. In this manner, the human factor provides insights based on experience, judgment, and contextual intelligence that are hard to incorporate into automated systems.

The fusion of automatic and human-based decision-making methods results in a hybrid decision-making model, which is a combination of efficiency and flexibility. Hybrid models automate low-risk decision processes while retaining manual decision processes for high-risk events. Thus, this dual-process model allows decision processes to be both efficient and context-sensitive, allowing the decision process to function effectively within different environments.

From the viewpoint of control systems, hybrid systems constitute multi-layered control schemes, whereby lower layers perform faster but less intelligent activities, whereas upper layers execute slow but intelligent processes.

6.6.4 Trade-Off Between Risk and Delivery Speed

Balancing risk management and delivery speed represents a major challenge in DevSecOps. According to previous analysis, higher levels of control, for example, through more strict policies or more advanced validation and monitoring procedures, lower the risk of system problems; however, they decrease the speed of delivery and responsiveness as well. Focusing on fast delivery, on the contrary, means lowering the amount of controls and thereby increasing the risk of vulnerabilities and errors. Thus, risk management and delivery speed represent a critical trade-off inherent to any software delivery system.

The approach of risk-based decision-making helps address the trade-off described above, allowing for proportionate risk management. Instead of restraining all operations in terms of the same controls, the system calculates how risky the operation is and does what needs to be done. Operations that have been identified as low risk, for example, small modifications of coding or small modifications of configurations, can proceed unhindered by any extra constraints and continue to operate efficiently.

Through proportionality, the security measures would be used only where required, making the policy applicable on a proportional basis where it should only be imposed where it should be. Thus, using this approach, the system can be operated with high velocities and at the same time be secure.

Under the control theory paradigm, this system corresponds to the state-dependent approach to system management. Under this approach, actions taken by a system depend on its state. Risk is considered a state-related characteristic and therefore becomes a control variable for the system's performance. When the risk level is low, the system enters the permissive state of operation where speed and delivery of results are important. With growing levels of risk, the system moves into a more restrictive regime.

Most importantly, the proportional approach changes the goal of DevSecOps completely. Security should not aim to reduce all risks to zero. Rather, risk management becomes a tool to help deliver results with a proper balance of speed and control. Figure 6-3 presents a risk-based decision model in which security signals and policy thresholds determine whether a deployment action is allowed, restricted, or blocked.

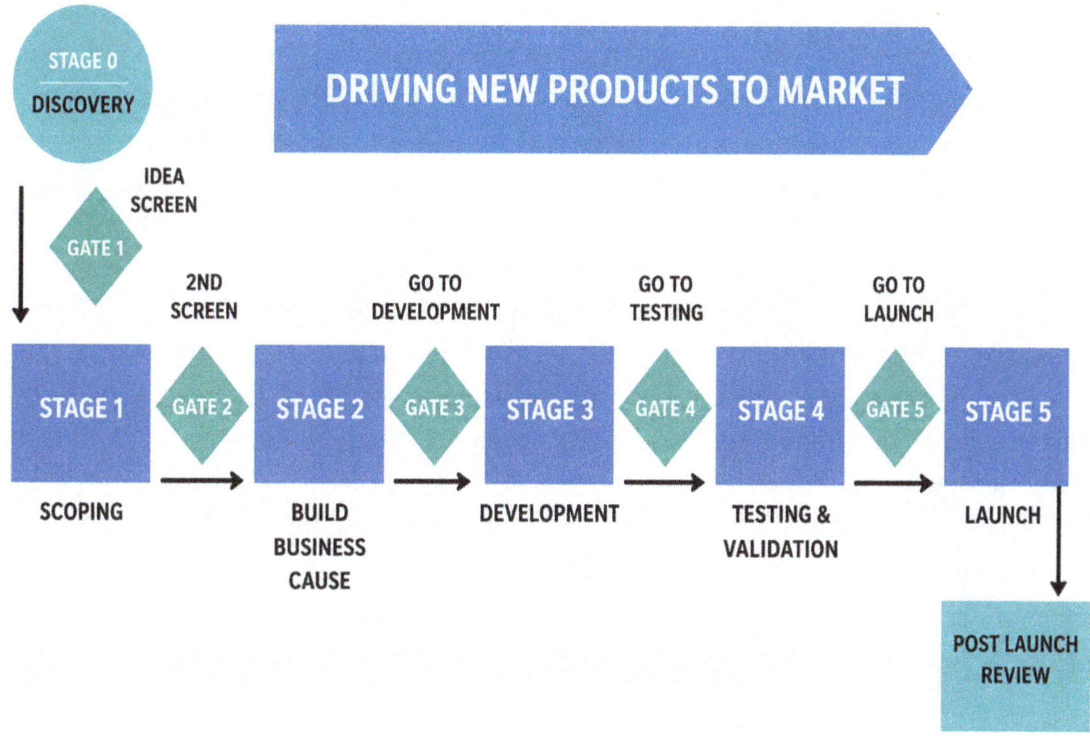

Figure 6-3. *Risk-Based Decision Model in CI/CD*

This risk-based decision model uses security signals and policy thresholds to allow, restrict, or block deployment actions.

Section Summary

Through this section, risk-based decision-making has been revealed as one of the critical elements in control-driven DevSecOps solutions. By using the risk-based approach, decisions are made with respect to the current state of operations and the current context within which operations are taking place. This means that, unlike the evaluation techniques used in other methods, risk-based decision-making allows for flexibility.

The main idea is that binary decision models do not work in today's ever-changing environment since they cannot adequately accommodate variations in risk level and contexts. Risk-based decision-making does not suffer from such shortcomings because risk scoring makes it possible to make decisions in a continuously changing environment. In other words, there will always be an adjustment according to the degree of risk involved.

It is important to note that policies play a significant part in risk scoring and the decisions resulting from risk assessments. These decisions need to have clear policies that determine what the thresholds should be. Through the policies, decision-making processes can continue in a controlled manner despite continuous changes.

In addition, the application of hybrid decision models was noted as an essential aspect of the design. By blending automated decision-making with human decision-making, such models combine rapidity and uniformity with flexibility and context sensitivity, allowing systems to respond to all types of situations.

Lastly, it was highlighted that the adoption of risk-based strategies would allow organizations to effectively reconcile the need for security with the need to deliver quickly. In doing so, security controls can be applied selectively rather than indiscriminately.

These considerations set up the theoretical framework for analyzing the impact of decisions on actuation, a topic discussed in the following section.

6.7 Security-Driven Actuation Mechanisms

In a DevSecOps control architecture, actuation is the process of translating decisions into actionable changes in the system itself. After laying out the process by which security events are detected and analyzed in earlier segments, the efficiency of the system can be determined by the way these decisions are implemented. Actuation in a security context allows for constant alignment with risk boundaries through the ability to make timely, accurate, and situation-specific interventions.

Traditional systems have generally involved security interventions being manually carried out after delays; however, in the context of DevSecOps, actuation is an automated process inherent in the continuous integration and delivery processes of the system itself. Actuation is essentially the execution component of the control process, implementing preventive, corrective, and adaptive measures depending on the current state of the security environment.

6.7.1 Preventive Actuation

The essence of preventive actuation is in preventing the occurrence of a state that can be hazardous to the system. This approach entails the implementation of policies through which actions are assessed and approved before they are undertaken to ensure compliance with established requirements.

Deployment blocking based on reaching specified vulnerability levels can serve as one illustrative example. In case such security issues arise during the course of assessing proposed actions, the process will be stopped so that risk does not enter the system. Other forms of preventive actuations include restriction of the use of configuration management, access control, and infrastructure operations, which do not comply with set conditions.

In effect, prevention falls under feedforward control, in which actions are limited beforehand, depending on the outcome of their assessment.

6.7.2 Corrective Actuation

While certain controls help prevent potential problems in systems, there are times when corrections have to be made to maintain system stability. This is where corrective actuation comes into play, by bringing back the system to a balanced and secure state.

Corrective actuation is exemplified in rollback procedures, where the system will return to its prior stable state following any problems encountered during deployment. In addition, automated patches for vulnerabilities will correct any existing security risks within the system.

By nature, corrective actuation is reactive, reacting to any issues that may arise. However, the effectiveness of corrective actuation increases when applied in a closed-loop control system because feedback signals allow the system to detect deviations and make necessary adjustments quickly.

Corrective actuation acts like a negative feedback loop from a control standpoint.

6.7.3 Adaptive Actuation

Whereas preventive measures and corrective measures serve the purpose of control, they are frequently inadequate to control in dynamic environments in which conditions are continuously changing, and so are risks. Here, adaptive actuation helps the system to modify its action according to changes in environmental conditions.

Some examples of adaptive techniques are dynamic adjustments in terms of the strength of controls employed. The strength of certain policies could be changed depending on risks. For instance, the rate at which something is deployed could be limited if there were high risks involved.

Other instances of adaptive techniques include risk-based approaches that would deploy the system according to risk conditions. These techniques are designed to minimize risk and exposure of the system and could involve techniques such as incremental or phased rollout of software or systems.

Adaptive actuation corresponds to advanced control techniques in which the response of the system is continuously modified to ensure stability and efficiency in the process.

6.7.4 Automated Incident Response

In cases where the frequency is too high for human response, the speed required to resolve security incidents can exceed the capabilities of human interaction. Automating the process of resolving security incidents expands the potential scope of actuation.

Such automation begins with a security signal, such as those generated by intrusion detection, anomaly detection, or the detection of policy violations. These signals trigger an action that includes isolation, access revocation, resource downsizing, or remediation.

Inclusion in CI/CD enables automated incident response to take place within the same control environment as the rest of the processes of delivery. As such, the automated response takes place without the risk of becoming uncoordinated with other activities.

The ability of the system to respond automatically to incidents improves its resilience due to reduced response time and consistency in implementation. Nevertheless, such systems have the risk of becoming problematic when triggered unnecessarily. Table 6-2 summarizes the principal actuation types, their purpose, and representative examples.

Table 6-2. *Security Actuation Types*

Actuation Type	Purpose	Example
Preventive	Avoid an unsafe state	Block deployment
Corrective	Restore stability	Rollback
Adaptive	Adjust system behavior	Throttle rollout

Section Summary

This section examined how security-driven actuation mechanisms translate decisions into system behavior within DevSecOps environments.

The key insights are as follows:

- Actuation is the action layer in the security control system.
- Preventive controls ensure the absence of undesirable states even before their occurrence.
- Corrective controls restore balance when disturbances happen.
- Adaptive controls allow for flexible responses depending on the current situation.
- Automation of incident handling contributes to rapid and consistent control actions.

These results highlight the importance of actuation as a key element in closed-loop DevSecOps systems.

6.8 DevSecOps and System Stability

Stability is an essential goal in the process of software development using control-oriented principles. The term denotes a system's ability to operate consistently despite all sorts of changes that occur. In the case of DevSecOps, stability does not depend only on performance and availability, but to a great extent, it depends on how well the concept of security is included in the control process. When properly implemented, security can serve as a means for achieving greater stability because it ensures that the system's behavior stays within safe borders.

To comprehend the relation between DevSecOps and stability, one must study both sides of the issue – the stabilizing effect of security as well as the failure modes that may arise due to improper integration of security.

6.8.1 Security as a Stabilizing Force

Stability is maintained in control systems by keeping system variables bounded and ensuring that deviations are addressed promptly. The role of security here is to provide a risk-based constraining approach, which prevents the system from reaching a condition where it could become unstable.

Security systems maintain the system's stability by imposing risk thresholds and constraining actions in accordance with policy guidelines. This way, security helps prevent any action such as deployment, configurations, and access management from adding any risks to the system.

Moreover, feedback mechanisms are introduced through the use of detection systems. These detection systems help detect and address any deviations from what is expected of the system, thus helping improve its stability. For instance, security systems may use anomaly detection tools to monitor network traffic for any unusual activity.

This shows how security acts as a negative feedback controller to correct any deviations from equilibrium (Åström & Murray, 2008).

6.8.2 Instability from Poor Security Integration

Although security can help in stabilizing systems, its wrong implementation can lead to the destabilization of the system.

One way in which instability can be introduced is through delays in feedback generation and processing. As a result, the measures for addressing a problem will come too late and will fail to eliminate it, leading to propagation. A small time delay could cause considerable deviations in the state of a system operating at high frequencies due to an accumulation of changes over time.

Overreactions based on signals that are either insufficiently strong or unreliable pose another threat. Since security processes generate a lot of feedback, and some of it will be irrelevant, responding aggressively to such inputs by blocking deployment or rolling back will cause unnecessary disruptions.

Such overreaction is similar to overcorrection in control systems. As a result, the process can become unstable and experience many interruptions. These include multiple deployment attempts, configuration adjustments, and scale changes.

Therefore, it is crucial to have the necessary measures calibrated so that overreactions do not happen.

6.8.3 Balancing Security and Performance

A major problem in implementing DevSecOps is reaching an optimum point between enforcing security and system performance. As much as there is a need for strict security protocols to maintain system stability, too many constraints might negatively impact the performance and response capability of the system.

Strict protocols might cause delays and inefficiencies in deployment activities which may lead to bottleneck formation and eventually compromise the performance of the system. Too much security enforcement might make some necessary changes impossible to implement, resulting in the inability of the system to respond effectively to changing conditions.

Too little security on the other hand increases risk levels and decreases stability, leading to poor performance in the long run. Effective DevSecOps implementation thus requires proportionality and adaptation in security enforcement processes.

This entails ensuring that the security protocols enforced in a system are proportionate and adaptive depending on the environment and risks involved at a given time. The objective in DevSecOps implementations is therefore to optimize the stability-responsiveness trade-off in systems engineering. Figure 6-4 contrasts stable and unstable system responses, showing how feedback quality determines whether the system converges to a steady state or oscillates.

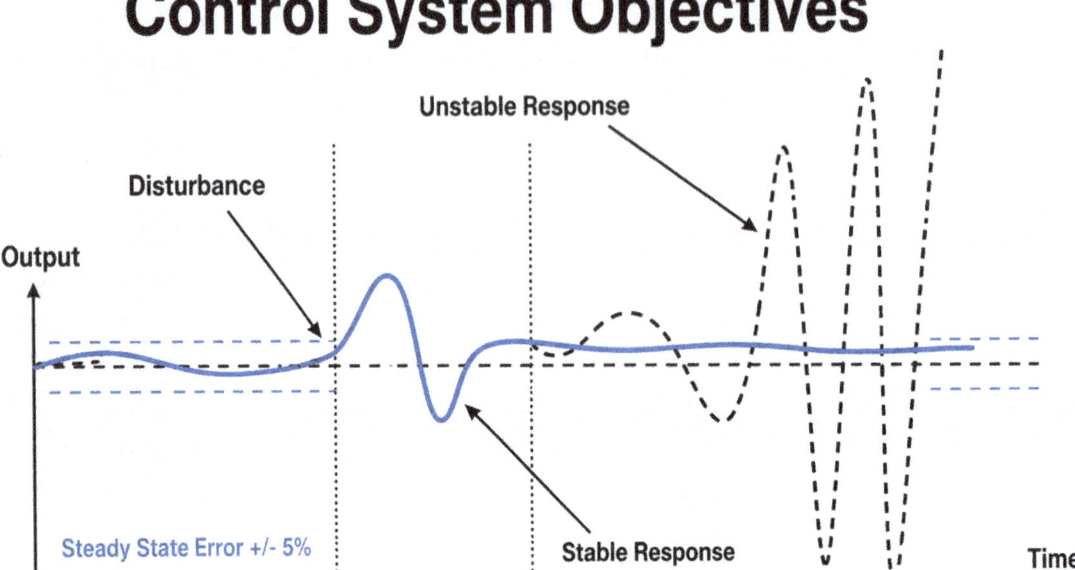

Figure 6-4. *Security Impact on System Stability*

This figure shows the impact of security integration on system stability, showing stable convergence, delayed response, and oscillatory behavior under varying feedback quality.

Section Summary

In this section, we investigated the correlation between DevSecOps and stability, focusing on the stabilization effect of security and the dangers associated with bad integration. The key insights are as follows:

- Security acts as a stabilizing force by enforcing constraints and enabling feedback-driven control.
- Delayed detection reduces control effectiveness and introduces instability.

- Overreaction to weak signals can produce oscillatory system behavior.
- Balancing security and performance is essential for maintaining stability.

These findings reinforce the importance of designing DevSecOps systems as well-calibrated control systems, where security mechanisms support both stability and efficient operation.

6.9 Scaling DevSecOps Across Systems and Teams

As software delivery becomes more widespread, covering many different teams, services, and environments, the complexity of the security management process grows. In order for DevSecOps to work on a larger scale, it has to transform from a local phenomenon into a distributed system of controls that will be able to preserve consistent security across various settings. This change will involve several challenges related to the proper organization of the policy-setting process, platform design, and feedback mechanisms that should enable effective security management despite the need for scalability.

When DevSecOps operates in a large-scale environment, security can no longer be limited to one pipeline and one particular team. Instead, it should operate on various platforms that differ in terms of their security needs and dependencies.

6.9.1 Distributed Security Challenges

Among the problems involved in scaling DevSecOps is the fact that there will be several teams that will run in different environments. The use of different sets of tools, procedures, and methods of deploying applications means that there will be different ways of implementing and enforcing security measures.

These differences will cause fragmentation whereby the implementation of security measures is inconsistent from one environment to another. As a result, even when there are similar vulnerabilities in these environments, there may be inconsistent approaches to addressing them, which makes it easy for them to proliferate and lead to system-wide risks.

The number of environments such as production, development, and cloud environments further complicates the governance issues due to the differences in environmental requirements. From the perspective of control systems theory, these are examples of decentralized controls that have to be coordinated to achieve specific goals.

6.9.2 Standardization of Security Policies

The following is one way in which the above problems can be solved: organizations need to adopt standardized security policies that lay down a consistent baseline for their security efforts. With standardization comes uniformity in defining and implementing security protocols and measures, thereby ensuring more reliability on an organizational level.

Policy as Code (PaC) is a concept that plays an essential role in achieving standardized security policies. PaC makes sure that there are policies that can be implemented consistently, as they are written in code and therefore machine-executable. These policies can be easily version-controlled, centralized, and shared.

Even at a large scale, organizations should understand that standardization should not equate to rigidness. On the contrary, the implementation of standardized security policies creates a baseline constraint within which teams have enough room to maneuver.

6.9.3 Platform-Based Security Control

Scaling DevSecOps is about more than just policy standardization; it's about having a means to enforce those policies in a consistent manner throughout distributed systems. Platform-based security control meets this challenge by offering a way to build a centralized layer wherein the policy tools and enforcement are incorporated into a single layer.

In this case, a common platform, which can be built through platform engineering approaches, becomes the control plane for the security function (CNCF, 2022). The platform integrates security controls into infrastructure and delivery systems used by different teams, thereby ensuring consistent application of security measures.

The concept of centralized enforcement is not necessarily about limiting the autonomy of teams. In fact, it provides a means for them to execute operations in a decentralized manner, albeit under some common constraints. This avoids duplication of efforts and facilitates governance of security measures.

As far as the control systems go, a common platform becomes the central control mechanism that coordinates the actions of the distributed parts under certain constraints.

6.9.4 Consistency Across Environments

It is essential to have uniformity across all systems to ensure the continued effectiveness of the security controls as systems evolve. Without uniformity, there will be inconsistencies in terms of the level of security offered by systems, since there will be vulnerabilities addressed in some systems but not in others.

Consistency will be achieved by aligning technology with the organization. First, technology needs to have policies that can work seamlessly in different environments, while at the same time accommodating differences in environments, considering critical constraints. The organization needs to have a shared vision concerning security practices.

Unified observability systems will facilitate this process since they gather information about logs, metrics, and traces from all environments. The resulting information gives a clear picture of how the system works and its current security status. Such information will be useful for ensuring consistent surveillance of system security and reacting to security incidents appropriately.

Consistency does not always mean sameness in all procedures. Flexibility is essential in the operation of systems on a local level, but the systems must also adhere to global rules during their local operations. Table 6-3 summarizes the main scaling challenges and their corresponding solutions.

Table 6-3. *DevSecOps Scaling Challenges and Solutions*

Challenge	Solution
Inconsistent enforcement	Policy as Code
Tool fragmentation	Platform integration
Visibility gaps	Unified observability

Section Summary

In this section, we have explored the difficulties and ways to scale DevSecOps across distributed architectures and groups.

The main takeaways include the following:

- Complexity in maintaining consistency in security controls due to distributed architectures.
- Policy standardization ensures a common framework for governance.
- Powerful control using platforms ensures consistent execution even in distributed architectures.
- Environment consistency is crucial for stability and security.

It can be concluded from these results that DevSecOps scaling demands the transition from fragmented processes to platform-based controls that ensure consistency.

6.10 Security as Continuous Control, Not a Phase

Shift left security, which involves focusing on security within the development cycle early on, has been instrumental in the formation of DevSecOps. While this approach is an excellent method for building on the legacy model of security validation, it has its limitations. Similar to shift-left thinking, which focuses on past stages, the notion of considering security as a characteristic of certain delivery stages, rather than as an attribute of operations, is further reinforced.

In high-frequency and constantly changing systems, a phase-based view is not adequate. Security risks are not just created during development or deployment, but they continue to change with the changes of systems and their interaction as systems interact and operate in diverse environments. Security, therefore, cannot be limited to specific checkpoints but has to be integrated into the fabric of the system lifecycle.

Such a change of perspective results in a more holistic model whereby security is viewed as an ongoing control operation. In this model, security is involved in all phases of the delivery process such as development, integration, deployment, and runtime, and it offers continuous assessment and control of system behavior. Instead of authenticating security at a single point, the system continuously checks its health, evaluates risk, and implements remedial or preventive actions as required.

Constant surveillance is at the center stage of facilitating this model. Through the incorporation of observability and security feedback, systems can have real-time visibility of their operational and security posture. Such visibility enables the detection of developing risks and enables adaptive responses to keep systems stable. Critically, monitoring is a process rather than a goal and an element of a continuous feedback loop, in which information is continually employed to inform decision-making and actuation.

Adaptation is also of great essence. Security mechanisms have to adapt as the conditions of the system and threat landscape change. Fixed controls and policies cannot work in dynamic environments, but systems need adaptive constraints and decision logic that address the present condition. This makes sure that security is upheld without overly limiting system performance and flexibility.

DevSecOps systems have this degree of integration that is not found in classical methods through the integration of security in the control loop. Security is no longer independent of the functioning of the system; it affects the way of decision-making and the performance of actions. This integration allows systems to have a tolerable risk level and facilitates continuous delivery and quick innovation.

Key Insight

Security is not a stage in delivery - it is a continuous control function that operates across the entire system lifecycle.

6.10.1 Section Summary

In this part, the concept of security was shifted from that of a phase in the delivery process to that of a control function.

The important learnings include the following:

- The "shift-left" strategy facilitates early detection but not continuous risk reduction.
- Security needs to be incorporated throughout the system life cycle.
- Continuous monitoring ensures immediate visibility and reaction.
- Adaptation maintains security efficacy in dynamic environments.

These concepts reiterate the main thesis of the chapter, which is that efficient DevSecOps systems should consider security not as a task, but as a component of system control.

6.11 Chapter Summary

This chapter re-conceptualized DevSecOps as a risk, security, and system stability management control mechanism in continuous delivery settings. It has gone beyond tool-based and stage-based understandings and asserted that security should be envisioned as a dynamic and embedded aspect of system functioning. DevSecOps, in this context, is not just the application of security practices to pipelines, but the application of a closed-loop control architecture where security is a constant control over system behavior.

The main contribution of the chapter is a conceptualization of security as a constraint, as a feedback mechanism, and as a control objective. Security, as a constraint, characterizes the frontiers of permissible system behavior, avoiding shifts to unsafe or high-risk states. As feedback, it gives real-time visibility of system conditions in terms of detection mechanisms and monitoring systems. Being a control objective, it defines the desired state of undertaking acceptable risk levels and balancing operational performance. It is the combination of these functions that allows security to act as an intrinsic part of system control and not an external validation layer.

The chapter also showed that closed-loop security modeling is critical in contemporary software delivery. DevSecOps systems provide real-time risk control through the constant gathering and analysis of security indicators, implementation of policy-based decisions, and automated response systems via pipelines. This closed-loop architecture facilitates the ongoing risk management processes, which enable systems to detect, assess, and react to the emanating threats as they occur. It is also conducive to adaptive decision-making, in which actions change with current system state and contextual risk, as opposed to fixed rules or binary outcomes.

Notably, the strategy has a direct impact on the stability and resilience of the system. Security mechanisms can be used to ensure predictable system behavior in the face of constant change by aligning feedback, decision-making, and actuation into a single control loop. The outcome is a delivery system that is not only secure but can work efficiently at scale, striking a balance between speed and safety.

Overall, the chapter confirms that to achieve effective DevSecOps, it is not necessary to add security tools, but rather to create integrated control mechanisms where security is regularly implemented, tested, and improved. Such a view offers a basis to construct software delivery systems that are agile and robust enough to be stable and secure in dynamic and complex environments.

References

Åström, K. J., & Murray, R. M. (2008). Feedback Systems: An Introduction for Scientists and Engineers. Princeton University Press.

Bass, L., Weber, I., & Zhu, L. (2015). DevOps: A Software Architect's Perspective. Addison-Wesley.

Beyer, B., Jones, C., Petoff, J., & Murphy, N. R. (2016). Site Reliability Engineering: How Google Runs Production Systems. O'Reilly Media.

Cloud Native Computing Foundation. (2022). Cloud Native Security Whitepaper (v2). CNCF.

Forsgren, N., Humble, J., & Kim, G. (2018). Accelerate: The Science of Lean Software and DevOps. IT Revolution Press.

Humble, J., & Farley, D. (2010). Continuous Delivery: Reliable Software Releases through Build, Test, and Deployment Automation. Addison-Wesley.

Microsoft. (n.d.). DevSecOps Maturity Model. Microsoft Docs.

National Institute of Standards and Technology. (2020). Systems Security Engineering (NIST SP 800-160, Vol. 1, Rev. 1).

Ogata, K. (2010). Modern Control Engineering (5th ed.). Prentice Hall.

OWASP Foundation. (n.d.). OWASP Top 10 and DevSecOps Guideline.

CHAPTER 7

Decision-Making Inside Delivery Systems

7.1 Chapter Objective

Special attention will be paid to the influence exerted on decisions by policy frameworks that are versioned, tested, enforced consistently, auditable, and aligned with accountable risk ownership, as well as by risk management practices and the operational context of the delivery system.

The chapter considers decision-making from the perspective of a closed-loop control architecture in which observability and security sensors provide feedback on system state, policy engines evaluate that feedback against risk thresholds and governance rules, and pipeline actuators execute the resulting decisions. By structurally integrating these three elements and considering risks, threshold values, and current system conditions, decisions become adaptive and context-sensitive rather than predetermined NIST (2020), NIST (2023).

The chapter argues that decisions should be understood through the lens of their importance for delivering control, adaptation, and scalability across software delivery systems. Properly designed decision-making systems do not merely react to changes but actively shape and govern them.

7.2 Introduction: Decision-Making as the Core of System Control

It has undergone a lot of transformation due to the emergence of ideas like continuous integration, continuous delivery, and DevSecOps. These types of approaches have

S. Bobba and N. S. Vummaneni, *CI/CD as a Control System*, https://doi.org/10.1007/979-8-8688-2842-3_7

ensured the presence of a high level of automation within software development and operations management practices. Although much has changed in the modern implementation model due to the adoption of the new trends, there has been a wrong concentration on automation as the most critical element of performance and success. Automation provides much of the execution, orchestration, and validation capability within modern delivery systems, but it is decision logic that determines when, how, and under what conditions that automation should operate. In this sense, decisions form the governing core of the system, while automation serves as the mechanism through which those decisions are carried out.

However, the main problem of the modern implementation model is the fact that all the decisions made are implicit. Very little attention is paid to the decision-making process, which leads to decision-making based on scripts and tools. Decisions can be conditioned by certain conditions and policies and can be made automatically; however, the crucial issue is the fact that these decisions remain implicit but define the flow of the processes taking place in the system. This creates a transparency and governance problem because critical decision logic remains hidden inside tools, scripts, and default configurations where it cannot be readily inspected, tested, or audited.

This is one of the shortcomings that arise from a wider gap in thinking. There has been a lot of emphasis put on automating functions and tool integration, but there has not been much emphasis placed on decision-making processes. Systems can carry out their functions in an efficient manner, but they have no way of determining whether their actions are suitable in the existing situation. It is especially difficult when working in environments that change continuously, since decisions have to be flexible enough to respond to changing states.

Applying control systems theory as an architectural model rather than a literal equivalence to continuous physical plants, decision-making serves as the critical link connecting feedback with actuation. Feedback provides information about the present state of the system, while actuation introduces modifications. Decision-making interprets feedback data and determines what actions should be taken, functioning as the governing logic of the system. Without structured decision-making procedures, feedback cannot be translated into proportionate responses, and actuation becomes uncoordinated and potentially counterproductive.

In delivery environments where organizations seek to optimize flow under acceptable thresholds of risk, reliability, compliance, and recovery capability, the significance of decision-making is accentuated by the volume and frequency of changes. Decisions in such settings are not discrete events but a continuous stream of occurrences distributed across pipelines, policy engines, and runtime environments. Each individual decision carries some impact on system behavior, and the aggregate effect of all decisions shapes the system's operational performance, stability, and risk posture.

As the number of decisions increases, particularly in high-frequency environments, systems handling sensitive workloads, and organizations operating at mature platform levels, the disadvantages of ad hoc decision-making become operationally significant. Decisions that lack a structured process behind them may conflict with one another, produce unforeseen outcomes, or fail to respond proportionately to changing conditions.

To overcome these difficulties, decision-making must evolve into controlled control logic for software delivery systems. It will mean designing the decisions that will be made and ensuring they have explicit parameters. Strategic decision-making is associated with improved transparency, consistency, and flexibility and allows for more adaptive responses by a system to varying conditions.

Within this model, decision-making is linked with feedback processes, constraints, and actuation techniques in an integrated control architecture. Policies, when versioned, tested, enforced consistently, auditable, and aligned with accountable risk ownership, provide the governance context within which decisions are made. Feedback from observability and security systems supplies current data on the system state. Actuation mechanisms ensure that the resulting decisions are implemented through proportionate and timely actions. Together, these elements help produce decisions that are not only appropriate in substance but also well-timed relative to the current system conditions.

These changes carry substantial practical significance. When decision-making is established as a central component of system operation, it contributes to improved control, stability, and scalability through specific mechanisms: structured decisions reduce the gap between system state and corrective action, constraint-aligned logic prevents transitions into unsafe states, and consistent decision processes enable reliable behavior across distributed environments. Under these conditions, decisions become operational means through which organizational objectives are pursued.

Key Argument

Software delivery systems are not defined by automation alone – they are defined by how decisions are made, evaluated, and executed under continuous change.

7.2.1 Section Summary

This section established decision-making as the central control function within modern software delivery systems.

The key insights are as follows:

- Automation alone does not determine system behavior; decision logic governs how feedback is interpreted, how constraints are applied, and how actuation is triggered, thereby shaping stability through the coordination of these elements.
- Implicit and tool-driven decisions reduce transparency and control.
- Decision-making links feedback from observability and security sensors to actuation through pipeline mechanisms, with policy engines serving as the decision layer that evaluates signals and determines responses.
- Environments optimizing delivery flow under acceptable risk, reliability, and compliance thresholds face increased decision complexity and volume.
- Decision systems need to be structured so that feedback latency, control thresholds, constraint alignment, and remediation behavior work together to support stability, adaptability, and scalability.

These concepts serve as the basis for the subsequent discussion, which applies control systems theory as an architectural model for reasoning decision-making in software delivery rather than as a literal equivalence to continuous physical systems.

7.3 Decision-Making in Control Systems Theory

Control systems theory, applied here as an architectural model rather than a literal equivalence to continuous physical plants, provides a productive framework for comprehending decision-making within modern software delivery. Under this model, decision-making is not a secondary activity but the primary mechanism through which system behavior is governed. Controllers analyze feedback signals, compare them with predetermined criteria, and determine what actions are needed to guide the system toward its desired state.

When applied as an architectural model to software delivery frameworks, this construct maps productively onto CI/CD pipelines, policy engines, and DevSecOps approaches, provided the policies governing decision logic are versioned, tested, enforced consistently, auditable, and aligned with designated risk ownership. Under these conditions, decisions are made continuously, informed by the current state of the system at each point of evaluation.

7.3.1 Decision as Control Action

In classical control theory, which serves here as an architectural model, the function of the controller includes the interpretation of feedback information and the determination of an adequate response to maintain system stability. This requires a defined mapping between the observed state of the system and a corresponding action, governed by preset objectives and constraints.

Signals representing the current state of the system are fed to the controller as inputs. These may include deviations from desired behavior, environmental changes, or anomalous conditions. For these signals to support sound decisions, they must be timely, correlated across relevant sources, de-duplicated to reduce noise, and interpreted against defined SLOs or policy thresholds rather than treated as inherently reliable raw data. Based on this processed information, the controller determines what corrective or adaptive actions are needed. These actions are carried out through actuators, which modify system behavior and generate additional feedback.

In software delivery systems, decision-making performs an analogous function. Feedback from observability platforms, security scanning tools, and runtime monitors is processed by decision-making mechanisms embedded within pipelines and policy engines. For these mechanisms to deliver genuine control, the policies they enforce must be versioned, tested against representative scenarios, applied consistently across environments, auditable for traceability, and aligned with designated risk ownership.

The mapping of observed system state into action choices represents the core of decision-making as a control process. This mapping determines how feedback signals are translated into proportionate responses, how control thresholds trigger corrective actions, and how remediation behavior is coordinated across distributed components. Without such structured mapping, feedback cannot be transformed into effective actions, and the system's ability to regulate itself through architecture, workload management, and dependency coordination is materially impaired.

7.3.2 Deterministic vs. Adaptive Decision Models

For the purposes of this discussion, decision-making models in control-oriented delivery systems can be grouped into two broad categories, deterministic and adaptive, while acknowledging that the full spectrum of control approaches also includes optimal, stochastic, predictive, and hybrid methods. Each category carries distinct strengths and limitations.

Deterministic decision-making models use predetermined rules and logic that specify what action should be taken for a given set of inputs. Under ideal conditions and within a fully specified rule set, the same input produces the same output. In practice, however, enterprise delivery systems may require exception handling based on risk context, environment, service criticality, or operational circumstances, which can introduce variability even within nominally deterministic frameworks. Deterministic models are straightforward to implement in stable and predictable conditions, making them suitable for static policies, threshold-based gates, and pre-planned deployment processes.

The principal limitation of purely deterministic models is that, when implemented without runtime feedback or contextual inputs, they cannot adapt to changing conditions. In such implementations, contextual factors are not considered, and decisions may prove too restrictive during stable periods or insufficiently protective when environmental volatility increases. For instance, a fixed deployment rule may block low-risk changes unnecessarily under calm conditions while permitting changes that carry elevated risk during periods of system stress.

Adaptive decision-making models, by contrast, adjust their behavior based on the current state of the system. In software delivery, adaptive decisions may take the form of dynamic risk tolerance levels, contextual policy adjustments, or feedback-driven modifications to deployment tactics. These models contribute to stability by aligning decision thresholds with observed system conditions, such as current workload, dependency health, feedback latency, and remediation readiness, rather than relying on static assumptions that may no longer reflect the operational reality.

This tension reflects the broader design challenge of balancing predictability with adaptability. Deterministic techniques improve repeatability and make decision behavior easier to audit, but may lack the flexibility to respond to changing conditions. Adaptive approaches enhance responsiveness to runtime dynamics but introduce additional complexity in design, testing, and governance. A well-balanced system employs both: deterministic logic provides a stable and auditable foundation, while adaptive mechanisms supply the flexibility needed to accommodate conditions that fall outside predetermined rule sets.

7.3.3 Decision Boundaries and Constraints

Decision-making, however, does not operate in an unconstrained space. Applying control theory as an architectural model, the delivery system faces decision-making constraints that define its safe operating envelope. These constraints are designed to prevent decisions from driving the system into unsafe or non-compliant states.

In software delivery systems, decision-making constraints include policies, governance frameworks, and risk tolerance levels. For these constraints to function as effective controls, the underlying policies must be versioned, tested, enforced consistently across environments, auditable, and aligned with designated risk ownership. When these conditions are met, constraints meaningfully bound the decision space and determine which actions are permissible. For instance, a constraint might prevent deployment of software whose assessed risk score exceeds a defined threshold.

The most critical function of decision-making constraints in software delivery is to define and enforce the safe operating envelope of the system. The decision process must reconcile the need for operational flexibility with the requirement that decisions remain within boundaries established by versioned, tested, and consistently enforced policies, so that governance norms and risk limits are not violated (Meadows, 2008).

Applying control systems theory as an architectural model, decision logic is the mechanism that guides system behavior within the boundaries established by constraints, translating observed conditions into actions that keep the system within its defined operating envelope. Figure 7-1 illustrates decision-making in a control system as a closed feedback loop, in which the set point is compared with a measured signal to produce an error that the controller acts upon to keep the process variable close to the desired value (Åström & Murray, 2008).

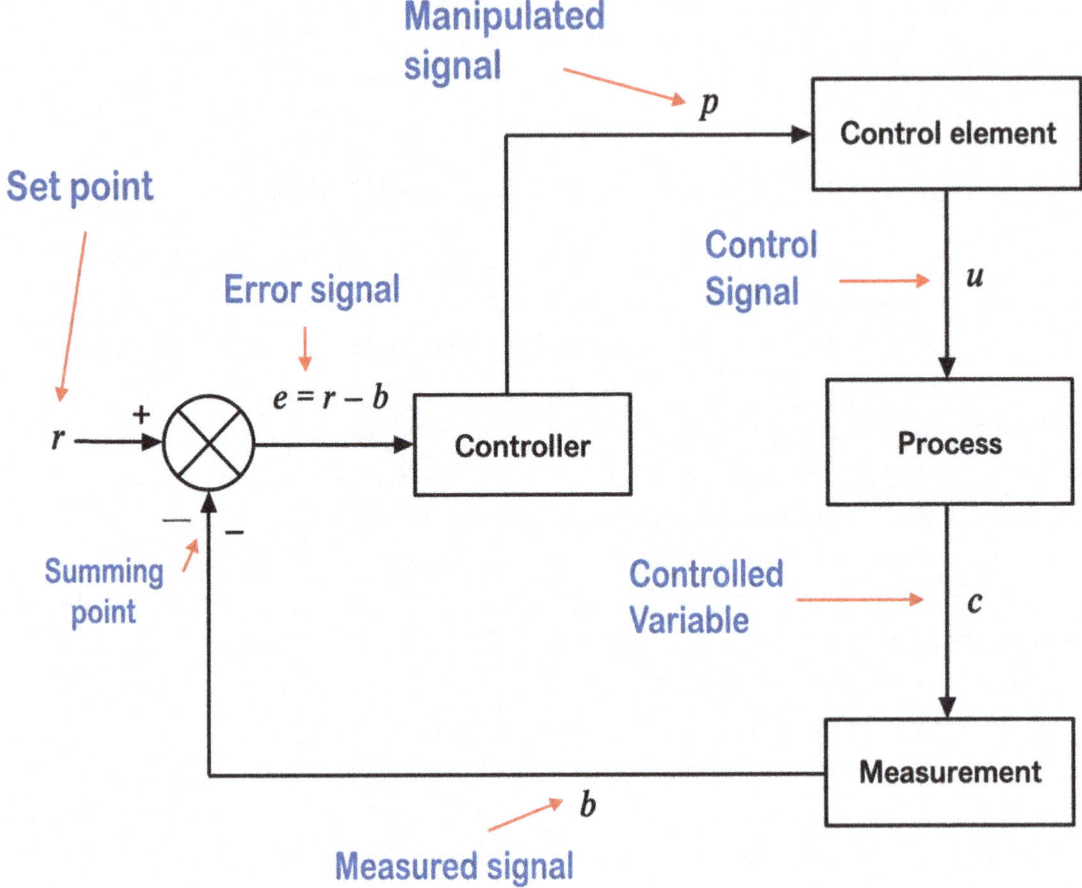

Figure 7-1. *Decision-Making in a Control System*

The diagram above illustrates decision-making within an architectural model derived from control systems theory, applied here to software delivery rather than as a literal representation of a continuous physical system. Feedback signals indicating system state are supplied as inputs to the decision-making layer, where policy-driven rules evaluate the situation against defined goals and constraints. The decision layer produces action directives that are implemented through pipeline actuators. Constraint boundaries limit the available decision space, helping ensure that the resulting actions remain within safe and governable parameters.

Section Summary

This section established decision-making as a fundamental component within the control system architectural model adopted throughout this book, providing the theoretical basis for its role in software delivery while recognizing that software delivery systems are discrete, distributed, and socio-technical in ways that distinguish them from classic continuous-process examples.

The key insights are as follows:

- Decision-making functions as the core control action linking feedback to actuation.
- Deterministic and adaptive models offer complementary approaches to decision design.
- Constraints, when codified in versioned and testable policies that are enforced consistently and auditable for traceability, define the decision space and support safe system operation.
- An effective decision system should be predictable, flexible, and controllable.

These guidelines form the basis of studying decisions in the CI/CD and DevSecOps pipeline, which will be discussed in the following section.

7.4 Decision Points in CI/CD and DevSecOps Pipelines

Within software delivery systems that are control oriented, decision-making is not centralized in a specific point within the process but rather spread throughout the lifecycle of the delivery pipeline itself. In CI/CD and DevSecOps environments, there are several distinct processes involved, and each contains several decision points where behavior is assessed and an action is taken as a result. It is within these decision points that the control structure exists.

It is crucial to understand how and where decisions take place within software delivery system design. In high-frequency environments, systems handling sensitive workloads, and organizations operating at mature platform levels, the structure, visibility, and coordination of decision points materially influence system performance and robustness.

7.4.1 Types of Decision Points

Decision points in software delivery systems can be classified by their position in the delivery lifecycle: pre-deployment, deployment-time, and post-deployment phases. Each phase performs a distinct control function, and in systems where runtime behavior, workload patterns, and dependency interactions create material operational risk, the coordinated operation of all three phases contributes to overall system stability.

Pre-deployment decision-making is the first level of decision-making. In this case, the input artifacts such as source code, configuration, and dependencies of the application are checked before deployment into the system. The decisions made on the pre-deployment stage deal with prevention and are aimed at excluding the risks of introducing unstable elements into the system through the application of certain quality criteria to the inputs.

Deployment decisions are taken during the actual implementation of changes. They encompass rollout strategy selection, scaling adjustments, and the application of runtime constraints. For these decisions to function as effective controls, the policies governing them must be versioned, tested, enforced consistently, auditable, and aligned with designated risk ownership. Unlike pre-deployment decisions, which focus on approval or rejection, deployment decisions are concerned with managing how changes are introduced and propagated through the system.

Post-deployment decision-making represents the final tier in the decision hierarchy. During this stage, system behavior is closely monitored to determine whether the implemented changes are producing the intended outcomes. Decisions at this stage may include maintaining the current state, initiating a rollback toward a previously known-good operating condition, or reconfiguring system parameters. It should be noted that in distributed or stateful architectures, rollback may not fully restore prior behavior due to factors such as database migrations, message queue state, cache invalidation, external side effects, or dependency changes; rollback is therefore best understood as a recovery mechanism rather than a guaranteed reversal.

In delivery environments where runtime conditions, workload variability, and cross-service dependencies create material operational risk, these stages form a layered and interdependent decision-making process whose coordination directly influences system stability and reliability.

7.4.2 Explicit vs. Implicit Decisions

A further way of categorizing decision points is based on how they are formulated and implemented in the system, which plays an essential role in comprehending the quality of a system's decision-making process.

Explicit decisions are those that are formally defined and deliberately engineered into the system. They are enabled by predefined policies, rules, and decision-making logic that specify criteria and actions, provided those policies are versioned, tested, enforced consistently, auditable, and aligned with designated risk ownership. Because explicit decisions are visible and controllable, their behavior can be inspected, analyzed, and refined through iterative feedback.

Implicit decisions arise from interactions between system components, including configuration tools, default settings, and inherited behaviors. These decisions are not formally defined but emerge from the way the system has been assembled and configured. While implicit decisions may function acceptably under predictable conditions, they carry materially higher risk in high-frequency delivery environments, systems handling sensitive workloads, and architectures where runtime behavior can diverge significantly from design assumptions, because they are difficult to detect, audit, or systematically improve.

The first danger in implicit decision-making lies in the possibility of a hidden decision rule. There is no certainty about the way in which this system works if there is no knowledge concerning the process of decision-making. In addition, such circumstances could lead to inconsistencies in the process of making decisions.

Applying control systems theory as an architectural model, explicit decision-making increases the controllability and observability of the delivery system by making decision logic visible, testable, and auditable. Implicit decision-making, by contrast, reduces these properties by embedding consequential logic in locations that are difficult to inspect or govern.

7.4.3 Frequency and Distribution of Decisions

A distinguishing feature of contemporary software delivery is the volume and decentralization of decision-making. Where organizations seek to optimize flow under acceptable levels of risk, reliability, compliance, and recovery capability, CI/CD and DevSecOps processes generate a continuous stream of decisions distributed across multiple system layers Google (2022) and CNCF (2023).

At one level, micro-level decisions include evaluating test results, checking conditions defined by versioned and auditable policies, and adjusting deployment-related parameters. These decisions are made rapidly and often automatically, forming an essential part of continuous delivery processes. Their effectiveness as controls depends on whether the policies governing them are tested, enforced consistently, and aligned with accountable risk ownership (Kim, Humble, Debois, & Willis, 2021).

Simultaneously, decision-making is distributed across multiple systems and components, including pipelines, policy engines, runtime environments, and monitoring platforms. For this decentralized architecture to function as coherent control rather than fragmented logic, the policies governing each component must be versioned, tested, enforced consistently, auditable, and aligned with a shared governance framework and designated risk ownership (Humble & Farley, 2010).

Decision design is made even more important due to the fact that there is a high frequency of decision-making along with distribution (Forsgren, Humble, & Kim, 2018). Lack of coordination among individuals involved in decision-making could result in their decisions colliding and, hence, creating instability. A good system will solve the problem of non-coordination of decisions. Table 7-1 summarizes the key decision points that arise across the software delivery process (Bass, Weber, & Zhu, 2015).

Table 7-1. *Decision Points in Software Delivery*

Decision Stage	Decision Type	Impact
Pre-deployment	Validation	Prevent risk
Deployment	Execution control	Manage rollout
Post-deployment	Evaluation	Ensure stability

Section Summary

This section examined the structure and characteristics of decision points within CI/CD and DevSecOps pipelines.

The key insights are as follows:

- Decision-making is distributed across multiple stages of the delivery lifecycle.

- Pre-deployment, deployment-time, and post-deployment decisions serve distinct control functions.
- Explicit decision logic enhances transparency and control, while implicit logic introduces risk.
- High-frequency and distributed decisions increase system complexity.
- Coordinated decision design is essential for maintaining stability and scalability.

These findings highlight that decision points are not isolated elements but integral components of a broader control system, shaping how software delivery systems operate under continuous change.

7.5 Decision Models in Software Delivery Systems

The decision-making process in software delivery systems is carried out via different decision-making models which describe how feedback is understood and which decisions are made based on such understanding. These decision models are important elements of software delivery systems because they influence their architecture, flexibility, and reactivity, enabling them to function efficiently in an environment of constant change. Over time, there has been a development of different decision models from more static to much more dynamic and intelligent.

Different decision models are used to solve specific problems of dealing with the state of the system, risk, and uncertainty. Although decision models may be examined separately, they are usually combined into hierarchies of decisions.

7.5.1 Rule-Based Decision Models

Rule-based decision models are considered the most primitive forms of decision-making within software delivery systems. They utilize predetermined rules that establish mappings from certain conditions to particular actions, where, upon detecting a given condition, a specific action is always performed in a deterministic way.

Predictability and repeatability are the key strengths of rule-based decision models. The logic behind them is easily visible and understandable, and as such, the models themselves are highly consistent. Rule-based decisions within CI/CD pipelines are implemented via policy check, validation gate, and conditional execution components.

The downside of using rule-based models lies in their static nature. Since the rules are fixed and do not change based on new information, such as workload, risk environment, or even external variables, rule-based decisions can be too permissive or too restrictive, failing to properly balance between these two extremes.

Rule-based decision models in control systems translate to deterministic controllers that function well in a stable environment but fail in the case of changing dynamics of the system.

7.5.2 Risk-Based Decision Models

Unlike the rule-based model, the risk-based decision model goes further to consider the risk involved when an action is taken. The risk involved is evaluated continuously, and this is used in making decisions about what action to take.

The level of risk involved in an action is evaluated using a rating scale. The scoring involves various factors, including the risk severity, system criticality, and circumstances under which the change is proposed. The score generated is compared to a threshold level defined by policies and used in decision-making.

With the risk-based model, decision-making can be much finer. Unlike in rule-based decision-making, the model allows for discrimination between changes with low and high risk, thereby enabling proportional decisions. For instance, in the case of low-risk changes, little restriction can be imposed, whereas high-risk changes may require validation before implementation.

The risk-based decision model provides a flexible but controlled way of decision-making. It allows for fine-tuning of decisions based on the state of the system. This makes the decision process one of continuous control.

7.5.3 Feedback-Driven Decision Models

The feedback-based approach is another way to increase the flexibility of decision-making systems by taking into account the state of the system at each moment in time when making decisions. Feedback-based decisions are continuously based on various types of feedback such as performance, observability, and security data.

In contrast to other models that use rules or rely only on risk analysis, the feedback approach stresses dynamism in decision-making. The decisions in a feedback-based model are not only based on some threshold values. Instead, decisions are continuously modified according to changes in the state of the system.

For instance, deployment and scaling may take place depending on real-time information about performance and traffic. Such constant interaction of decisions with feedback data results in the flexibility of the system.

It is necessary to mention that feedback-based decisions can be considered a type of closed-loop control in the field of control systems theory.

7.5.4 Machine-Assisted Decision Models

Due to the growing complexity of software distribution systems, machine-assisted decision models have been put in place, employing artificial intelligence and machine learning tools for improved decision-making. Such models process huge amounts of data and use the results to discover patterns, find anomalies, and assist in decision-making.

As it relates to machine learning technologies, their strength lies in anomaly detection, predicting risks, and optimizing deployment policies. Machine learning models learn from both historical data and real-time input, thus discovering patterns that would be missed by other models based solely on thresholds or rules Goodfellow, Bengio, & Courville (2016).

There are certain disadvantages related to the use of machine learning algorithms. Firstly, they are much more complex, which makes it difficult to comprehend the process of decision-making. Another issue connected to them concerns their dependency on the quality of the input data. That is why, in combination with other techniques, decision-making with the help of a machine is used. The involvement of a person in the process plays an important role as well (Sculley et al., 2015).

As a control approach, such methods represent the shift toward intelligent control, which includes feedback along with learning and prediction elements in the decision-making process. Figure 7-2 presents the decision-model spectrum, ranging from rigid, deterministic rule-based AI, through hybrid approaches, to implicit, language-based AI, highlighting the strengths and limitations of each along the continuum.

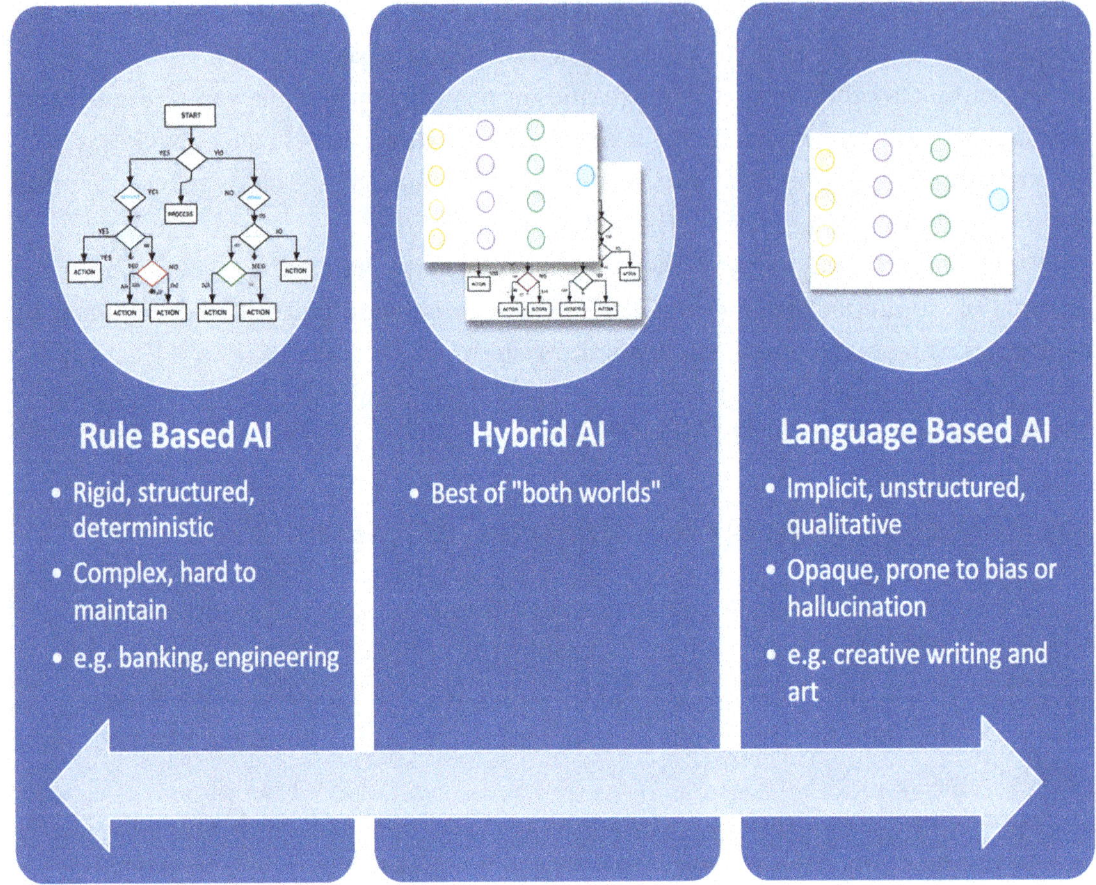

Figure 7-2. *The spectrum of decision models ranges from*

Spectrum of decision models from rule-based deterministic approaches to adaptive risk- and feedback-driven methods and AI-assisted intelligent systems.

Section Summary

This section examined the evolution and characteristics of decision models in software delivery systems.

The key insights are as follows:

- Rule-based models provide predictability but lack flexibility.
- Risk-based models enable proportional and context-aware decisions.
- Feedback-driven models support real-time adaptation and closed-loop control.

- Machine-assisted models enhance decision-making through learning and prediction.
- Effective systems combine multiple decision models to balance control and adaptability.

These results provide the basis for examining the process by which decisions are actually made, especially when considering automation and human supervision, which will be discussed in the following section.

7.6 Automation vs. Human-in-the-Loop Decision-Making

The decision-making aspect within software delivery systems has gradually become something of an area between automation and human intuition. With developments in CI/CD and DevSecOps methodologies, organizations have to think not only about what decisions need to be taken but also about how to make such decisions and who should be making them. Here comes the main challenge in designing control-oriented systems, which is how to reconcile the fast-paced decisions made by automated systems with the context-awareness of human decision-making.

In terms of a control-oriented system, this reconciliation comes down to reconciling the determinism of the system's operation with its adaptiveness to changing conditions. Automated decision-making allows for quick and consistent responses, whereas humans in the loop provide additional room for interpretation and flexibility.

7.6.1 Fully Automated Decisions

The full automation of decision-making is the most immediate form of the application of the principles of control within software distribution systems. Under such conditions, decisions are being performed only based on predetermined rules, policies, and algorithms, without any involvement of humans. Such an approach appears to be more efficient for high-frequency environments since under these conditions, decisions have to be made quickly and uniformly across systems of any scale Kahneman (2011).

The main benefits of the automation are its speed and consistency. Automation implies that decisions can be made instantly as soon as feedback signals appear and, therefore, enables a continuous delivery cycle. Moreover, due to the elimination of any variations that could occur due to human interaction, such decisions can be performed consistently regardless of the environment.

Nevertheless, despite its benefits, the approach is subject to many restrictions since the logic applied by automated solutions remains predetermined. This could lead to overly rigid decision-making, wherein decisions are taken without taking into account any contextual nuances. In a constantly changing environment, rigidity in decision-making could lead to wrong decisions, including deployment failures that are not necessary and an over-constriction of the system's performance parameters Taleb (2007).

The accuracy and reliability of input information and the decision-making process of automation are also vulnerable to errors. This is because any mistake in the policies governing decision-making and the information derived from feedback would be amplified throughout the automation system. From the perspective of control systems, this is the danger of overdependence on deterministic control.

7.6.2 Human-in-the-Loop Models

Human-in-the-loop decision-making is a technique whereby humans intervene in the decision-making loop and incorporate their judgment into the decision process. As a result, the decision-making takes into consideration not only the available data but also the context and experience.

The major benefit of such an approach is its capability to deal with more complicated scenarios. Human beings are able to interpret signals that are unclear for machines, take into account the general context of the system, and make sophisticated decisions that cannot always be made automatically.

At the same time, human intervention into the process of decision-making means the introduction of delays. While the automated decision-making process takes place instantly, humans need some time to make decisions after receiving recommendations and analyzing information. It creates certain limitations in a highly demanding environment.

Human judgment could be another source of variability because people perceive similar conditions in their own ways. Such variability affects the way system operation becomes unpredictable, especially in cases of distributed systems.

Control systems theory suggests that human decision-making adds flexibility to system operation at the expense of decreasing its speed and responsiveness.

7.6.3 Hybrid Decision Systems

The shortcomings of either fully automated or completely manual decision-making models have led to the adoption of hybrid models within today's software delivery platforms. Hybrid models make it possible for platforms to deliver efficiency as well as the capability to deal with challenging environments.

Hybrid models allow for routine and non-critical decisions to be made using automation. However, critical decisions are escalated to human operators who review such decisions manually and provide their approval or rejection. This model makes it possible to apply human judgment in cases where it would add the most value.

Escalation models are important components of hybrid models because they define the point at which human operators must intervene in decision-making processes. Escalation points are usually determined by critical factors, such as risks, uncertainty, or policy violations. For instance, an activity with low risk could be approved using automation, but a high-risk activity would require human approval.

The hybrid model also allows for progressive decision-making, wherein decisions are made at different levels of analysis. The system can start with automated analysis and then be reviewed by a human operator when critical decisions need to be made.

In the domain of control systems, a hybrid system is a control system that utilizes both deterministic and adaptive control approaches. Table 7-2 compares the main decision models, contrasting their characteristics, strengths, and limitations.

Table 7-2. *Decision Models Comparison*

Model	Advantage	Limitation
Automated	Fast, consistent	Limited context
Human-in-loop	Flexible	Slower
Hybrid	Balanced	More complex

Section Summary

This section examined the trade-offs and integration of automated and human-driven decision-making within software delivery systems.

The key insights are as follows:

- Automation is efficient and consistent but lacks the element of contextual awareness.
- Human-in-the-loop strategy allows flexibility and the application of human intelligence but introduces the factor of time inconsistency.
- Hybrid decision-making is a combination of the two strategies.

Decision design is dependent upon the alignment of decision models with the system's risk, complexity, and environment.

Such outcomes indicate that when making decisions in current delivery systems, one should not make a choice between technology and human intervention, but rather use both strategically in order to enable stability and scalability amid changes.

7.7 Decision Latency and System Stability

In control-based delivery systems, the concept of decision-making cannot simply be reduced to which decisions get made; rather, the critical factor of timing must also be considered. Timing in decision processes is known as decision latency, and it holds an extremely important place in the determination of system stability and responsiveness, as well as its effectiveness. As was shown in the previous sections, decision-making acts as the bridge between feedback and actuation. However, the introduction of latency causes the decision process to introduce a time delay into this equation.

As such, in environments characterized by high frequency and dynamics of change, even a small delay in the feedback-action link may result in a misalignment between changes occurring in the system and actions taken in response to these changes. In other words, misalignment results from an inability of the decision process to react fast enough.

7.7.1 Decision Latency in Control Systems

Latency, sometimes called time delay, is defined as the duration from when a system's state is detected until a correction is performed in classical control theory. The reason behind such latency can be attributed to either sensing issues, calculation time, or actuator latency. However, regardless of the source of latency, the gap between the true state of the system and the controller's response reduces the efficiency of the control.

Introduction of latency brings about new dimensions in the whole process of control. This is because the controller acts on the basis of past information, and thus, its decisions may end up being inconsistent with the real condition of the system. The situation gives rise to a phase lag, where action may be delayed too much for it to serve any useful purpose. In certain cases, this phase lag could result in the instability of the system (Ogata, 2010).

As theoretical studies reveal, the presence of latency decreases the stability reserve of a process. The longer the delay period, the more susceptible a process becomes to disturbances and the less its ability to remain stable. It is essential to consider this effect in the development of delivery systems of software, as here all changes are fast and there are plenty of feedback loops.

It is therefore possible to define the decision latency in such a case as the inefficiency of the control function due to time considerations.

7.7.2 Impact on Software Delivery Systems

The implications of latency in decision-making are most evident when applied to modern software delivery platforms, where the software operates in an environment marked by constant changes and frequent deployments.

The first consequence of this latency is related to delayed corrective actions, which happen when decisions are made too slowly compared to the speed of changes that occur within the software. For example, while performance issues have been picked up by the software and are flagged by its monitoring tools, a proper solution may come late, meaning that by the time something is done about the problem, the software has suffered its consequences.

On the other hand, reducing latency, without paying due attention to decision quality, may result in another kind of instability within the software platform. Making quick, yet poorly informed decisions can often be detrimental to the system, since such actions may be triggered by false positives.

The result is an important compromise between speed and accuracy of decision-making, where speed comes at the cost of accuracy and vice versa. Decisions have to be timely yet correct, which necessitates striking the proper balance between these two considerations in any effective control process.

In fast-paced environments, however, the relationship between latency and the nature of a dynamic system takes on a whole new layer of complexity. Continuous integration and continuous delivery chains create a constant stream of modifications that must be assessed and acted upon. Without adequate latency consideration, such decisions could be taken in respect of old system states, creating a chain reaction of mismatches and errors.

To illustrate this point, suppose several deployment operations are carried out in short succession. The high decision latency could mean that any corrections made following the previous modifications have been applied following the changes to the system state by another deployment, causing the actions to cancel each other out.

7.7.3 Synchronization with Feedback and Actuation

In order to address latency issues, the process of decision-making should be properly synchronized with both the feedback and the actuation components.

The process of synchronization within control systems takes into account the proper coordination of sensing, decision-making, and actuation processes.

Synchronization in software delivery systems entails various aspects of importance:

Firstly, feedback systems should provide data in a timely manner with minimal noise levels. It means that observability platforms, monitoring, and security should be adjusted in a way to decrease delays and noise to enable decision logic to operate on exact information.

Secondly, decision-making should be optimized to enable efficient and timely processing. Such optimization may entail minimizing overhead and maximizing efficiency of decision-making by applying specific evaluation techniques, for instance, incrementally, event-driven decision, caching, etc.

Thirdly, the actuator needs to be able to act swiftly and in synchronization. The CI/CD process, deployment engines, and runtime engines need to make these decisions without causing further delay.

The interplay between the above-mentioned elements results in what may be referred to as a temporal control loop, with each phase timing being an important factor affecting the system performance. Disruption in the relationship between the feedback, decision, and actuation processes can lead to instabilities, even if individually each element functions properly.

The idea of temporal coherence plays an essential role here. All of the elements of the system must follow a synchronized timeline. Figure 7-3 shows the effect of decision latency on stability, illustrating how a controlled variable responds to a disturbance over time and how varying system gain produces overdamped, critically damped, and underdamped behavior.

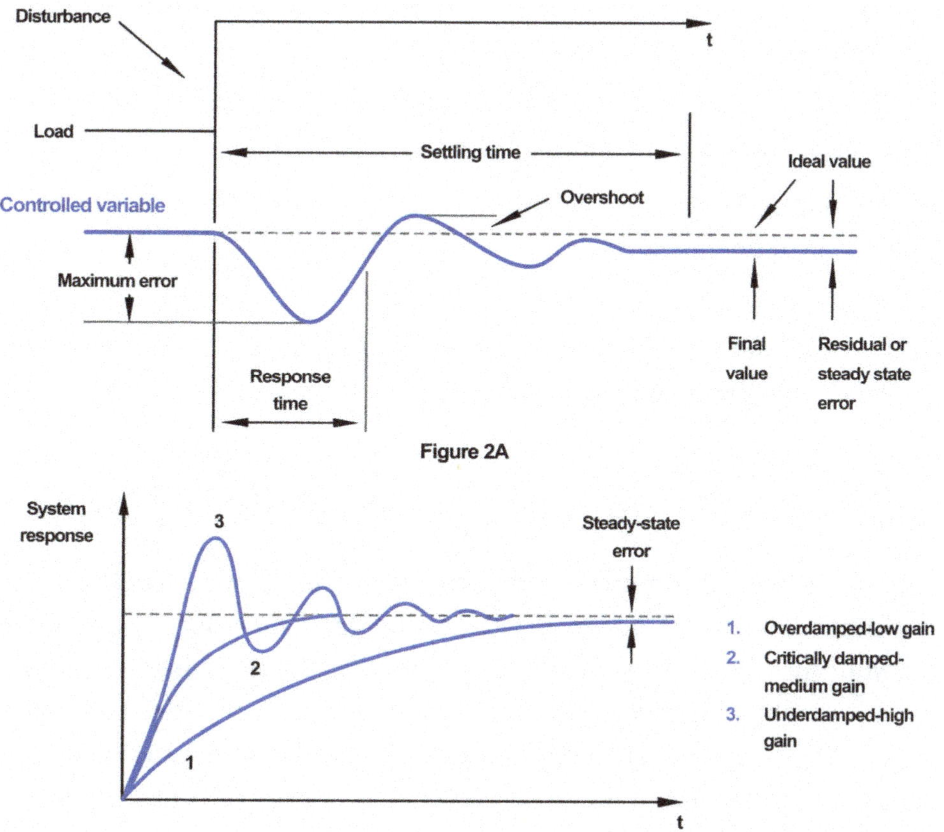

***Figure 7-3.** Effect of Decision Latency on Stability*

This figure shows the impact of decision latency on system stability, showing smooth convergence, delayed response, and oscillatory or divergent behavior.

Section Summary

This section examined the role of decision latency as a critical factor influencing system stability in software delivery environments.

The key insights are as follows:

- Decision latency represents the delay between feedback and action within the control loop.
- Increased latency reduces control effectiveness and can destabilize system behavior.
- Slow decisions lead to delayed correction, while fast but uninformed decisions introduce instability.
- Synchronization between feedback, decision-making, and actuation is essential for maintaining stability.
- Temporal alignment and coherence are critical design considerations in high-frequency systems.

Such results confirm that good decision-making cannot be limited to just rationality and structure, but timing is equally important and needs to be handled in order to build sustainable, adaptive, and scalable software delivery frameworks.

7.8 Decision Errors and System Failure Modes

In the control-oriented SD process frameworks, the quality of system performance is ultimately determined by the quality of decision-making that influences its behavior. However, while the role of decision-making in providing for a link between feedback and actuation was emphasized earlier, the importance of understanding decision-related error and how it propagates to system failure cannot be overstated. Decision errors are related to the malfunctioning of the control process in terms of the discrepancy between actions taken and system conditions, limitations, or goals.

As opposed to traditional approaches to fault diagnosis and failure analysis, decision-driven models take into account both the logic and temporal aspects of system response. In a modern CI/CD or DevSecOps environment characterized by distributed, automated, and continuous decision-making, even minor errors may have far-reaching consequences, manifesting themselves in the form of failure in different parts of the system. In addition to technical defects, such decision errors may often reflect underlying problems with feedback or policy implementation.

7.8.1 Types of Decision Errors

The errors in decision-making in software delivery systems can be classified into three main types which include incorrect decisions, delayed decisions, and missing decisions. Both types are failures in the control process and can be characterized by different implications for system behavior.

The wrong choices are made when the system chooses an action that is not related to the real state or demands of the system. This can be due to faulty reasoning, a misunderstanding of feedback, or wrong policy analysis. As an illustration, a deployment can be done without critical vulnerabilities, or a rollback can be caused without reason based on false-positive indicators. Mistakes in decision-making are especially hazardous as they actively drive the system in unwanted directions.

Delayed decisions are due to a large time interval between the occurrence of a condition and action implementation. Latency causes the misalignment of the system state and response, as explained in the section "Decision Latency and System Stability." There is no strong possibility that delayed decisions are wrong, just that they are untimely. Even the right choice may turn out to be wrong in a dynamic environment when implemented late.

Missing decisions are the lack of action that is necessary. The system in this instance does not react to a situation that needs to be addressed. This can be a result of policy coverage gaps, failure in detection mechanisms, or failure of communication between the system components. Missing decisions are of great concern, especially because they enable issues to continue and get out of control.

These three types underline that the errors in decisions are not restricted to erroneous logic, but also include errors in timing and completion, which are the fundamental elements of effective control.

7.8.2 Causes of Decision Failure

Decision-making mistakes cannot happen in a vacuum. There are fundamental flaws in the system design, feedback processes, or operations that cause decision failures in software delivery systems. Below are some factors that often lead to such failures.

First, there is the issue of faulty feedback. For decision-making to be effective, the system needs to have access to reliable information regarding its state at any given point in time. With feedback information being faulty, the decisions the system makes could easily be wrong. Incorrect feedback can generate false alarms that can make the system take action that is unnecessary or even harm the entire system operation. This would be a lack of observability in control system terms, which affects the controllability of the system.

Second, decision failures could arise from inadequate policy formulation. Policies represent the logical approach that the system will use to make decisions. They are composed of rules that set decision thresholds and criteria for deciding whether certain conditions exist.

Complexity is another important issue when it comes to decision-making within software distribution systems. Larger and larger-scale systems involve the growing distribution and connectivity of software delivery systems. Consequently, decision-making processes may span several pipelines, services, and even platforms with varying logics, which can lead to emerging system properties that are hard to understand and control.

The aforementioned complexity of systems leads to potential inconsistencies in decision-making processes that are often fragmented or replicated in several parts of the software system. Complex software systems can suffer from synchronization problems in which decisions that are made in different parts of the software distribution system might contradict each other.

Among other causes of decision problems in software delivery systems are poor testing of decision-making logic and inadequate monitoring of decision-making processes.

7.8.3 Impact on System Behavior

Decision errors not only affect individual decisions but also the entire system's behavior and stability. For control systems, decision errors may result in a number of failure modes, such as instability, oscillation, and cascade effects.

First, decision errors could lead to the occurrence of instability in a system, which means that the system would not be able to stay in one condition. Erroneous or delayed decisions may drive the system to operate differently, causing it to underperform, make errors more frequently, or become vulnerable to security threats.

In addition to that, decision errors could also result in oscillations in a system, which means that the system will continuously switch between different conditions due to overcompensation. For instance, fast iterations of deployment and rollback processes are likely to happen if the system overreacts to information feedback.

Cascading failure is another very important mode of failure, where mistakes propagate from one part of the system to other parts, causing large-scale disruption. Decision errors such as updating the wrong configuration or scaling services improperly in the distributed environment may start a cascade that will affect many services and become increasingly problematic due to the speed and automation in the delivery process.

Mistakes made in decision-making can cause system drift, where the system state does not match desired states after a while. This happens because the decisions were either too slow or were never made in the first place.

As can be seen from the point of view of control theory, mistakes made in decision-making break the balance among feedback, decision, and actuation, which causes disruption of behavior regulation and thus becomes the reason for instability. Table 7-3 outlines common decision failure patterns and their typical causes.

Table 7-3. *Decision Failure Patterns*

Failure Type	Cause	Impact
Incorrect decision	Faulty logic	Instability
Delayed decision	Latency	Drift
Missing decision	Lack of control	System failure

Section Summary

This section examined the nature, causes, and consequences of decision errors within software delivery systems.

The key insights are as follows:

- Decision errors represent failures in logic, timing, or completeness of the control process.
- Incorrect, delayed, and missing decisions each produce distinct system risks.

- Poor feedback quality, weak policy design, and system complexity are primary causes of decision failure.
- Decision errors can lead to instability, oscillation, cascading failures, and system drift.
- Effective system design requires continuous monitoring and refinement of decision processes.

These results demonstrate that decision-making does not only act as an enabling device but may also result in error. It follows that a resilient system should not only rely on good decision-making processes but also incorporate detection and recovery measures for any mistakes made in decision-making.

7.9 Designing Effective Decision Systems

In today's world, the success of modern software delivery systems does not depend on the presence of automation, but rather on the nature and structure of the decision-making systems underlying automation. From the above discussion, it becomes clear that decision-making is the key to controlling any system's automation, with feedback being one of the key inputs into the decision-making process.

The process of designing decision-making systems is dependent on a number of factors, which include system dynamics, feedback dynamics, contextual information, and constraints. In addition, the process of designing decisions needs to be viewed not only in terms of making the right decision but also in terms of making the decision quickly and consistently in order to achieve specific goals and objectives.

In this section, we will explore the process of developing decision-making systems from a structured perspective.

7.9.1 Principles of Decision Design

There are certain key design concepts upon which efficient decision systems rely in order to function effectively. Clarity and alignment are two of the most crucial of such design concepts.

A clear and transparent design means that decision logic is clearly defined and can be seen and understood by others. When decision-making processes are complex because of the involvement of many different elements, it is often hard to grasp what kind of decisions are being made, especially in the case of failure. Transparent decisions enhance observability and auditability and make it easier for designers to improve the decision process through iterative feedback.

Another important concept of efficient decision systems is alignment. Every decision system should align itself with the greater goals of the whole company: performance goals, security needs, etc. There may be cases when a company makes decisions that are not aligned with its goals and, on the contrary, prevent it from reaching its aims efficiently. Such decisions will create a conflict of interest.

In terms of control systems theory, the principles are reflective of the design process of a well-designed controller, with inputs, outputs, and logic being clearly laid out for the purposes of the system. If that is not done, then even proper decisions might yield improper results.

7.9.2 Feedback-Aware Decision Logic

The feedback mechanism needs to be tightly coupled with the decision systems in order to ensure that all actions taken reflect the current state of the system. With feedback-aware logic, decisions can go beyond rule-based executions and become dynamic and contextual in nature.

This means leveraging information from observability tools through real-time data from various sources, including metrics, logs, traces, and security information. Such information allows decision systems to understand their current operational state and the state of the overall system at any particular moment. This makes decision-making more contextual rather than dependent on fixed assumptions.

Such a feedback mechanism becomes especially relevant when decisions need to be made in a variable environment with some degree of uncertainty. Thus, for instance, a decision regarding the deployment of software could be made based not just on the quality of the code, but also on the current load of the system, error rate, and dependencies on other systems.

Nevertheless, when incorporating feedback into the system, some issues arise from factors such as signal quality, latency, and noise. The system should include measures for filtering, weighting, and verifying the feedback signal to avoid basing decisions on erroneous signals. Otherwise, the system becomes prone to instabilities due to its reactions to transient signals.

From the viewpoint of control theory, the feedback-informed decision-making approach increases the agility of the controller, allowing it to align itself with the system dynamics.

7.9.3 Constraint-Aligned Decisions

Decision-making systems should have clear boundaries so that all the activities carried out during decision-making are within reasonable limits. Such boundaries are set using constraints. Decision-making in the context of the decision-making boundary requires that the decisions made are within a safe and acceptable range.

Constraint-oriented decision-making implies that the decisions made are appropriate for the situation at hand and comply with policies, governance principles, and risk tolerance levels. Constraints such as policies, governance structures, and risk thresholds are essential in determining the logic used in decision-making, which prevents activities from causing instability, security problems, and policy infringement.

The idea of safe operating zones is critical in constraint-oriented decision-making. The system can operate freely within the safe zone, while outside the zone, the decisions made will be controlled.

However, it is equally important to note that there should be flexibility within the constraints. This is because the environment being dynamic, there will always be a need for change in the constraint itself according to the environment. This means that in case of a risky environment, strict constraints are set, and in a safe environment, loose constraints are set.

In terms of control systems, constraints act as the limit to how the system behaves.

7.9.4 Scalability of Decision Systems

As software delivery processes scale across teams, services, and environments, decision-making processes need to scale as well to preserve consistency and efficacy. Scalability poses significant technical and organizational challenges, as the ability to operate at scale mandates that decision systems be capable of functioning within distributed and heterogeneous environments.

A major requirement for operating at scale is distributed decision-making, which involves executing decisions within separate system components such as pipelines, services, and platforms. Although the ability to make decisions across different parts of the system provides great flexibility, it also creates inconsistencies. Decision-making in distributed settings involves ensuring that decisions are consistent with each other.

In order to standardize the process of decision-making, there must be some coordination mechanisms used in order to coordinate policies in a single entity. For example, Policy as Code can prove to be quite instrumental in creating decision-making processes that scale. Another important aspect to consider is that of consistency in multiple environments. The decision-making process must ensure that consistency in the same situation is maintained regardless of the environment.

In the context of scalable decision systems, performance is also a critical consideration. As the number of decisions grows, systems need to be able to handle feedback and decision-making logic without causing delays. Event-based architecture, distributed computing, and caching are some methods that can be used to enhance performance in scalability scenarios.

From the perspective of control systems, scalability also entails coordinated control of the various components involved. Table 7-4 presents the core design principles for building sound decision mechanisms.

Table 7-4. *Decision Design Principles*

Principle	Description	Benefit
Clarity	Transparent logic	Predictability
Adaptability	Context-aware decisions	Flexibility
Alignment	Matches system goals	Better outcomes
Scalability	Works across systems	Consistency

Section Summary

This section established a comprehensive framework for designing effective decision systems in software delivery environments.

The key insights are as follows:

- Decision systems must be explicitly designed as control architectures, not implicit rule sets.
- Clarity and alignment ensure transparency and consistency in decision-making.

- Feedback-aware logic enables context-sensitive and adaptive decisions.
- Constraint alignment ensures safe and controlled system behavior.
- Scalability requires distributed coordination and consistent policy enforcement.

These tenets clearly show that efficient decision-making systems are the basis for stability, adaptability, and scalability in contemporary software development. By incorporating feedback loops, constraints, and scalability in the design of decision-making systems, businesses can develop systems that do more than just react to change; they can influence the behavior of the system itself.

7.10 Decision as a Driver of System Behavior

Decision-making in control-oriented software delivery systems is viewed as a reactive process – a response to the state of the system or the signals received from the system. Nevertheless, this understanding overlooks its essential nature. The decisions made do not react to the system state but create it, shape it, and keep transforming it. In today's world of CI/CD and DevSecOps practices, the decision-making process becomes the primary means of evolving, constraining, and stabilizing the behavior of the software delivery system.

In essence, every software delivery system is based on a series of decisions that dictate the way how inputs affect the outputs, i.e., how actions will be performed in response to the inputs. The effect that the input has on the output depends, first of all, on the decisions made during the process. Thus, in the course of time, particular patterns of decision-making emerge that define how the system operates in the changing environment, manages risks, and keeps its balance.

The first area in which decisions affect the behavior of systems includes the interaction of policies and decision-making. The former defines rules that constrain the way decisions can be made, while the latter involves the actual execution of decisions. Overall, policy and decision logic combine together to create a consistent system of actions that defines its behavior. For instance, a stringent security policy and decision-making logic may result in the development of secure yet inefficient systems. In their turn, more flexible policies may result in quick solutions but also increased vulnerability to possible risks. In other words, system behavior cannot be regarded as an intrinsic property of the system itself but as a result of decisions being made.

Another important influence of decisions on system behavior is related to the way systems evolve. Traditionally, systems undergo changes only occasionally. However, current systems deliver updates based on continuous integration and delivery. As a result, decision-making becomes an ongoing process of adjusting system behavior and creating conditions that facilitate its further evolution.

Continuous decision-making enables systems to be dynamic and adjust accordingly to changes in their environment, including varying workloads, threats, and demands. Nevertheless, it comes with increased complexity, since the accumulation of several decisions made can lead to the emergence of the system. In cases where decision rules are carefully defined, the continuous decision-making process ensures evolutionary change in the system. In other situations, where decision-making rules are not properly defined, the result might be a form of drift and instability.

It is important to note that decision-making within systems can influence patterns in either direction, depending on what decisions have been made repeatedly by the system. For example, decisions that continuously scale out, or frequently reverse changes, can create feedback loops that enforce the pattern. The decision process thus influences not just what happens at the time of decision-making but also in the long term, because patterns are reinforced by repeated decision rules.

When we consider the system from a control theory standpoint, decision-making becomes the very process that determines the nature of the response function of the system – a function that specifies how the system responds to external disturbances, how fast it reaches its target states, and how stable it remains through changes. In this way, any modification of the decision-making rules necessarily changes the behavior of the system itself.

Additionally, decision-making affects the stability and flexibility trade-off. A system based on static decision-making rules tends to become stable but is unable to respond to new changes. At the same time, a dynamic decision-making system might easily react to disturbances but become unstable in its functioning.

This is further emphasized by the difference between continuous decisions and static processes. In static processes, there is always an already specified process flow that exists independent of the system state, resulting in predictable yet rigid system behavior. On the other hand, decision systems incorporate feedback, contextual information, and constraints into each step of a process, allowing for adaptable system behavior. The change from static systems to decision-making systems is one of the most significant changes made within software delivery systems.

In summary, decision-making can be described as the core element that defines the way a system behaves, which includes its adaptation and maintenance. Decision systems determine not only the actions taken within the system but also the ways in which these actions are impacted by the dynamics and constraints of the system. Through decision systems, the relationship between feedback, policy, and actuation becomes defined.

Key Insight

Decisions do not respond to system behavior – they define and shape it.

7.10.1 Section Summary

This section emphasized the central role of decision-making in shaping system behavior within software delivery systems.

The key insights are as follows:

- Decision-making functions as the primary mechanism driving system evolution.
- Policies and decision logic jointly define system behavior.
- Continuous decision processes enable dynamic adaptation under continuous delivery.
- Repeated decision patterns create feedback loops that influence long-term system dynamics.
- Effective decision design balances stability and adaptability.

The above understandings further illustrate the fact that decision-making is not an afterthought to be included in the software delivery process system, but an essential aspect that guides the functioning of the system.

7.11 Transition to Autonomous and Intelligent Delivery Systems

The history of software release processes has seen the steady trend from manual processes to automation and lately to autonomous systems. This progression is not merely related to the growth of automation, but rather involves the very essence of decision-making in terms of its formation, evaluation, and implementation. Namely, in the evolving process, the development of decision-making is accompanied by its reinforcement by means of intelligence-based systems.

A crucial part in making such a shift in decision-making is played by artificial intelligence (AI) tools for enhancing the decision-making process. In particular, the use of machine learning models within software delivery systems is aimed at improving the process of decision-making through the analysis of operational data. The technology can help to detect patterns, discover abnormalities, and identify some insights into the likely outcomes of various actions taken. For example, an AI model might be used for predicting the likelihood of failures in the system based on previous data.

AI-assisted decision-making differs greatly from automation in its ability to predict and adapt. Intelligent algorithms possess the possibility to adjust their actions according to the newly acquired data, while rule-based algorithms are bound by deterministic logic. Therefore, software delivery systems capable of intelligent decision-making are better suited for rapid changes in the environment that cannot be managed with preexisting strategies.

However, using AI technology in decision-making systems entails a number of difficulties caused by probabilistic approaches adopted by machine learning algorithms. In such cases, their actions become unpredictable and difficult to monitor.

Closely associated with AI-assisted decision-making systems are self-regulating systems. The key feature of self-regulating systems is that decision-making, feedback, and actuation processes take place within a closed-loop system that does not require any human supervision. Self-regulating delivery systems have the ability to autonomously alter resource allocation, deploy necessary measures, impose necessary security, and self-repair.

These systems embody the principle of autonomous control in the sense that the system is capable of functioning in such a way that stability and optimal performance occur on their own. In other words, for example, a self-governing system may be able to detect a problem, identify the cause of the problem, alter the settings of the system, and assess the outcome of this change autonomously.

However, the use of autonomous systems poses many challenges associated with the risks and governance of such systems. As decision-making becomes autonomous, errors and their consequences become increasingly critical. Inaccuracies in the model, bias in training data, and discrepancies between the goal of the system and the decision process could have severe implications for the system's stability, security, and governance.

Firstly, the key problem with AI-based decision-making refers to the lack of transparency in the decision-making process. As opposed to decisions based on pre-established rules, decisions taken by AI may create additional difficulty with respect to understanding the rationale behind certain decisions.

In order to handle such difficulties effectively, it will be necessary to apply appropriate mechanisms of governance so as to make sure that decisions taken by the machine will remain within certain limits. Such governance tools could consist of limiting the policy, constantly supervising decisions, and involving human beings in case of risky decisions.

Another important issue that needs to be considered is the consistency between the intelligent system and the objectives pursued by the organization and/or society as a whole. In other words, the decision system should be constructed in such a way that its operations lead to the achievement of not only technical but also security, reliability, and other important goals.

Finally, from the control system's point of view, the transition to autonomous delivery systems signifies a move toward higher-order control, where the decision-making process involves learning and adaptation functions. However, the presence of these functions implies a need for the development of meta-control systems that will monitor and manage the functioning of the decision system itself.

In essence, the move toward automated and intelligent distribution channels is a representation of the natural evolution of software delivery to become more efficient, scalable, and flexible. Nevertheless, it is also a realization of the importance of designing and managing such systems to prevent loss of control.

7.11.1 Section Summary

This section examined the transition from automated to autonomous and intelligent software delivery systems.

The key insights are as follows:

- Decision-making through AI enhances decision quality through prediction and pattern identification.
- Self-governance mechanisms ensure continuous and flexible control without much human intervention.
- Autonomy enables scaling and flexibility, but it brings its share of dangers too.
- Governance, transparency, and goal alignment are essential for intelligent system management.
- An important aspect of intelligent system design is restricting its autonomy.

This shows that the way ahead for software delivery is not just in automation but also in the creation of intelligent control systems which would be adaptable, self-learning, and able to cope with change.

7.12 Chapter Summary

In summary, decision-making emerges as the fundamental control function in contemporary software delivery, acting as the critical juncture between feedback and actuation. Contrary to the traditional definition of pipelines as mere executors of functions, the chapter argues that behavior in a delivery pipeline can only be understood in the context of how decisions are made within the system. While automation helps to make decisions possible, it is in the quality of decision-making processes that we find the basis for good system performance.

The importance of decision-making to the stability of the delivery process is a key topic discussed in the chapter. Proper decision-making involves not just making the correct decisions, but doing so at the right time, based on appropriate feedback. The process of decision-making can thus enable the system to reach its intended state. Failure on any aspect of the decision-making process contributes to system instability and inefficiency.

The chapter also stressed that decision-making occurs in the context of an integrated control process comprising feedback, constraints, and actuation. Feedback gives real-time information on the condition of the system, thus enabling evaluations. On the other hand, constraints set the limits within which the system can perform, thereby ensuring the safety and compliance of any decision made by the system. Actuation mechanisms put the decision into effect, turning decisions into changes in the system. An efficient system can only be achieved through the proper alignment and coordination of the above processes in the form of a closed-loop control.

Furthermore, the chapter explored the evolution of decision systems as they progress from one model to another. The models included rule-based systems, risk-based systems, feedback systems, and machine-based systems, among others. The chapter also noted the need for human–machine balance and effective management of the challenges arising from decision lag, decision errors, and system complexity.

At the end of the day, the chapter shows that effective decision-making systems can bring about agility, adaptability, and scalability in delivery. The inclusion of real-time feedback, the matching of constraints, and efficient functioning in decentralized networks allows decision systems to make sure that systems behave properly despite external changes. This is critical in making sure that modern delivery platforms are fast and stable.

To conclude, decision-making in software delivery systems is not just an auxiliary activity but rather the fundamental process for managing the behavior of the system. The knowledge discussed in the chapter will go a long way in helping develop decision systems for continuous delivery with stability and security in mind.

References

Åström, K. J., & Murray, R. M. (2008). *Feedback Systems: An Introduction for Scientists and Engineers.* Princeton University Press.

Bass, L., Weber, I., & Zhu, L. (2015). *DevOps: A Software Architect's Perspective.* Addison-Wesley.

Forsgren, N., Humble, J., & Kim, G. (2018). *Accelerate: The Science of Lean Software and DevOps: Building and Scaling High Performing Technology Organizations.* IT Revolution Press.

Goodfellow, I., Bengio, Y., & Courville, A. (2016). *Deep Learning.* MIT Press.

Humble, J., & Farley, D. (2010). *Continuous Delivery: Reliable Software Releases through Build, Test, and Deployment Automation.* Addison-Wesley.

Kahneman, D. (2011). *Thinking, Fast and Slow.* Farrar, Straus and Giroux.

Kim, G., Humble, J., Debois, P., & Willis, J. (2021). *The DevOps Handbook* (2nd ed.). IT Revolution Press.

Meadows, D. H. (2008). *Thinking in Systems: A Primer*. Chelsea Green Publishing.

NIST (2020). *Risk Management Framework for Information Systems and Organizations*. National Institute of Standards and Technology.

NIST (2023). *Artificial Intelligence Risk Management Framework (AI RMF 1.0)*. National Institute of Standards and Technology.

Ogata, K. (2010). *Modern Control Engineering* (5th ed.). Prentice Hall.

Sculley, D., et al. (2015). *Hidden Technical Debt in Machine Learning Systems*. Advances in Neural Information Processing Systems (NeurIPS).

Taleb, N. N. (2007). *The Black Swan: The Impact of the Highly Improbable*. Random House.

Google (2022). *Site Reliability Engineering: How Google Runs Production Systems*. O'Reilly Media.

CNCF (2023). *Cloud Native Security Whitepaper*. Cloud Native Computing Foundation.

CHAPTER 8

Failure, Instability, and Recovery

8.1 Chapter Objective

Autonomous software delivery systems are discussed in this chapter as an evolved type of control architecture, building on top of CI/CD and DevSecOps approaches and advancing them further toward self-regulation and intelligent self-learning. Thus, software delivery is not seen here as a set of automated actions only; instead, it is interpreted as a sophisticated control system, which becomes increasingly sophisticated due to the introduction of machine learning capabilities that enable improved feedback, decisions, and actions Mitchell (1997).

The chapter highlights the evolution of control architectures to autonomous systems and how autonomy can assist software delivery systems in balancing competing operational objectives such as delivery speed, reliability, stability, security, and compliance when supported by high-quality telemetry, policy enforcement, and human oversight. Moreover, the role of autonomy in system architecture design is explained, with emphasis placed on the fact that autonomy does not mean control elimination but its enhancement at a different level of sophistication.

8.2 Introduction: From Automated to Autonomous Systems

The contemporary software delivery systems have experienced a radical change as they have evolved into highly automated pipelines as opposed to manual processes. Automation has facilitated organizations to improve delivery velocity, reliability, and

S. Bobba and N. S. Vummaneni, *CI/CD as a Control System*, https://doi.org/10.1007/979-8-8688-2842-3_8

scalability while operating within acceptable risk, governance, and recovery boundaries, which is the cornerstone of current DevOps and DevSecOps (Forsgren, Humble, & Kim, 2018). Nevertheless, with the increasing complexity, scale, and dynamism of systems, the shortcomings of the classical models of automation are becoming more visible.

Fundamentally, rule-based automation is driven by predefined logic, which involves taking action because of static rules and conditions. Although this method works well in stable and predictable environments, it can hardly adjust to situations experiencing uncertainty, variability, and rapid change. Tool-centric and isolated automation implementations often struggle to incorporate broader operational context beyond predefined rules and thus are limited to managing complex or unforeseen situations. Consequently, they can either have too strict controls that impede the performance of the system or not respond adequately to the risks arising.

Static automation alone is insufficient in highly dynamic cloud-native and distributed environments that require continuous feedback, adaptive control, and context-aware decision-making. This has contributed to the increasing demands of adaptive and self-regulating systems of delivery. In comparison to conventional automation, adaptive systems consider feedback in their decision-making and can therefore change behavior dynamically based on system state. Such systems go beyond the implementation of predetermined workflows to proactively process cues, assessing circumstances, and choosing actions according to the current situation. This change is an evolution of mere performance to smart control.

Autonomous systems may incorporate learning mechanisms that improve decision quality over time using historical and real-time operational data, provided that sufficient validation, governance, and safety controls are in place.

Autonomous systems build on the principles of control theory by adding learning and prediction to the control loop. The decision-making in such systems is not constrained to set rules but rather based on patterns, trends, and insights of the data. This can help systems estimate the likelihood of certain classes of operational problems and take preventive action when confidence thresholds and governance policies permit. An example is that an autonomous delivery system can do things like modify deployment strategies based on the predicted risk levels, allocate resources optimally based on usage patterns, or take preventive measures prior to failures.

Notably, autonomy does not negate the necessity of control; on the contrary, it improves it. Autonomous systems are typically designed to operate with predefined operational, security, compliance, and risk boundaries enforced through policies, approval mechanisms, and human oversight processes. This brings in the concept of controlled autonomy whereby systems are provided with the capacity to evolve and learn, but within well-established limits that ensure safety, compliance, and stability.

The transition to autonomy also comes with new difficulties. The more complex the systems are and the less deterministic the decision-making process is, the more important the issues of transparency, governance, and trust become. To make autonomous systems act in ways that are predictable and stay on track with the goals to be achieved, it is necessary to have strong design, monitoring, and oversight systems. Effective governance requires policies to be versioned, testable, auditable, consistently enforced, and aligned with organizational risk ownership models.

Finally, the emergence of automated systems to autonomous systems also marks one of the most significant changes in the delivery of software. It is an expression of a transition of systems that implement a fixed logic to systems capable of adapting operational behavior through feedback-driven learning and policy-constrained optimization mechanisms. This change has been motivated by the necessity to cope with rising complexity and the need to remain fast, reliable, and secure in today's software environments.

Key Argument

Automation follows predetermined logic, but autonomy allows systems to be capable of making context-sensitive decisions and adjusting their behavior according to feedback and learning.

8.3 Foundations of Autonomous Systems in Control Theory

The move toward self-governing software delivery systems is inspired by principles from control theory and applied as an architectural model for software delivery systems. Conventional control systems rely on feedback control to ensure that behaviors in the system can be regulated, thereby stabilizing the system and converging to desired states. Self-governing systems take this a step further, providing the necessary components for the system to learn from feedback and improve its performance.

Self-regulation is an aspirational capability of autonomous systems, though its effectiveness depends heavily on telemetry quality, operational constraints, governance mechanisms, and continuous validation.

8.3.1 Autonomy as Advanced Control

Autonomous control can be viewed as an extension of traditional control approaches by incorporating behavior, feedback-driven learning, and policy-governed optimization mechanisms. Traditional controllers perform tasks by means of predetermined rules or parameter values and cannot improve operations. Autonomous controllers have an advantage over traditional counterparts in the fact that they modify operations depending on feedback.

Self-regulation is an important objective of autonomous systems, although its effectiveness depends heavily on telemetry quality, governance control, validation process, and operation constraints. Software delivery systems with self-regulatory mechanisms can monitor their state and implement corresponding measures to ensure stable functioning. Examples of such actions include scaling up resources, making decisions about further deployment, etc.

Adaptability is an important characteristic of autonomous controllers operating in dynamic delivery environments. An adaptive controller can respond not only to instantaneous stimuli but also detect patterns and trends related to them. A delivery system could determine that some types of deployments lead to failures and change its decision rules according to those findings.

This is also reinforced by the continual learning done through feedback. Learning mechanisms with autonomous systems use historical operational data to improve future decision quality under validated and policy-constrained conditions. Some of the methods that can be used in learning include statistical learning, machine learning, or reinforcement learning, and any other method that would ensure the system becomes better with time. The control loop will change from being a reaction mode to a learning mode.

From a control systems perspective, the shift is from static control loops toward adaptive feedback systems in which telemetry collection, decision policies, and operational actuation are continuously refined based on observed system behavior.

Closed-Loop Intelligence

Another important capability of autonomous systems is the incorporation of data-driven decision support into closed-loop controls. In conventional closed-loop controls, feedback, decision-making, and actuation are included in the cycle. The addition of learning to the closed-loop control of autonomous systems gives rise to what is termed closed-loop intelligence, which incorporates the use of feedback to drive intelligent actions.

Closed-loop learning occurs when operational telemetry such as metrics, logs, traces, and runtime events is analyzed and integrated into decision policies that influence deployment, scaling, rollback, or remediation actions. An example here would be gathering historical performance information about a particular system so that the autonomous system would know how to roll out when deployed.

One possible technique for closed-loop learning in autonomous systems is reinforcement learning, although many enterprise delivery platforms rely more heavily on supervised learning, anomaly detection, predictive analytics, and rule-based orchestration because of explainability and operational safety requirements.

Moreover, there are other adaptive optimization techniques that need to be considered. They involve adjusting system parameters to attain the best possible performance in the face of varying conditions. A delivery system, for example, can constantly update its deployment limits, scalability limits, or security parameters depending on the actual results being observed.

By incorporating intelligence into the control mechanism of the software system, its efficiency in dealing with unpredictable conditions is improved greatly. In addition, this helps the system make predictions based on the present situation. Such predictions are necessary since this makes it possible for the system to adapt to anticipated future scenarios effectively.

8.3.2 Objectives of Autonomous Systems

The design and functioning of autonomous systems revolve around a series of fundamental objectives that are aimed at defining desirable behaviors of these systems. The achievement of such objectives allows an increase in the efficiency of systems while guaranteeing their safety and stability.

One of the primary objectives of autonomous systems is maintaining operational stability. It means that an autonomous system should demonstrate stable functioning despite any environmental changes. This implies a tendency for the system to reach desirable states and stay in those states. In terms of software delivery, it involves ensuring proper functioning and preventing any failure.

Another objective of autonomous systems is improving the operational efficiency and throughput while remaining within acceptable risk, reliability, and governance boundaries. An autonomous system should strive to achieve maximum efficiency and throughput through constant analysis of the current performance of the system and modification of control parameters accordingly.

The final goal is risk management. Autonomous systems should operate within predefined risk tolerances enforced through policy control, governance processes, and human oversight mechanisms. Risk management involves consideration of the security of the autonomous system as well as the compliance and operational constraints. Risk-based control enables better performance without compromising the integrity of the system Meadows (2008).

It should be noted that these goals are interrelated and might conflict with each other. For instance, improved performance may entail risks, while risk-based control may result in inefficiencies. Autonomous systems attempt to balance competing operational goals dynamically using telemetry, policy constraints, and risk-aware decision-making mechanisms.

From a control systems perspective, these goals represent operational objectives used as architectural guidance. Autonomous systems build on these goals through learning and adaptation (Ogata, 2010). Figure 8-1 illustrates an autonomous control loop augmented with a learning component, which allows the system to adapt its behavior over time rather than relying on fixed control logic.

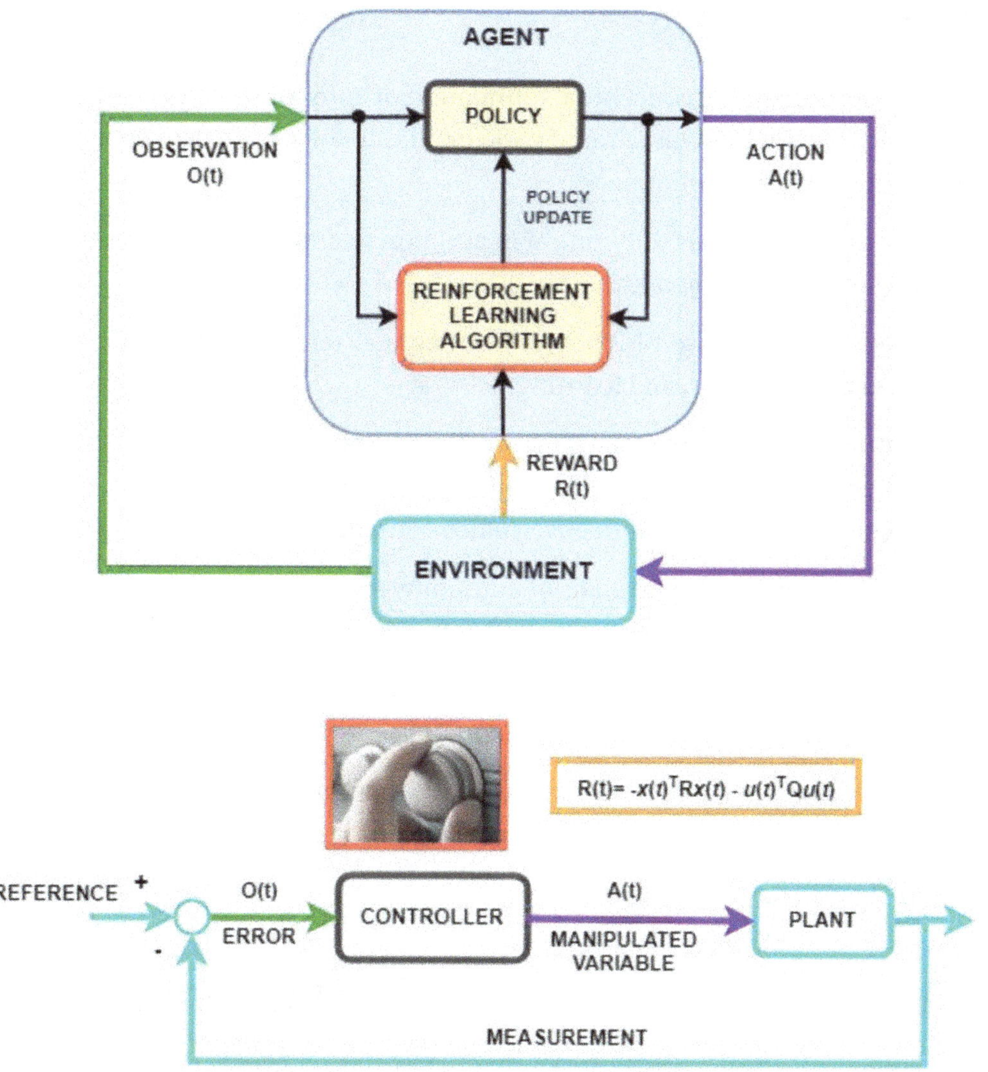

Figure 8-1. *Autonomous Control Loop with Learning Component*

This figure shows a closed-loop control system integrating telemetry feedback that facilitates decision-making, learning mechanisms, and adaptive actuation to improve operational quality over time.

Section Summary

This section established the conceptual foundation of autonomous systems using control theory as an architectural framework for adaptive software delivery systems.

The key insights are as follows:

- Autonomy includes self-control in addition to conventional controls through adaptation and learning.
- Intelligence in closed-loop systems integrates telemetry feedback, predictive analysis, and learning.
- Autonomous systems may improve their decision quality over time through validated feedback-driven optimization and learning mechanics operating with governance constraints.
- The three fundamental goals of autonomy include maintaining stability, improving efficiency, and managing operational risks.
- By using learning in control, the system can function in unpredictable and complex situations.

The above-discussed ideas form the theoretical background of the use of artificial intelligence and machine learning in software delivery systems, which will be discussed in the next chapter.

8.4 AI and Machine Learning in Software Delivery

The application of artificial intelligence and machine learning to software delivery control processes can be viewed as a significant evolution in terms of decision-making, optimization, and risk management. The difference between traditional DevOps and DevSecOps approaches and those involving AI is that AI systems possess data-driven, adaptive, and predictive qualities that make control processes more effective.

When dealing with modern, complex, changing, and big data environments in software delivery processes, purely rule-based strategies may fail to capture the full operational context. Thanks to their ability to analyze large amounts of data and detect patterns in them, artificial intelligence systems allow for making decisions and constantly optimizing processes within these environments.

8.4.1 Role of AI in Decision-Making

AI can improve the quality of decision-making when delivering software solutions with sufficient telemetry, validation, and governance. The most important contribution of artificial intelligence lies in the ability to conduct predictive analysis. For instance, models can predict the probability of deployment problems, identify the potential performance bottlenecks, or detect security threats in advance. Such a capability helps systems act preventively and thus mitigate the associated risks Bishop (2006).

Anomaly detection is one area where AI and statistical learning techniques can support operational decision-making. Anomalies can be defined as unexpected changes in the regular behavior of a system that might be caused by different factors, including a security threat or a configuration issue. Machine learning algorithms can recognize previously unseen patterns of unusual behavior and help identify the risks faster than traditional techniques.

Such capabilities substantially enhance decision-making because they enable it to be driven by relevant information. The decision-making process does not rely only on pre-established criteria; instead, it uses current parameters and makes decisions accordingly.

8.4.2 Learning from System Behavior

One of the key strengths associated with machine learning lies in the system's ability to learn from its own behavior, enabling adaptive optimization based on historical operational behavior and validated feedback signals. Any software delivery system produces lots of data thanks to logs, metrics, traces, and security signals. ML models can analyze this information and find connections, patterns, and dependencies that would not have been seen using traditional methods Géron (2019).

For instance, finding patterns in system behavior can help the system find relationships between a particular action taken and the results of this action. In other words, the system will learn from the experience and know what actions should be avoided in the future, as these actions cause negative effects on the system or on its behavior.

Historical data usage plays a key role here as well, since such usage provides opportunities for making the system smarter by analyzing previous behaviors, incidents, and outcomes. The process of decision-making gets improved each time because decisions are made based on learning.

In other words, software delivery systems become adaptive systems with decisions being constantly improved through the accumulation of knowledge.

8.4.3 Types of Learning Models

Machine learning algorithms are employed differently in software delivery systems based on their unique purposes in dealing with different problems, data sets, and challenges.

Supervised learning algorithms require a large data set with labels in place, which means the input variables and outputs must be present in the historical data. Such an algorithm is useful for predicting whether the deployment process will be successful, detecting security flaws in a program, or predicting certain performance measures. Supervised learning techniques learn from instances in order to make reliable predictions about future instances.

Unsupervised learning techniques don't need labeled information, but nevertheless, they can identify patterns in the data that are important for the process under consideration. Lack of labeling allows finding those patterns that otherwise could remain hidden from the analyst. In software delivery systems, unsupervised learning will allow identifying anomalous behavior, clustering, and other patterns that could signal security threats or inefficiencies in the performance of the system Kim, Humble, Debois & Willis (2021).

Reinforcement learning represents one possible approach for adaptive optimization, although many enterprise delivery systems prefer simpler and more interpretable methods because of governance, explainability, and operational safety considerations. According to this technique, the machine will undertake certain actions, and then will get either rewards or punishment for these actions. Using reinforcement learning, the machine learns how to perform actions that yield desirable outcomes (increased efficiency, increased stability, etc.). This approach is useful in solving problems related to dynamic optimization, such as resource allocation and parameter adjustments (Bishop, 2006; Goodfellow, Bengio, & Courville, 2016).

All these learning approaches make an integral set of techniques for infusing intelligent behavior in the delivery systems. Table 8-1 summarizes the main AI techniques applied in software delivery systems, along with their roles and typical use cases.

Table 8-1. *AI Techniques in Software Delivery Systems*

Technique	**Application**	**Benefit**
Predictive Analytics	Deployment risk prediction, performance forecasting	Proactive decision-making
Anomaly Detection	Identifying security threats and system irregularities	Early risk detection
Supervised Learning	Classification and prediction tasks	High accuracy with labeled data
Unsupervised Learning	Pattern discovery and anomaly detection	Detection of unknown issues
Reinforcement Learning	Adaptive optimization and decision-making	Continuous improvement

Section Summary

This chapter examined the contributions of AI and machine learning in the improvement of software delivery systems by means of data and adaptation abilities.

The important takeaways from this chapter include the following:

- AI aids in decision-making based on predictions in software engineering.
- The learning model utilizes system behavior data to improve efficiency.
- Pattern recognition combined with historical data could contribute to the proactive management of systems.
- Multiple learning models exist to address diverse requirements, including optimization and forecasting.
- Integration of AI in systems converts software delivery systems into learning-based control.

These concepts are the foundation for the adoption of intelligent decision-making models, which will be examined in the following chapter.

8.5 Autonomous Decision-Making Models

Self-directed decision model solutions constitute a paradigm shift in the way condition assessments and decision selections are executed by software delivery systems. Within conventional DevOps and DevSecOps operations, decisions are typically made based on static policies and predefined decision rules. Such methods offer predictability, but they are inflexible. In the face of increasing complexity and unpredictability in modern computing systems, rule-based decision models are inadequate for capturing and analyzing the wide range of possibilities that exist in the real world.

This chapter explores the development of decision models from rule-based models to learning-based models and the incorporation of risk-aware intelligent reasoning capabilities within such decision frameworks.

8.5.1 From Rule-Based to Learning-Based Decisions

Standard deployment systems rely on deterministic decision systems using policies and conditions. This means that the decision model will operate according to predetermined rules and policies without accounting for the dynamism that may affect its decision-making process. For example, if tests need to be done before deployment, if thresholds are not breached, the system will continue to be predictable in terms of decision processes and action to be taken.

The problem with such types of deterministic decision models is that they are usually static. As such, the decision model will be unable to consider outside influences that may affect the functioning of such decision models. Two consequences will arise from such a decision-making system: Firstly, the decision model will tend to err on the side of caution when making decisions, to the extent that it will take overly cautious decisions. Secondly, the decision model cannot identify possible threats.

Secondly, a learning-based decision model makes decisions based on the analysis of data collected during the operation of the software delivery system. The model will learn from historical data and make predictions regarding whether certain deployments are appropriate at a particular time based on current circumstances.

The transformation from static to adaptive decision-making can be seen as part of the move toward data-based control from deterministic control, which is characterized by ongoing adjustments based on the dynamics of the system. The learning-based approach allows systems to cope better with uncertainties.

8.5.2 Risk-Aware Intelligent Decisions

Risk awareness is one of the important components of making autonomous decisions. In contrast to conventional systems, which have only two states, risk-aware systems take into account the effect an action might have on the system and make the decision according to its magnitude. Predictive risk scoring can play an important role in making autonomous decisions by using the data about previous cases as well as the present circumstances in order to predict the possible risks of a particular action.

For example, deployment may be rated based on code or package dependency change, server loads, and prior experience. Therefore, an action may be rated as having low risk, moderate risk, or high risk.

Other than prediction rating, context-based decision-making is also a feature of the software which is used by the program in order to adapt to its prevailing conditions. Context-based decision-making considers numerous factors before deciding on the next course of action to take, including the state of the system and the environment, among others. For this reason, the same deployment may be carried out depending on the prevailing conditions or otherwise, for example, if the system is overloaded.

This is how intelligent decision-making can be made by autonomous systems using both prediction and context information. In this case, the principles behind control systems apply since decisions are made based on the state of the system.

8.5.3 Self-Optimizing Decision Systems

At the highest level of autonomous decision-making, there are self-optimizing systems. Such systems constantly improve their decision algorithms by analyzing the results of previous decisions. They are not dependent on any model, but constantly tune their behavior based on feedback received from the environment.

The continuous optimization process involves the evaluation of previously obtained results and the adjustment of the decision model. Thus, if certain approaches or tactics for deploying the system lead to a positive outcome, then in the next steps, the same tactic can be preferred. On the contrary, if some actions lead to an undesirable effect, then the decision algorithm can be changed.

One of the main features of self-optimizing systems is feedback-based refinement. This involves using feedback information to change the models that the system relies upon. It can be a retraining of machine learning models, setting new risk parameters, or other actions necessary for improving the decision model.

Such systems mark a breakthrough in control theory since they allow incorporating learning into the control algorithm. As a result, systems will be able to react both to current and future changes in the environment (Russell & Norvig, 2021).

But there is a need to take into account certain limitations when designing such a system. If no limitations are imposed, the self-optimization of a system can lead to undesirable outcomes. It is important that any system should act according to its goals and be transparent in decision-making. Figure 8-2 presents the evolution of decision models from rule-based control to AI-driven approaches, contrasting a reinforcement-learning agent that updates its policy from rewards with a traditional control system that relies on error correction and manual tuning.

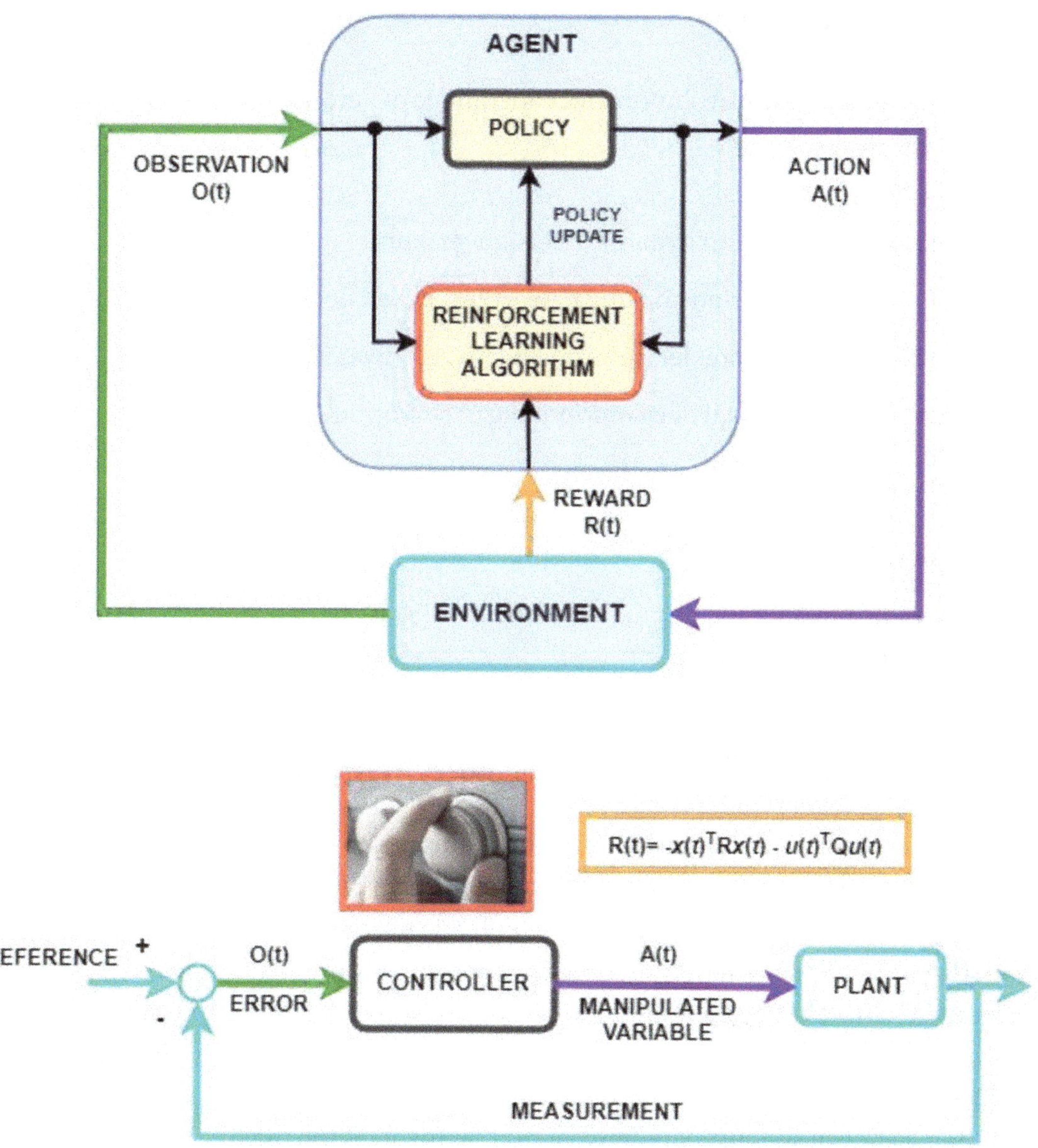

***Figure 8-2.** Evolution of Decision Models (Rule-Based → AI-Driven)*

This figure shows the progression of decision models from rule-based control to AI-driven approaches.

Section Summary

This section examined the evolution and capabilities of autonomous decision-making models in software delivery systems.

The key insights are:

- From rule-based to dynamic decision-making
- From static decision-making to learning-based decision-making
- From risk-unaware decision-making to risk-aware decision-making
- From conventional decision-making to self-optimizing decision-making
- From conventional decision-making to autonomous decision-making

This sets the basis for the discussion of the intelligent actuation mechanism, which will be explained in the next section.

8.6 Intelligent Actuation Mechanisms

Intelligent actuation denotes the action layer of autonomous software delivery frameworks, whereby decisions obtained from learning frameworks are executed as intelligent actions in a context-aware and predictive manner. Conventional actuations within CI/CD processes follow an approach that is mostly predictable, whereby actions are executed as a result of static conditions like deployment, scaling, or rollbacks. On the other hand, intelligent actuations have a feedback loop through which the actions are modified in real time according to predictive insights or system behavior.

Within a control systems paradigm, actuation involves the manipulation of systems to achieve desired behaviors. Through intelligence, this action becomes more sophisticated than the mere execution of tasks, as it can be used to adapt the system's behavior. Intelligent actuation will be examined with regard to the following dimensions: adaptive deployments, predictive actuation, and autonomous incident handling.

8.6.1 Adaptive Deployment Strategies

Adaptive deployment approaches go beyond conventional approaches by introducing feedback and dynamic adaptation into the deployment process. Unlike using preconfigured patterns like canary or blue-green deployment patterns, an adaptive approach makes use of performance metrics and other factors to influence how the deployment should progress.

The first important characteristic of adaptive approaches is the dynamic adjustment of rollouts. In this regard, rollouts can be adjusted according to how well they are performing. For instance, a rollback may be required if the initial phases of deployment reveal some problems. On the other hand, successful phases of rollout can encourage accelerated rollout. This way, decisions regarding the deployment process can be made in light of ongoing events in real time.

Intelligent scaling is another important feature of adaptive approaches. In this case, system resources can be scaled up or down according to traffic predictions done using machine learning approaches. This way of doing things ensures better resource utilization and increased efficiency of the system.

Adaptive actuation is important since it ensures stability of the system and also efficient delivery by incorporating feedback and prediction into the deployment methods.

8.6.2 Predictive Actuation

The concept of predictive actuation signifies the transition from a reactive approach to a proactive one, in which the control actions are performed with regard to predicted future states of the system instead of addressing already occurred incidents. The technique utilizes the power of predictive analysis and machine learning models for identifying possible risks, performance bottlenecks, or imminent failure.

Predictive actuation implies that certain control actions are executed based on the anticipated behavior of the system using historical and current data. For example, certain patterns of activity, which predict system degradation or malfunction, could be identified in advance using machine learning techniques. As a result, the system will take preventative action that could include adjustment of configuration settings, change of resource allocation schemes, and rethinking of deployment.

Such prevention of possible problems improves the resilience of the system by preventing failures from occurring. Predictive actuation does not wait for problems to happen but takes action to mitigate the risk of the problem becoming actual. Therefore, the technique is in line with the control theory that relies on the prediction of possible outcomes to ensure optimal system behavior.

Predictive actuation increases the efficiency of the control loop due to its timeliness and accuracy.

8.6.3 Autonomous Incident Response

Autonomous incident management would be considered among the leading cases of using intelligent actuation, with systems being able to detect, diagnose, and fix problems on their own without any form of human intervention. In conventional settings, incidents are usually managed manually, which could lead to delays and a lack of consistency in the process. However, autonomous systems allow for quick and effective handling of incidents thanks to automation and learning.

One of the main areas of autonomous operations is self-healing, where systems would heal themselves without requiring any human input. When new versions of software lead to problems within the system, it might be rolled back to an older, more stable version. The same is true when performance becomes poor due to certain factors.

Remediation that is automated takes this one step further, and it involves fixing the problems themselves, not just their symptoms. Automated remediation may rely on runbooks, diagnostics, policy engines, statistical models, or ML-assisted recommendations, depending on the operational risk and incident type. With experience, the machine will learn and become better at handling similar issues Burns, Grant, Oppenheimer, Brewer & Wilkes (2016).

Incident response automation makes systems more resilient and allows them to recover faster in case of problems because they don't depend on people to solve them. They also help them run better by saving time for humans to do more important things. Table 8-2 outlines the principal types of intelligent actuation and their characteristics.

Table 8-2. *Intelligent Actuation Types*

Type	Function	Example
Adaptive Actuation	Adjusts actions based on real-time feedback	Dynamic rollout adjustment during deployment
Predictive Actuation	Anticipates future system states and acts proactively	Pre-scaling resources based on predicted demand
Corrective Actuation	Restores system stability after disruption	Automatic rollback after failed deployment
Autonomous Actuation	Executes self-healing and remediation actions	Restarting services or applying patches automatically

Section Summary

This section explored the evolution of actuation mechanisms from static execution to intelligent, adaptive, and autonomous systems.

The key insights are as follows:

- Smart actuation facilitates context-based and adaptive actuation of system activities.
- Adaptive system deployment techniques ensure system stability through adaptive measures using feedbacks.
- Predictive actuation makes it possible to proactively manage the system through the anticipation of system activities.
- Autonomous incident management improves resilience through self-healing and remediation.
- Smart actuation makes pipelines smart control systems.

The above-listed concepts lay down the basis for feedback learning and system adaptation in autonomous systems, which is discussed in detail below.

8.7 Feedback Learning and System Adaptation

Learning and adaptability is what enables software delivery through autonomous systems to be superior to other systems. Feedback control systems have been found to rely on feedback to correct mistakes. In contrast, autonomous systems take a leap forward by using feedback to correct errors, learn from them, forecast, and optimize the behavior of the system.

In order for autonomous systems to remain balanced and optimized, it is essential that they learn from feedback due to the constant changes in their complex environment. This chapter explores how feedback drives continuous improvement, how feedback quality affects model accuracy, and how learning can inform control strategies.

8.7.1 Learning from Feedback Loops

Feedback is an important concept for classical control systems and contemporary autonomous systems as well. In classical systems, feedback is used to measure deviations and take corrective actions in response. In autonomous systems, feedback allows achieving a more general objective - continuous learning and improvement.

Every interaction made by the system - whether a deployment, scaling, or remediation activity - produces information reflecting the results of previous decisions. Such information becomes part of machine learning algorithms and is used to assess the performance of certain decisions. With time, continuous improvement becomes possible due to the fact that the system gets better at making decisions based on historical experience.

This process of continuous learning and improvement means that, for instance, when a specific approach to deploying an app always works well, the system tends to use such an approach next time around. Similarly, when some decision leads to undesirable results, it will be adjusted next time around because of the feedback received previously. As we see, there appears to be a feedback loop, which makes system development continuous.

From the point of view of control theory, it means that adaptation of the system to new conditions takes place instead of a reaction to deviations.

8.7.2 Feedback Quality and Model Accuracy

Learning in an autonomous system is highly dependent on the quality of the feedback signal. With high-quality feedback signals, the system has accurate, timely, and meaningful information about itself, which can be used for effective decision-making. Poor-quality feedback may decrease the efficiency of the learning algorithm and affect decision-making negatively.

Various attributes determine the quality of feedback signals. For software delivery systems, observable data from metrics, logs, traces, and security signals can be used as feedback sources. However, if any of the aforementioned data signals are noisy or delayed, then learning will become ineffective and erroneous.

In the case of anomaly detection, for instance, false alarms can exaggerate system risks, making learning and decisions too cautious. Meanwhile, the absence of feedback about certain events may lead to overlooking problems and passing risks to other parts of the system.

High-quality feedback depends greatly on the ability to validate, filter, and correlate data through mechanisms like anomaly detection scoring, signal consolidation, and cross-verification across sources. Timing feedback in relation to decisions and actions must also be done to ensure that the learning models get high-quality information to learn from.

From the perspective of learning systems, feedback quality significantly affects how accurate and generalized models become. This means that when high-quality data is used, the models learn and make accurate predictions, but low-quality data will only result in biased and inaccurate models. Figure 8-3 shows the feedback learning loop in autonomous systems, in which the agent uses observations and rewards from the environment to continuously update its policy and improve its decisions.

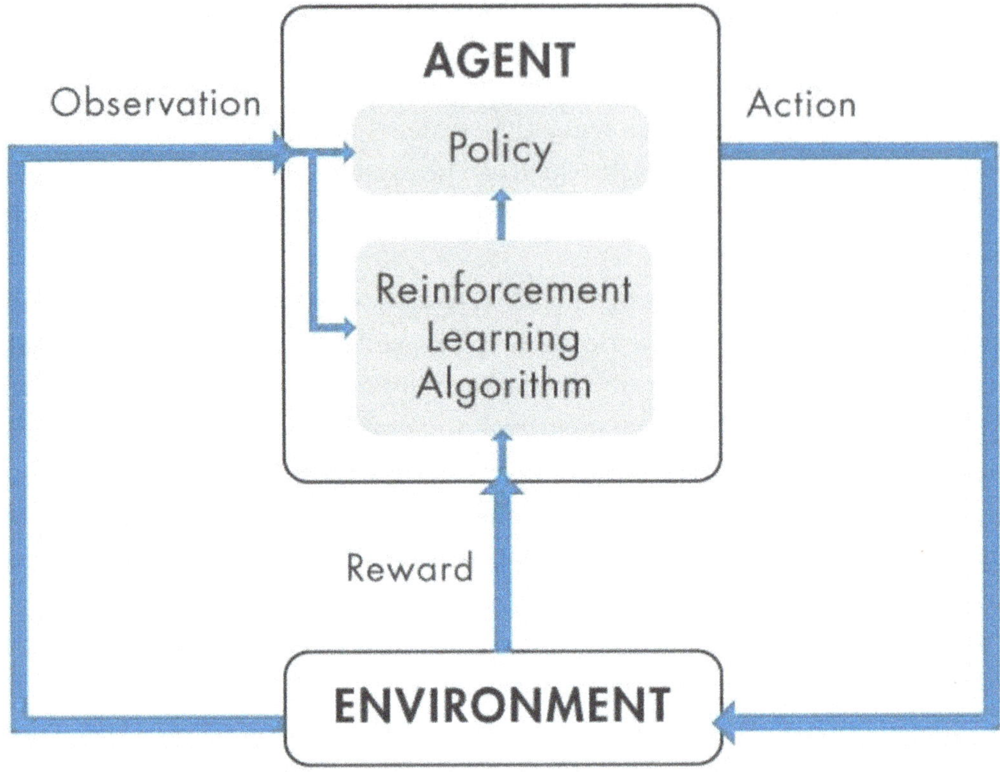

Figure 8-3. *Feedback Learning Loop in Autonomous Systems*

This figure shows a feedback-driven learning loop integrating system observation, model update, decision-making, and adaptive actuation in autonomous systems.

8.7.3 Adaptive Control Based on Learning

Adaptive control can therefore be viewed as an implementation of learning within a control system that enables the system to make changes based on the lessons learned from its experiences. Autonomous software delivery systems are capable of making changes to the parameters, policies, and decisions based on the system's environment.

There are several ways in which adaptive control works, and dynamic tuning of the control system is one such mechanism. It involves continually adjusting the control parameters based on changes to the environment and future predictions. The system can thus learn and adjust parameters, such as the threshold for deployment, scaling policy, or risk limit.

Adaptive control also enables the system to adapt over time. As the nature of the work changes, the system can also change its strategies for managing resources. The same can happen if there are emerging risks in the environment.

It is important to note that adaptive control should work under certain constraints in order to maintain stability and safety. Although learning allows for adaptability, it may result in undesirable outcomes if there is no limit to the amount of adaptation. Thus, autonomous agents need to include constraint-based learning, whereby the agent adapts according to certain constraints and goals.

Control theory shows that adaptive control increases efficiency by allowing an adjustment of system behavior toward desired outcomes. Through learning within the control loop, systems attain more efficiency and stability.

Section Summary

This section explored how feedback-driven learning enables continuous adaptation and optimization in autonomous software delivery systems.

The key insights are as follows:

- Feedback loops form the bedrock of continual learning and system improvements.
- Learning through feedback helps systems improve their decision-making processes.
- The quality of feedback affects both the accuracy of models and system stability.
- Adaptive control is a process where systems can change their behavior by learning.
- Learning-enabled control helps systems function in dynamic environments.

The aforementioned concepts lay the groundwork for the analysis of autonomous systems, and these are discussed in detail in the following section.

8.8 Stability and Risk in Autonomous Systems

As automated software delivery becomes increasingly complex, the issue transforms from facilitating automation to managing stability when learning-based control takes place. Autonomously controlled systems carry many strengths such as adaptation, prediction, and optimization; on the other hand, their strengths may become potential sources of problems for which the systems should be effectively managed. In contrast to traditional, deterministic systems whose behaviors can be expected according to certain regulations and limitations, autonomous systems run on probability and dynamic decision-making processes.

In terms of control theory, stability refers to the capacity of the system to converge toward desired states, avoiding oscillation or divergence due to changes in conditions. When it comes to autonomous systems, the stability issue implies that, in addition to the regulation of feedback and actuation, proper management of learning processes and decision constraints is also necessary. This part focuses on the risks associated with autonomously made decisions, stability management processes, and human governance.

8.8.1 Risks of Autonomous Decision-Making

Autonomous decision-making poses several challenges, owing to the nature of data-based decision-making algorithms and adaptive learning approaches employed in these systems. One such risk posed by autonomous decision-making is that of overfitting, whereby the decision models are highly fitted to historical patterns, thus rendering them unable to work efficiently in situations where the system behavior shifts. This creates a vulnerability in the decision-making framework, since the decision made by the model will be inaccurate in such cases.

The other major challenge is the problem of emerging unintended behaviors from the system. Autonomous decision-making systems are engineered to maximize certain objectives within an environment. In some instances, such objectives are ill-defined or improperly specified; as such, the system may find a means to meet the objective, which could lead to undesired outcomes.

Further, autonomous systems can develop feedback loop magnification effects, whereby erroneous feedback can create feedback loops, leading to increased errors and poor decisions. When learning is based on erroneous input, there is a risk that erroneous feedback will be learned repeatedly, causing degradation in system performance over time. The quality of feedback provided to an autonomous system must always be ensured (Sculley et al., 2015).

Such risks emphasize the need for proper planning and control over autonomous systems.

8.8.2 Maintaining Stability

To keep an autonomous system stable, there must be some form of control in place to regulate its operations. Among the best ways to achieve this goal is through constraint enforcement. This strategy allows system operations to be bound by certain limits, which ensures that it remains stable and operates safely. The constraints that should be considered here may include the risks associated with system operations, their performance levels, security, and adherence to regulations.

Another key aspect that should be considered in ensuring that an autonomous system stays stable is the safety mechanism. This refers to the tools that ensure that an autonomous system does not enter into any unstable state. Some of the examples of such mechanisms include rollback options, circuit breakers, redundancy systems, and others.

The alignment of the learning process with the control purpose is another important element of stability. Autonomous systems must guarantee that their models will be regularly tested and updated, considering the conditions existing now. Regular model testing, re-learning, and evaluation contribute to achieving proper alignment and avoiding its divergence.

Considering the control theory principles, the stability of autonomous systems can be reached by means of applying the concepts of feedback, constraints, and adaptive control (Åström & Murray, 2008).

8.8.3 Human Oversight in Autonomous Systems

Regardless of the advancements that have been made in automation and artificial intelligence, human intervention plays an essential role in the operation of autonomous systems. While machines can handle the collection of information and the execution of decisions efficiently, there might be situations in which they lack the necessary context and moral perspective to make the right decisions.

The use of governance mechanisms enables the autonomous systems to run effectively and in accordance with the organization's objectives. The policies, audit procedures, and mechanisms put in place for the evaluation of decisions contribute significantly toward achieving this goal. Moreover, human intervention through the governance mechanism ensures that transparency in decision-making is achieved.

The need for human intervention becomes more pronounced in situations where there are high risks involved; in such instances, human intervention acts as part of a human-in-the-loop approach. It ensures that all decisions made have been well thought through.

In addition, there are methods of overseeing autonomous processes. They ensure transparency in decision-making processes and give room for intervention when required. This guarantees safe operation and efficiency of autonomous systems NIST (2020) and NIST (2023).

Finally, the purpose is not to substitute human intervention but to enhance it. The system will be able to make simple decisions independently, while human intervention will play a crucial role in making strategic decisions. Table 8-3 presents the key risks associated with autonomous systems and their corresponding mitigation strategies.

Table 8-3. *Risks and Mitigation Strategies in Autonomous Systems*

Risk	Cause	Mitigation Strategy
Overfitting	Excessive reliance on historical data	Model validation, regular retraining
Unintended Behavior	Misaligned objectives or incomplete constraints	Clear policy definition, constraint enforcement
Feedback Noise	Low-quality or inconsistent signals	Signal filtering, data validation
Model Drift	Changes in system behavior over time	Continuous monitoring and updating
Over-automation	Lack of human oversight	Human-in-the-loop governance

Section Summary

This section examined the challenges of maintaining stability in autonomous software delivery systems and the risks associated with learning-driven control.

The key insights are as follows:

- Autonomous decision-making can be problematic in terms of overfitting and unpredictable behaviors.

- Stability is achieved through constraint implementation and safety measures.
- The provision of quality feedback is necessary to avoid propagating errors.
- Human monitoring helps ensure governance and accountability.
- Good autonomous systems achieve an optimal balance between learning and control.

The above principles lay the basis for discussing governance and ethics in autonomous delivery systems in the following section.

8.9 Governance and Ethics in Autonomous Delivery

As learning-based decision-making is achieved in software delivery systems that operate autonomously, it becomes imperative to apply rules of governance and ethics to maintain safety, accountability, and compliance. It is true that in autonomous software delivery, the decision-making process is autonomous, and the decisions made by these systems are based on data, models, and policies that keep evolving. Nevertheless, while decision-making makes things more efficient and adaptable, some new issues come up.

In the case of control systems, one may view the process of governance as a constraint layer that establishes limits of operation of the system itself. For the autonomous system, it becomes necessary to develop additional control measures that will be aimed at making decisions ethical and understandable. This section is devoted to the problem of accountability in artificial intelligence-based decisions, their ethical aspects, and regulations.

8.9.1 Accountability in AI-Driven Systems

Accountability is one of the fundamental requirements in the context of autonomous systems. It ensures that decisions can be traced, explained, and analyzed. Traditional systems have an inherent advantage in this regard because decision-making processes follow predetermined guidelines, and actions are undertaken by people. However, AI systems use intricate models, which can generate results that cannot always be interpreted.

One of the important elements of accountability is traceability. Decision traceability implies creating documentation concerning the decision-making process. The documentation should include input parameters, the decision-making model, and the actions taken. Traceability allows organizations to retrace decision processes and understand what factors impacted the final decision.

Traceability would require the deployment of logging, monitoring, and model explainability features. In one instance, logging could be done through risk scores, policy assessment, and model output for every action taken. Model explainability features would provide more accountability to understand the process behind the model's decision-making process.

There would be the problem of accountability that will entail identifying who is responsible for the decisions made by the system. The organization, in any case, must figure out how to govern itself so that it can understand who will be held accountable for designing and implementing the system.

8.9.2 Ethical Considerations

It is essential to consider ethical issues in the design and use of autonomous delivery systems. Since autonomous systems tend to make decisions more frequently, the problem of their ethics should be considered as well.

First, the problem related to bias should be discussed. This issue appears when the training data used by the machine learning algorithm is incomplete or insufficient. In this case, one can expect that the algorithm will work based on wrong data. It is worth noting that certain problems associated with bias could be observed in software delivery systems, for example, regarding risk assessment, policy enforcement, and priority of certain actions.

In addition to that, the issue of transparency can also be considered one of the ethical issues. The requirement of transparency involves informing people about the processes of decision-making. Therefore, it goes without saying that transparency implies that the process of decision-making through the machine learning algorithms should be transparent and clear for understanding.

As for the ethical issues related to the risk involved, they imply that risks should be minimal. Therefore, it is important to develop systems that pose no risk and pose no danger. Ethical factors have to be integrated into the decision-making processes so that decision-making does not endanger anybody.

8.9.3 Regulatory and Compliance Challenges

The increase in AI and automation in software delivery processes causes various problems related to regulations and compliance issues. In the first place, it is necessary to comply with the legislation and make sure that the autonomous system works legally.

Firstly, one should mention the problem of compliance with changes in legislation. There are certain guidelines developed by governments and regulators related to AI and automation technologies, and companies have to keep up with these changes.

The problem of auditability and verifiability of an autonomous system can be mentioned as well. Organizations may face a situation when they need to provide proof of certain boundaries set forth by their system as well as prove the legitimacy of results obtained through its application.

In addition, the regulation problems of cross-regulation must be addressed since software delivery systems tend to operate in many jurisdictions, each having different regulations. Only by means of standardization and centralization will such a task of consistency be achievable.

Taking into consideration the issue of control systems concerning autonomous systems, we may say that regulations act as the boundary conditions imposed upon the autonomous system. Thus, the autonomous system should include these boundary conditions in its operation.

Section Summary

This discussion addressed issues regarding the governance and ethics of autonomous software delivery platforms.

The important takeaways from this section include the following:

- Accountability is ensured through tracing decision-making, understanding the reasoning behind it, and assigning responsibility.
- Ethical practices are aimed at minimizing bias and being fair and transparent.
- Self-regulation occurs when there is a set of ethical and risk-based limits in place.

- The regulatory aspect affects how the platform functions due to constraints imposed on it.
- The governance process facilitates the balance between governance and autonomy.

This list captures the essential points necessary for establishing balance in autonomous systems.

8.10 Human–AI Collaboration in Delivery Systems

Since the development of software delivery tends toward greater autonomy, it will be more conducive to architectures that enhance rather than displace human participation in decision-making processes. Human–machine collaboration is an example of a hybrid model where machines are used to take advantage of their efficiency in decision-making due to the ability to make decisions quickly, in large quantities, and to recognize patterns. Humans are then used to address the inefficiencies of machine-based decision-making by handling uncertainties and the context of business decisions.

Where complex decision-making is concerned, especially when many decisions need to be made quickly, AI decision-making models tend to be highly effective and valuable because they can process large amounts of data fast and recognize useful patterns. On the other hand, AI decision-making models often lack the ability to handle uncertainties and the context of business decisions.

8.10.1 Augmented Decision-Making

Augmented decision-making refers to the use of AI technologies to enhance and support the decision-making process carried out by people rather than substitute it entirely. In this case, the machine learning algorithms would analyze the data, generate predictions, and give recommendations which will then be considered by the human being who takes the ultimate decision.

In delivery software systems, the examples of augmented decision-making could comprise but not necessarily be limited to evaluating risks of deployment, priority setting of resolving incidents, and optimizing the performance of the system. For example, the machine learning algorithm may look through previous deployments and estimate the risks of a current one. The results of such an analysis would then be looked at by the engineers or operators who might also consider other factors not included in the analysis.

The quality of the decisions made would thus be improved as the recommendations made by the algorithm would be considered together with other factors that operators have in mind.

8.10.2 Human-in-the-Loop for Critical Control

Whereas many decisions made in autonomous systems may be automated, some decisions are better left to be made by humans because of their riskiness, uncertainty, and significant impact. In order to prevent potential problems in such situations, human-in-the-loop (HITL) models are used to ensure that all critical decisions are examined and validated by human operators prior to execution.

The use of approval gates, exception management, and escalation procedures is a common practice in relation to human interventions into CI/CD pipelines and DevSecOps processes. For example, the detection of a risky deployment as a result of a model's predictions might imply the introduction of an extra review step that should be performed by engineers. Likewise, a suspicious state of the system detected by means of monitoring and runtime analytics might require human involvement in assessing the situation and choosing the right course of action.

HITL models serve to protect the system from mistakes, unintended consequences, and limitations of the decision-making model itself.

Nevertheless, there are obvious trade-offs in relation to such models insofar as they imply slower system operation due to human interventions.

8.10.3 Balancing Autonomy and Oversight

The proper balancing of the level of autonomy with oversight is one of the most essential things for an effective software delivery system of today. If there is too much autonomy in terms of automation, it will result in a lack of control, low levels of transparency, and greater risks. At the same time, if there is too much oversight performed by a person, it may hinder the system's scalability and make it inefficient. One should try to ensure that in such a system, autonomy and oversight are two complementary elements, but not opposing things.

There are a number of ways to ensure such balancing such as a tiered decision-making process. Decisions made in accordance with this approach are evaluated according to their degree of risk and complexity. While low-risk decisions and operations of routine nature are autonomous and thus executed at the highest speed and scale, moderate-risk decisions require augmented decision-making when artificial intelligence offers recommendations, which are later reviewed by humans. As for critical situations and high-risk decisions, they require full oversight from humans.

Another element that can help in balancing is feedback loops, which promote machine and human learning.

From the point of view of control theory, the interaction between humans and AI brings into play the concept of control hierarchy. In the control hierarchy, the process of automated control is relegated to the lower level, while human decision-making is elevated to the upper level, which helps make decisions more resilient.

Key Insight

Autonomy improves system capabilities, but successful software delivery systems reach their highest level of functionality and stability when there is an appropriate balance between artificial intelligence and human decision-making.

8.11 Transition to Fully Autonomous Systems

From automation to autonomy in software deployment processes, it is neither sudden nor quick; rather, it is a journey characterized by gradual developments in the ability of the systems to learn and make decisions. While automation serves as the basis upon which systems can reliably and repeatably perform actions (Humble & Farley, 2010), autonomy refers to the ability of the systems to learn and adapt to changing situations without requiring constant human intervention. As such, transitioning from one state to another necessitates careful and measured steps.

8.11.1 Gradual Adoption of Autonomy

The incorporation of autonomy into software delivery systems has to be done gradually, providing organizations with an opportunity to test the capabilities of the system and learn how reliable and accurate it is. The beginning steps will usually include using analytics for making decisions based on the available data in conjunction with automation processes. In this way, AI systems will contribute to decisions but not control them directly, which would help companies test their efficiency.

When systems advance, they will become capable of not only providing information but also executing certain operations independently. These will often be actions like scaling up and down, minor configuration changes, and low-stakes deployments, all of which are performed using the knowledge gained from machine learning algorithms.

The gradual approach helps mitigate the risk of problems with the system and provides companies with an opportunity to introduce governance policies gradually.

8.11.2 Hybrid Systems as an Intermediate Stage

Hybrid systems constitute an essential transitional phase toward complete autonomy. Hybrid systems integrate the elements of automation, learning-oriented decision-making processes, and human decision-making to form layers of decision-making.

In hybrid systems, low-complexity and low-risk decisions will be made autonomously through the use of ML-based models for consistency and fast processing. High-complexity and risky decisions, however, should be subject to human approval before execution. In such a way, organizations will be able to scale up the benefits of automation while having sufficient control over their processes.

In addition, hybrid systems make it possible to ensure continuous learning and improvements of models since information about the decision-making process of both humans and automated systems can contribute to such improvements. Gradually, with increasing confidence in the ability of the model to make correct decisions, autonomy can be extended accordingly.

Finally, from the perspective of control systems theory, hybrid systems can be considered as multi-layered control systems, in which automation and adaptability will be integrated in the lower levels of control, while human approval will take place at the upper levels.

8.11.3 Future of Self-Regulating Delivery Systems

The main objective of this shift is the design of completely autonomous and self-regulating delivery systems that would be able to regulate their activities with little or no human intervention at all. In self-regulating delivery systems, feedback, decision-making, and actuation will all be intertwined with learning procedures, thereby making constant refinement and improvement possible.

In terms of self-regulation, what sets these kinds of systems apart is their capacity to achieve stability despite being constantly faced with changing conditions. Self-regulating systems will be able to adapt by altering their deployments based on risks anticipated, allocating resources based on demands, and implementing preventative measures against possible system failure.

Advances in technology in fields like artificial intelligence, machine learning, and control theory have made a great contribution to the creation of such systems, enabling the development of advanced systems as well as increasing prediction accuracy. Yet, there are still some matters like trust, transparency, and accountability that must be taken into account to fully automate such processes.

In the future, self-governing delivery systems may change the approach toward software engineering. Instead of developing rule-driven automation systems and operating them manually, businesses will be able to design intelligent systems capable of governing themselves and performing various tasks on their own.

Section Summary

This section examined the transition from automated to fully autonomous software delivery systems.

The key insights are as follows:

- Autonomy is adopted gradually through incremental capability development.
- Hybrid systems provide a critical intermediate stage, balancing automation and human oversight.
- Learning-driven systems enable adaptive and scalable decision-making.
- Fully autonomous systems integrate feedback, learning, and actuation for continuous self-regulation.
- The future of software delivery lies in intelligent, self-optimizing systems governed by robust control and policy frameworks.

8.12 Chapter Summary

The chapter furthered the control-oriented approach to software delivery by defining autonomous systems as the next in the line of control systems, to which intelligence, learning, and adaptation are integrated into the feedback loop. Based on the principles of CI/CD, DevOps, and DevSecOps, it showed that contemporary delivery systems no longer focus on performing a set of pre-established workflows but have the ability to self-regulate, make predictive decisions, and self-optimize.

One of the key contributions of this chapter is the incorporation of artificial intelligence into control architectures which changed the process of decision-making and actuation into dynamic and data-driven tasks. By allowing the systems to examine the intricate patterns, predict future conditions, and make situation-based decisions that enhance performance and resilience, AI makes the systems better. This deterministic-based logic change to intelligent control contributes to the effective functioning of the system in the conditions of uncertainty and rapid change.

Another key aspect highlighted in the chapter is the importance of feedback learning in facilitating continuous adaptation. Autonomous systems can make their control loop more refined by including learning mechanisms that enable better decision-making and operational effectiveness as time passes. Feedback is no longer taken only to take corrective action but also as a source of knowledge that leads to the evolution of the system in the long term.

Nonetheless, the inception of autonomy also puts the significance of stability, constraints, and governance into focus. The boundaries of autonomy systems should be well-defined to achieve safe and foreseeable operation. The required structure to avoid instability, unintended behavior, and misalignment with organizational objectives is constraint mechanisms, policy enforcement, and governance structures.

Finally, the autonomous software delivery systems allow new kinds of capabilities that transform the way systems are designed and used. These systems enable adaptive control, where the changing conditions can be adjusted dynamically; predictive decision-making, where the risk and performance can be managed in advance; and scalable intelligent delivery, where the systems can scale efficiently and remain stable and secure.

Overall, this chapter confirms that control theory, artificial intelligence, and system governance come together, which is the future of software delivery, a way to build intelligent, self-regulating systems that can deal with complexity without losing reliability and performance.

References

Åström, K. J., & Murray, R. M. (2008). *Feedback Systems: An Introduction for Scientists and Engineers*. Princeton University Press.

Bishop, C. M. (2006). *Pattern Recognition and Machine Learning*. Springer.

Burns, B., Grant, B., Oppenheimer, D., Brewer, E., & Wilkes, J. (2016). *Borg, Omega, and Kubernetes*. ACM Queue, 14(1), 70–93.

Géron, A. (2019). *Hands-On Machine Learning with Scikit-Learn, Keras, and TensorFlow*. O'Reilly Media.

Goodfellow, I., Bengio, Y., & Courville, A. (2016). *Deep Learning*. MIT Press.

Humble, J., & Farley, D. (2010). *Continuous Delivery: Reliable Software Releases through Build, Test, and Deployment Automation*. Addison-Wesley.

Kim, G., Humble, J., Debois, P., & Willis, J. (2021). *The DevOps Handbook* (2nd ed.). IT Revolution Press.

Meadows, D. H. (2008). *Thinking in Systems: A Primer*. Chelsea Green Publishing.

Mitchell, T. M. (1997). *Machine Learning*. McGraw-Hill.

NIST (2020). *Risk Management Framework for Information Systems and Organizations*. National Institute of Standards and Technology.

NIST (2023). *Artificial Intelligence Risk Management Framework (AI RMF 1.0)*. National Institute of Standards and Technology.

Ogata, K. (2010). *Modern Control Engineering* (5th ed.). Prentice Hall.

Russell, S., & Norvig, P. (2021). *Artificial Intelligence: A Modern Approach* (4th ed.). Pearson.

Sculley, D., et al. (2015). *Hidden Technical Debt in Machine Learning Systems*. Advances in Neural Information Processing Systems (NeurIPS).

CHAPTER 9

Scaling Control Across Teams and Platforms

9.1 Chapter Objective

This chapter looks into the process of scaling up software delivery control systems across teams, services, and platforms, taking feedback, decision-making, actuation, and constraints beyond localized pipelines to create an organizational system. Scaling delivery is not only a matter of infrastructure or deployment throughput; it also requires coordinated control.

In microservices-based environments with cloud-native platforms and DevSecOps approaches, there is a shift toward a distributed nature and interdependence of the software delivery control systems. Individual teams use their own pipelines, tools, and decision processes; nevertheless, they collectively influence related system states across services, environments, and platforms. In such an environment, stability and consistency require alignment of all these different parts asww a control system. This chapter looks into the alignment of all those different parts within a common control system.

9.2 Introduction: From Local Optimization to System-Wide Control

The contemporary software delivery patterns have enhanced the efficiency of teams at a significant level due to automation and continuous integration, as well as quick deployment pipelines. Now individual teams can optimize their workflows, minimize lead times, and deploy more often. But as organizations grow, the limitations of isolated

S. Bobba and N. S. Vummaneni, *CI/CD as a Control System*, https://doi.org/10.1007/979-8-8688-2842-3_9

optimization become increasingly evident, especially when governance, observability, and policy enforcement mechanisms are not consistently coordinated across teams. What may be effective at the level of an individual team or service is not necessarily going to be the best at the system-wide level Sigelman et al. (2010).

Fragmented control structures can emerge when teams independently implement pipelines, policies, and operational practices without shared governance standards, policy validation, or coordinated observability mechanisms. Every team can adopt their pipelines, policies, and decision logic which results in discrepancies in the way the systems are constructed, tested, and deployed. This autonomy leads to flexibility and speed, but can also cause misaligned goals, redundant effort, and conflicting actions within the organization. An example is a deployment plan that is ideal in a service might cause instability when it interacts with other services on which it depends.

The difficulty is amplified in settings where there exist distributed architectures and interdependent systems. An example of such systems is microservices-based systems which are comprised of many services that will develop independently but need to work as a unit. In tightly coupled or runtime-dependent environments, changes within one component may propagate across dependent services, potentially affecting performance, reliability, or security characteristics. Control that is not coordinated could lead to the emergence of instability, breakdowns, and unpredictable behavior of the system.

Scaling CI/CD and DevSecOps approaches brings about additional complexity. While it may be possible to replicate pipelines, the control structures that make the pipelines run need to be coordinated to ensure consistency. Control gaps may emerge when governance policies, observability standards, and enforcement mechanisms are inconsistently implemented, versioned, validated, or audited across teams and platforms.

This underscores the importance of coordinated control of distributed systems. Instead of viewing each pipeline as a system on its own, organizations can use control theory concepts as an architectural model for coordinating distributed delivery systems, in which feedback, decisions, and actions are synchronized between teams. This entails the implementation of common observability structures, uniform decision frameworks, and uniform policy implementation systems that cut across the system.

Moving to an integrated control architecture is a major paradigm shift away from the isolated pipeline approach to software delivery design and management. This architectural model treats pipelines as coordinated components within a broader distributed delivery system, where every action gets informed by a system-wide feedback and has goals that are aligned with organizational objectives. This method will allow organizations to be stable and consistent and facilitate decentralized decision-making and fast delivery.

From a control-oriented architectural perspective, scaling introduces coordination, propagation, and synchronization challenges across feedback signals, decision processes, and operational actions. Feedback should be summarized and compared across services, decisions should take into consideration system-wide context, and actuation should be coordinated to ensure that there are no unintended interactions. These issues can be mitigated by a composite of architectural design, governance models, and platform-level abstractions that can facilitate scalable control Meadows (2008).

Ultimately, scaling software delivery is not only about increasing deployment frequency or throughput but also about maintaining reliability, governance, recovery capability, and operational stability at scale. It is concerned with making sure that systems that become large and complex still remain coherent, stable, and predictable. This necessitates the extrapolation of control principles to more than individual pipelines up to the organization as a whole so that distributed systems can act as a single entity.

Key Argument

Scaling software delivery is not only about increasing throughput but also about maintaining reliable and coordinated operational control within acceptable risk and governance boundaries.

9.3 Distributed Control Systems in Software Delivery

As software delivery platforms evolve and grow in terms of teams, services, and other aspects, they can be analyzed using concepts inspired by distributed control systems as an architectural abstraction. As opposed to centralized control systems, which have a single authority in decision-making, distributed control systems involve many partial decision mechanisms whose functioning leads to the system's stability and effectiveness.

Within current DevOps/DevSecOps environments, each respective team/service or pipeline within an organization may be considered as the local controller, which makes decisions according to its local feedback process. However, it is important to understand that operational decisions within one service or pipeline may influence dependent services, shared infrastructure, or runtime behavior across the broader environment. This implies that, besides ensuring independence and autonomy of the different parts, it is also necessary to guarantee the coherence of the entire system.

The current subsection addresses some key structural elements and problems associated with distributed control.

9.3.1 Centralized vs. Distributed Control

Another consideration that is critical in scaling software delivery is to decide if it is wise to use centralized control or decentralized control. Both controls come with their advantages and disadvantages.

In case one decides on a centralized control model, then this will imply the existence of a central controller who makes decisions regarding the various parts. Decision consistency can improve when policies are centrally defined, versioned, validated, auditable, and enforced consistently across environments. It becomes much easier to monitor and govern systems under centralized control as it becomes possible to do so from one central point.

However, centralized control suffers major setbacks concerning scalability and responsiveness. The central controller will become a bottleneck in large systems because it can become a bottleneck if feedback volume, operational complexity, or decision scope exceeds its processing capacity. Centralized control may also lack consideration of other teams within the organization, thus not taking advantage of the organization's decentralization (Newman, 2015).

In the case of decentralized control, there are multiple controllers who base their decision-making processes on feedback from each constituent part. This approach can improve scalability and flexibility in environments where localized operational decisions are appropriate within defined governance and coordination boundaries.

However, there are multiple challenges involved in the process of distributed control, which mostly include the problem of coordination and consistency. In case decisions cannot be synchronized properly, they will conflict with each other and result in problems in other parts of the system. For example, service deployment decisions might contradict each other.

Undoubtedly, the difference between the two types of control is that of a compromise between consistency and autonomy. It should be acknowledged that successful implementations use a mixed approach.

9.3.2 Hierarchical Control Structures

The remedy to these limitations caused by total centralization or decentralization lies in applying hierarchical coordination models inspired by control system principles. This is because it allows for coordination to happen at different layers of the system while maintaining independence.

In a hierarchical approach to management, control is divided into three major layers:

- Team-level control, where each team individually controls its pipeline, decision, and actuation
- Platform-level coordination, where shared platform services, versioned policies, and enforcement mechanisms establish common operational capabilities and governance boundaries
- Organizational-level governance, where enterprise standards, risk ownership models, and policy frameworks define global operational objectives and constraints

All three layers can be viewed conceptually as coordinated operational control layers with feedback, decision-making, and actuation mechanisms, respectively. However, they work together and form a multi-layered control system wherein decision-making and constraints flow down layer after layer.

Understanding how policies, feedback, and operational decisions propagate across hierarchical coordination layers is critically important in distributed delivery environments. Goals set at the organizational level need to be transformed into constraints for activities at the lower levels to ensure that the decisions made there conform to the organization's policies and goals. Similarly, information at the lower levels needs to aggregate upward to make high-level strategic decisions possible.

Such a hierarchical setup makes coordination at an organizational scale possible due to decentralization of control. It allows flexibility to work independently within certain predefined limits while helping maintain alignment with broader organizational objectives in environments involving shared infrastructure, runtime dependencies, or cross-service operational impact.

From the viewpoint of control systems, hierarchical coordination models can improve operational stability by balancing local autonomy with broader organizational coordination (Ogata, 2010).

9.3.3 Coordination Across Services

The first challenge is in relation to the interdependence between the involved services in distributed software delivery systems, where various components tend to share their data and operations context. It follows that the interactions among these services are rather complicated and may involve changes in one service triggering changes in the behavior of another service. It is vital, therefore, for the sake of efficient system operation to have proper coordination among these services.

One significant challenge involves managing dependencies between services sharing infrastructure, APIs, data stores, or operational workflows. For instance, a change in the core service will trigger changes in other services depending on the functionality of the former service. Coordination in such a case is required in order to ensure that everything is done properly and consistently.

Cross-service coordination depends on timely, correlated, de-duplicated, and policy-aware observability signals derived from metrics, logs, traces, and runtime telemetry.

Another important consideration in this regard is the timing of the actuation process, which is particularly important in environments involving tightly coupled deployments, shared dependencies, or coordinated runtime changes. For example, certain coordination schemes may have to be developed to ensure that the services deployed work well together, as well as the rollback processes to consider all the dependencies involved.

The challenge of coordinating activities in distributed systems also involves the issue of delays and other communication problems because operational telemetry, coordination signals, and deployment decisions often need to propagate across multiple dependent services and infrastructure layers.

In the context of control systems, coordination across services involves integrating telemetry feedback, deployment decisions, dependency-aware policies, and operational actions across interdependent services. In order to ensure that there is stability in the overall process, care needs to be taken to coordinate all aspects of the feedback process and decision-making. Figure 9-1 illustrates a distributed control architecture for software delivery, organizing the key capability areas that support autonomy and alignment across product and engineering value streams.

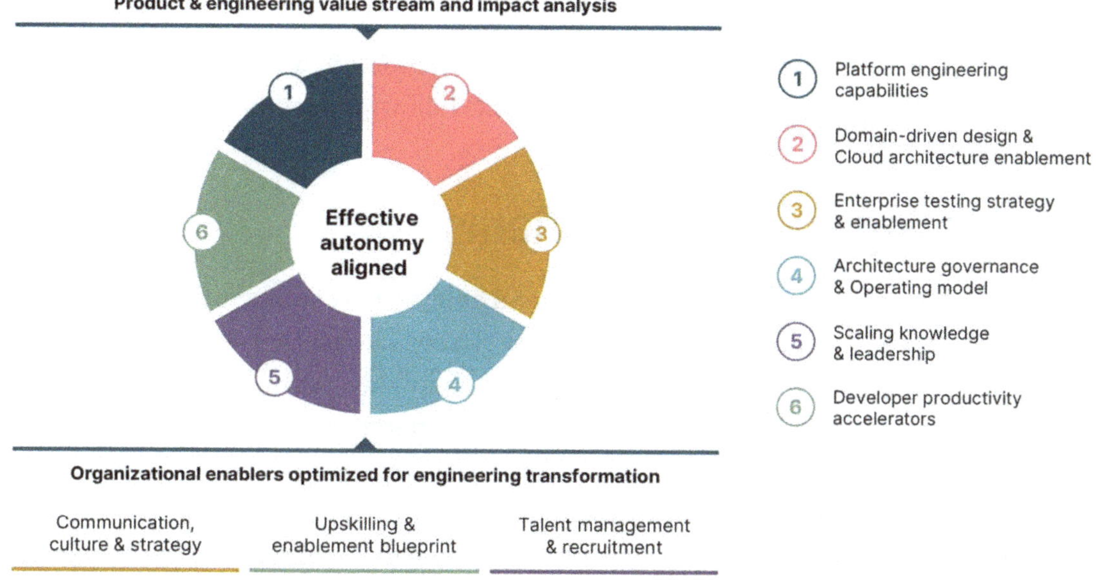

Figure 9-1. *Distributed Control Architecture in Software Delivery*

This figure shows distributed delivery coordination architecture illustrating telemetry feedback, policy-driven decisions, and operational actuation across teams, services, and platform layers.

Section Summary

This section examined how software delivery systems can be conceptually modeled using distributed control system principles.

The key insights are as follows:

- Scaling provides distributed control, in which many controllers function within teams and services.
- Centralized governance is designed to improve consistency but restricts scalability, whereas distributed control improves autonomy but necessitates coordination.
- The hierarchical control paradigm allows for scalability within coordination through teams, platforms, and organization levels.

- Services coordination is necessary in order to handle dependencies in a distributed manner.
- Distributed control involves coordinating feedback, decisions, and actuation processes within the system.

These ideas form the basis of a discussion of how feedback systems can be scaled in a distributed manner, which we will examine in the following section.

9.4 Scaling Feedback Systems

Feedback systems collect, process, correlate, and analyze operational telemetry within distributed delivery environments, where signal quality, latency, correlation accuracy, and policy interpretation significantly affect decision quality. With growth in scale, feedback systems are becoming more complex and generate more information. The simple and compact flow of information limited to a particular pipeline or service transforms into multiple data flows coming from across an organization.

The process of scaling feedback systems is ensuring that feedback signals are timely, correlated, de-duplicated, policy-aware, interpretable, and operationally actionable. The failure to properly scale will lead to inconsistent and unreliable information, thus reducing the quality of decision-making and control of the process. This chapter discusses scaling in terms of observability, processing signals, and maintaining consistency across teams.

9.4.1 Observability at Scale

Observability provides telemetry inputs that support feedback-driven operational decisions and actuation processes within modern delivery systems. The term includes metric collection and analysis, as well as logging and tracing. In turn, all of the above allow gaining insight into system performance, which is critical at the enterprise level when working with large amounts of information.

Metrics provide quantitative telemetry regarding system performance and operational behavior, though their usefulness depends on signal quality, SLO alignment, correlation accuracy, and collection latency.

Logs provide contextual event data describing system operation, especially when normalized, correlated, and connected to operational policies and runtime conditions.

Traces track request flows across distributed services and become most effective when correlated with metrics, logs, dependency mappings, and SLO-aware operational analysis.

When scaling the system, the amount of telemetry volume, signal diversity, and correlation complexity increases substantially, requiring special approaches to monitoring, management, and analysis. Special tools are required to integrate, analyze, and aggregate data from different sources and combine signals. This allows creating a picture of the system state by correlating data from multiple sources.

Observability unification supports near-real-time monitoring and alerting when signals are sufficiently timely, correlated, and aligned with operational thresholds and policies. By incorporating observability into the control loop, it will be easier to keep track of the status of systems and make better decisions.

Nonetheless, scalability is accompanied by issues such as large data volumes, data storage, and processing. Therefore, the issue of scalability is connected to the need for the management of data, which requires scalable solutions and high efficiency of processing.

9.4.2 Signal Aggregation and Correlation

Feedback signals in distributed systems come from many sources, each of which provides partial operational visibility with varying levels of accuracy, latency, and contextual relevance. In order for such information to be useful for management purposes, these signals need to be consolidated and correlated in order to get valuable conclusions.

Aggregation of signals involves collecting, correlating, filtering, and prioritizing telemetry data to obtain a holistic picture of the current state of affairs. This allows for recognizing patterns and tendencies that would otherwise go unnoticed. For instance, some problems associated with a particular service can have an indirect cause in a change that was made in another service.

Correlation of signals involves identifying operational dependencies and causal relationships across metrics, logs, traces, runtime events, and policy violations.

The key problem facing such systems relates to reducing noise. The larger a system becomes, the greater volume of data it will produce. Much of this data will be unnecessary and redundant. Too much noise could hinder critical signals and cause delays or incorrect responses. Filtering, detecting anomalies, and prioritizing are some of the approaches required for achieving good signals.

Achieving good signal qualities is also necessary for solving problems of false positives and false negatives. False positives could make one think that the system's state is different from what it actually is. False negatives would also misrepresent the state. High-quality signals will facilitate good decisions, but bad-quality signals will encourage overreaction or underreaction.

Control system analysis reveals that better signal aggregation and correlation increase the system's controllability and observability.

9.4.3 Feedback Consistency Across Teams

Consistency in the process of collecting, interpreting, and utilizing feedback information becomes particularly crucial as the scope of feedback systems extends to the whole team of developers. Otherwise, each development group would use its own metrics and measurement methods, producing an inconsistent picture of the system state and decisions being made.

Standardized feedback collection and processing means developing universal metrics, logs, traces, and other techniques employed within the company to facilitate the feedback process. Standardization will ensure the compatibility of feedback signals and allow using them in creating an integrated observability mechanism. On the other hand, the existence of standardized processes makes it easier for the development process to be undertaken collaboratively through a series of established practices.

Visibility, which is one of the other key principles involved in collecting feedback through collaboration, refers to sharing the data collected among all developers. Here, the developers get to understand how their decisions impact the system as a whole and are able to decide more effectively since they will be evaluating their decisions in relation to other services.

Consistency is also helpful in governance and the implementation of the policy. Consistency ensures that the feedback provided is used in implementing consistent constraints and decision-making standards in order to achieve consistency with the organization's objectives. At the same time, consistency should be achieved alongside flexibility. Table 9-1 summarizes the main feedback challenges that arise at scale, along with strategies for addressing them.

***Table 9-1.** Feedback Challenges and Solutions at Scale*

Challenge	Description	Solution
Data Volume	Large amounts of metrics, logs, and traces	Scalable observability platforms
Signal Noise	Irrelevant or redundant data	Filtering and anomaly detection
Fragmentation	Disparate tools and metrics across teams	Standardized observability frameworks
Latency	Delays in feedback processing	Real-time data pipelines
Inconsistent Interpretation	Different teams interpret signals differently	Shared dashboards and common metrics

Section Summary

This section examined how feedback systems scale in distributed software delivery environments and the challenges associated with maintaining effective observability.

The key insights are as follows:

- Observed scalability necessitates an integrated approach to metrics, logging, and tracing in distributed systems.
- Observed integration platforms give a complete view of the system's operation.
- The process of combining and correlating signals converts data into information.
- Signals need to be of good quality for proper decision-making.
- Standardization and visibility facilitate the consistency of feedback across departments.

The principles above define the basis for scaling decision-making in distributed systems. This is discussed further in the following section.

9.5 Scaling Decision-Making Across Teams

As the delivery processes grow beyond individual companies, decision-making itself moves from being an individual, pipeline-specific process to becoming a distributed control process involving several teams, services, and platforms. At this point, there is a fundamental shift where decisions cannot exist in isolation, but are interconnected in such a way that together they define system behavior. There are now additional considerations about coordination, consistency, and governance in cases where different teams have autonomy yet work within a single system context.

There are clear requirements for decision-making at this level. Decision points need to be distributed effectively. Policies need to provide decision rules and make sure that all the decisions can stay coordinated despite being distributed. Conflicts need to be managed effectively too. This section considers these requirements.

9.5.1 Distributed Decision Points

In current CI/CD and DevSecOps pipelines, decision points are necessarily distributed in the pipeline architecture. Every individual team has its own pipelines, which consist of decision points in the form of validations, deployments, risk assessments, and runtime actions. Such decisions may be performed by each individual team according to their own feedback.

This decentralized approach allows for enhanced flexibility and efficiency in decision-making, as decisions can be made closer to the point of execution, without depending on central authorities.

However, such an approach poses major problems with regard to coordination. An individual decision point can have implications for others, as it will create undesired side effects. For instance, deployment decisions in one pipeline can create incompatibilities with other services that depend on this service, or poor allocation of resources between pipelines can negatively impact system efficiency.

The issue of incomplete awareness is another challenge in the distributed model, since decisions are made on limited data. Teams lack knowledge of the entire system and cannot consider all its aspects when making decisions about its operations.

To solve these challenges, teams require a feedback and coordination framework that allows them to have complete visibility of the system.

9.5.2 Policy-Driven Decision Standardization

In order to maintain coherence at each distributed point of decision-making, policy-based decision standardization is used by organizations wherein decision-making processes are established by adopting common policies within the organization. Here, common policies serve as common decision frameworks whereby decisions made by various units within an organization are aligned with overall organizational goals and risk profiles.

An important component for achieving such alignment is Policy as Code wherein decisions are represented in computer-readable code and integrated with existing decision-making process pipelines. As far as examples go, security-related policies could contain rules regarding what vulnerability threshold is deemed acceptable, while operational policies could provide instructions for deployment and rollback procedures.

Policy-driven standardization provides several benefits:

- **Consistency**: Guarantees that decisions are made according to the same criteria throughout the teams
- **Scalability**: Ensures that policies can be enforced in larger and more complicated systems
- **Traceability**: Provides an opportunity for auditing and analyzing decisions
- **Governance**: Keeps decisions in accordance with organizational norms and limitations

It is important that policies should be made in an adaptive way. Having too many rigid policies can limit any innovations, which means that the organization will not react properly to changes in its surroundings. On the other hand, having too much flexibility means that the necessary constraints will be difficult to impose. Therefore, there has to be a balance in this aspect.

In the control system approach, policies represent decision constraints.

9.5.3 Managing Decision Conflicts

Decision conflicts occur naturally in distributed environments, where several teams and systems work with conflicting interests, constraints, and objectives. Decision conflicts may stem from

- **Incompatible policies**: Conflicting requirements from various policies.
- **Conflicting goals**: For example, optimizing performance vs. minimizing risk.
- **Resource competition**: Several services may vie for limited resources.
- **Incongruent timing**: Decision-making based on incongruent data points.

Without proper management, decision conflicts can result in conflicting decisions, poor performance, or even system instabilities. Conflict management is thus crucial for building scalable decision infrastructures.

There are several possible approaches to decision conflict management, including defining a hierarchy of policy priorities and decision objectives. For instance, compliance and security policies may take priority over performance considerations in sensitive environments.

Another approach involves using coordination mechanisms, whereby control is delegated to a higher layer. Such coordination mechanisms are used for evaluating decisions in the context of dependencies across the system.

Conflicts may be identified and resolved using the feedback-driven approach, where the decisions are informed by the data collected from the functioning of the system. In cases where conflicting decisions are made, leading to poor performance of the system, feedback information could be used to correct these decisions.

A consensus model could be employed in which many systems or stakeholders would participate in the process of making decisions. This helps achieve more alignment of objectives but also makes the process complex and lengthy.

In summary, conflict management depends on the development of good policies for making decisions along with feedback processes. Figure 9-2 presents a distributed decision-making model in which multiple rule authors develop policies in parallel that are merged, approved, and released into a shared decision repository.

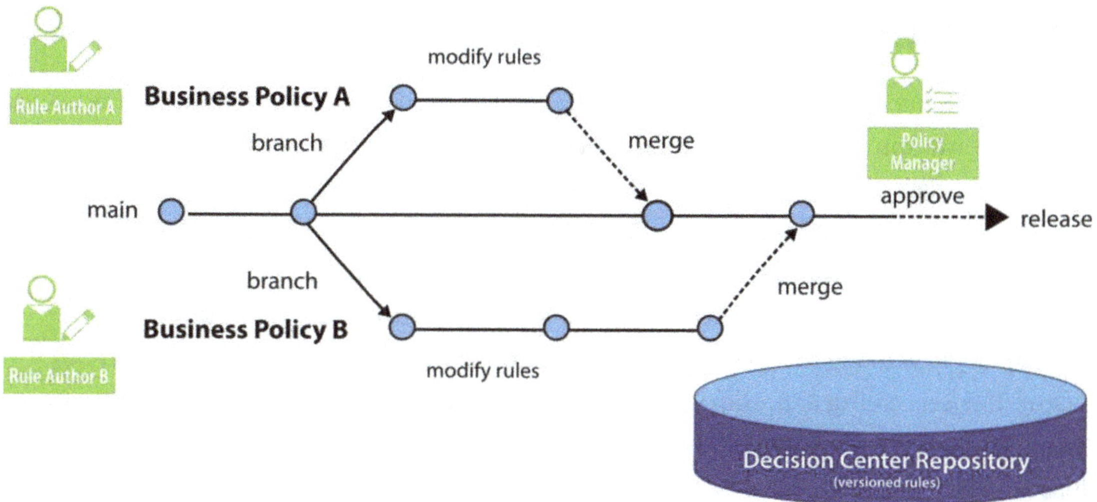

Figure 9-2. *Distributed Decision-Making Model*

This figure shows a distributed decision-making model illustrating decentralized pipeline decisions coordinated through shared policies and feedback mechanisms.

Section Summary

This section examined how decision-making scales across distributed teams and the mechanisms required to ensure coordination and consistency.

The key insights are as follows:

- Decision-making gets delegated to various pipelines and teams in scalable architectures.
- Decentralized decision nodes make scalability easier, although coordination issues emerge.
- Standardization of policies ensures alignment in systems.
- Decision disputes come from conflicting priorities and need to be managed.
- Scaling depends on feedback, policy management, and coordination.

The above-mentioned principles constitute the framework within which actuation mechanisms can be scaled in distributed systems, as further detailed in the following section.

9.6 Scaling Actuation Mechanisms

Actuation, the actualization of decisions via deployments, changes in configurations, and manipulation of the infrastructure, becomes a cross-service, cross-team, cross-environment activity in large-scale software delivery systems. Actuation becomes a cross-system process rather than a local pipeline step as systems grow into more distributed environments. It is imperative to ensure that actions performed by systems do not cause unforeseen effects elsewhere, yet remain fast and independent.

This section discusses how coordination, consistency, and containment can be ensured when scaling actuation, so changes can be applied in a safe and effective manner across environments. The concepts discussed include coordinated deployments, platform-level actuations, and techniques for bounding the effects of problems.

9.6.1 Coordinated Deployments Across Services

Today's software applications consist of several services that are interdependent on each other, meaning that changing one service may have implications for other services. It follows that coordination is required when making changes to an application since it would not make sense to change one service at the cost of compromising another.

Multi-service deployments necessitate multi-service deployment strategies because, unlike the case of single-service deployment, multi-service deployment cannot take place separately from each other but needs proper sequencing and synchronizing. The canary, blue-green, and progressive deployment strategies, among others, are therefore applied in a multi-service environment.

For instance, an implementation process may entail the gradual deployment of services in a coordinated manner, such as first deploying some selected services to observe their effect before moving further. However, the coordination process can also be facilitated by a dependency-aware approach to deployment, whereby the links among the different services are taken into consideration.

The dependency-aware approach typically involves the implementation of strategies such as versioning, backward compatibility, and feature flags to ensure that while the services may be developed separately, they work well together.

9.6.2 Platform-Level Actuation

As scale increases, it becomes more common for actuation to move away from each pipeline and become a part of the infrastructure itself. This is a key concept in platform engineering where standardized execution environments, pipelines, and services help achieve efficient control over operations.

Under this approach, infrastructure serves as the common control layer that allows you to abstract the process of managing applications and services as well as enforce consistency. IaC and API-driven actuation allow you to automate and standardize processes.

Here are the key benefits of platform-level actuation:

- **Consistency**: Standardized operation of services across all teams and processes.
- **Scalability**: Infrastructure makes it easy to run large numbers of instances.
- **Governance**: Platform-level enforcement of policies and constraints.
- **Efficiency**: Ability to use reusable components and avoid duplication.

For example, the platform may offer pre-built deployment templates, scaling automation, and even observability features out of the box.

However, platform-driven actuation must balance between being too rigid and flexible. On one hand, overly rigid platforms might limit the freedom of teams, whereas on the other hand, not being standardized enough might lead to chaos. In this regard, successful platforms impose guardrails, not constraints, on teams.

9.6.3 Limiting Blast Radius at Scale

Failures have the potential to spread rapidly within such environments, leading to cascade failures and making the systems highly unstable. It is imperative that such failures do not become problematic due to spreading, and this is an essential part of scalable actuation. There are many ways through which this can be achieved, and one of them includes isolation, which entails the partitioning of the systems into pieces of codes which can fail individually without collapsing the entire system.

- Service isolation, whereby services run separately from each other and have minimal shared state
- Isolation on the infrastructure level, like separate environments or separate clusters
- Deployment isolation, wherein changes are deployed only to parts of the system

Another approach to introducing change involves rolling out changes in a controlled manner, watching their impact on the system, and proceeding from there.

Fail-safes such as rollback strategies, circuit breakers, and redundancy help contain the issue. The reason for employing these strategies is that, in case problems occur, they can be detected early enough and sorted out.

When viewed from the perspective of control systems, constraining the blast radius requires designing actuation procedures that limit the disturbance and do not amplify it. Table 9-2 outlines the principal actuation strategies used in distributed systems.

Table 9-2. *Actuation Strategies in Distributed Systems*

Strategy	Description	Benefit
Coordinated Deployment	Synchronizing deployments across services	Ensures compatibility and system stability
Dependency-Aware Actuation	Considering service dependencies during deployment	Prevents integration failures
Platform-Level Actuation	Using shared infrastructure and pipelines	Enables consistency and scalability
Progressive Rollout	Gradual deployment with monitoring	Reduces risk and enables early detection
Isolation Strategies	Segmentation of services and environments	Limits failure propagation
Automated Rollback	Reverting changes upon failure detection	Restores system stability quickly

Section Summary

This section examined how actuation mechanisms scale across distributed software delivery systems and the strategies required to ensure safe and effective execution.

The key insights are as follows:

- Actuation in a distributed context becomes a systemic process.
- Multiservice systems need coordination and awareness of dependencies.
- Platform engineering offers a common control plane for actuation scalability.
- It is important to restrict the blast radius to avoid failures spreading.
- Controlled deployment and isolation improve system robustness.

This set of principles is the basis of the discussion about scaling of governance and constraints in the next section.

9.7 Governance and Constraints at Scale

With scaling of software delivery processes to include cross-functional team collaboration, service coordination, and platform integration, there is also a shift from point control to an organization-wide approach to governance and constraints management. For a smaller software delivery pipeline, governance can be implemented by means of centralized constraints and policies. However, as we scale our processes and introduce more complexity, governance has to become decentralized and operate on the level of distributed, independent units that have their own pipelines, tooling, and processes.

When thinking of our systems from a control systems perspective, governance represents a constraint layer for our software delivery systems. Constraints make sure that all actions performed by any unit in a software delivery pipeline are consistent in terms of performance, quality, security, etc. Thus, as part of scaling our systems, we need to implement solutions to define, propagate, enforce, and adapt constraints.

In this chapter, we will discuss policy enforcement in a multi-team environment, approaches to governance, such as federated vs. centralized models, as well as constraints propagation.

9.7.1 Policy Enforcement Across Teams

However, in large enterprises, numerous teams work separately, and their tasks include the creation and launch of their own services. As this approach leads to rapid innovation and high efficiency, it also creates opportunities for inconsistency in operations and control. Thus, policy enforcement by teams becomes necessary to maintain consistency between all activities.

Standard governance patterns make it possible to create a uniform model of operation by establishing policies on various aspects. Such policies concern security issues, compliance, the development process, and the behavior of operations. They allow companies to provide consistent restrictions for their teams, irrespective of the technologies used by them.

The concept of policy as code makes it possible to implement policy enforcement in a consistent way by means of automating this process. Thus, security policies will prevent from launching vulnerable applications or infrastructure components, while compliance policies will require all teams to go through certain audit stages regardless of the pipeline utilized.

Cross-team compliance is done through incorporating the enforcement of policies into the control mechanism of software delivery tools. The feedback received from security checks, performance indicators, and audits is compared against policies, and decisions are taken based on them. This guarantees that compliance is a process rather than an event.

The enforcement of policies among teams calls for the reconciliation of consistency and flexibility. Consistent policies are important in achieving effective governance; however, it is equally essential to allow the teams to adjust their policies to the context in which they work.

9.7.2 Federated vs. Centralized Governance

One key factor when scaling governance is whether to adopt centralized or federated governance, each of which has its strengths and weaknesses.

Centralized governance means that decisions and policies related to governance are handled centrally by an organizational unit or platform. The major benefit of this form of governance is that it is consistent and tightly controlled since all teams operate under the same set of guidelines. In other words, centralized governance is easy to audit since there is uniformity in how things are done.

The downside of centralized governance is that it lacks flexibility because decision-making powers are not distributed among teams. On the other hand, federated governance means that teams operate with a certain degree of freedom regarding policies. Teams in federated governance are able to set their policies based on the guidelines provided by the organization.

Coordination and consistency become significant problems within a federated form of governance. Lack of coordination will make it impossible for the groups to come up with conflicting policies, contrary to the organizational policy, thus causing inefficiencies and increased risk.

The hybrid form of governance has been popularly applied to overcome such problems. In the hybrid form of governance, the organization

- Have centralized core policies (such as security policies)
- Have local policies implemented by the teams

In this way, the organization can balance its need for control while still providing flexibility and independence for the teams.

In the context of control systems theory, the hybrid model can be thought of as a multilevel constraint system where global constraints determine the scope of the system, whereas local constraints allow the system to adapt.

9.7.3 Constraint Propagation Across Systems

In distributed software delivery systems, constraints should be propagated in a coherent manner among various teams, services, and platforms in order for their behavior to be consistent. Propagation of constraints consists of mapping high-level policies and goals into lower-level rules that should be enforced by all participants.

One of the biggest problems in such propagation lies in the need for consistency of constraints in heterogeneous environments. Teams can use different tools and frameworks, which makes it hard to maintain a uniform set of policies. In order to solve this problem, companies resort to utilizing standard interfaces and platforms that allow enforcing policies uniformly.

Another important problem lies in policy drift. Policies may change over time because some participants update their rules while others remain unchanged. Such situations can result in inconsistencies and gaps in policy enforcement NIST (2020) and NIST (2023).

Policy drift prevention calls for mechanisms for ongoing coordination and verification of constraints. They include

- Policy management systems that act as a one-stop shop for all policies
- Policy validators that check whether policies have been consistently implemented
- Ongoing monitoring that identifies departures from established constraints

The dissemination of constraints also entails making sure that policies have been properly applied and executed within the system. Policies need to be translated into executable rules within the pipelines, platforms, and services Burns et al. (2016).

From a control systems viewpoint, the propagation of constraints makes sure that all feedback loops within a control system function within identical limits, resulting in stable operation. Without consistent constraints, distributed control systems become inconsistent, thus unstable. Figure 9-3 shows the governance model for distributed systems, in which a central governance hub distributes policies to managed clusters that enforce them locally and map technical controls to compliance standards.

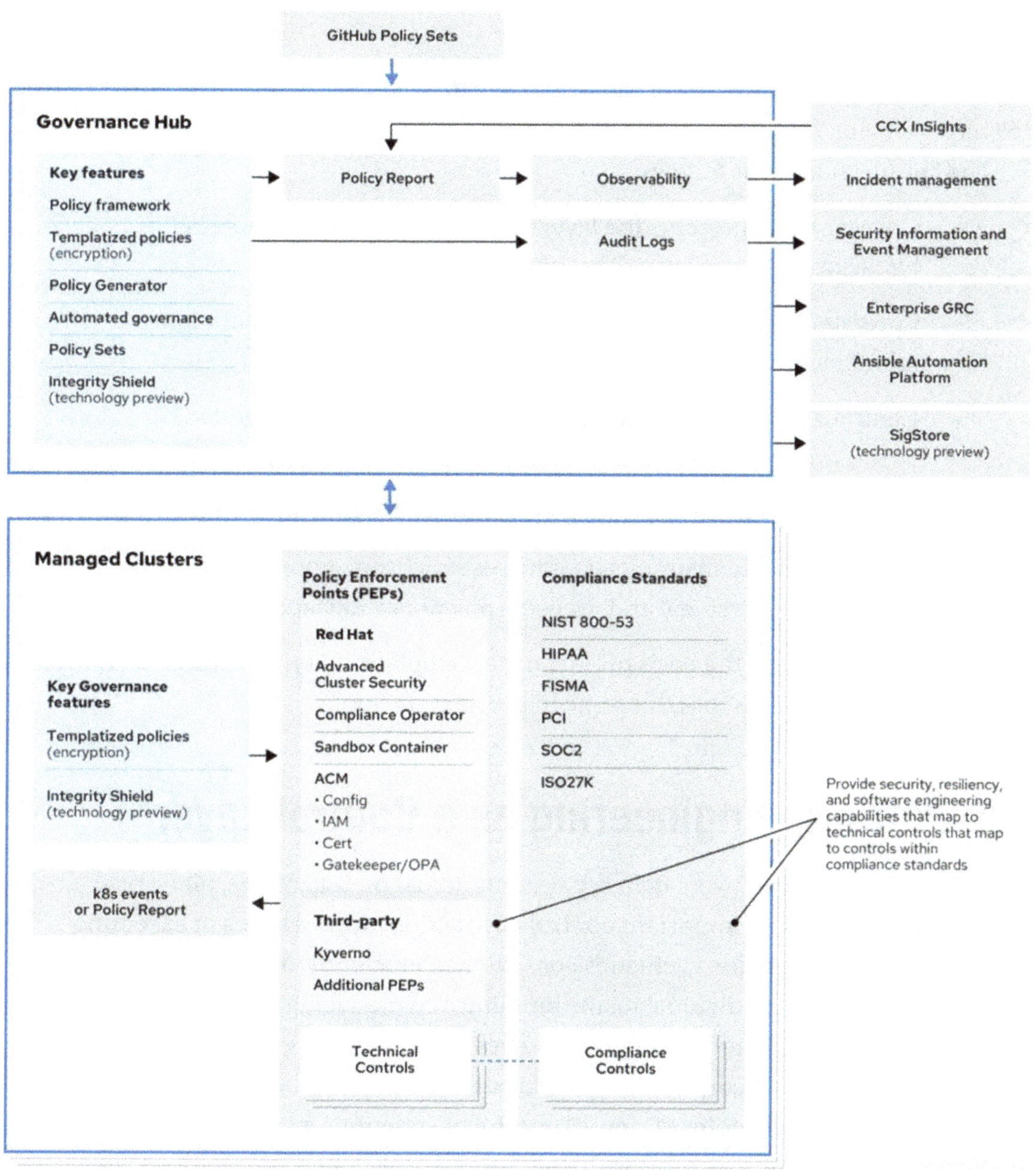

Figure 9-3. *Governance Models in Distributed Systems*

This figure compares of centralized, federated, and hybrid governance models illustrating trade-offs between consistency, autonomy, and scalability.

Section Summary

This section examined how governance and constraints scale across distributed software delivery systems.

The key insights are as follows:

- Governance represents the layer of constraints that guarantees the behavior of the system stays within acceptable limits.
- Consistency in policy implementation across the team guarantees adherence.
- Centralized governance allows consistency, whereas federated governance promotes autonomy.
- Hybrid governance combines both consistency and autonomy.
- Propagation of constraints guarantees synchronization among decentralized systems and prevents any policy deviation.

All these points form the basis of learning about platform engineering for controlling scalability, and we will discuss this topic in the next section.

9.8 Platform Engineering as a Control Layer

In line with increased software delivery systems across organizations, platform engineering becomes an important control abstraction layer in terms of executing development and operations activities consistently, efficiently, and in a controlled fashion. Unlike having individual teams building and managing their respective pipelines and tooling, platform engineering helps in abstracting such tools and creating common services that incorporate control abstractions into the delivery process.

When seen from the point of view of control abstractions, platforms become intermediary control abstractions within systems where policies, limitations, and overall goals of organizations get translated into actual capabilities. In other words, organizations become capable of operating at scale in an autonomous fashion while maintaining system control at all times.

This chapter will explore control abstractions in platforms, the balance between consistency and autonomy, and the role of standardization in systems.

9.8.1 Platforms as Control Abstractions

The platforms provide abstractions that package complexity into reusable services and build control into their very essence. This makes it easier for developers to focus on developing the application itself without worrying about how it will run effectively. This may be achieved via IDP solutions by providing an ecosystem that consists of certain pipelines and tools to deliver software.

IDPs will integrate everything like CI/CD pipelines, infrastructure, security management, and more into one dashboard. With that in mind, everyone will receive the same control plane where the processes, decisions, and actions will be done in a similar manner.

With standardized pipelines and tooling in place, this becomes easier to achieve. Instead of adapting processes according to the particular needs of every team, platforms will offer ready solutions that are consistent with best practices and guidelines. For example, a ready deployment pipeline will include security, performance, and rollback mechanisms.

Through abstraction, variability is minimized, and complexities are mitigated to allow predictable and reproducible behavior from systems. On the other hand, abstraction also provides the groundwork for incorporating complex functionalities such as policy enforcement, decision automation, and actuation intelligence.

In the realm of controls, platforms function as controllers and constraint enforcers to ensure that all activities performed in the systems comply with the policies set.

9.8.2 Enabling Consistency and Autonomy

Another issue with scaling the software delivery process is maintaining both consistency throughout the enterprise while simultaneously ensuring that the teams have the autonomy necessary to do the work. Platforms help resolve this issue by introducing a concept of practical operational guardrails implemented through policy-driven constraints, which means that teams are free to make decisions as long as these decisions are made within reasonable boundaries.

The concept of guardrails refers to rules set up inside the platform that impose restrictions on what actions can be taken by the team. In other words, guardrails provide teams with the ability to make choices that will benefit their project without violating any important rules, including compliance issues and security policies.

On the contrary, very restrictive platforms limit the freedom of decision-making of development teams due to a too strict workflow and limited options for adaptation to the specific conditions.

Platforms allow teams to manage resources, provision services, deploy them, and take care of other tasks independently while still being consistent because all the actions performed are within the boundaries of organizational policies. Platforms provide teams with opportunities to manage resources and perform other activities autonomously using standardized interfaces.

Thus, platforms offer self-service with built-in controls and guardrails.

9.8.3 Scaling Through Standardization

Standardization is an essential concept in platform engineering, whereby the delivery systems can scale effectively by limiting variations and encouraging reuse. Platforms can ensure that the behaviors of the delivery systems are predictable because they set patterns, templates, and components.

Using reusable components like pipeline templates, infrastructure modules, and deployment techniques enables teams to develop their systems based on already available solutions instead of reinventing them. In addition, reusability enables teams to implement solutions using best practices.

Standardization makes it easy to govern and enforce compliance policies. Since policies are integrated into standardized components, implementation can be automatic and effortless. Consequently, there is less need for supervision since compliance is ensured.

However, standardization should be created in a way that enables the platform to evolve and adapt. For example, as changes happen, platforms must be updated or extended. To enable this, platforms should use modular and versioned architectures for continuous development Kim et al. (2021).

When considering control systems, standardization makes systems predictable and stable.

Table 9-3 presents the key benefits of platform engineering for distributed software delivery.

***Table 9-3.** Platform Engineering Benefits*

Benefit	Description	Impact
Consistency	Standardized pipelines and tooling across teams	Predictable system behavior
Scalability	Reusable components and templates	Efficient scaling of delivery systems
Governance	Embedded policies and constraints	Continuous compliance and control
Autonomy	Self-service capabilities with guardrails	Faster and more flexible team operations
Efficiency	Reduced duplication and operational overhead	Improved productivity

Section Summary

This section examined the role of platform engineering as a control layer in scaling software delivery systems.

The key insights are as follows:

- Platforms serve as control abstractions where governance and execution capabilities are embedded within.
- Developer platforms support standardized and scalable distribution processes internally.
- Guardrails offer a means to strike a balance between standardization and the autonomy of teams.
- Self-service models boost efficiency without compromising control.
- Standardization facilitates scalability, predictability, and governability of the system.

These guidelines form the basis for comprehending failure propagation in distributed systems and building resilience, which is discussed in the following section.

9.9 Failure Propagation and Systemic Risk

When software distribution systems expand to include multiple services in a distributed network, without adequate isolation and containment mechanisms, an individual failure may propagate across dependent services and infrastructure components. In tightly connected systems, a disturbance to one element can cascade throughout the rest of the system, increasing the magnitude of the problem. This type of behavior is known as failure propagation and can present difficulties for controlling such systems.

Failure is defined as an occurrence that acts as a disturbance affecting the steady-state operation of the system in control theory. With regard to a distributed system, the interconnectivity of components means that disturbance has paths through which it could travel in the entire system, and this may cause the occurrence of cascading failure events.

This part focuses on cascading failure events and how to limit the occurrence of such failures in the system.

9.9.1 Cascading Failures in Distributed Systems

Cascading failures happen when a failure in one component leads to a sequence of subsequent failures in other components. In distributed software architectures, this typically happens due to dependencies among services, in which actions of one influence another.

For example, failing one service may disrupt other services using its functionalities. They will be overloaded, slowed down, or become unable to function correctly. This creates a feedback loop of degradation in which the issues multiply and cause a massive disruption throughout the system.

The failure propagation is especially prominent in systems with

- High coupling between the services
- Sharing of the resources used by services, for example, a database or shared infrastructure component
- Processes communicating in a synchronous manner
- Ineffectiveness of isolating failure

In addition to this problem, there may be problems arising from incorrect or delayed feedback which will lead to wrong actions being taken in order to solve the problem. For instance, if the system thinks that high loads are the steady state, it will end up scaling and throttling incorrectly.

If looked at through a systems control theory, a cascading failure will be termed as a situation where positive feedback takes place, meaning disturbance amplification takes place.

9.9.2 Containment Strategies

Containment is key to avoiding the spreading of disruptions and isolation of the system from further damage in case of failures. Containment strategies should be utilized to prevent the spread of disturbances.

Isolation is one of the most common strategies, involving the decoupling of different components in order to minimize their interference in case of failures. There are several ways to achieve isolation, namely

- Service-level isolation, involving decoupling of services via clear interfaces
- Isolation on infrastructure level, e.g., using separate clusters, or environments
- Boundary of failure domain, restricting failure scope

Segmentation is another technique of containment, which implies breaking down the system into segments, allowing better control over individual parts of it. Traffic can be segmented according to certain criteria, for instance, according to geographical locations, so that a failure of one environment does not influence the entire system.

Circuit breakers and rate-limiting techniques are also commonly used in order to avoid further problems in case of system failure. Circuit breaker mechanism detects failure of dependent service and interrupts calls to it, whereas rate limiting manages request traffic.

In addition, progressive release strategies like canary release and feature flagging minimize the effect of any changes by restricting their scope to a limited part of the system. Should there be any problem, the changes can then be reverted without affecting the rest of the system.

This is because the above methods change the behavior of the system, shifting it from a disturbance-amplifying state to a disturbance-absorbing state.

9.9.3 Resilience Through Control Design

Further to containment, attaining stability will require building resilient control systems where resilience is one of the objectives in the control process. Resilience refers to the ability of systems to continue functioning and recover rapidly after experiencing any disturbance.

One of the main characteristics of resilient systems is redundancy. In this approach, important parts are replicated such that the entire system can keep working even when there is a failure in certain areas. The redundancy process can be applied to infrastructure, data, and services. This implies that the occurrence of problems does not lead to the total collapse of the system.

The second characteristic of resilience is a fail-safe. Fail-safes are mechanisms through which systems can enter a safe condition whenever there is a failure. Examples of fail-safes include rollbacks on failed deployments, service degradation, and switching to alternate sources.

Finally, from the control systems' point of view, resilience entails designing negative feedback systems. Negative feedback systems entail designing the control process such that disturbances are counteracted and stability is maintained.

Also very significant to consider is adaptive resilience, which involves learning from past mistakes and building on them for improvement over time. This entails learning from the mistakes made during the process and modifying the system's control strategy accordingly so that any future problems can be effectively addressed Beyer et al. (2016).

In summary, resilience should not be considered as one isolated trait of the system, but rather an outcome of all the components. Figure 9-4 illustrates failure propagation versus containment through the circuit-breaker pattern, whose closed, open, and half-open states prevent repeated failures from cascading through the system.

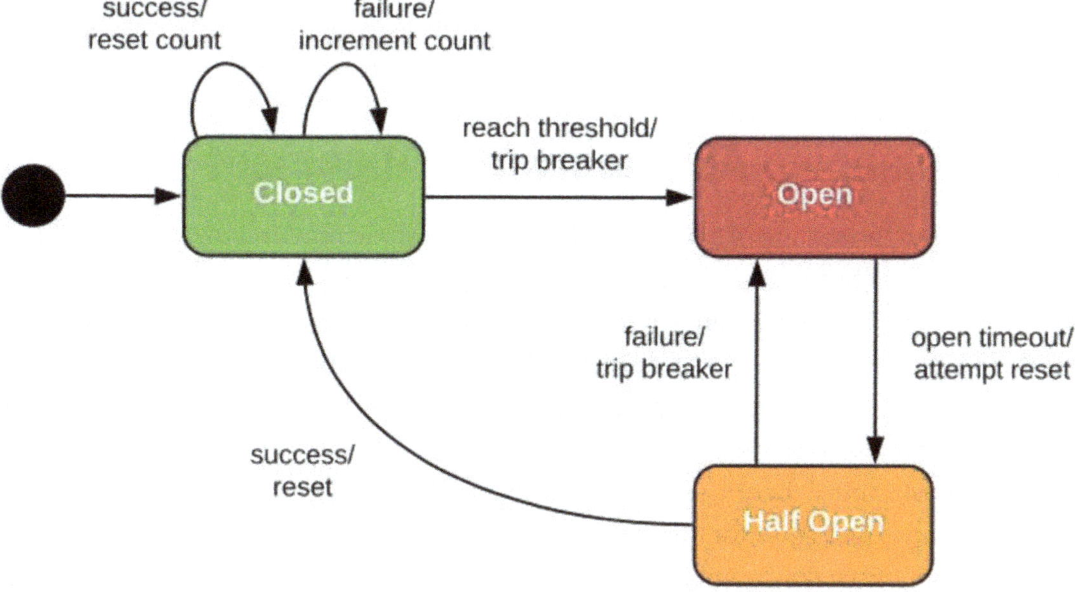

Figure 9-4. *Failure Propagation vs. Containment*

This figure compares of failure propagation and containment in distributed systems, illustrating how isolation and control mechanisms limit cascading effects.

Section Summary

This section examined the dynamics of failure propagation in distributed systems and the strategies required to manage systemic risk.

The key insights are as follows:

- As distributed systems are prone to chain reactions caused by their dependencies.
- A failure that results in a failure amplification will cause a system instability, unless mitigated.
- The containment measures include isolation, segmentation, and circuit breakers that inhibit spreading.
- Resilience involves redundancy, fail-safes, and adaptation.
- Sound system design turns systemic threats into manageable occurrences.

The above ideas constitute the theoretical base needed to understand how autonomy and alignment are balanced among team members.

9.10 Balancing Autonomy and Alignment

With respect to the scaling of software delivery processes across organizations, perhaps one of the biggest hurdles faced by modern DevOps and DevSecOps environments revolves around finding a balance between autonomy and alignment of teams across the entire system. Modern DevOps and DevSecOps approaches rely on decentralization so that individual teams can act independently, make quick decisions, and fine-tune their processes.

In terms of control theory, such a situation would mean striking a balance between localized control and goals for the entire system. Individual teams, acting as localized controllers, would make decisions on the basis of their own feedback loops and needs. However, the decision-making process within those teams influences the functioning of the entire system.

9.10.1 Team Autonomy vs. Organizational Consistency

Autonomy for teams is a critical ingredient for scalability and innovation. Giving teams ownership over their services, pipelines, and decision-making allows for faster cycle times, greater agility, and better ownership. Autonomous teams are able to respond to changes in requirements quickly and optimize their process flow without depending on any form of centralization.

Excessive autonomy, on the other hand, leads to inconsistencies both in terms of practices and behavior in the organization. Team members may utilize different toolkits and have different measures and policies, among other aspects, that lead to inconsistencies in control systems. These tend to be difficult to coordinate, insecure, and inefficient. Conversely, one strength of consistency is predictability. With a common policy for all team members, communication will be easier. The organization will also have predictable behavior, which will make it easy to manage. On the downside, consistency leaves little space for innovation.

As such, the solution lies in finding a middle ground where both factors are accounted for.

9.10.2 Shared Goals and Control Frameworks

It is necessary to create common objectives and control systems that could affect the decisions and actions of these autonomous groups. Objectives define what must be accomplished by all teams to achieve the stability of the system, its appropriate functioning, ensuring its safety, and system compliance.

Objectives provide the criteria for making decisions and ensure that all local decisions have a global impact. Thus, teams may pursue the goal of quick deployment, but this does not mean that their decisions should have a negative impact on the stability and safety of the system. Defining particular objectives means the indication of consistent system actions.

The control scheme provides tools and methods that can help achieve the set objectives. This scheme involves the following items:

- Policies and constraints
- Feedback mechanisms
- Decision models
- Actuation

At the same time, it is important to note that control schemes are supposed to meet the different needs of each team. From the standpoint of control systems, objectives become control targets, while the control scheme helps realize control goals.

9.10.3 Alignment Through Policy and Feedback

Among the two primary approaches for establishing alignment are the use of policies and the use of feedback. The former defines the limits of acceptable behaviors within which the various teams must operate in order to achieve organizational goals, while the latter represents the input used to judge the operation of the system.

In policy-driven alignment, teams ensure that their actions are consistent and aligned with one another despite being decentralized. This is accomplished by building policy enforcement into the infrastructure, including the use of pipeline and platform-based solutions, often in the form of Policy as Code, allowing organizations to impose consistent policies on the security, compliance, and operations aspects of the systems they develop.

Feedback-driven alignment, on the other hand, allows teams to gain insight into the current state of the system and the consequences of their actions. This is achievable by leveraging a common observability framework that offers data relating to performance, failure, dependency, and numerous other factors. This way, it becomes possible for different groups to modify their approach based on how their activities impact the other elements in the network.

Key Insight

Scaling software delivery requires not only distributing control across teams but also ensuring alignment through shared objectives, policies, and feedback, enabling independently operating systems to function as a coherent and stable whole.

Section Summary

This section examined the balance between autonomy and alignment in distributed software delivery systems.

The key insights are as follows:

- Team autonomy enables scalability and responsiveness but can lead to fragmentation if not aligned.
- Organizational consistency ensures stability and coordination across systems.
- Shared goals and control frameworks align local decisions with global objectives.
- Policy enforcement and feedback integration enable continuous alignment.
- Effective systems balance autonomy and alignment to achieve both flexibility and control.

9.11 Transition to Organization-Wide Intelligent Systems

The evolution from team-level delivery pipelines to intelligent enterprise systems is a change in structure from optimizing in isolation to controlling in unison through learning. For individual groups, instrumentation, enforcement of policies, and optimization toward their own targets within services take place. At a larger scale, there is a need to federate, standardize, and inject intelligence into these individual control mechanisms so that what happens in one part of the system aligns with the goals set by the entire system.

9.11.1 From Team-Level Systems to Enterprise-Wide Control Systems

The team-level system can work efficiently as a controller using the feedback provided by that specific service. But the problem lies in distributed systems where there are interdependencies between services; hence, a team-level system cannot optimize for the entire organization. There needs to be a control structure across teams, platforms, and governance levels of an enterprise.

This transition involves the following:

- Harmonize feedback using observability throughout the organization (metrics, logs, traces, and security signals) to form a single picture of the system's state.
- Standardize decision logic by means of Policy as Code and common risk models to ensure that all pipelines use the same criteria.
- Coordinate actuation between services and environments, such as awareness of dependencies and coordinated rollout of updates.
- Enforce constraint propagation from governance layers to execution layers to preserve consistent constraints on security, compliance, and performance.

The result is that pipelines shift from individual execution engines to become parts of a distributed control system wherein local decisions can be made based on global behavior and affect global behavior at the same time.

9.11.2 Integration of AI Across Distributed Environments

In the evolutionary process, the coming phase entails the use of AI and machine learning as technologies that are embedded throughout processes such as decision-making, coordination, and optimization. Unlike the previous phases, AI is not limited to specific services or pipelines but utilizes data that has been aggregated through the entire system.

Key integration patterns include the following:

- **Large-scale predictive analytics**: Risk prediction and forecasting of the likelihood of incidents and capacity requirements by leveraging organizational data
- **Multi-service anomaly detection**: Anomaly correlation among various services in order to identify potential risks
- **Global risk assessment**: Assessing change risk based on multi-faceted criteria (including code, dependencies, runtime, and impact analysis) to take proper action
- **Thresholds and policy adaptation**: Threshold adjustment for each of the controls based on observation of effects and changing circumstances
- **Optimization through reinforcement learning**: Policy optimization through reinforcement learning of the best possible rollout strategy, scaling, and mitigation efforts

In order to apply these features, the organization should put in place a proper MLOps and modeling governance practice including data quality management, model validation, monitoring for model drift, and model explainability (Sculley et al., 2015).

9.11.3 Future of Scalable Intelligent Delivery

Fully realized, organization-wide intelligent systems exhibit characteristics of self-regulating control architectures:

- Continuous monitoring through a combination of observability and security telemetry
- Smart decision-making that integrates policies, risk assessment, and predictions
- Multiservice actuation that is aware of dependencies and involves controlled rollouts
- Learning-based adaptation that iteratively improves models, policies, and control through feedback

Such systems make possible the predictive and proactive nature of operations, moving away from the traditional reactive approach toward incidents and toward anticipation. Systems can, for instance, proactively manage capacity prior to demand surges, adapt rollout policies based on risk predictions, or segregate components from failures.

However, advancing toward full autonomy requires robust governance and guardrails:

- Constrained autonomy to ensure that actions do not exceed certain risk and compliance parameters
- Human intervention in cases involving high risks or uncertainty
- Transparency and traceability to keep the process trusted and accountable
- Standardized platforms with embedded controls but that also support autonomy within teams

The longer-term trend is not toward eliminating human control altogether, but toward elevating humans into positions responsible for governance and oversight, leaving more mundane tasks to intelligent control systems.

Section Summary

This section outlined the transition from team-level delivery systems to **enterprise-scale intelligent control systems**.

The key insights are as follows:

- Scaling involves combining local pipelines into a coherent and organization-wide control system.
- AI improves control through its ability to make adaptive decisions in a distributed environment.
- Control in enterprise-level systems entails having integrated feedback and policy coordination, as well as actuation.

- Intelligent delivery systems move toward self-control, ensuring optimal performance, risk management, and stability.
- Proper adoption of such technology relies on governance, restrictions, and human supervision.

9.12 Chapter Summary

This chapter explored scaling in software delivery systems in terms of control theory and showed that scaling in both size and complexity of system demands more than just increased infrastructure capacity; it demands distributed but coordinated control. When organizations are growing in terms of teams, services, and platforms, the control functions like feedback, decision-making, and actuation should be running in harmony to achieve stability and predictability.

A valuable takeaway is that scale inherently leads to the emergence of control structures that are distributed, with multiple teams being semi-independent controllers. However, while such decentralization enables efficiency and creativity, it comes with the danger of inconsistency and fragmentation. As such, successful scaling depends on the capacity to coordinate the decentralized units among one another.

The chapter underscored the need to ensure there was congruence in feedback, decisions, and actuation across systems. Feedback should be combined and visible across services to have a precise picture of the system state. Standardized policies and common models should be used in making decisions in order to be consistent. Actuation has to be synchronized to take into consideration interdependencies and prevent unintended interactions. These factors combine to create a complete control loop, which functions throughout the organization.

Governance becomes an important component as the limiting aspect that guarantees that the system's behavior remains within accepted parameters. Rather than limiting freedom, effective governance actually facilitates freedom by providing a framework and enforcement of policies, enabling teams to become self-governing but still consistent with the objectives of the organization. This harmony is particularly evident in hybrid governance models, which involve centralized standards and decentralized execution.

The second platform engineering capability mentioned in the chapter is platform engineering as a facilitator of scalable control. By reducing variability and ensuring consistency during execution, platforms provide standardized workflows, reusable modules, and embedded governance capabilities. This allows organizations to scale efficiently while maintaining control and freedom.

Lastly, scaling successfully allows organizations to gain stability in their teams, stability in governance, and scalability as well as resilience in their delivery systems. Organizations can create a system that is coherent, adaptable, and resilient as it scales by treating software delivery as a distributed control problem.

References

Åström, K. J., & Murray, R. M. (2008). *Feedback Systems: An Introduction for Scientists and Engineers*. Princeton University Press.

Beyer, B., Jones, C., Petoff, J., & Murphy, N. R. (2016). *Site Reliability Engineering: How Google Runs Production Systems*. O'Reilly Media.

Burns, B., Grant, B., Oppenheimer, D., Brewer, E., & Wilkes, J. (2016). *Borg, Omega, and Kubernetes*. ACM Queue, 14(1), 70–93.

Kim, G., Humble, J., Debois, P., & Willis, J. (2021). *The DevOps Handbook* (2nd ed.). IT Revolution Press.

Meadows, D. H. (2008). *Thinking in Systems: A Primer*. Chelsea Green Publishing.

Newman, S. (2015). *Building Microservices*. O'Reilly Media.

NIST (2020). *Risk Management Framework for Information Systems and Organizations*. National Institute of Standards and Technology.

NIST (2023). *Artificial Intelligence Risk Management Framework (AI RMF 1.0)*. National Institute of Standards and Technology.

Ogata, K. (2010). *Modern Control Engineering* (5th ed.). Prentice Hall.

Sculley, D., et al. (2015). *Hidden Technical Debt in Machine Learning Systems*. Advances in Neural Information Processing Systems (NeurIPS).

Sigelman, B. H., et al. (2010). *Dapper, a Large-Scale Distributed Systems Tracing Infrastructure*. Google Research.

CHAPTER 10

Designing Delivery Systems That Evolve

10.1 Chapter Objective

In this chapter, concepts inspired by control theory, DevSecOps, and adaptive software systems are combined as an architectural model for designing software delivery systems capable of continuous evolution through feedback, learning, and coordinated operational adaptation. Instead of considering the process of evolution as one requiring regular interventions or major transformations, this chapter considers the evolution of such delivery systems as an intrinsic part of the process of their design and operation, where feedback loops, decision mechanisms, and actuation processes are all involved.

The reality of the world of modern software development is characterized by ongoing changes and dynamics in many domains, from workload fluctuations to changing threats, from changing infrastructure to a constantly updated code base. If these delivery systems are to operate effectively, they should not only adapt to the changes in the environment but also learn from it and evolve as necessary.

At the same time, continuous evolution must be governed carefully because excessive adaptation, poor signal quality, delayed feedback, unstable dependencies, or overly aggressive remediation behavior can negatively affect operational stability and reliability.

The following chapters will examine the possibility of building such systems using a combination of the discussed approaches.

S. Bobba and N. S. Vummaneni, *CI/CD as a Control System*, https://doi.org/10.1007/979-8-8688-2842-3_10

10.2 Introduction: From Static Systems to Evolving Systems

Conventional software delivery systems have been predominantly designed as fixed, preset systems, with behavior determined by preset workflows, set policies, and deterministic decision logic. Although this strategy offers predictability and control, it brings about high levels of limitation in environments where change is great and complexities are on the rise.

In immature, isolated, or heavily tool-centric implementations, adapting operational logic dynamically can become difficult because workflows, policies, and decision rules are tightly coupled to predefined assumptions and manual operational processes. Rules and policies are usually pre-specified, depending on assumptions regarding system behavior and operating conditions. But with the changing nature of systems, these assumptions are not necessarily true anymore, and the result is outdated or ineffective decision-making. As an example, a deployment policy that is optimized to work well in a stable environment might not be sufficient during periods of varying workload or new security threats.

The scale and interdependence of modern architectures are also difficult to handle with the help of static systems. The move toward microservices, cloud-native infrastructure, and distributed platforms requires software delivery systems to coordinate across many different components, each with its own behavior and dependencies. Such environments have too many possible interactions, which would not be represented by fixed rules, and thus have only a limited responsiveness and a higher risk of failure.

These challenges are also compounded by the complexity of the software systems that are increasingly becoming more complex. Observability systems, including metrics, logs, traces, and runtime events, generate large volumes of telemetry data whose usefulness depends on signal quality, latency, correlation accuracy, de-duplication, and alignment with operational objectives and policy thresholds. This information represents an ever-evolving state of the system that cannot be effectively addressed through the application of only statistical methods. Rather, systems need to be able to process this data on the fly and change their behavior based on it.

These limitations emphasize the need for continuous adaptation and learning. Evolving systems use feedback to apply refinement to their behavior with time, to respond to new conditions, and to improve performance. This includes the incorporation of learning processes within the control loop whereby systems are able to study previous results, find patterns, and optimize future decisions.

From an architectural perspective inspired by control system concepts, evolution can be viewed as an extension of feedback-driven operational coordination, where systems not only respond to deviations but also refine decision strategies, policies, and operational behavior over time, in which the system does not just correct deviations, but also changes its own control logic in response to the behavior that is observed. This makes the system an adaptive and learning-enabled system rather than a static controller which can be continuously improved.

In mature platform implementations, evolution increasingly becomes an integrated operational capability rather than a separate or infrequent transformation process. Properly structured delivery systems involve feedback, learning, and adaptation mechanisms at all levels of operation. Policies are not fixed but constantly improved; decision models are not fixed but change with new information; and actuation mechanisms are not fixed but change dynamically according to the system conditions.

But there are new challenges when it comes to facilitating evolution. Adaptive behavior must be implemented carefully because excessive policy changes, delayed feedback, unstable dependencies, or aggressive remediation actions can introduce operational instability, inconsistent behavior, or unintended side effects. Unconstrained learning may result in overfitting, undesired behaviors, or system oscillations. As such, moving systems should have clear limitations and governance systems that ensure that the changes do not lose focus with regard to system goals.

Finally, the process of turning the non-evolving systems into evolving ones is a radical change in software delivery design. Rather than designing systems that implement predetermined logic, organizations need to design systems that can learn, adapt, and continuously improve. This transformation allows delivery systems to be effective in the face of complexity and change, which enables long-term scalability and resilience.

Key Argument

In large-scale, high-change, or operationally sensitive environments, software delivery systems increasingly benefit from architectures capable of continuous adaptation, learning, and controlled operational evolution.

10.3 Evolution as a Control System Property

For control systems-oriented software delivery solutions, evolution cannot be considered as a periodic addition to the functionality of the solution; rather, in mature delivery platforms, evolution is increasingly treated as an ongoing operational capability rather than an occasional enhancement process. Standard control systems can be defined as systems designed for the maintenance of stability and deviation correction. But in highly dynamic environments, it is important for systems to adapt the control strategy itself depending on current conditions.

Thus, evolution becomes a logical step forward in the development of traditional control solutions when feedback-based control does not just lead to the adjustment of some parameters; rather, feedback contributes to refining decision-making strategies, operational policies, and actuation mechanisms when those controls are versioned, validated, audited, and consistently enforced across environments, Such an approach makes sense in the framework of modern control theories such as adaptive and learning control systems.

These approaches suggest that control solutions should evolve depending on the feedback from the controlled processes. In the case of software delivery, evolution can be seen as continuous optimization of decision-making processes and learning about possible issues that might arise in the course of the software delivery process.

10.3.1 Feedback-Driven Evolution

Feedback concepts provide a useful architectural abstraction for understanding how adaptive software delivery systems coordinate telemetry, operational decisions, and remediation behavior across distributed environments. In conventional systems, feedback is utilized to sense deviations and make adjustments as necessary. In evolutionary systems, however, feedback goes beyond mere corrections; rather, it helps achieve constant learning and improvement of the system.

The use of feedback is abundant in software delivery systems, where feedback is derived from observability telemetry such as metrics, logs, traces, deployment events, and security signals, provided that those signals are timely, correlated, policy-aware, and operationally actionable. These signals allow for creating an image of what happens in a system, representing its performance characteristics, patterns of failure, and dynamics. Through integrating these signals into learning capabilities, it is possible for systems to learn and improve their future actions based on previous observations and evaluations.

A feedback-based evolution involves iterative cycles of

1. **Observation**: Gathering information about system states and behavior
2. **Evaluation**: Analyzing outcomes against operational objectives, versioned policies, governance requirements, and acceptable risk thresholds
3. **Learning**: Identifying operational patterns and refining models or policies through validated, auditable, and governance-aware update mechanisms
4. **Adaptation**: Making decisions based on learning insights

This process turns feedback into a driver of change rather than simply a source of adjustments. If a certain deployment approach constantly results in performance deterioration, then this feedback should help to recognize that fact and adopt an alternative strategy.

From the point of view of control theory, it implies that feedback supports both operational error reduction and the continuous refinement of decision models, policies, and remediation strategies. It not only helps in enhancing the accuracy of results but also makes it more robust, which means that the system can operate effectively despite changes in the environment.

It must be remembered, though, that the evolution process through feedback needs accurate, timely, and appropriate feedback for it to be effective. This means that inaccurate feedback can result in wrong decisions.

10.3.2 Adaptive and Self-Tuning Systems

Adaptive and self-tuning systems extend feedback-driven operational models by enabling controlled adjustments to parameters, policies, and decision logic under governance, validation, and observability constraints. Unlike traditional control mechanisms, adaptive systems can be viewed as flexible in terms of control strategies that depend on current performance and changes in the environment.

Examples of adaptive control within software delivery systems include the following:

- Dynamic policy adjustments based on validated risk indicators, performance objectives, governance requirements, and operational telemetry
- Dynamic deployment patterns that are adapted in response to changing feedback
- Self-tuning resource scaling strategies that optimize resource scaling according to patterns of resource usage
- Decision models based on machine learning algorithms

Such capabilities help achieve continuous performance and robustness optimizations that are difficult to achieve in static or weakly adaptive implementations relying exclusively on predefined configurations.

A critical aspect of learning-based optimization includes techniques related to reinforcement learning, which allow estimating results of specific actions and adjusting decision rules in order to optimize specific goals. For instance, in controlled or simulated environments, reinforcement learning techniques may help explore deployment optimization strategies when safety constraints, rollback mechanisms, and governance controls are in place.

The issue of model adaptation also deserves attention, which means that the system adapts models in response to new conditions. The result will be such that decision-making processes will be relevant and accurate and based on updated models.

Model adaptation requires careful validation because inaccurate telemetry, delayed feedback, unstable dependencies, or excessive policy adjustments can introduce overfitting, inconsistent operational behavior, or instability across distributed environments.

From an architectural perspective informed by adaptive control concepts, adaptive delivery systems can improve operational flexibility and responsiveness when governance, observability, and policy coordination mechanisms are implemented effectively.

10.3.3 Stability vs. Adaptability Trade-Off

Adaptability and operational stability must be balanced carefully because distributed delivery systems depend on workload behavior, dependency structures, telemetry latency, remediation timing, and policy coordination. Although adaptability allows the system to react to its environment and perform better, the lack of control over this process might create instabilities or unwanted behaviors.

Using control system concepts as an architectural abstraction, stability in software delivery environments refers to maintaining predictable and reliable operational behavior despite changing workloads, failures, or environmental disturbances.

- **Adaptability**: Quick responses to new scenarios
- **Stability**: Consistency and predictability

Rapid or poorly validated adaptation may cause inconsistent operational behavior when decisions rely on noisy, delayed, weakly correlated, or transient telemetry signals.

In order to resolve this dilemma, evolving systems require mechanisms designed to reduce the likelihood of unsafe or unstable adaptation. Some examples would be

- Limitations that restrict the degree of change
- Filtering of signals to remove any noise
- Consequences and testing in order to make sure that adaptations result in intended effects
- Micro-updates that slowly implement changes to avoid disruption

As far as control systems theory is concerned, operational feedback mechanisms should integrate telemetry collection, policy evaluation, decision logic, and controlled actuation processes in ways designed to dampen excessive reactions and reduce instability risks. Nevertheless, it is necessary to have sufficient space for adapting to major changes in the environment.

Lastly, it is obvious that achieving an effective balance between adaptability and operational stability is especially important in high-change, high-scale, or runtime-sensitive delivery environments. Stability without adaptation leads to stagnation and obsolescence, while adaptability without stability results in chaos and instability. Figure 10-1 illustrates evolution in a feedback control system, in which an outer loop adjusts the controller's parameters based on auxiliary measurements while the inner loop maintains normal error correction.

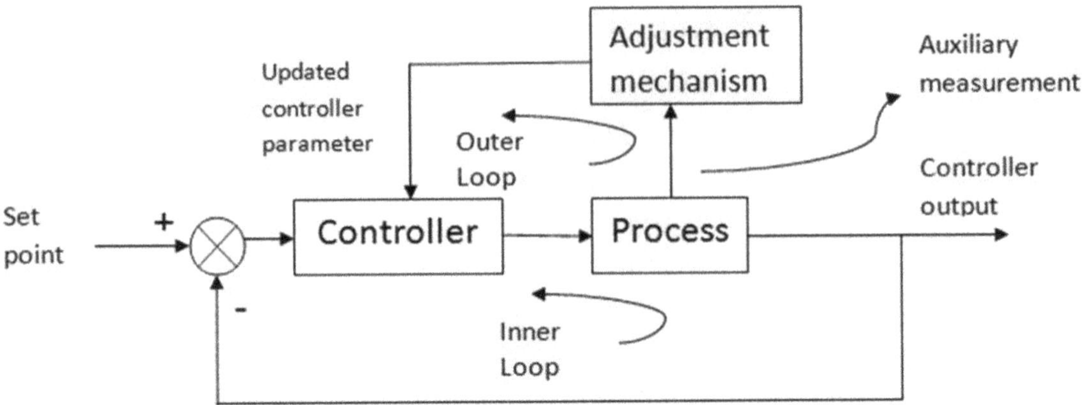

Figure 10-1. *Evolution in a Feedback Control System*

This figure shows an architectural model illustrating how telemetry feedback, policy evaluation, learning mechanisms, and operational actuation can support both corrective actions and adaptive system evolution in distributed delivery environments.

10.3.4 Section Summary

This section established evolution as a fundamental property of control-oriented software delivery systems.

The key insights are as follows:

- Evolution results from learning through feedback and adaptation.
- Integrated telemetry, policy evaluation, decision logic, and operational actuation mechanisms support continual system improvement through iterative feedback-driven refinement.
- Adaptive systems constantly tune themselves to optimize performance.
- Learning leads to improved optimization and resiliency.
- Controlled evolution requires balancing adaptability with operational stability through validated policies, bounded remediation behavior, telemetry quality controls, and governance-aware operational coordination.

This forms the basis of our discussion on designing adaptive systems, which we will explore further in the subsequent section.

10.4 Designing for Continuous Learning

Continuous learning acts as the process that ensures continuous adaptation, optimization, and resilience in developing software delivery systems. While feedback helps in gaining insights into how the system operates, learning involves translating operational insights into improved decision-making, validated policy updates, and refined actuation strategies implemented through governed and auditable operational processes. Consequently, learning must be incorporated in system design in such a way that each iteration in its operations leads to an improvement in the overall functioning of the system.

Learning becomes an intrinsic aspect of system design as opposed to being an external activity. Instead of involving a separate process of feedback analysis and update, learning becomes integrated into operational feedback mechanisms where telemetry collection, policy evaluation, decision logic, and actuation processes continuously refine system behavior over time.

10.4.1 Learning from Feedback Data

Continuous learning rests upon the efficient exploitation of feedback data, which describes the dynamic nature of software delivery systems. The primary sources of operational learning data are observability signals whose effectiveness depends on telemetry quality, latency, correlation accuracy, de-duplication, and alignment with operational objectives.

- **Metrics**: Quantitative telemetry related to latency, throughput, saturation, availability, and error behavior, provided the signals are timely, correlated, and aligned with SLOs or operational thresholds
- **Logs**: Event-related data that provide some contextual information about the system's activity
- **Traces**: Distributed request-flow telemetry used to analyze service dependencies, execution paths, and operational bottlenecks across interconnected systems

In total, such information gives a multidimensional picture of how the system behaves and allows for identifying patterns and anomalies and assessing the effects of decisions taken.

One crucial aspect related to learning design is distinguishing between two types of learning processes, namely, historical learning and real-time learning:

- Historical learning is based on analyzing data collected during a particular period in order to detect patterns and tendencies and improve the system's operation by taking relevant actions, such as optimization of deployment strategies and refinement of validated, versioned, and auditable operational policies.
- Real-time learning relies on timely, correlated, policy-aware telemetry signals capable of supporting operational decisions in fast-changing environments.

But the success of learning hinges on the quality of data that is used. If noisy, inaccurate, or late data is collected, then it could result in erroneous inference and poor decisions. So, data filtering and validation should be employed so that the learning process uses good-quality data.

From the standpoint of control systems, telemetry feedback improves operational visibility and supports more informed modeling, coordination, and decision-making across distributed delivery systems

10.4.2 Incorporating AI and ML Models

In order to scale the learning process, mature delivery platforms may incorporate artificial intelligence (AI) and machine learning (ML) capabilities into operational decision-support architectures when governance, validation, explainability, safety constraints, and human oversight mechanisms are appropriately established. By applying machine learning, systems can handle large volumes of data and identify various complex patterns, thus making predictive decisions.

A typical example of the application of machine learning is represented by the concept of predictive analytics, which suggests forecasting possible system behaviors. In this regard, for example, one can mention such predictions as

- Detection of deployment risks based on code modification and dependencies
- Capability prediction by analyzing the system load
- Proactive detection of possible failures based on previous experience

With respect to predictive analytics, it should be noted that ML helps systems make decisions proactively rather than reactively, based on the forecasts of what will happen in the nearest future.

Another popular concept is associated with reinforcement learning, according to which systems learn how to act optimally in certain situations by making decisions and receiving feedback based on actions taken. In this case, for instance, a system may learn the best way to perform deployment by analyzing the results of applying different deployment techniques.

Machine learning algorithms can also provide the functionality of anomaly detection for the identification of anomalies that deviate from typical operation and might require further attention.

Nevertheless, embedding AI/ML algorithms in a delivery system presents various challenges associated with algorithmic accuracy, interpretability, and governance. These will include constant testing and monitoring of AI/ML systems to ensure that they continue functioning properly. The decision-making process must be comprehensible, particularly when there is risk involved.

In terms of control theory, AI/ML models can function as adaptive decision-support components when data quality, model latency, explainability, and governance controls remain within acceptable operational limits

10.4.3 Feedback Loops for Improvement

Continuous learning, in this regard, is achieved by way of closed-loop learning systems, in which the feedback received is used to improve the operation of the system. Here, the use of learning becomes a key part of the control loop that connects observations, decision-making, and actuations.

The following steps characterize the operation of a closed-loop learning system:

1. **Feedback gathering**: Observation of the system state using various measurements and metrics

2. **Analysis and learning**: Using models and algorithms to learn from the data collected

3. **Decision improvement**: Improving the decision-making, policy implementation, or parameters

4. **Actuation**: Implementation of the action based on the refined decisions

5. **Evaluation**: Assessment of results and input of feedback back into the system

Through such a loop, improvements can be incrementally and iteratively achieved.

One of the main advantages of closed-loop learning systems is the capability for continuous improvement of decisions being made. This includes updating deployment policies depending on their success rate, optimizing the scale-up based on use cases, or enhancing security controls as per new threats.

Crucially, it is important to design learning loops that will ensure stability and reliability of the process. In case the learning process is left uncontrolled, there will be undesirable consequences such as oscillation and overreaction to temporary inputs. Ways of addressing this problem include

- Gradual changes through incremental updating
- Trying out and validating the changes made
- Staying consistent with the system objectives

In the context of control systems, learning loop control can be seen as an enhancement of the traditional concept of feedback control. Table 10-1 summarizes the main learning mechanisms used in delivery systems.

Table 10-1. *Learning Mechanisms in Delivery Systems*

Mechanism	Description	Benefit
Historical Learning	Analysis of past system behavior	Long-term optimization and trend detection
Real-Time Learning	Immediate adaptation to current feedback	Rapid response and dynamic adjustment
Predictive Analytics	Forecasting future system states	Proactive decision-making
Reinforcement Learning	Learning optimal strategies through outcomes	Continuous improvement of decisions
Anomaly Detection	Identifying deviations from normal behavior	Early detection of issues
Closed-Loop Learning	Continuous feedback-driven refinement	Adaptive and self-improving systems

10.4.4 Section Summary

This section established continuous learning as a core capability of evolving software delivery systems.

The key insights are as follows:

- Continuous learning turns feedback into system enhancements.
- Metrics, logging, and tracing offer the basis for learning.
- AI/ML models facilitate scalable and predictive learning.
- Continuous learning loops embed learning within control loops.
- Successful learning demands an equilibrium between flexibility and stability/governance.

This set of principles forms the basis of our understanding of the evolution of decision systems, discussed further in the following section.

10.5 Evolution of Decision Systems

Within the context of developing software delivery systems, decision-making is no longer a deterministic and rigid procedure, but one that is characterized by dynamism and adaptation. With an increasing level of system complexity as well as changing dynamics, the decision logic must be developed for the sake of effectiveness. The process of development turns decision systems into adaptive and learning-oriented elements capable of responding to uncertainty, enhancing performance, and mitigating risks.

Looking at the matter from the point of view of control systems theory, decision systems become the fundamental controller whose job is to transform feedback into actuation. In deterministic systems, the controller remains fixed and operates on rules. In the case of adaptive and evolving systems, the controller is itself mutable because it learns. This section will analyze how decisions shift from being determined to adaptive, the concept of continuous optimization, and governance.

10.5.1 From Static Policies to Adaptive Policies

Software delivery approaches that have been practiced before depended on rule-based decision policies. The rule-based approach refers to a software decision policy that explicitly defines the actions or decisions as deterministic functions. The policy outlines various conditions that permit, constrain, or alter any action to take place. Although these decision policies ensure predictability and easy implementation, their applicability is constrained in many ways.

The decision policies assume that software environment conditions will be accurately predicted and encoded beforehand. This is not the case in contemporary software environments since software environment conditions are always uncertain, unpredictable, and interdependent. This implies that the software environment changes rapidly, hence making rules redundant. Adaptive policies provide a way out of such situations by providing more dynamic decision criteria. This includes considering system history, environment feedback, and forecasts when evaluating various software decision parameters. For instance:

- Decision parameters such as deployment policies may adapt depending on system status.
- Security policies are adapted whenever there is a security threat.
- Resource management decisions are changed after analyzing usage history.

The transformation of rule-based policies into adaptive policies entails the adoption of continuous control techniques in place of the discrete controls employed previously.

One of the advantages associated with such a transition is that it enhances a system's capability to accommodate uncertainty and variations. Nonetheless, such policies complicate the process due to their dynamic nature, meaning there will be a need for verification and explanation processes.

10.5.2 Continuous Policy Optimization

The development of decision-making systems is based on the continuous optimization of policies, which entails improving decisions through the learning process. As a result, the logic of the policies is kept up-to-date with regard to their goals.

Policy optimization includes the adaptation of the parameters, thresholds, and constraints that determine the limits of the decisions. Some examples include

- Adjusting the risk thresholds considering the number of incidents experienced
- Correcting the performance constraints according to the workload variations
- Modifying the deployment criteria, taking into account the success factors accumulated throughout the experience

The changes to policies are made on the basis of feedback information analyzed using various techniques, including statistical analysis, machine learning algorithms, and reinforcement learning techniques.

Using learning to adjust policies enables decision-making systems to go beyond fixed designs and keep on optimizing decisions. Thus, for example, reinforcement learning can be used to find an appropriate way to deploy solutions for achieving maximum stability and performance.

Nonetheless, continuous optimization should be carried out with caution because of possible complications, such as

- Overfitting, whereby policies are tailored excessively to recent data
- Instability, whereby policies frequently change and cause inconsistent behavior
- Policy drift, whereby decision-making deviates from organizational goals

In addressing such challenges, it is necessary for policy update processes to involve validation and monitoring frameworks to ensure the updates are both effective and safe. Incremental policy updates and simulations are common techniques employed to safeguard policy stability in optimization efforts.

From the standpoint of control systems, continuous policy optimization improves adaptive control capabilities and ensures optimal system performance under changing conditions.

10.5.3 Decision Governance in Evolving Systems

As decision systems develop, it is crucial to maintain control and accountability. Decision models that are adaptive and driven by learning bring in the element of complexity and uncertainty, so there is a need to have governance measures in place that will help decisions be consistent with the goals of the decision-making process.

Decision governance is defined by policies, procedures, and controls associated with decision-making, updating, and evaluation. Some of the main concerns associated with the governance of evolving decision systems include

- **Transparency**: Making sure that decision logic is explainable
- **Traceability**: Creating a trail of decisions and their evolution based on policies
- **Accountability**: Understanding who is responsible for what
- **Compliance**: Adherence to regulations

Policy as code is one of the fundamental aspects of decision governance because it allows for systematic definition, updating, and auditing of decision policies.

The other crucial dimension is the adoption of constrained decision frameworks, where adaptive policies run within the bounds of defined constraints. The constraints guarantee that, despite the changes in policies, they will always adhere to mandatory needs like security, safety, and compliance.

The human factor also forms part of the decision governance model. While simple choices may be programmed into the system, complex and doubtful cases require human intervention. The human-in-the-loop approach acts as a middle ground between the two approaches.

Lastly, in terms of control systems, the governance process acts as a supervisory control mechanism that controls the controller itself. Figure 10-2 presents the evolution of decision logic, showing how feedback, adaptive, and feedforward controllers work together with a reference model to maintain performance despite disturbances.

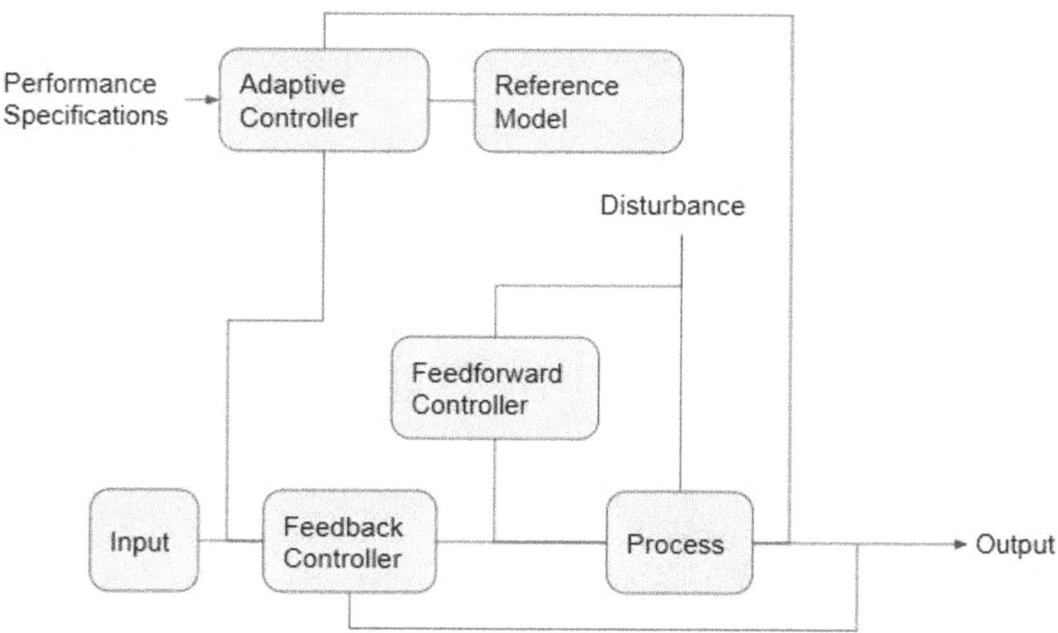

***Figure 10-2.** Evolution of Decision Logic*

This figure shows the evolution of decision systems from static rule-based policies to adaptive and learning-driven decision models.

10.5.4 Section Summary

In this chapter, we discussed the evolution of decision systems within software deployment environments and the means by which intelligent decision-making can take place.

The important points include the following:

- Decision systems evolve from fixed rule-based systems to adaptive and learning-based systems.
- Adaptive policies support context-based and flexible decision-making.
- Continuous improvement of policies supports the matching of decisions to system changes.
- The governance process is important to ensure control during adaptation.
- Decisions must be managed so as to balance flexibility and stability.

These considerations will form the basis for our discussion about actuation systems' evolution in the next section.

10.6 Evolution of Actuation Mechanisms

For the control-driven approach in software delivery systems, the actuation phase is the layer that turns decisions into tangible system actions such as deployments, scaling, configurations, and remediations. As systems develop, there is also a need for developing new forms of actuation processes from static and rigid processes to adaptive and intelligent ones that can also anticipate system conditions in advance.

The current approach of actuation is based on executing workflows that have been set up beforehand, with little variability or change involved. Nevertheless, systems need new forms of actuation processes that would not only be capable of adapting to system changes but that would also be able to operate automatically and make predictions about future conditions. In essence, actuation becomes part of the process of control within feedback and learning loops.

This section highlights how actuation evolves in response to system needs.

10.6.1 Adaptive Deployment Strategies

Adaptive deployment strategy refers to the change from static deployment strategies to dynamic deployment strategies. Static deployment strategies involve the adoption of pre-specified deployment strategies that are executed in a set manner, irrespective of the current status of the system. Dynamic strategies involve adjustments of the deployment strategies as a result of real-time evaluations of risk and other relevant factors.

Dynamic deployment strategies are one of the core elements involved in the process. Various methods for dynamic deployment include canary release, progressive delivery, and feature toggling. In the case of adaptive systems, these methods are enhanced through feedback mechanisms such that the speed, scope, and sequence of rollouts can change.

Some examples of how feedback can affect deployment include the following:

- Accelerate the process when the deployment so far has been successful.
- Halt or roll back the deployment when errors have occurred.
- Change the scope based on the current demands of the system.

Finally, there is adaptive scaling. Adaptive scaling involves the adjustment of resource allocation based on observed requirements.

These mechanisms allow for a trade-off between speed and security by introducing any changes to the system in an effective manner while maintaining stability at the same time. In terms of controls, adaptive deployment is a way of providing feedback-based actuation.

10.6.2 Self-Healing Systems

Self-healing is a method that extends actuator functions by incorporating self-recovery and self-correction for dealing with problems or any other anomalies in the process of functioning. In contrast to the need for manual interventions, self-healing systems recognize problems based on feedback information and correct those problems automatically.

Self-healing systems incorporate the following functions:

- Automatic rollback to a previous version of failed software deployment
- Automatic restarts and recoveries, for example, recovering from service failure or a failed container
- System parameter tuning, which enables the process to resume its normal operation
- Traffic rerouting, which means redirection of requests to avoid a failure point
- Adjustments in scaling to solve a problem and restore performance

Those processes are enabled by automatic monitoring and anomaly detection.

Considering the context of control systems, self-healing involves creating negative feedback in order to negate any disruptions that might occur within the system. This will enable self-healing in order to create a more resilient system.

Nonetheless, self-healing systems need to be designed in such a manner as to prevent any unintended consequences such as instability or overreaction. The process should be proportional to the problem, and its success should always be proven.

10.6.3 Predictive Actuation

The highest stage of development in terms of the actuation mechanism is predictive actuation, whereby the system can make predictions on future events, allowing the system to act accordingly rather than react to those future events. Predictive models, together with learning systems, can use historical and live data to make predictions on the behavior of a system.

Through predictive actuation, a system will be able to

- Scale its resources before there is an increase in demand
- Change the way of deployment based on how risky it might be in the future
- Stop failures by taking action based on early warnings
- Maximize performance by changing system settings in advance

In case a system predicts high traffic flow in the coming weeks, the system will have scaled its resources enough so that it won't face poor performance during that period. In other cases, predictive models will detect patterns that come just before failures occur, thus enabling the system to take proactive steps like adjusting the configuration.

Predictive actuation, when viewed from the control systems viewpoint, can be said to be a synthesis of feedforward control and feedback techniques, where not just the current situation but also the forecasted future situation influences decision-making Table 10-2 outlines how actuation strategies evolve across levels of system autonomy.

Table 10-2. *Evolution of Actuation Strategies*

Stage	Description	Characteristics	Benefit
Static Actuation	Predefined execution workflows	Fixed rules, no adaptation	Predictability
Adaptive Actuation	Feedback-driven execution	Dynamic rollouts and scaling	Flexibility and responsiveness
Self-Healing Actuation	Automated recovery mechanisms	Real-time remediation	Increased resilience
Predictive Actuation	Anticipatory system adjustments	AI/ML-driven predictions	Proactive optimization

10.6.4 Section Summary

In this part, the development of actuation systems used in software delivery was analyzed along with their potential for allowing adaptability and intelligence.

Key findings include the following:

- Actuation develops from a static process to an adaptive, self-healing, and predictive one.
- Adaptive delivery allows contextual and feedback-based processing.
- Healing systems can automatically recover from issues and increase resilience.
- A predictive actuation system can optimize operations and mitigate risks proactively.

- Modern actuation combines feedback and predictions to attain intelligent management.

These concepts are the basis of understanding risk management and stability in evolving systems, which will be further discussed in the following part.

10.7 Managing Risk in Evolving Systems

In the case of advancing toward adaptive and learning-capable software delivery systems, risk management is becoming more complicated and more important than ever before. While risks in static systems can be related to certain fixed sets of rules and behaviors, in the case of evolving software delivery systems, the risks will arise continuously as a result of the process of adaptation and learning.

From the point of view of a control system, evolution adds a higher order of uncertainty, which means that it is not only the state of the system that changes; the logic of the controller also undergoes change. In turn, there will be different types of risks, such as system instability, unintended system behavior, and failure to achieve the goals of the system.

This section considers some of the risks involved with the process of continuous adaptation, constraint-based evolution, and the control mechanisms for evolution.

10.7.1 Risks of Continuous Adaptation

Continuous adaptation allows for improved system performance, although it comes at the risk of failure to adequately mitigate these changes if appropriate controls are not implemented. One major risk factor is overfitting of learning algorithms or adaptation policies to recent data sets. Here, systems will work efficiently for current conditions, yet be incapable of dealing with shifts in the environment, thereby failing to offer robust and generalizable responses.

Another important risk of rapid and uncontrolled adaptation is instability. In any controlled process, stability is a condition where the process converges to its target. Yet, if there are too many adaptations in decision rules or action plans, the process could start to behave in an oscillatory fashion, thereby continuously compensating for errors due to excessive corrections from feedback. Such behaviors can lead to inefficient use of resources when making adjustments to scaling policies due to changing conditions.

There is also the risk of unintended behavior from evolving systems through learning algorithms. Learning algorithms may detect valid patterns that do not fit system goals. This problem is particularly important for reinforcement learning models, since the optimization of an objective function may lead to unwanted side effects if there are no appropriate constraints.

Moreover, the problems associated with data contribute to the formation of the risks mentioned above. The quality of feedback plays an important role in the process; any deviations from the norm (noise, incompleteness, bias) may negatively affect learning and lead to incorrect adjustment of the algorithm.

Another problem that increases the negative impact of the factors mentioned above is the delay in feedback. It may cause the system to respond to outdated data, which significantly reduces the efficiency of control actions.

10.7.2 Constraint-Aware Evolution

For adapting to be safe and effective, there is a need for the evolving system to adhere to specific constraints that limit the scope of acceptable behaviors. In constraint-aware evolution, these boundary conditions are built into the control mechanism in order to make sure that all the modifications are consistent with what the system is meant to achieve.

Constraints may include those

- Related to operations, such as performance limits and resource boundaries
- Constituting security constraints, in terms of vulnerability levels and access restrictions
- Tied to compliance issues
- Dealing with the risks, where certain levels of uncertainty are unacceptable

In essence, the constraints act as boundaries for controlling how the system evolves. For instance, while the deployment policy can adapt depending on the context, this is done in a manner that the risk levels do not exceed an agreed-upon threshold. In the case of scaling policies, any changes are made without exceeding the boundaries.

Boundary control involves

- Policy enforcement engines, which check for compliance with constraints
- Validation and testing environments, which measure the effects of modifications before implementation
- Revertive procedures, which undo any changes if constraints are not met

In the context of control systems theory, constraints offer assurance about stability by keeping the system inside a safe operational zone. Constraints function as negative feedback mechanisms that ensure an overly assertive or risky adaptation does not take place.

One should keep in mind that the constraints must be developed in such a manner that safety as well as adaptability are promoted. Excessive constraints will impede the evolution of the system, while insufficient constraints can result in hazardous outcomes.

10.7.3 Governance of Evolving Systems

Governance refers to the structures and processes that support the ongoing management of dynamic systems, such that the adaptation process can be made open, transparent, and accountable while aligning with higher-level goals. Governance in adaptive contexts goes beyond compliance monitoring to include oversight of learning processes, model behaviors, and system evolution.

A fundamental component of governance involves policy management, whereby rules and constraints are codified, versioned, and managed. Using Policy as Code techniques, governance can be embedded directly within pipelines and platforms to enforce consistency across systems.

In systems that involve AI/ML components, model governance is equally critical, including

- Validation, which ensures that models are accurate and reliable
- Detection of drift, which involves observing model performance over time
- Explainability, which makes decision processes understandable
- Auditability, which involves keeping track of all model behaviors and revisions

The role of human interaction in governing some processes of decision-making cannot be neglected, especially when facing highly risky or complex situations. With human-in-the-loop methods, people can keep an eye on the decisions made to ensure their validity.

Finally, feedback-based governance plays a key role in the process. It is required to provide that learning takes place based on valid data.

Regarding the approach of control systems, governance becomes the meta-element of control. Not only does it involve controlling the processes taking place inside the system and their functioning but also regulating the creation of such processes themselves. Figure 10-3 shows the safe evolution boundary model, in which AI systems are classified, assessed for risk, and governed through continuous monitoring and reassessment.

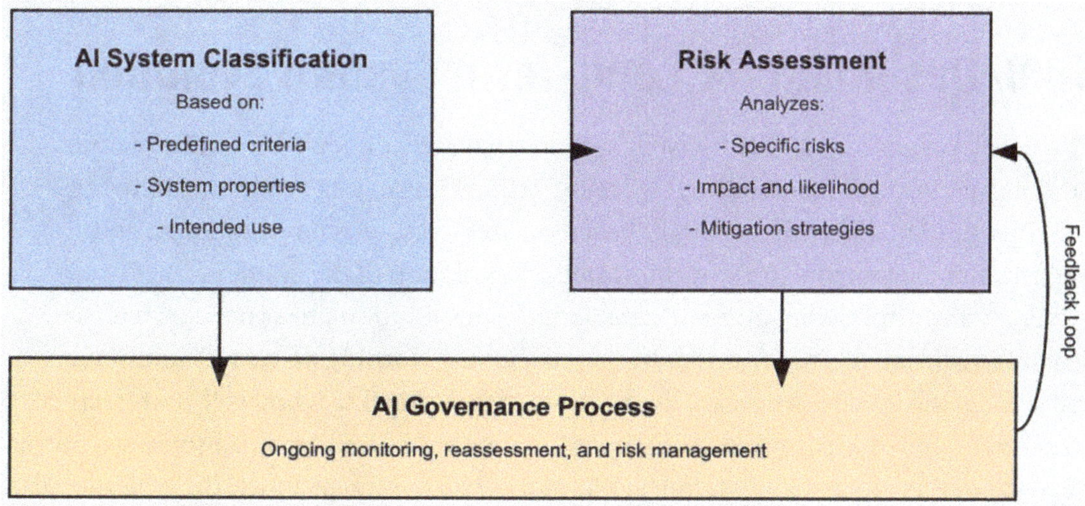

Figure 10-3. *Safe Evolution Boundary Model*

This figure shows the safe evolution boundary model illustrating how constraints define a stable operating region within which adaptive systems can evolve without compromising stability or safety.

10.7.4 Section Summary

In this section, we have looked at the issues involved as well as the means to address them while trying to deal with risk in emerging software delivery architectures.

The main points made here were as follows:

- Adaptation comes with its own risks, including over-fitting, instability, and unforeseen behaviors.
- Constraint-aware adaptation makes sure that the adaptation process stays within safe boundaries.
- Governance provides oversight, accountability, and direction for evolving architectures.

Proper risk management involves the incorporation of constraints, verification, and monitoring in the control process.

Safe evolution needs adaptability alongside stability and control, which is discussed further in the next section.

10.8 Designing for Long-Term System Evolution

The development of software delivery systems that can adapt well over time cannot be achieved through feedback and learning within control systems alone. It involves the construction of an infrastructure based on architectural, computational, and organizational elements to allow the sustained evolution of the system.

From a control theory point of view, long-term evolution poses new problems of scalability, sustainability, and consistency within the learning systems framework. As the scale of the system increases, learning algorithms need to work well, architectural structures need to accommodate changes incrementally, and organizational structures need to conform to system dynamics. Without such an infrastructure, the evolution of the system could become fragmented, unstable, or complex.

This section will consider the way modularity in architecture, scalable learning systems, and organizational consistency allow sustainable system evolution.

10.8.1 Modular and Composable Architectures

The basic necessity for any system architecture for evolving is the implementation of modular and compositional systems that allow for incremental modifications while not affecting the entire architecture's function. Monolithic systems are tightly integrated and hence pose a risk to any changes made because the modification will affect the entire architecture.

Modularity involves dividing the system into loosely connected modules or subsystems that define their boundaries clearly. The system is developed and evolved independently as a whole in such a way that each component can be upgraded or replaced independently of others in the system. For example, one can upgrade or replace a certain module without affecting the rest of the modules within the system.

Composability is an approach in which the system uses some pre-existing components to develop new capabilities. In composability, the system comprises some predefined and reusable components that work together to make up a system. Microservices, APIs, and infrastructure modules are examples of reusable components used to build software architecture.

In terms of controls, a modular architecture increases controllability and observability because each module can be controlled and observed separately. It is therefore easier to detect problems, intervene selectively, and evolve incrementally.

Design considerations when creating modular or composable systems include

- Low coupling, which means that there are few connections between the different modules
- High cohesion, meaning that each module has a well-defined role
- Standardized interfaces, making it possible for the modules to interact with each other
- Versioning and backward compatibility, allowing for gradual evolution

10.8.2 Scalability of Learning Systems

With the growth of the system, the learning processes themselves need to grow proportionally to accommodate an ever-increasing amount of data, system complexity, and other factors. A learning system that works efficiently on a smaller scale might be highly inefficient once it gets scaled up and thus will not work properly.

Some scalability issues in the context of learning systems can include the following:

- The amount of data produced by observability systems, which includes metrics, logs, and traces
- The complexity of the learning model, since it needs to be more complicated to cover all aspects of system behavior
- The computational resources needed for training, inference, and real-time analysis of data
- The distributed nature of the environment, as learning needs to take place within various services and platforms

For learning systems to overcome their scalability issues, the following solutions can be used:

- The processing of data using multiple nodes simultaneously
- The implementation of incremental and online learning
- The hierarchical structure of the learning system, which features service-level and global models
- The optimization of models and their compressions

The second equally important issue is the question of data management and quality control. As the number of learning systems increases, the need for data accuracy and relevance becomes even greater. Filtering, normalizing, and validating systems are needed to keep learning data at a high quality level.

From the viewpoint of control systems, scalable learning makes control processes adaptable amid growing system complexity.

10.8.3 Continuous Improvement Culture

However, along with technical design, the future development of systems is dependent on organizational alignment and culture. Continuous evolution of systems implies the implementation of a culture of continuous improvement based on feedback, learning, adaptation, and cooperation at all levels of technical process and operations.

Continuous improvement culture is characterized by the following aspects:

- Focus on data and analysis in order to guide actions
- An iterative approach in developing the system step-by-step

- Coordination among different teams to promote alignment
- Use of failures as sources of experience and improvement

Such an approach allows ensuring that the evolution of systems is not confined to the automation of routine processes only.

As far as the control is concerned, it is implemented by humans as meta-controllers that guide the evolutionary path of the system, review decisions, and update policies.

It is essential that organizational structures are designed in a way that allows for scalable governance and coordination, which means that teams have autonomy while still being able to work in line with system-wide aims. It can be achieved through

- Standardized approaches and standards, creating consistency among teams
- Feedback sharing, including through dashboards and reporting tools
- Knowledge transfer and training, allowing teams to benefit from new methodologies

This way, an environment for continuous improvement will be created. Table 10-3 presents the core design principles for safe system evolution.

Table 10-3. *Evolution Design Principles*

Principle	Description	Impact
Modularity	Decomposition into independent components	Enables incremental and safe evolution
Composability	Reusable and interoperable components	Supports scalability and flexibility
Scalable Learning	Efficient handling of data and model complexity	Maintains adaptive capability at scale
Data Quality	Reliable and relevant feedback inputs	Improves learning accuracy
Continuous Improvement	Organizational focus on learning and iteration	Sustains long-term evolution
Governance Alignment	Integration of policies and constraints	Ensures controlled and safe adaptation

10.8.4 Section Summary

This section examined the architectural, computational, and organizational foundations required for long-term system evolution.

The key insights are as follows:

- Evolving architecture that allows for modular and composable approaches.
- Scale in order to cope with the rising complexity and volume of information.
- Quality data is essential for efficient learning.
- The company's culture should facilitate ongoing improvement efforts.
- Long-term development needs synchronization of technical systems and organizational processes.

The above principles form the basis for the analysis of future evolution trends of delivery systems and will be discussed in more detail in the next section.

10.9 The Future of Evolving Delivery Systems

The direction of the delivery systems of software is moving toward systems that are completely self-regulated and self-optimizing, where sensing, decision-making, action, and learning take place constantly. Control theory, DevSecOps, and machine learning can be used to develop next-generation delivery systems that function as closed-loop systems with machine learning capabilities that ensure performance, mitigate risks, and respond to change automatically. This new development does not exclude humans; instead, it shifts human responsibilities from controlling activities to governance and designing control actions.

10.9.1 Autonomous, Self-Optimizing Systems

Next-generation delivery systems will be able to demonstrate characteristics of autonomy and self-optimization. Such systems will be capable of making decisions and executing actions based on real-time feedback and predictions. Specifically, they will be capable of

- Monitoring system states through unified observability (metrics, logs, traces, and security signals)
- Dynamically optimizing their decisions, adapting policies, thresholds, and strategies
- Conducting coordinated actuations (deployments, scaling, and remediations)
- Learning from past results, updating models and policies

The ability to evolve from reaction to anticipation will be particularly significant for future systems. They will increasingly make use of predictive signals such as capacity forecasts, risk scoring, and anomaly precursors. For instance, systems could automatically tune their deployment strategies according to estimated probabilities of failure or prepare for increased demand.

In general, however, such capabilities allow for the formation of control loops that are able to optimize themselves, which is done based on an objective function, such as reliability, latency, costs, and risk, among others. In this process, the system must always be aware of its limitations.

10.9.2 Integration of AI, Control Theory, and DevOps

Future delivery system architecture will be at the confluence of AI/ML, control theory, and DevOps:

- Control theory offers the mathematical model for stability, feedback, and dynamic behavior. It guarantees that the adaptive behavior stays well-defined and converges. The use of negative feedback, margins of stability, and robustness principles ensures a safe design of the adaptive loop.
- DevOps/DevSecOps offers the execution environment for decision-making through CI/CD, infrastructure as code, Policy as Code, and observability.
- AI and ML enrich the controller with predictive and policy-learning abilities.

Such an approach will be implemented as learning-enabled controllers deployed in delivery platforms:

- Predictive risk models guide deployment criteria and strategies.
- Anomaly detection models lead to proactive measures and guardrails.
- Reinforcement learning fine-tunes sequencing, scale, and rollback approaches.
- Adaptive threshold values are set according to past results and the present environment.

Implementing such an AI stack calls for MLOps in combination with platform engineering, namely, the creation of data pipelines for generating features, training, validating models, online prediction services, detecting model drifts, and rollback of models/policies. Governance systems (such as auditability, explainability, and versioning) make sure that decisions made by the AI are transparent and under control.

10.9.3 Human–AI Collaboration in Evolving Systems

With the advancement of autonomy, there will be the need for human–AI cooperation as opposed to automation. Humans are required

- To establish goals and constraints (like SLA, risk tolerance, etc.)
- To design architectures for controls and policies based on organizational intention
- To oversee decisions made under risky situations or conditions of uncertainty
- To interpret the decision-making process, especially when it produces surprising results
- To make improvements through continuous improvement from incident analysis

This brings us to a new form of decision-making:

- Automation for routine decision-making processes (where there is a lot of repetition but not much ambiguity)

- Human-in-the-loop for critical decision-making processes (where there is a lot of risk involved and a lack of certainty)

It is essential that there be an element of explainability and transparency in order for such collaborations to happen. Explainability means having an adequate explanation of the decision-making process, while transparency refers to making sure the decision-making process is clear by means of its inputs and outputs, tracking model changes, and policy updates.

10.9.4 Toward Organization-Wide Intelligent Control

In terms of the enterprise, new delivery mechanisms will operate as intelligence-based control systems for the entire organization:

- A holistic feedback mechanism allows for situational awareness throughout the system.
- The standardization of decision-making processes leads to a uniform understanding of risks and performance.
- The coordination of actuation ensures that any interdependencies between layers are taken into account, reducing systemic risks.
- The propagation of constraints provides governance at all levels.

This forms an overall control structure in which there is autonomy at all levels yet alignment with global goals.

10.9.5 Section Summary

- Future delivery platforms become autonomous self-optimization control loops.
- Artificial intelligence adds prediction and learning to control.
- The science of control gives assurance of stability and resilience, but DevOps scales the operation.
- A human–machine partnership achieves a proper balance between speed and responsibility.
- Systems-of-enterprise become integrated intelligent control structures.

10.10 Chapter Summary

In this chapter, it was determined that evolution is not a luxury addition to the software delivery system but an essential feature. It synthesized control theory, DevSecOps practices, and intelligent systems by showing that a high-performance delivery system needs to be designed to constantly adapt, learn, and improve in response to the changing environment, system behavior, and emerging risks.

One of the major themes of the chapter is that the adaptation is mainly driven by feedback and learning. The understanding of system behavior is based on observability data that is collected by using metrics, logs, traces, and security signals. This feedback, when embedded in learning mechanisms, can help systems to refine decision logic, optimize actuation strategies, and to evolve policies over time. This turns delivery systems from static execution engines into learning-enabled control systems that can continually improve.

Simultaneously, the chapter pointed out the fact that evolution should be well balanced with stability. The uncontrolled adaptation may bring about instability, oscillation, and unwanted behavior. The best way to reduce these risks is to have evolving systems with a constraint-aware design whereby all changes are made within set limits. This maintains the balance in the system and allows flexibility and responsiveness.

Governance was considered to be an important facilitator of safe evolution. Governance will make sure that adaptation stays within the organizational goals and regulation and operational limits through policy frameworks, model oversight, and validation mechanisms. Instead of limiting evolution, governance offers the structure and guardrails required to have a controlled and predictable system behavior.

It is also noted in the chapter that the evolving systems work on more than one dimension, among them being the decision systems, actuation mechanisms, and even the learning processes which should all be synchronized in a single control architecture. It is this integration that allows systems to react dynamically to feedback and provides coherence and alignment to distributed environments.

Finally, the design of delivery systems helps organizations to reach continuous improvement, adaptive decision-making, and resilience in the long term. These systems are more capable of managing complexity, uncertainty, and change and thus have sustainable performance and reliability over time.

Index

A

S. Bobba and N. S. Vummaneni, *CI/CD as a Control System*, https://doi.org/10.1007/979-8-8688-2842-3

B

C

D

E

F

G

H

I, J, K

L

M

N

R

S

T

U

V, W, X, Y, Z

GPSR Compliance
The European Union's (EU) General Product Safety Regulation (GPSR) is a set of rules that requires consumer products to be safe and our obligations to ensure this.

If you have any concerns about our products, you can contact us on

ProductSafety@springernature.com

In case Publisher is established outside the EU, the EU authorized representative is:

Springer Nature Customer Service Center GmbH
Europaplatz 3
69115 Heidelberg, Germany

www.ingramcontent.com/pod-product-compliance
Lightning Source LLC
Chambersburg PA
CBHW080246120826
49721CB00023B/418
9798868828416